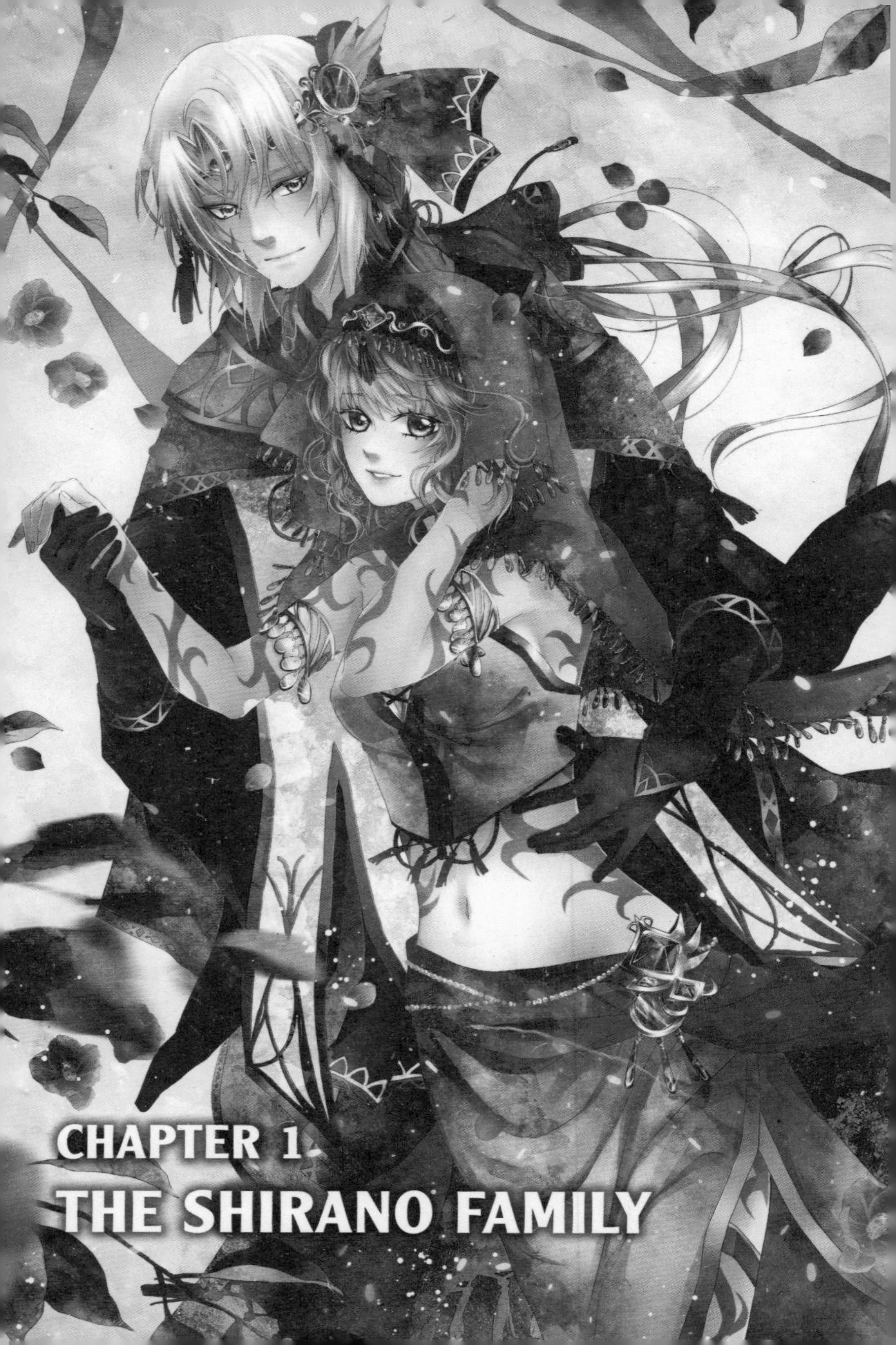
CHAPTER 1
THE SHIRANO FAMILY

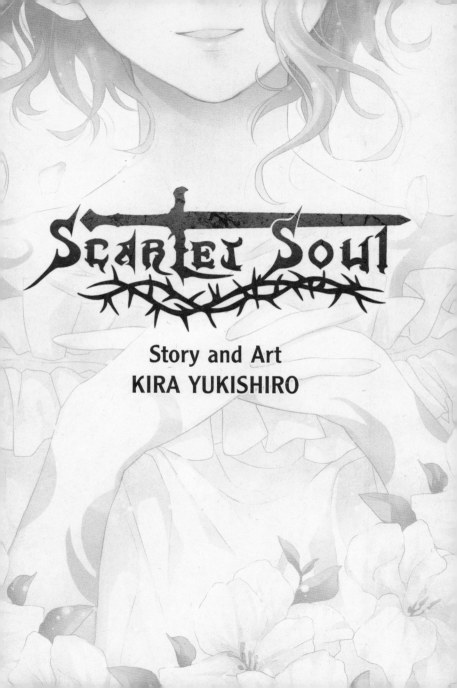

SCARLET SOUL

Story and Art
KIRA YUKISHIRO

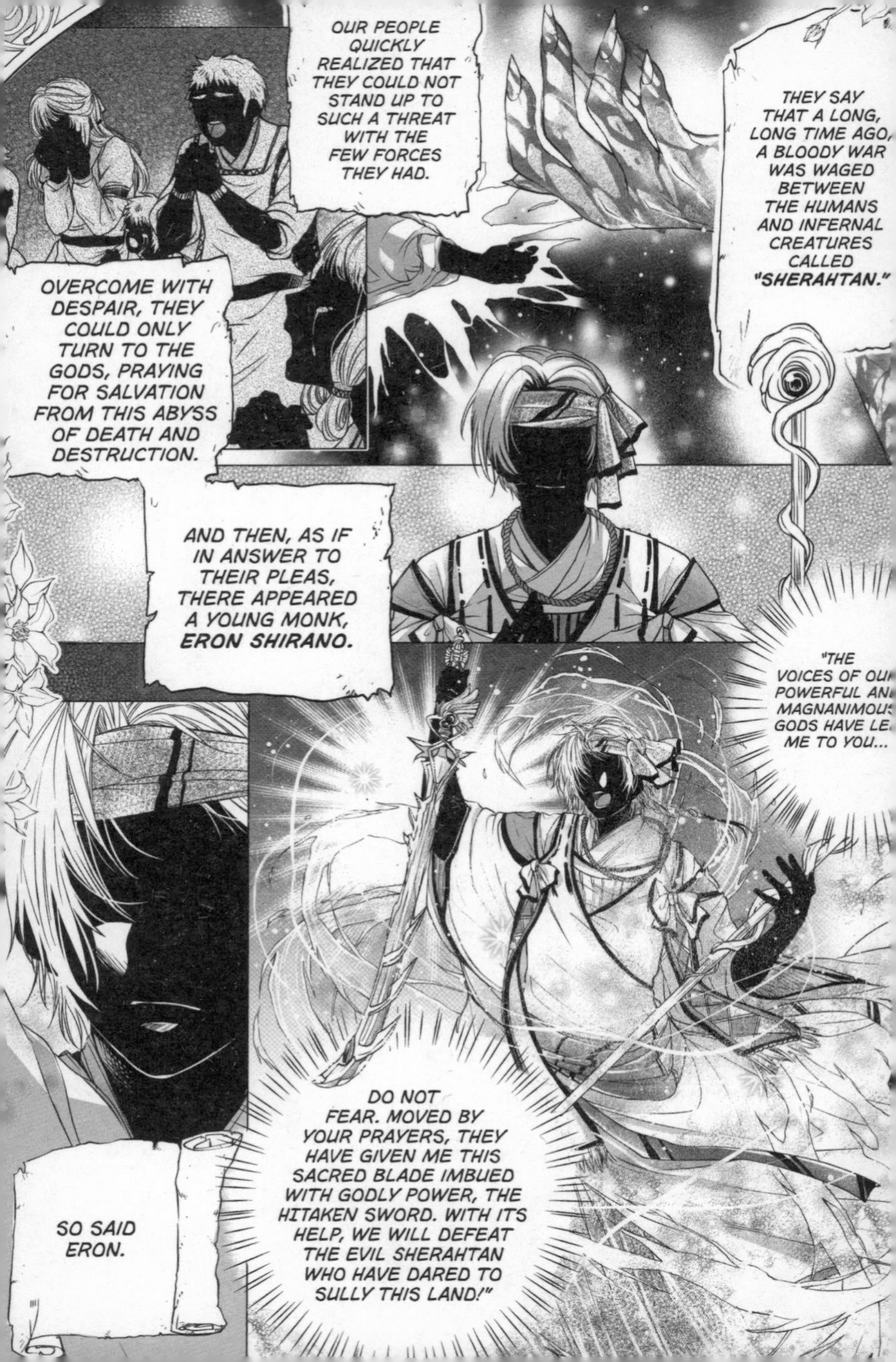
THEY SAY THAT A LONG, LONG TIME AGO, A BLOODY WAR WAS WAGED BETWEEN THE HUMANS AND INFERNAL CREATURES CALLED "SHERAHTAN."
OUR PEOPLE QUICKLY REALIZED THAT THEY COULD NOT STAND UP TO SUCH A THREAT WITH THE FEW FORCES THEY HAD.
OVERCOME WITH DESPAIR, THEY COULD ONLY TURN TO THE GODS, PRAYING FOR SALVATION FROM THIS ABYSS OF DEATH AND DESTRUCTION.
AND THEN, AS IF IN ANSWER TO THEIR PLEAS, THERE APPEARED A YOUNG MONK, ERON SHIRANO.
"THE VOICES OF OU POWERFUL AN MAGNANIMOU GODS HAVE LE ME TO YOU...
DO NOT FEAR. MOVED BY YOUR PRAYERS, THEY HAVE GIVEN ME THIS SACRED BLADE IMBUED WITH GODLY POWER, THE HITAKEN SWORD. WITH ITS HELP, WE WILL DEFEAT THE EVIL SHERAHTAN WHO HAVE DARED TO SULLY THIS LAND!"
SO SAID ERON.

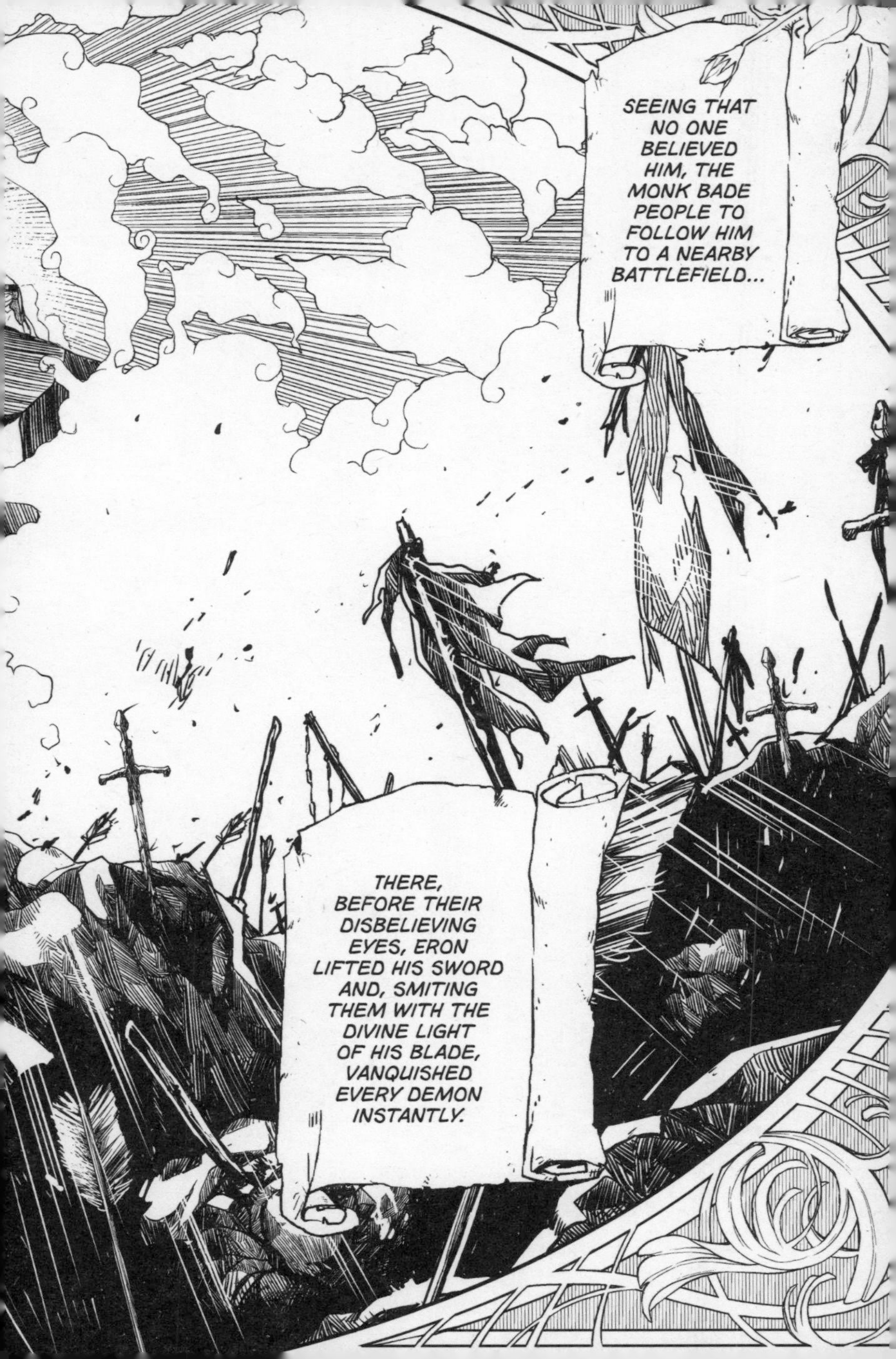
SEEING THAT NO ONE BELIEVED HIM, THE MONK BADE PEOPLE TO FOLLOW HIM TO A NEARBY BATTLEFIELD...
THERE, BEFORE THEIR DISBELIEVING EYES, ERON LIFTED HIS SWORD AND, SMITING THEM WITH THE DIVINE LIGHT OF HIS BLADE, VANQUISHED EVERY DEMON INSTANTLY.

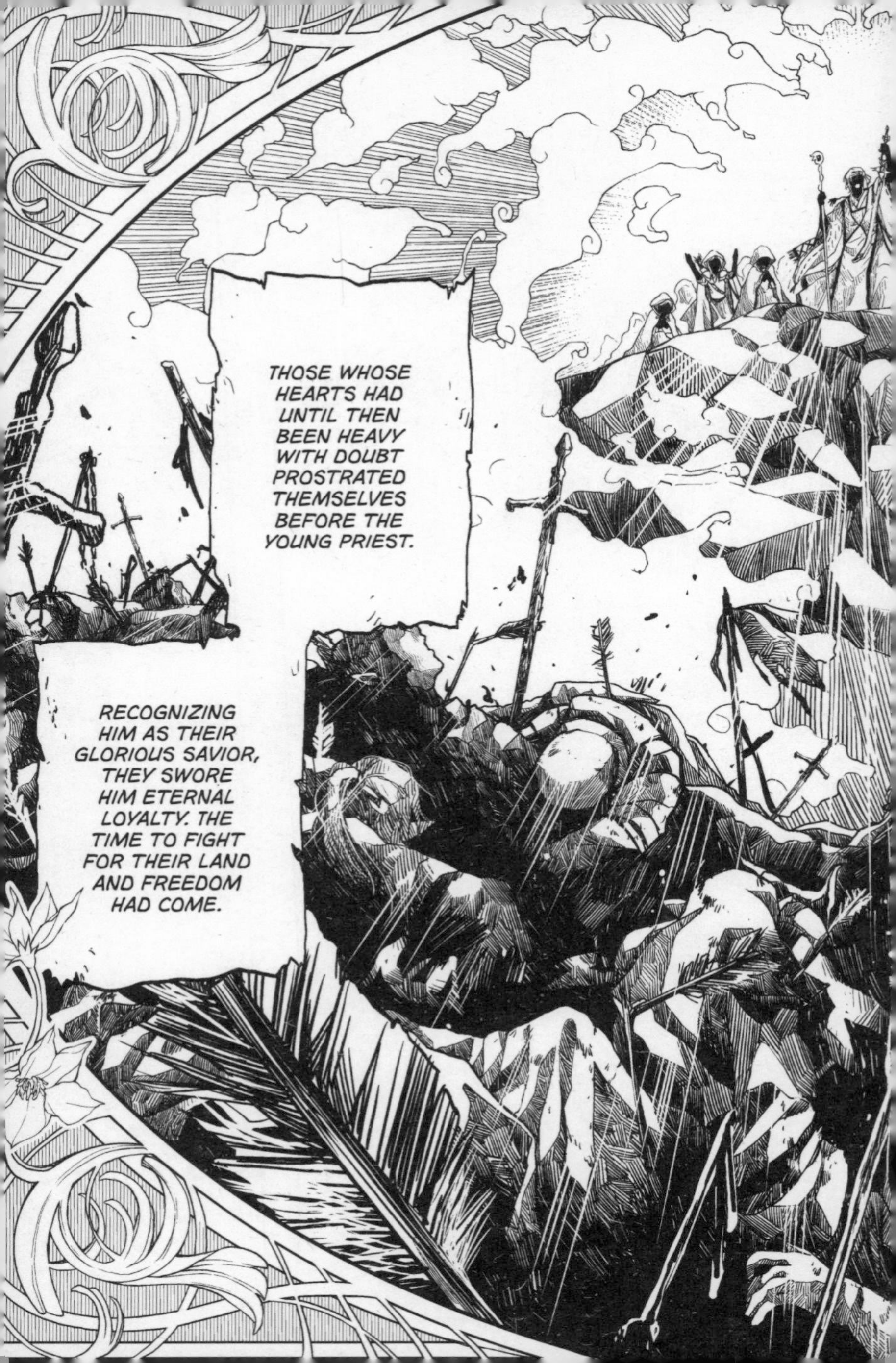
THOSE WHOSE HEARTS HAD UNTIL THEN BEEN HEAVY WITH DOUBT PROSTRATED THEMSELVES BEFORE THE YOUNG PRIEST.
RECOGNIZING HIM AS THEIR GLORIOUS SAVIOR, THEY SWORE HIM ETERNAL LOYALTY. THE TIME TO FIGHT FOR THEIR LAND AND FREEDOM HAD COME.

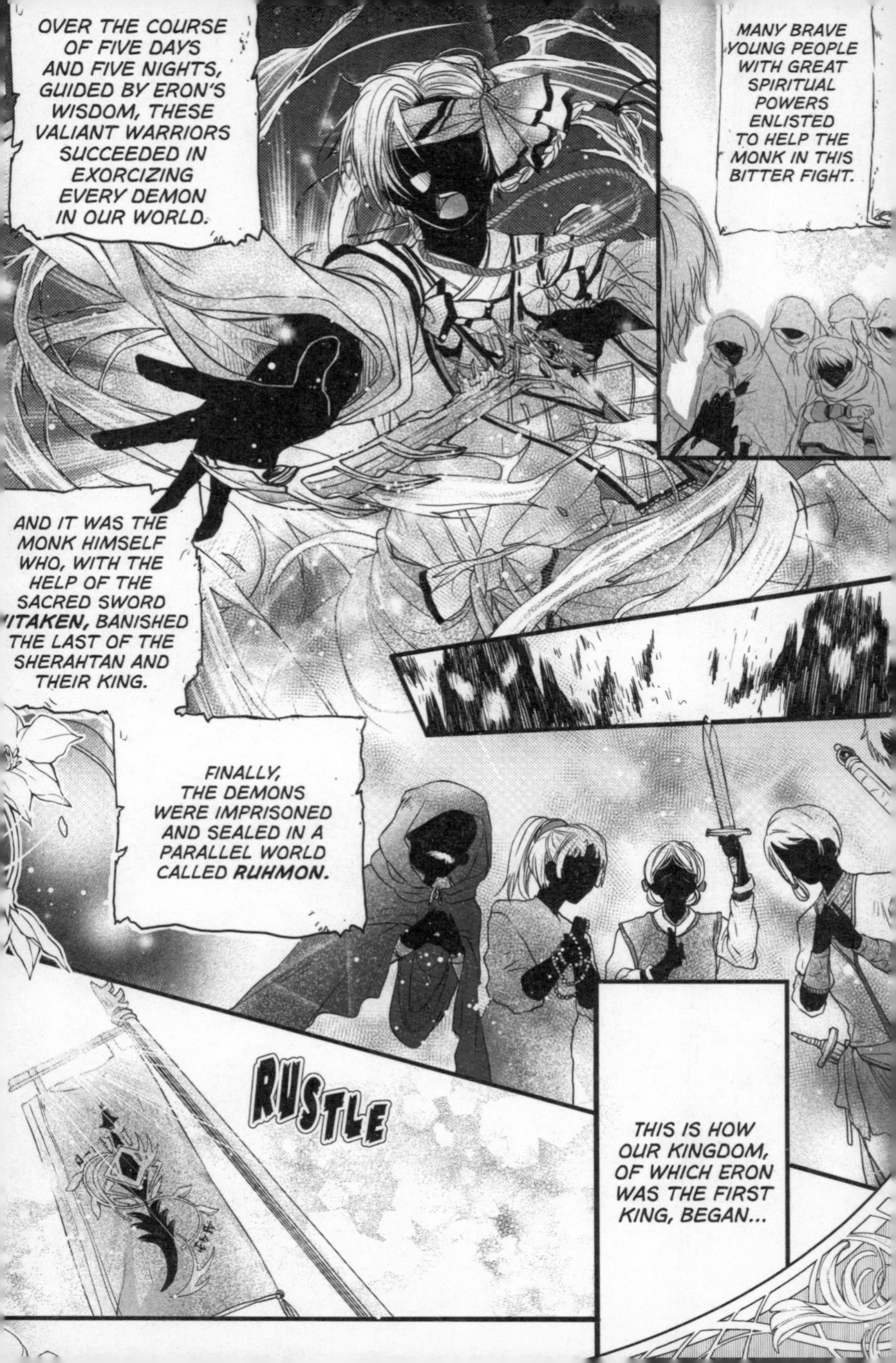
MANY BRAVE YOUNG PEOPLE WITH GREAT SPIRITUAL POWERS ENLISTED TO HELP THE MONK IN THIS BITTER FIGHT.
OVER THE COURSE OF FIVE DAYS AND FIVE NIGHTS, GUIDED BY ERON'S WISDOM, THESE VALIANT WARRIORS SUCCEEDED IN EXORCIZING EVERY DEMON IN OUR WORLD.
AND IT WAS THE MONK HIMSELF WHO, WITH THE HELP OF THE SACRED SWORD VITAKEN, BANISHED THE LAST OF THE SHERAHTAN AND THEIR KING.
FINALLY, THE DEMONS WERE IMPRISONED AND SEALED IN A PARALLEL WORLD CALLED RUHMON.
RUSTLE
THIS IS HOW OUR KINGDOM, OF WHICH ERON WAS THE FIRST KING, BEGAN...

Scarlet Soul

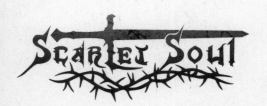

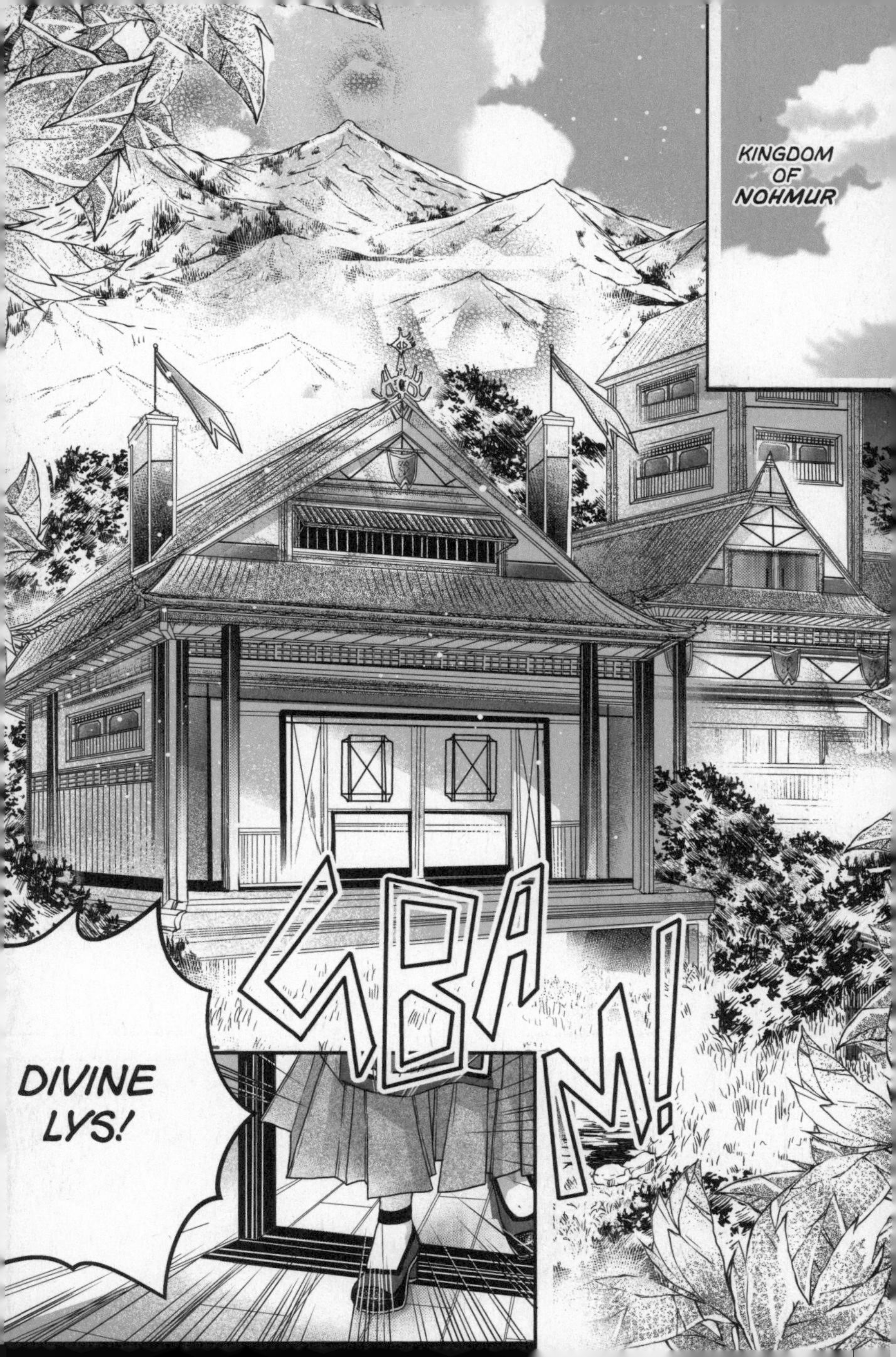
KINGDOM OF NOHMUR
SLAM!
DIVINE LYS!

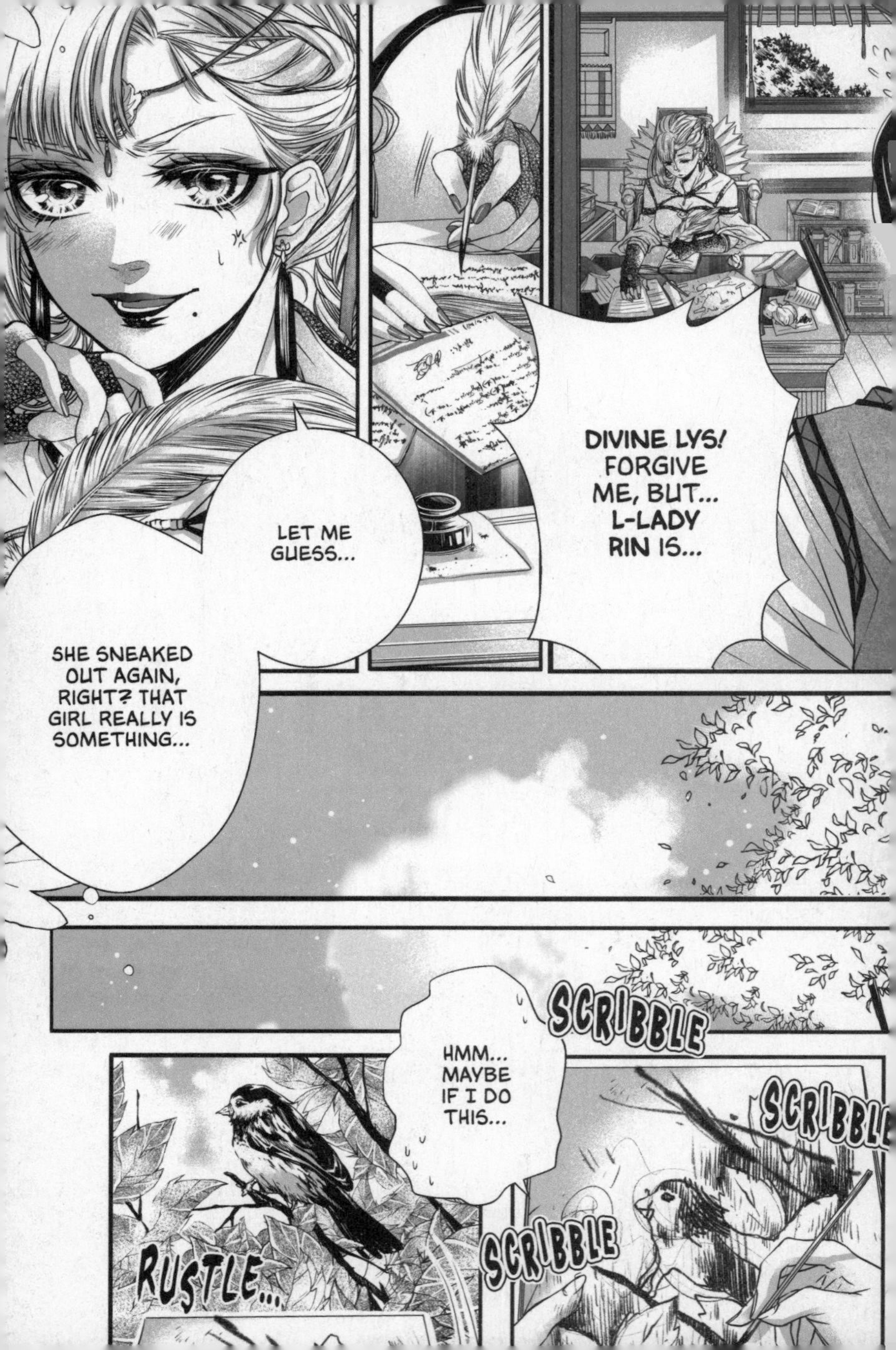
DIVINE LYS! FORGIVE ME, BUT... L-LADY RIN IS...
LET ME GUESS...
SHE SNEAKED OUT AGAIN, RIGHT? THAT GIRL REALLY IS SOMETHING...
SCRIBBLE
HMM... MAYBE IF I DO THIS...
SCRIBBLE
SCRIBBLE
RUSTLE...

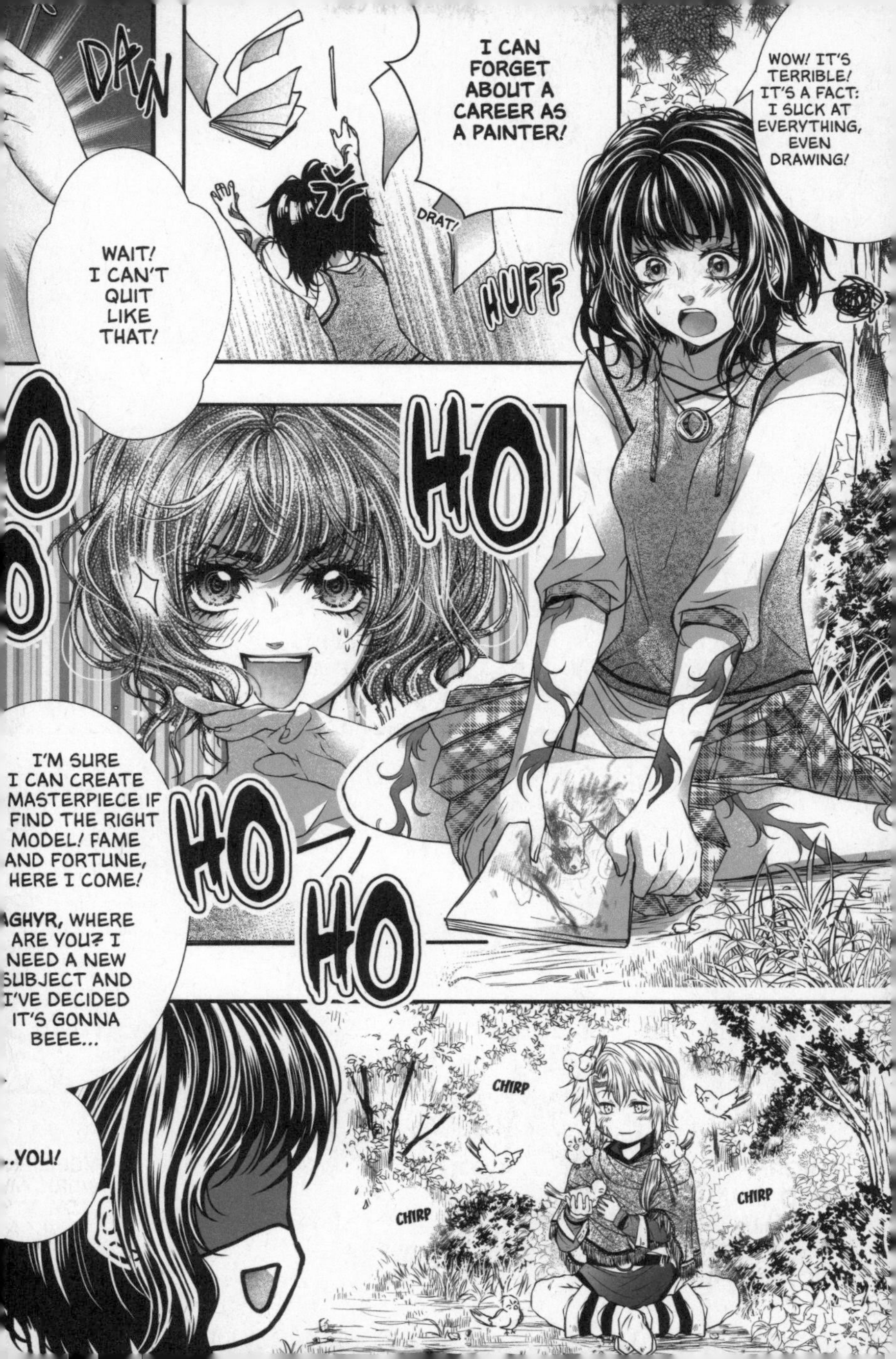
WOW! IT'S TERRIBLE! IT'S A FACT: I SUCK AT EVERYTHING, EVEN DRAWING!
I CAN FORGET ABOUT A CAREER AS A PAINTER!
DRAT!
HUFF
DAN
WAIT! I CAN'T QUIT LIKE THAT!
HO
HO
HO
HO
HO
I'M SURE I CAN CREATE MASTERPIECE IF FIND THE RIGHT MODEL! FAME AND FORTUNE, HERE I COME!
AGHYR, WHERE ARE YOU? I NEED A NEW SUBJECT AND I'VE DECIDED IT'S GONNA BEEE...
..YOU!
CHIRP
CHIRP
CHIRP

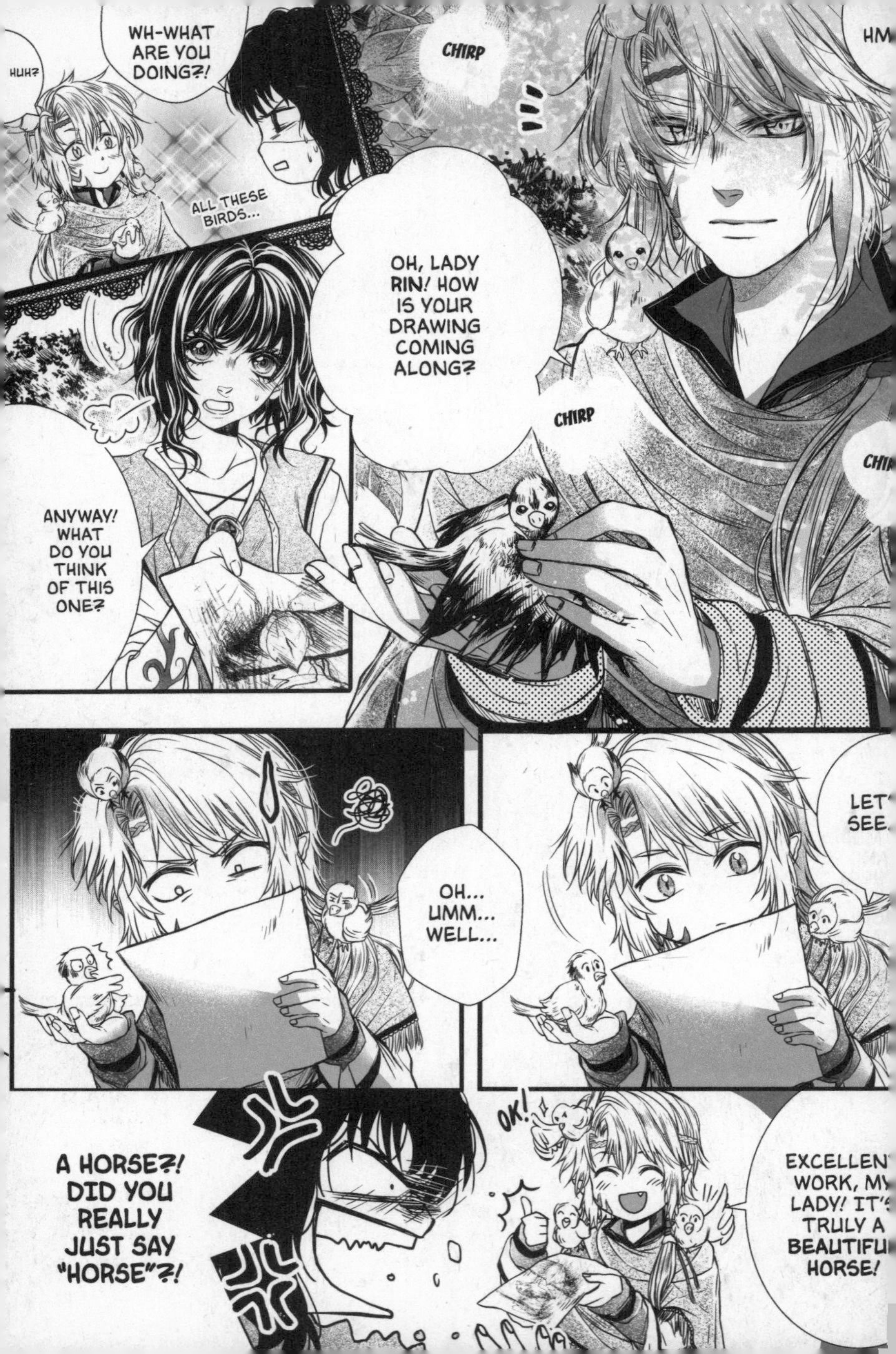
HM
CHIRP
OH, LADY RIN! HOW IS YOUR DRAWING COMING ALONG?
CHIRP
CHI
WH-WHAT ARE YOU DOING?!
HUH?
ALL THESE BIRDS...
ANYWAY! WHAT DO YOU THINK OF THIS ONE?
LET' SEE.
OH... UMM... WELL...
OK!
EXCELLEN WORK, MY LADY! IT'S TRULY A BEAUTIFU HORSE!
A HORSE?! DID YOU REALLY JUST SAY "HORSE"?!

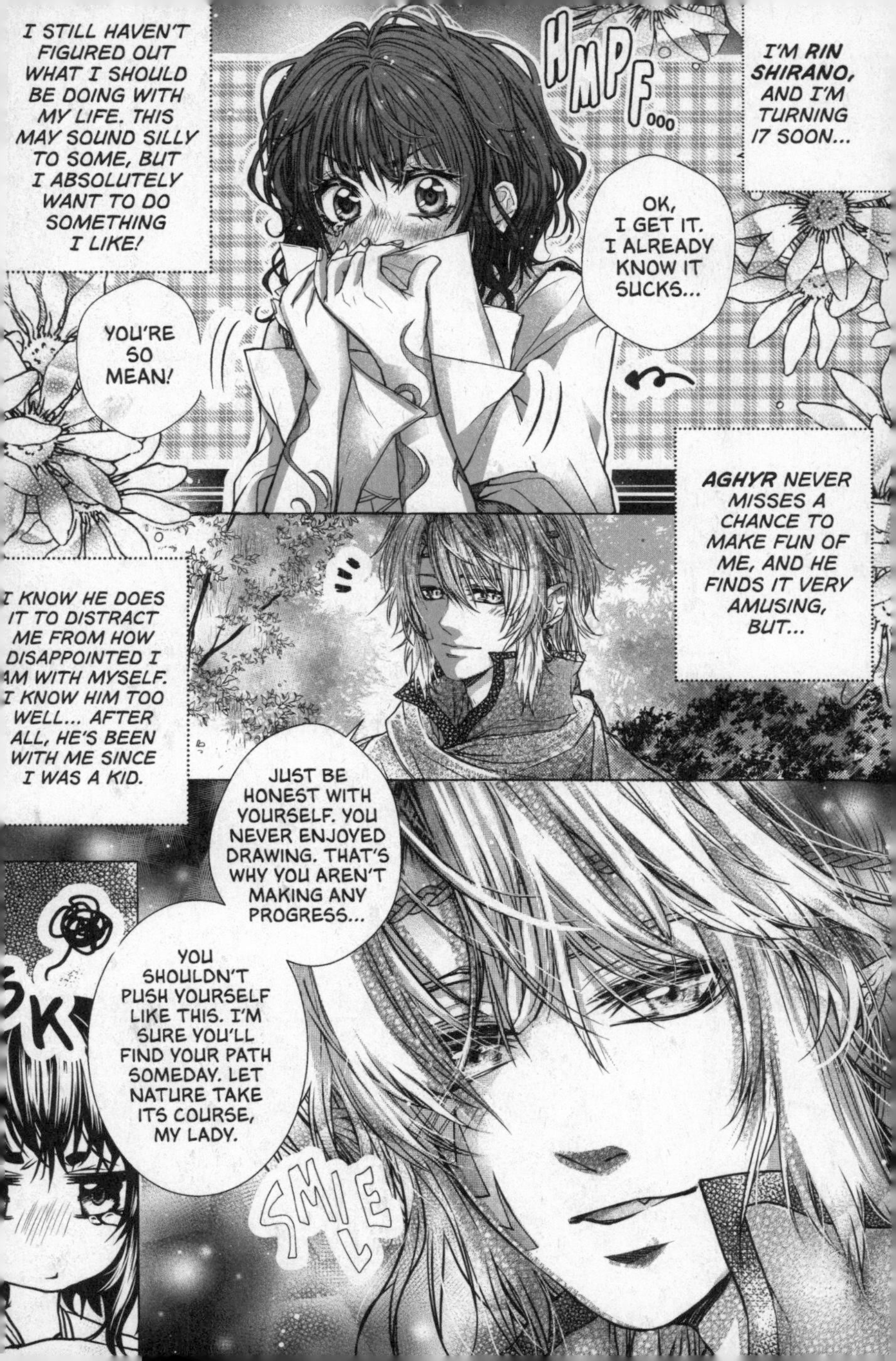
I'M RIN SHIRANO, AND I'M TURNING 17 SOON...
HMPF
I STILL HAVEN'T FIGURED OUT WHAT I SHOULD BE DOING WITH MY LIFE. THIS MAY SOUND SILLY TO SOME, BUT I ABSOLUTELY WANT TO DO SOMETHING I LIKE!
OK, I GET IT. I ALREADY KNOW IT SUCKS...
YOU'RE SO MEAN!
AGHYR NEVER MISSES A CHANCE TO MAKE FUN OF ME, AND HE FINDS IT VERY AMUSING, BUT...
I KNOW HE DOES IT TO DISTRACT ME FROM HOW DISAPPOINTED I AM WITH MYSELF. I KNOW HIM TOO WELL... AFTER ALL, HE'S BEEN WITH ME SINCE I WAS A KID.
JUST BE HONEST WITH YOURSELF. YOU NEVER ENJOYED DRAWING. THAT'S WHY YOU AREN'T MAKING ANY PROGRESS...
YOU SHOULDN'T PUSH YOURSELF LIKE THIS. I'M SURE YOU'LL FIND YOUR PATH SOMEDAY. LET NATURE TAKE ITS COURSE, MY LADY.
SMILE

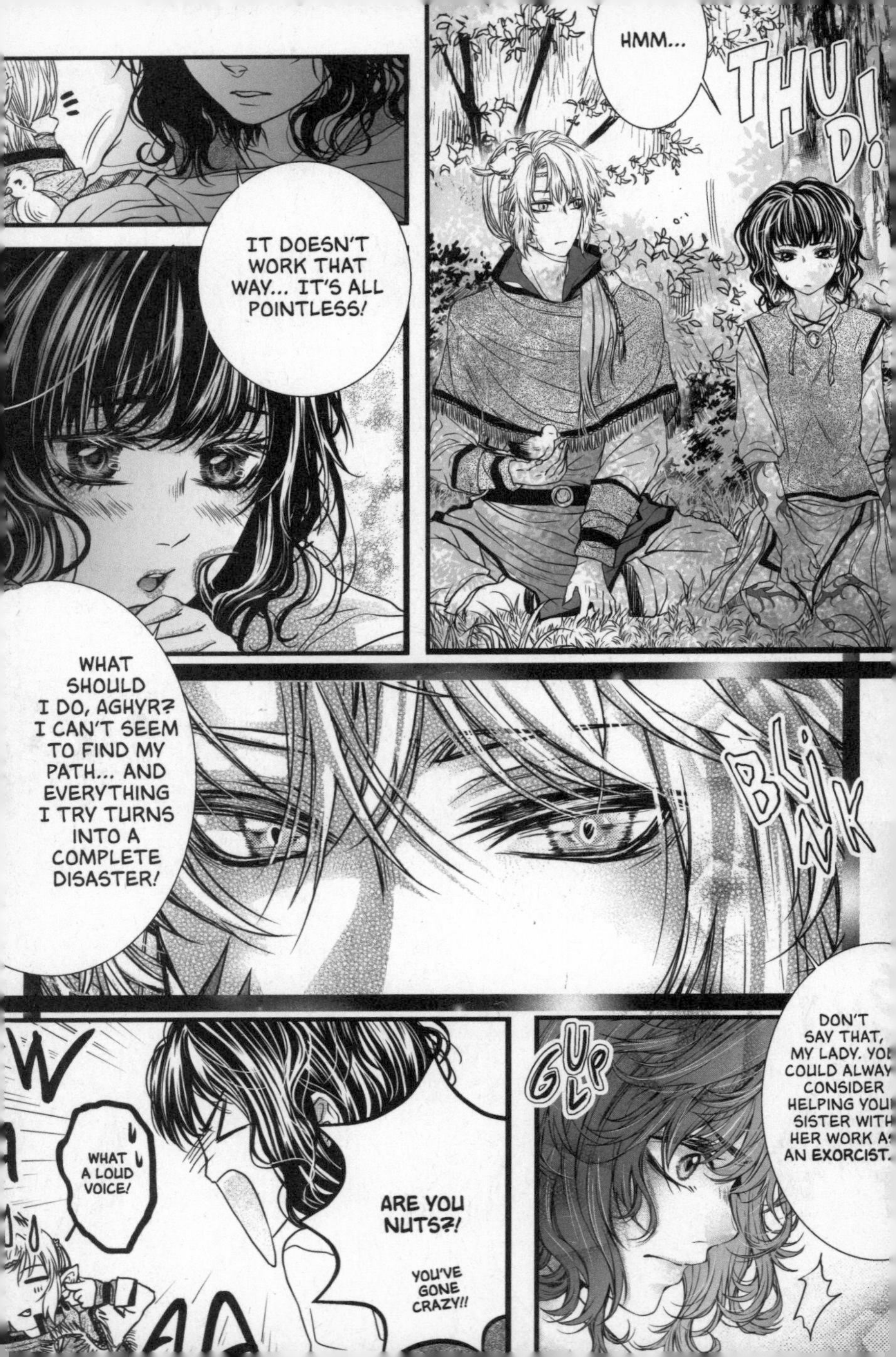
HMM...
THUD!
IT DOESN'T WORK THAT WAY... IT'S ALL POINTLESS!
WHAT SHOULD I DO, AGHYR? I CAN'T SEEM TO FIND MY PATH... AND EVERYTHING I TRY TURNS INTO A COMPLETE DISASTER!
BLINK
GULP
DON'T SAY THAT, MY LADY. YOU COULD ALWAYS CONSIDER HELPING YOUR SISTER WITH HER WORK AS AN EXORCIST.
ARE YOU NUTS?!
YOU'VE GONE CRAZY!!
WHAT A LOUD VOICE!

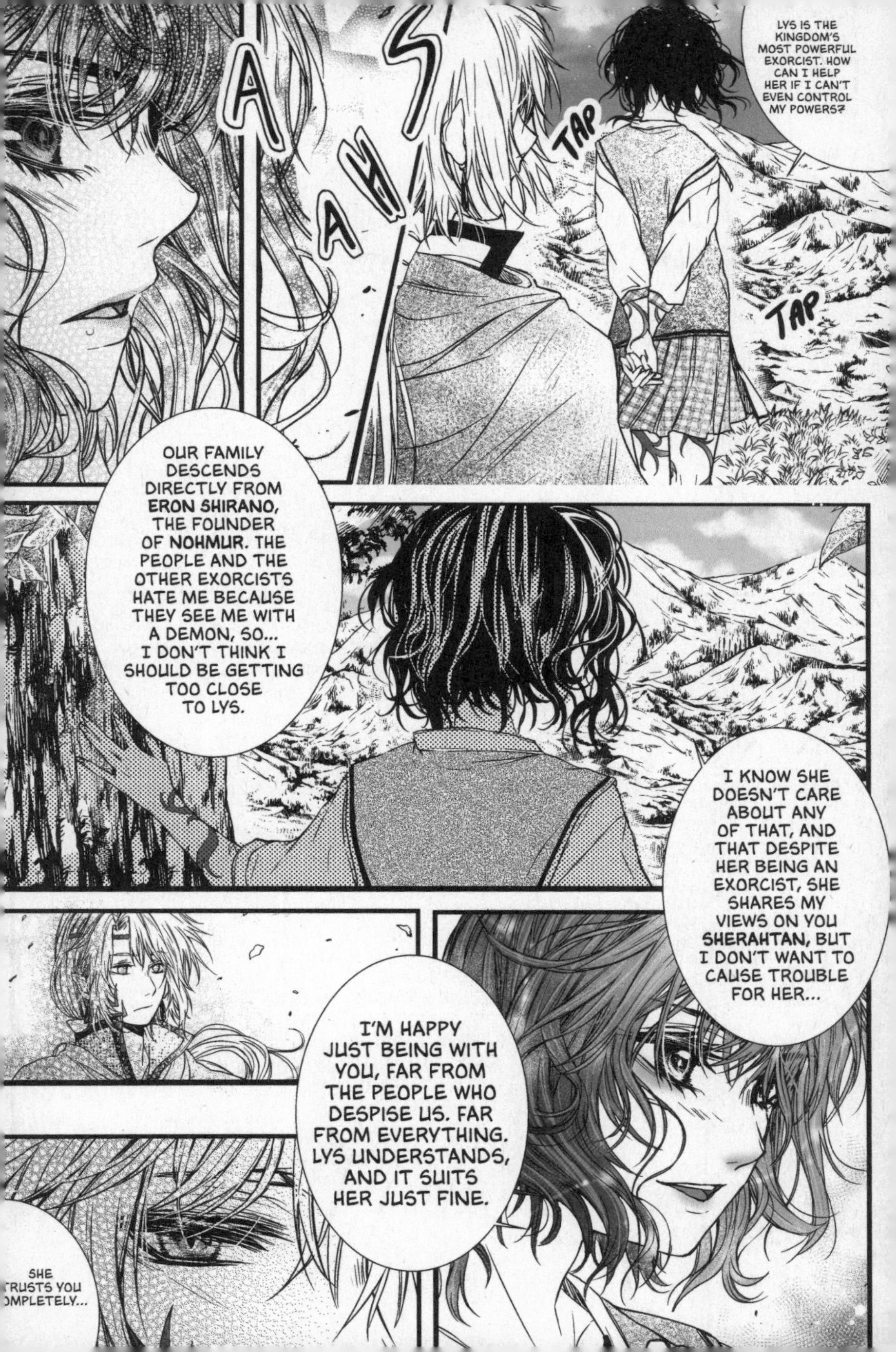
LYS IS THE KINGDOM'S MOST POWERFUL EXORCIST. HOW CAN I HELP HER IF I CAN'T EVEN CONTROL MY POWERS?
TAP
TAP
OUR FAMILY DESCENDS DIRECTLY FROM ERON SHIRANO, THE FOUNDER OF NOHMUR. THE PEOPLE AND THE OTHER EXORCISTS HATE ME BECAUSE THEY SEE ME WITH A DEMON, SO... I DON'T THINK I SHOULD BE GETTING TOO CLOSE TO LYS.
I KNOW SHE DOESN'T CARE ABOUT ANY OF THAT, AND THAT DESPITE HER BEING AN EXORCIST, SHE SHARES MY VIEWS ON YOU SHERAHTAN, BUT I DON'T WANT TO CAUSE TROUBLE FOR HER...
I'M HAPPY JUST BEING WITH YOU, FAR FROM THE PEOPLE WHO DESPISE US. FAR FROM EVERYTHING. LYS UNDERSTANDS, AND IT SUITS HER JUST FINE.
SHE TRUSTS YOU OMPLETELY...

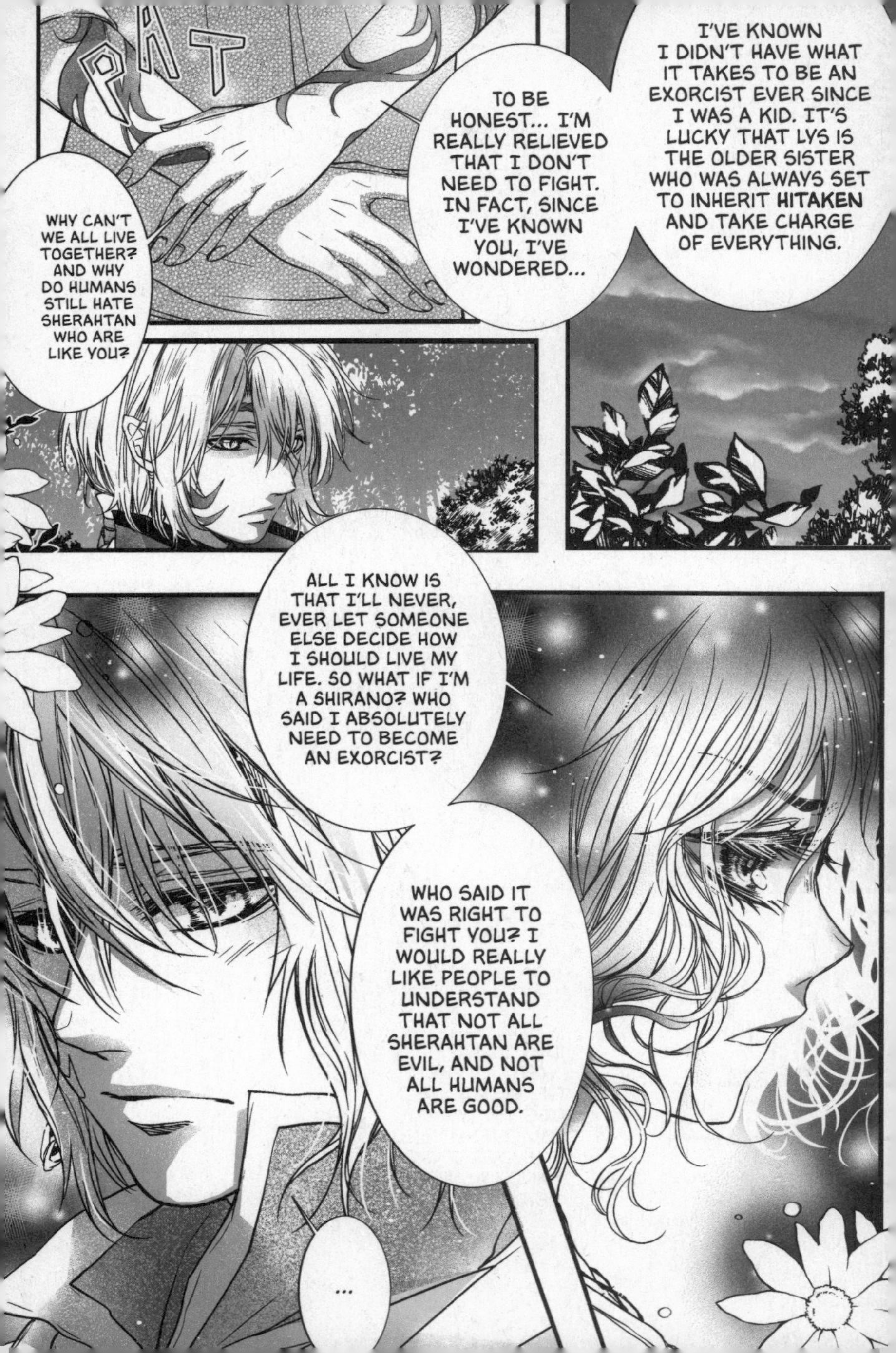
I'VE KNOWN I DIDN'T HAVE WHAT IT TAKES TO BE AN EXORCIST EVER SINCE I WAS A KID. IT'S LUCKY THAT LYS IS THE OLDER SISTER WHO WAS ALWAYS SET TO INHERIT **HITAKEN** AND TAKE CHARGE OF EVERYTHING.
TO BE HONEST... I'M REALLY RELIEVED THAT I DON'T NEED TO FIGHT. IN FACT, SINCE I'VE KNOWN YOU, I'VE WONDERED...
PAT
WHY CAN'T WE ALL LIVE TOGETHER? AND WHY DO HUMANS STILL HATE SHERAHTAN WHO ARE LIKE YOU?
ALL I KNOW IS THAT I'LL NEVER, EVER LET SOMEONE ELSE DECIDE HOW I SHOULD LIVE MY LIFE. SO WHAT IF I'M A SHIRANO? WHO SAID I ABSOLUTELY NEED TO BECOME AN EXORCIST?
WHO SAID IT WAS RIGHT TO FIGHT YOU? I WOULD REALLY LIKE PEOPLE TO UNDERSTAND THAT NOT ALL SHERAHTAN ARE EVIL, AND NOT ALL HUMANS ARE GOOD.
...

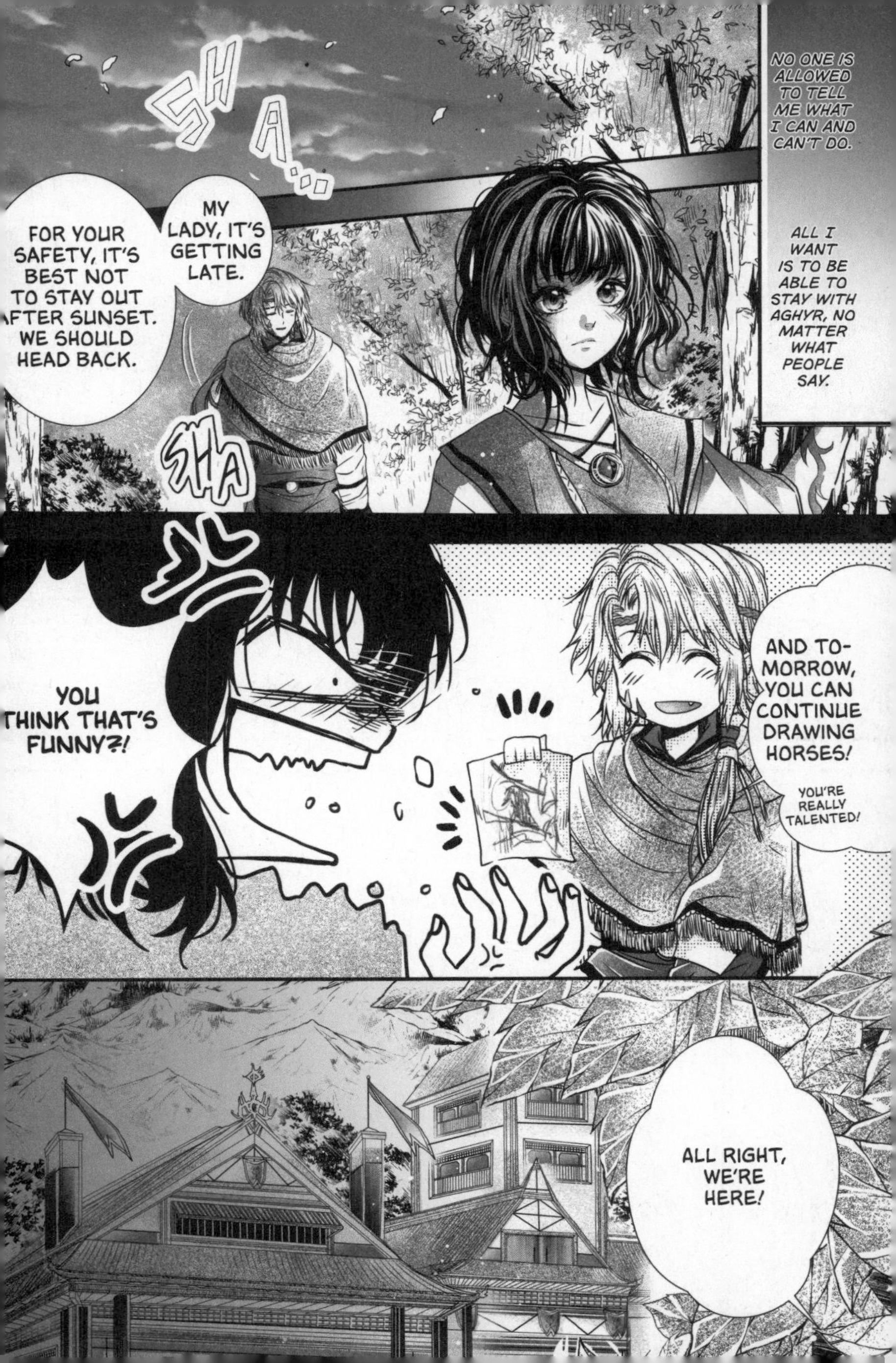

SHA...
NO ONE IS ALLOWED TO TELL ME WHAT I CAN AND CAN'T DO.
ALL I WANT IS TO BE ABLE TO STAY WITH AGHYR, NO MATTER WHAT PEOPLE SAY.
MY LADY, IT'S GETTING LATE.
FOR YOUR SAFETY, IT'S BEST NOT TO STAY OUT FTER SUNSET. WE SHOULD HEAD BACK.
SHA
AND TO-MORROW, YOU CAN CONTINUE DRAWING HORSES!
YOU'RE REALLY TALENTED!
YOU THINK THAT'S FUNNY?!
ALL RIGHT, WE'RE HERE!

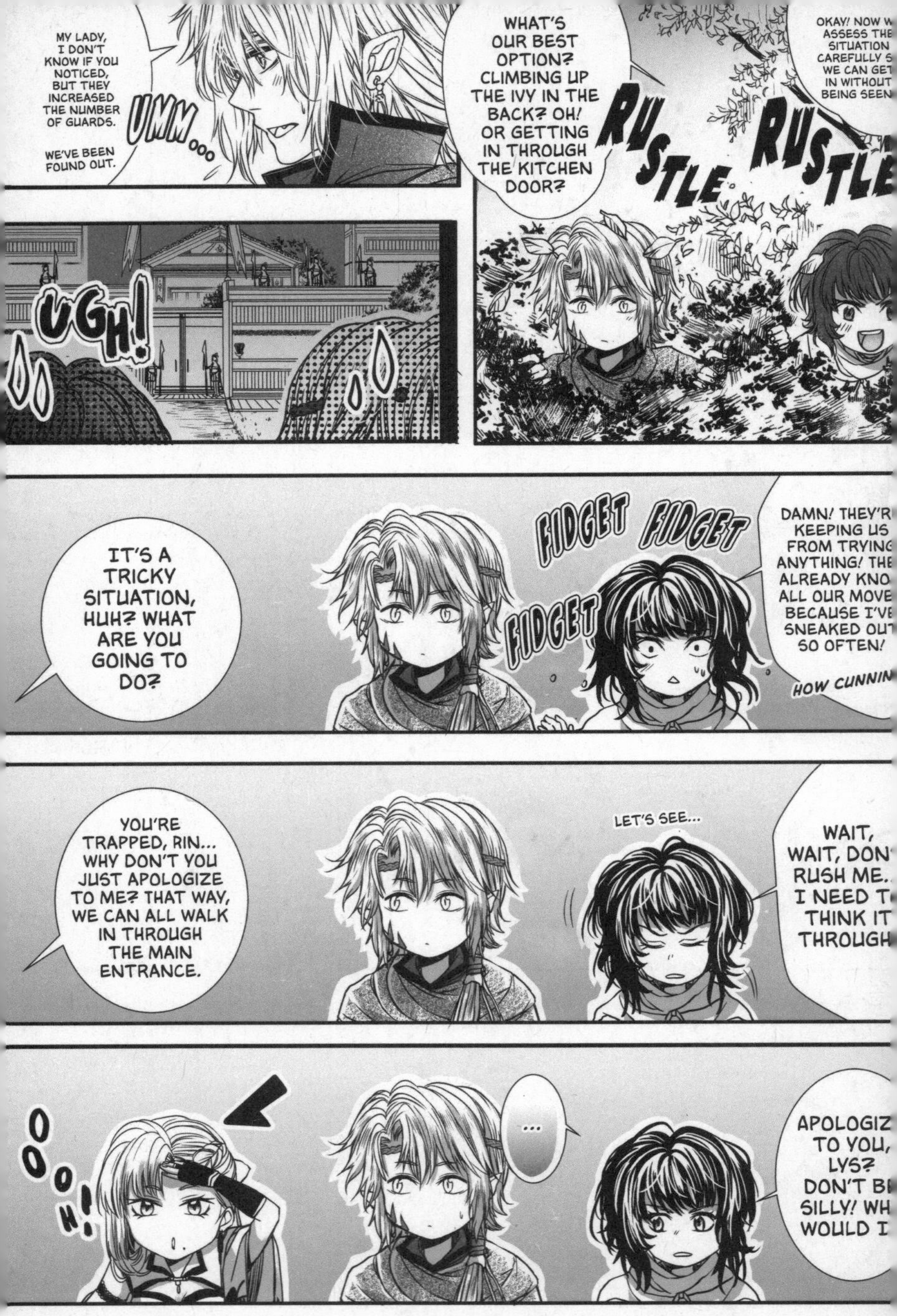
OKAY! NOW W ASSESS THE SITUATION CAREFULLY S WE CAN GET IN WITHOUT BEING SEEN
RUSTLE RUSTLE
WHAT'S OUR BEST OPTION? CLIMBING UP THE IVY IN THE BACK? OH! OR GETTING IN THROUGH THE KITCHEN DOOR?
UMM...
MY LADY, I DON'T KNOW IF YOU NOTICED, BUT THEY INCREASED THE NUMBER OF GUARDS.
WE'VE BEEN FOUND OUT.
UGH!
DAMN! THEY'R KEEPING US FROM TRYING ANYTHING! THE ALREADY KNO ALL OUR MOVE BECAUSE I'VE SNEAKED OUT SO OFTEN!
HOW CUNNIN
FIDGET FIDGET FIDGET
IT'S A TRICKY SITUATION, HUH? WHAT ARE YOU GOING TO DO?
WAIT, WAIT, DON RUSH ME.. I NEED T THINK IT THROUGH
LET'S SEE...
YOU'RE TRAPPED, RIN... WHY DON'T YOU JUST APOLOGIZE TO ME? THAT WAY, WE CAN ALL WALK IN THROUGH THE MAIN ENTRANCE.
APOLOGIZ TO YOU, LYS? DON'T B SILLY! WH WOULD I
...
OOOH!

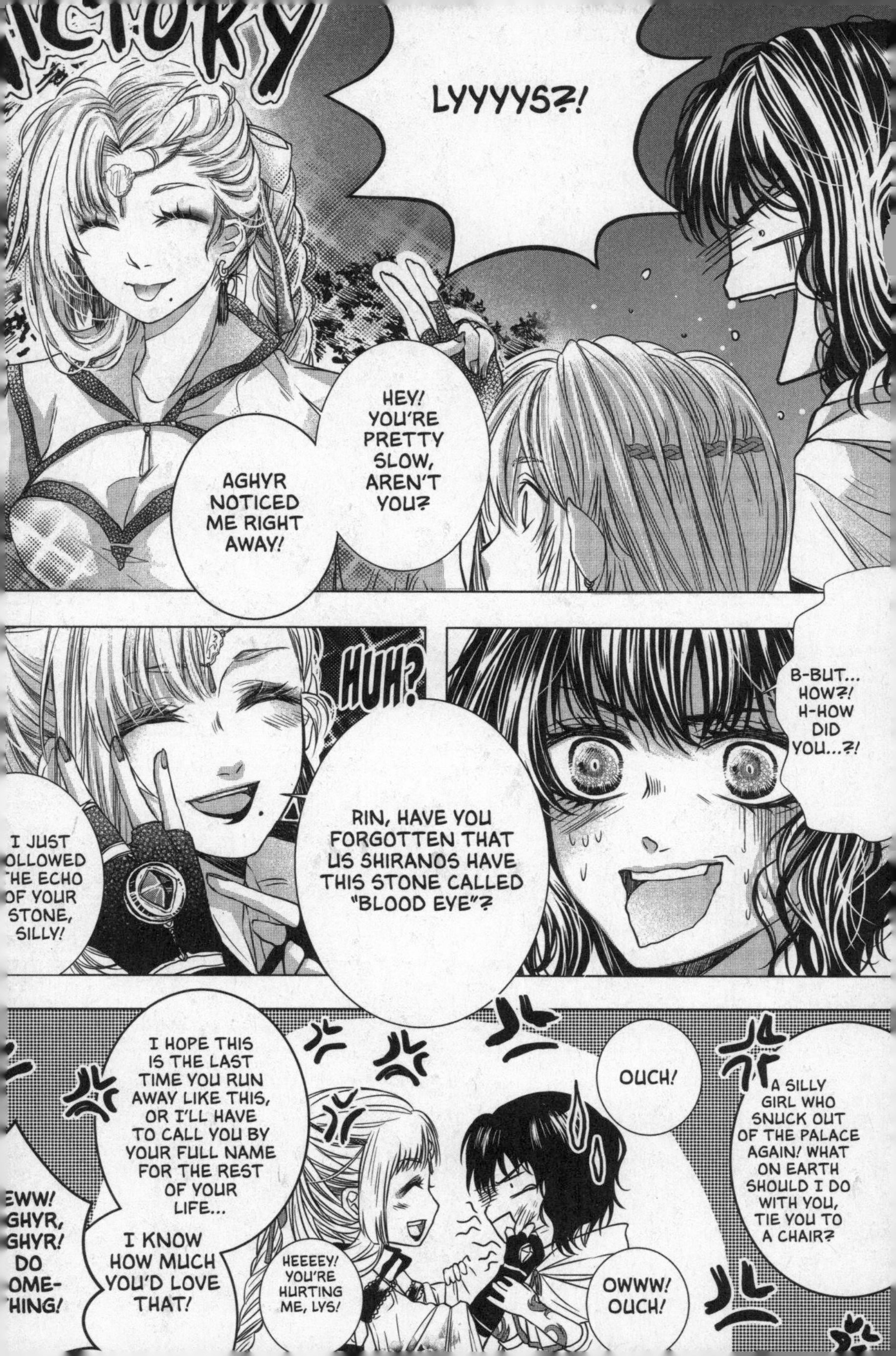
LYYYYS?!
ICTORY
HEY! YOU'RE PRETTY SLOW, AREN'T YOU?
AGHYR NOTICED ME RIGHT AWAY!
B-BUT... HOW?! H-HOW DID YOU...?!
HUH?
RIN, HAVE YOU FORGOTTEN THAT US SHIRANOS HAVE THIS STONE CALLED "BLOOD EYE"?
I JUST OLLOWED THE ECHO OF YOUR STONE, SILLY!
A SILLY GIRL WHO SNUCK OUT OF THE PALACE AGAIN! WHAT ON EARTH SHOULD I DO WITH YOU, TIE YOU TO A CHAIR?
OUCH!
I HOPE THIS IS THE LAST TIME YOU RUN AWAY LIKE THIS, OR I'LL HAVE TO CALL YOU BY YOUR FULL NAME FOR THE REST OF YOUR LIFE...
I KNOW HOW MUCH YOU'D LOVE THAT!
OWWW! OUCH!
HEEEEY! YOU'RE HURTING ME, LYS!
EWW! GHYR, GHYR! DO OME- HING!

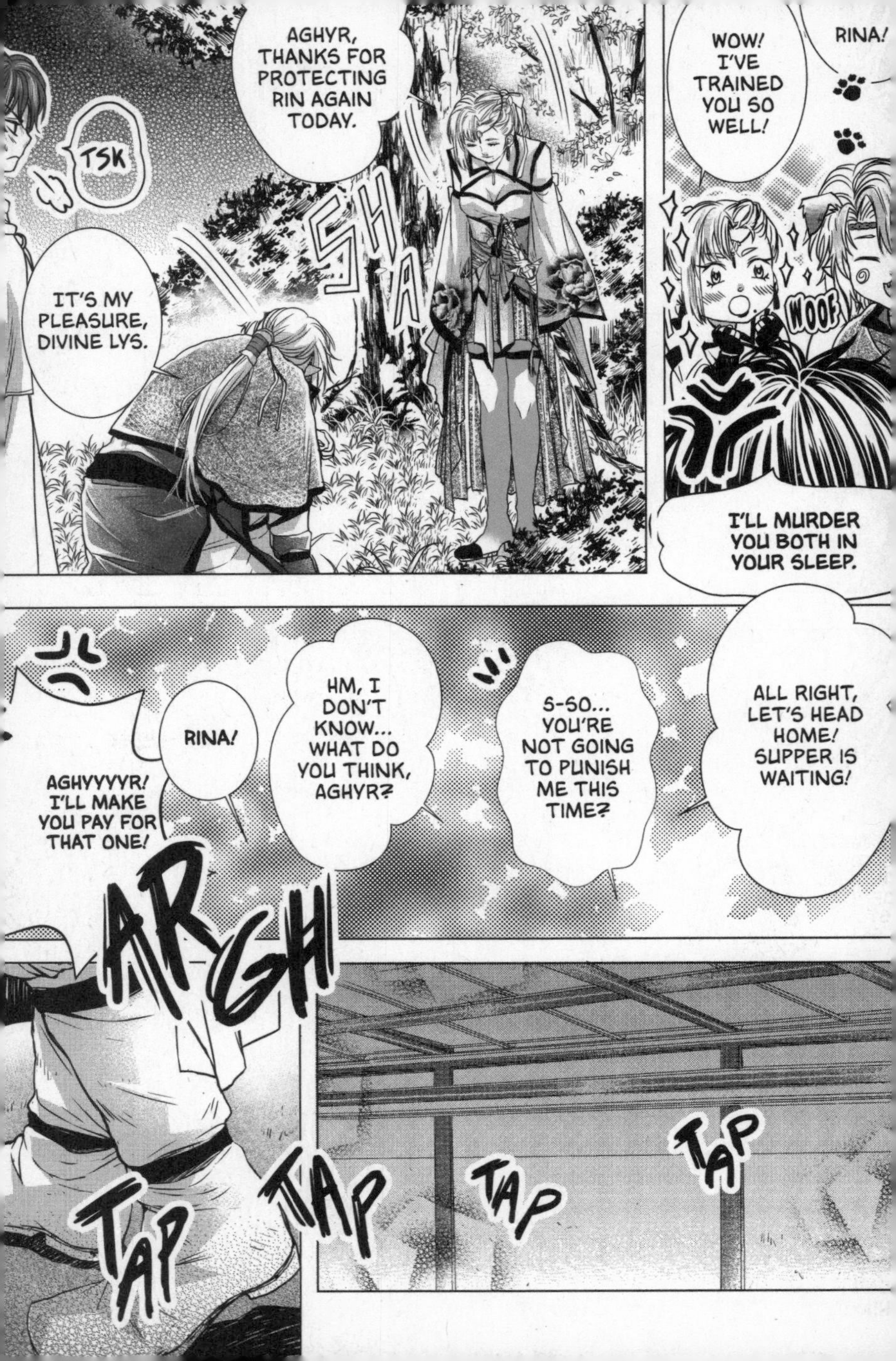
RINA!
WOW! I'VE TRAINED YOU SO WELL!
WOOF
I'LL MURDER YOU BOTH IN YOUR SLEEP.
AGHYR, THANKS FOR PROTECTING RIN AGAIN TODAY.
SHA
TSK
IT'S MY PLEASURE, DIVINE LYS.
ALL RIGHT, LET'S HEAD HOME! SUPPER IS WAITING!
S-SO... YOU'RE NOT GOING TO PUNISH ME THIS TIME?
HM, I DON'T KNOW... WHAT DO YOU THINK, AGHYR?
RINA!
AGHYYYYR! I'LL MAKE YOU PAY FOR THAT ONE!
TAP
TAP
ARGH
TAP
TAP

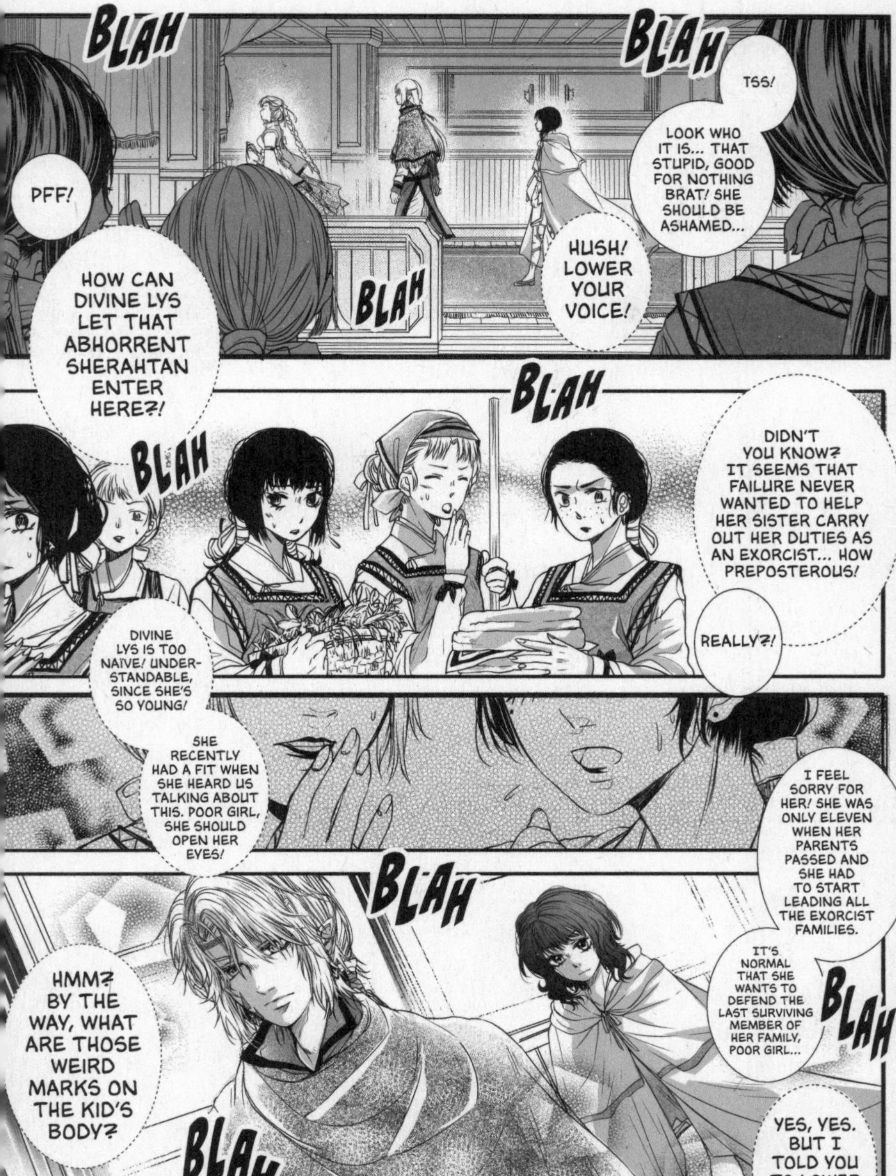
BLAH
TSS!
LOOK WHO IT IS... THAT STUPID, GOOD FOR NOTHING BRAT! SHE SHOULD BE ASHAMED...
HUSH! LOWER YOUR VOICE!
BLAH
BLAH
PFF!
HOW CAN DIVINE LYS LET THAT ABHORRENT SHERAHTAN ENTER HERE?!
BLAH
DIDN'T YOU KNOW? IT SEEMS THAT FAILURE NEVER WANTED TO HELP HER SISTER CARRY OUT HER DUTIES AS AN EXORCIST... HOW PREPOSTEROUS!
REALLY?!
BLAH
DIVINE LYS IS TOO NAIVE! UNDER-STANDABLE, SINCE SHE'S SO YOUNG!
I FEEL SORRY FOR HER! SHE WAS ONLY ELEVEN WHEN HER PARENTS PASSED AND SHE HAD TO START LEADING ALL THE EXORCIST FAMILIES.
SHE RECENTLY HAD A FIT WHEN SHE HEARD US TALKING ABOUT THIS. POOR GIRL, SHE SHOULD OPEN HER EYES!
BLAH
IT'S NORMAL THAT SHE WANTS TO DEFEND THE LAST SURVIVING MEMBER OF HER FAMILY, POOR GIRL...
BLAH
YES, YES. BUT I TOLD YOU TO LOWER YOUR VOICE!
HMM? BY THE WAY, WHAT ARE THOSE WEIRD MARKS ON THE KID'S BODY?
BLAH

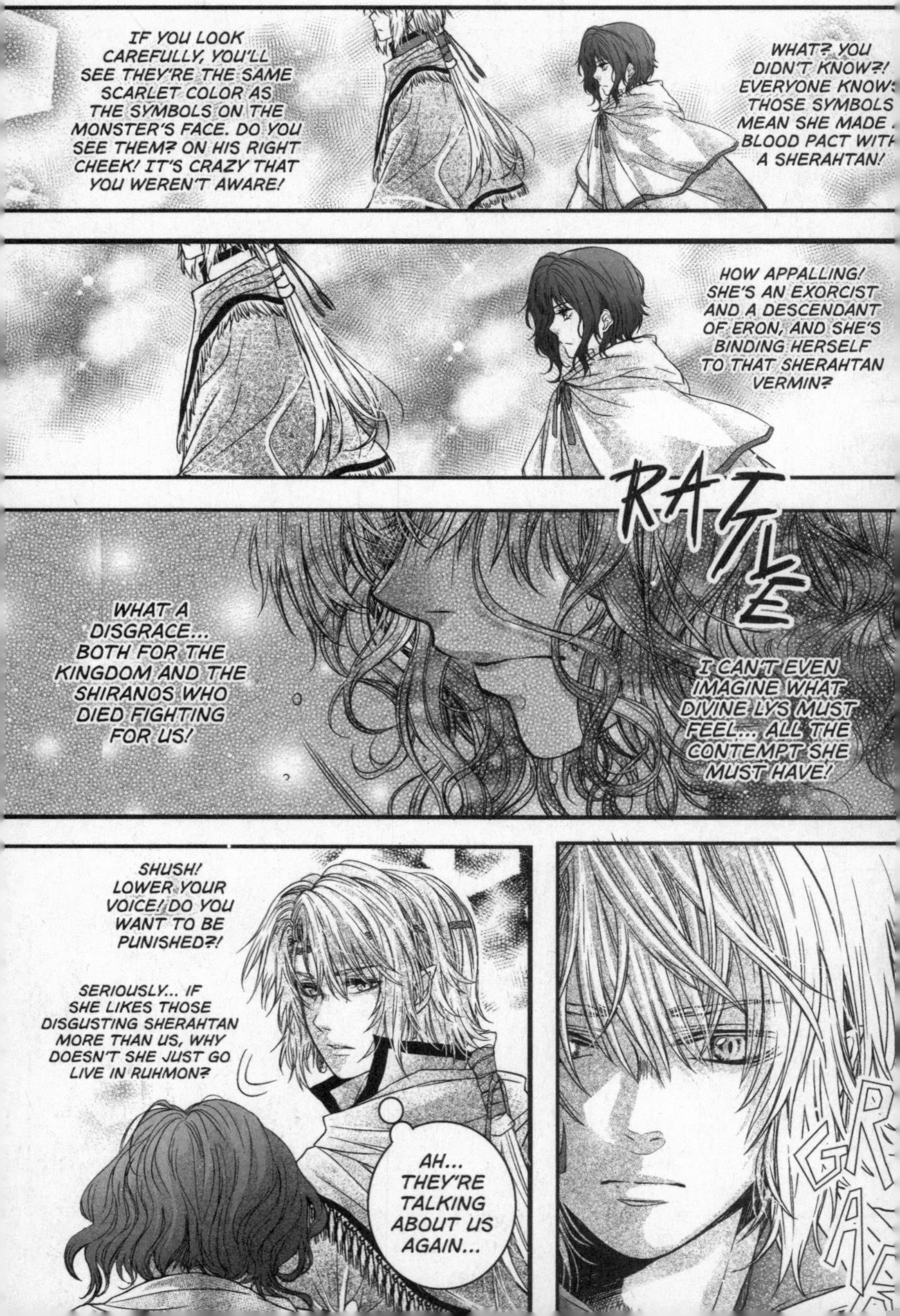

WHAT? YOU DIDN'T KNOW?! EVERYONE KNOWS THOSE SYMBOLS MEAN SHE MADE A BLOOD PACT WITH A SHERAHTAN!
IF YOU LOOK CAREFULLY, YOU'LL SEE THEY'RE THE SAME SCARLET COLOR AS THE SYMBOLS ON THE MONSTER'S FACE. DO YOU SEE THEM? ON HIS RIGHT CHEEK! IT'S CRAZY THAT YOU WEREN'T AWARE!
HOW APPALLING! SHE'S AN EXORCIST AND A DESCENDANT OF ERON, AND SHE'S BINDING HERSELF TO THAT SHERAHTAN VERMIN?
RATTLE
I CAN'T EVEN IMAGINE WHAT DIVINE LYS MUST FEEL... ALL THE CONTEMPT SHE MUST HAVE!
WHAT A DISGRACE... BOTH FOR THE KINGDOM AND THE SHIRANOS WHO DIED FIGHTING FOR US!
GRR
SHUSH! LOWER YOUR VOICE! DO YOU WANT TO BE PUNISHED?!
SERIOUSLY... IF SHE LIKES THOSE DISGUSTING SHERAHTAN MORE THAN US, WHY DOESN'T SHE JUST GO LIVE IN RUHMON?
AH... THEY'RE TALKING ABOUT US AGAIN...

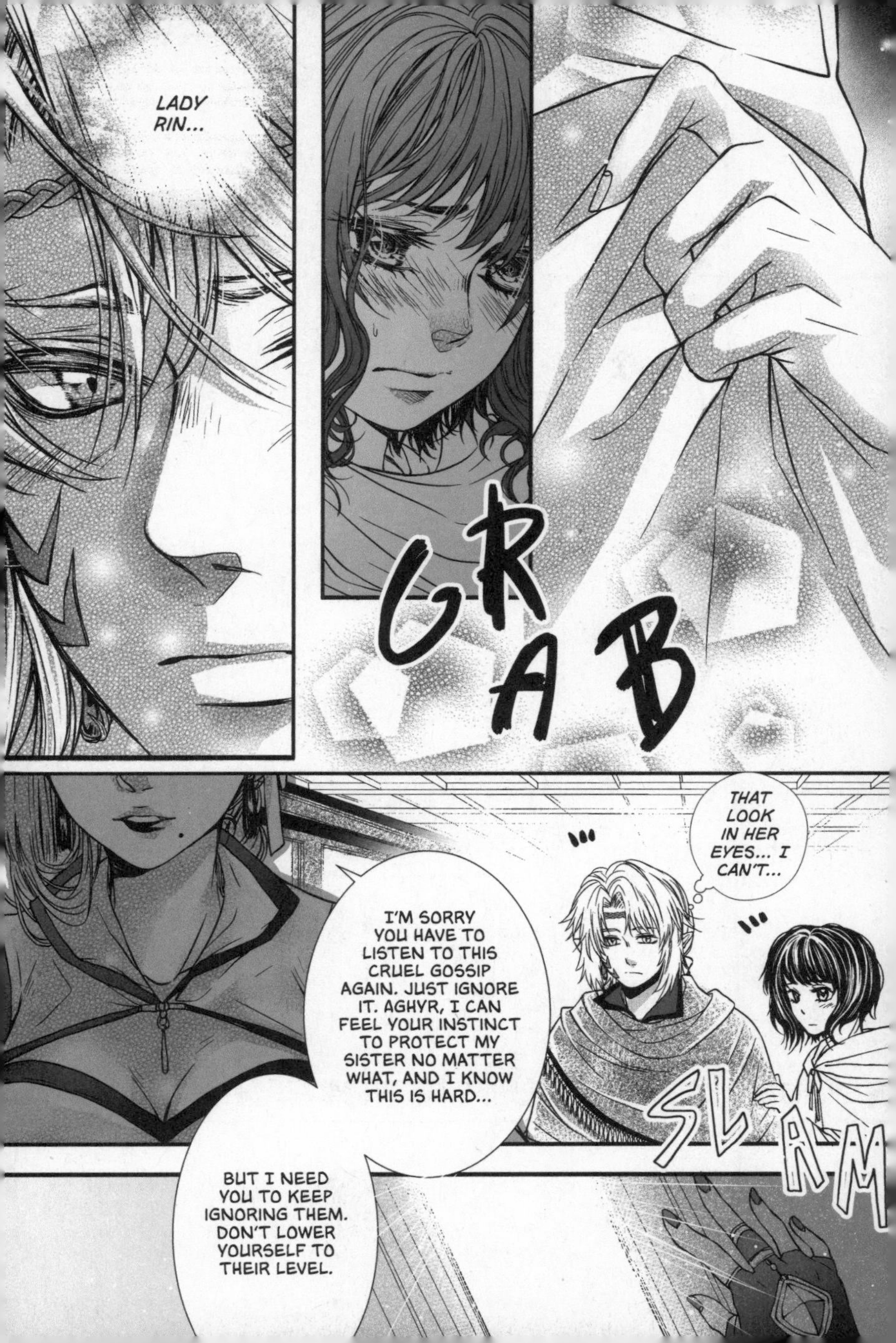
GRAB
LADY RIN...
THAT LOOK IN HER EYES... I CAN'T...
...
...
I'M SORRY YOU HAVE TO LISTEN TO THIS CRUEL GOSSIP AGAIN. JUST IGNORE IT. AGHYR, I CAN FEEL YOUR INSTINCT TO PROTECT MY SISTER NO MATTER WHAT, AND I KNOW THIS IS HARD...
BUT I NEED YOU TO KEEP IGNORING THEM. DON'T LOWER YOURSELF TO THEIR LEVEL.
SLAM

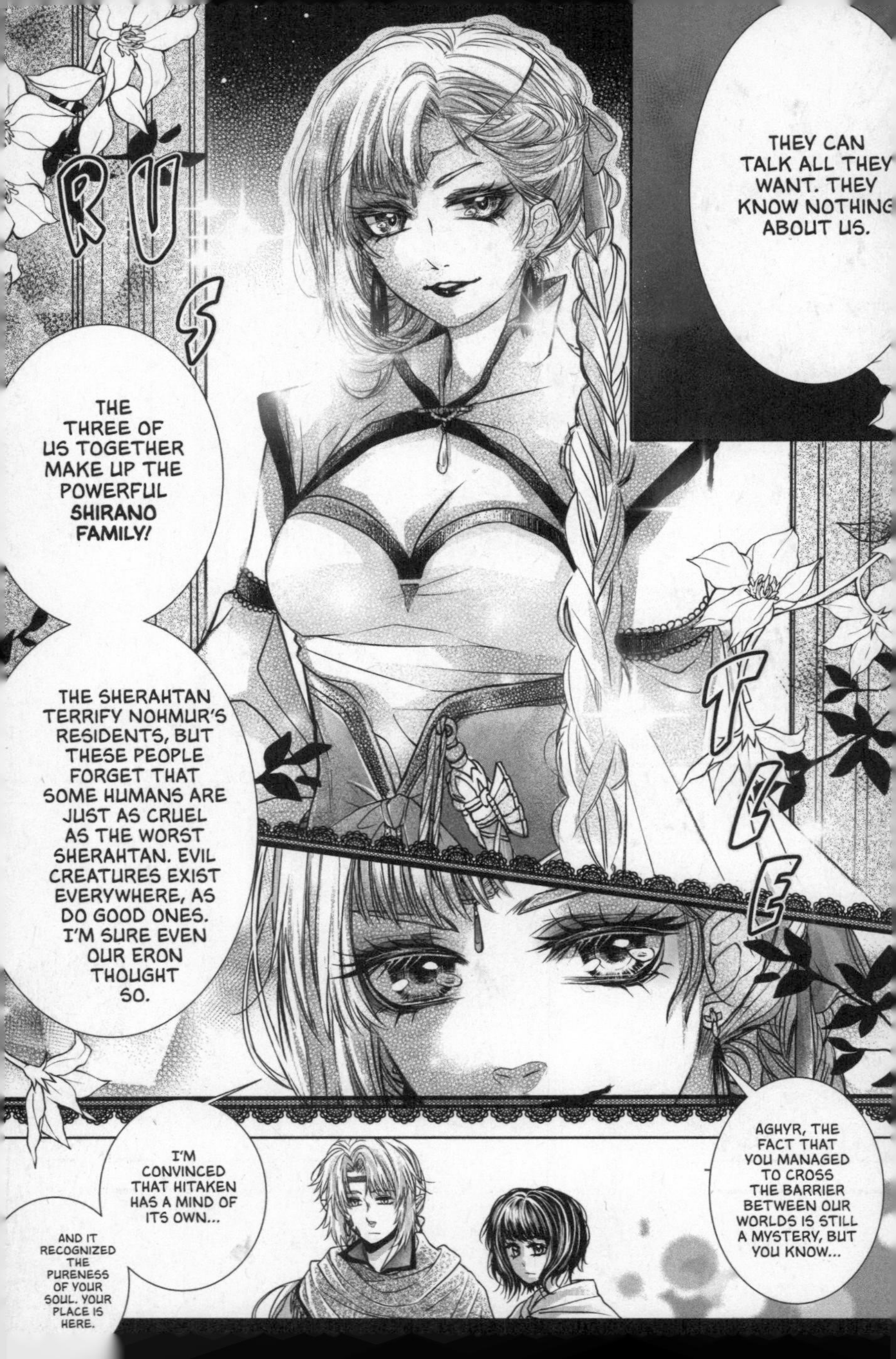
THEY CAN TALK ALL THEY WANT. THEY KNOW NOTHING ABOUT US.
RUS
TLE
THE THREE OF US TOGETHER MAKE UP THE POWERFUL SHIRANO FAMILY!
THE SHERAHTAN TERRIFY NOHMUR'S RESIDENTS, BUT THESE PEOPLE FORGET THAT SOME HUMANS ARE JUST AS CRUEL AS THE WORST SHERAHTAN. EVIL CREATURES EXIST EVERYWHERE, AS DO GOOD ONES. I'M SURE EVEN OUR ERON THOUGHT SO.
AGHYR, THE FACT THAT YOU MANAGED TO CROSS THE BARRIER BETWEEN OUR WORLDS IS STILL A MYSTERY, BUT YOU KNOW...
I'M CONVINCED THAT HITAKEN HAS A MIND OF ITS OWN...
AND IT RECOGNIZED THE PURENESS OF YOUR SOUL. YOUR PLACE IS HERE.

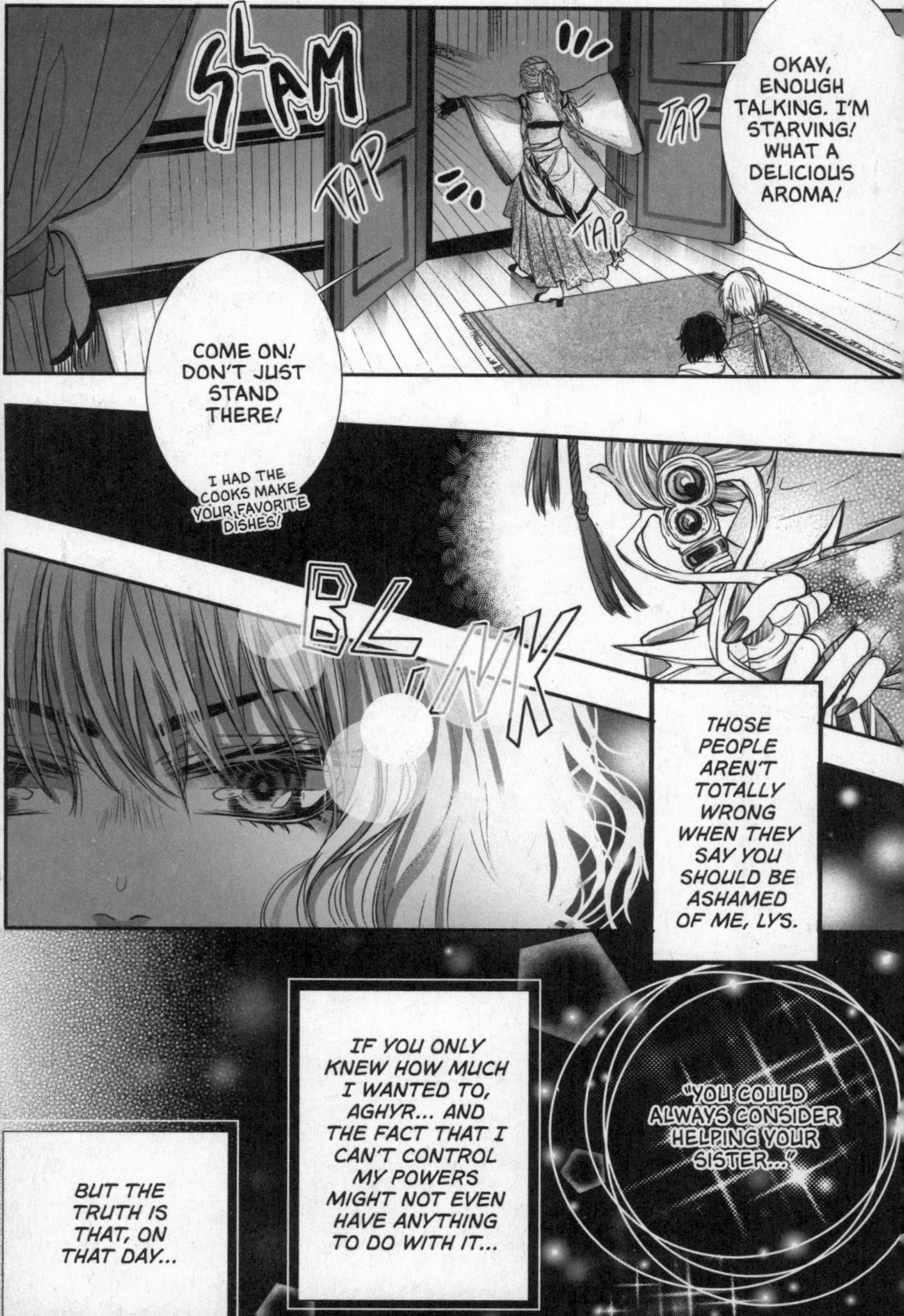
OKAY, ENOUGH TALKING. I'M STARVING! WHAT A DELICIOUS AROMA!
TAP
TAP
...
TAP
SLAM
COME ON! DON'T JUST STAND THERE!
I HAD THE COOKS MAKE YOUR FAVORITE DISHES!
BLINK
THOSE PEOPLE AREN'T TOTALLY WRONG WHEN THEY SAY YOU SHOULD BE ASHAMED OF ME, LYS.
"YOU COULD ALWAYS CONSIDER HELPING YOUR SISTER..."
IF YOU ONLY KNEW HOW MUCH I WANTED TO, AGHYR... AND THE FACT THAT I CAN'T CONTROL MY POWERS MIGHT NOT EVEN HAVE ANYTHING TO DO WITH IT...
BUT THE TRUTH IS THAT, ON THAT DAY...

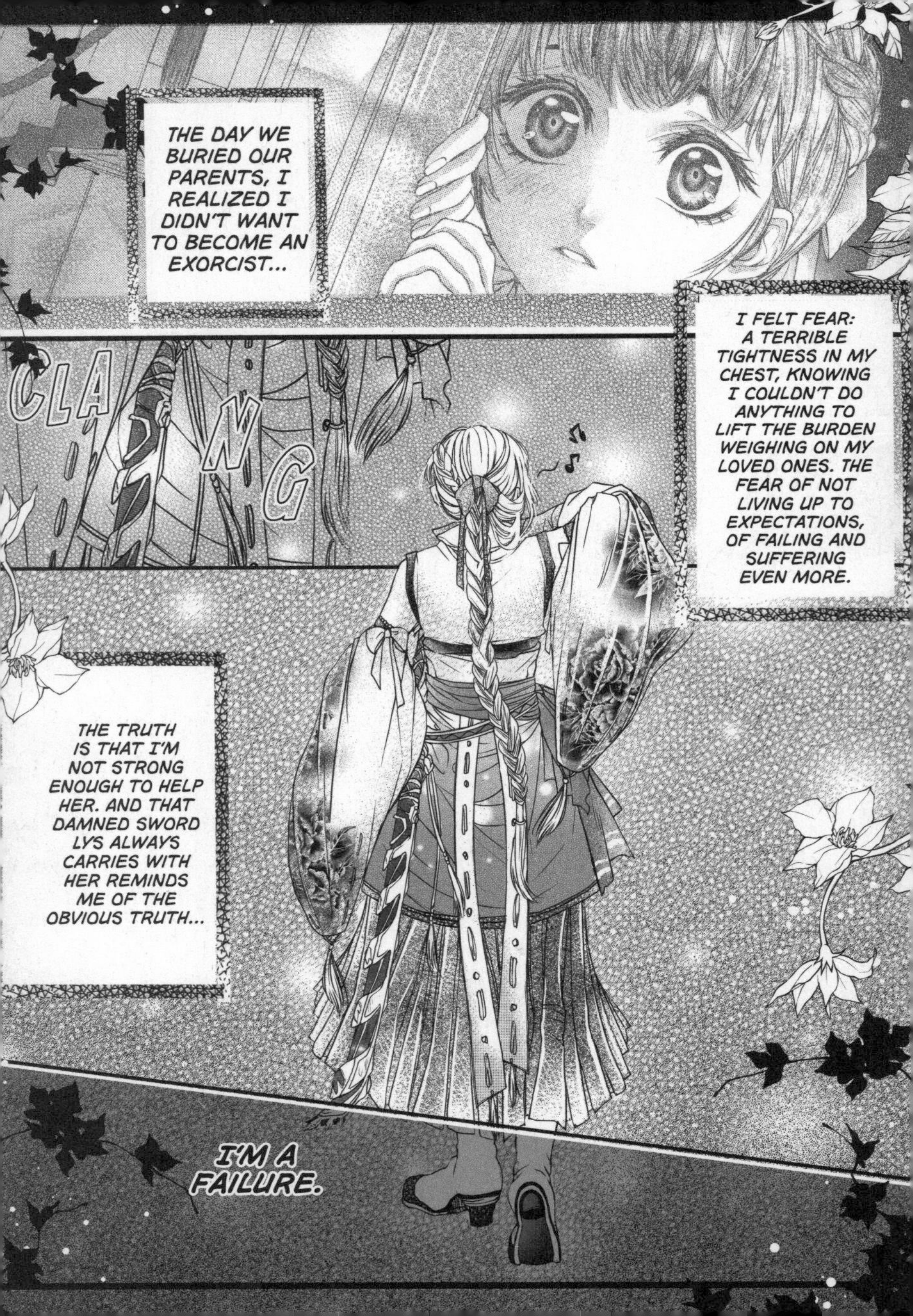
THE DAY WE BURIED OUR PARENTS, I REALIZED I DIDN'T WANT TO BECOME AN EXORCIST...
I FELT FEAR: A TERRIBLE TIGHTNESS IN MY CHEST, KNOWING I COULDN'T DO ANYTHING TO LIFT THE BURDEN WEIGHING ON MY LOVED ONES. THE FEAR OF NOT LIVING UP TO EXPECTATIONS, OF FAILING AND SUFFERING EVEN MORE.
CLANG
THE TRUTH IS THAT I'M NOT STRONG ENOUGH TO HELP HER. AND THAT DAMNED SWORD LYS ALWAYS CARRIES WITH HER REMINDS ME OF THE OBVIOUS TRUTH...
I'M A FAILURE.

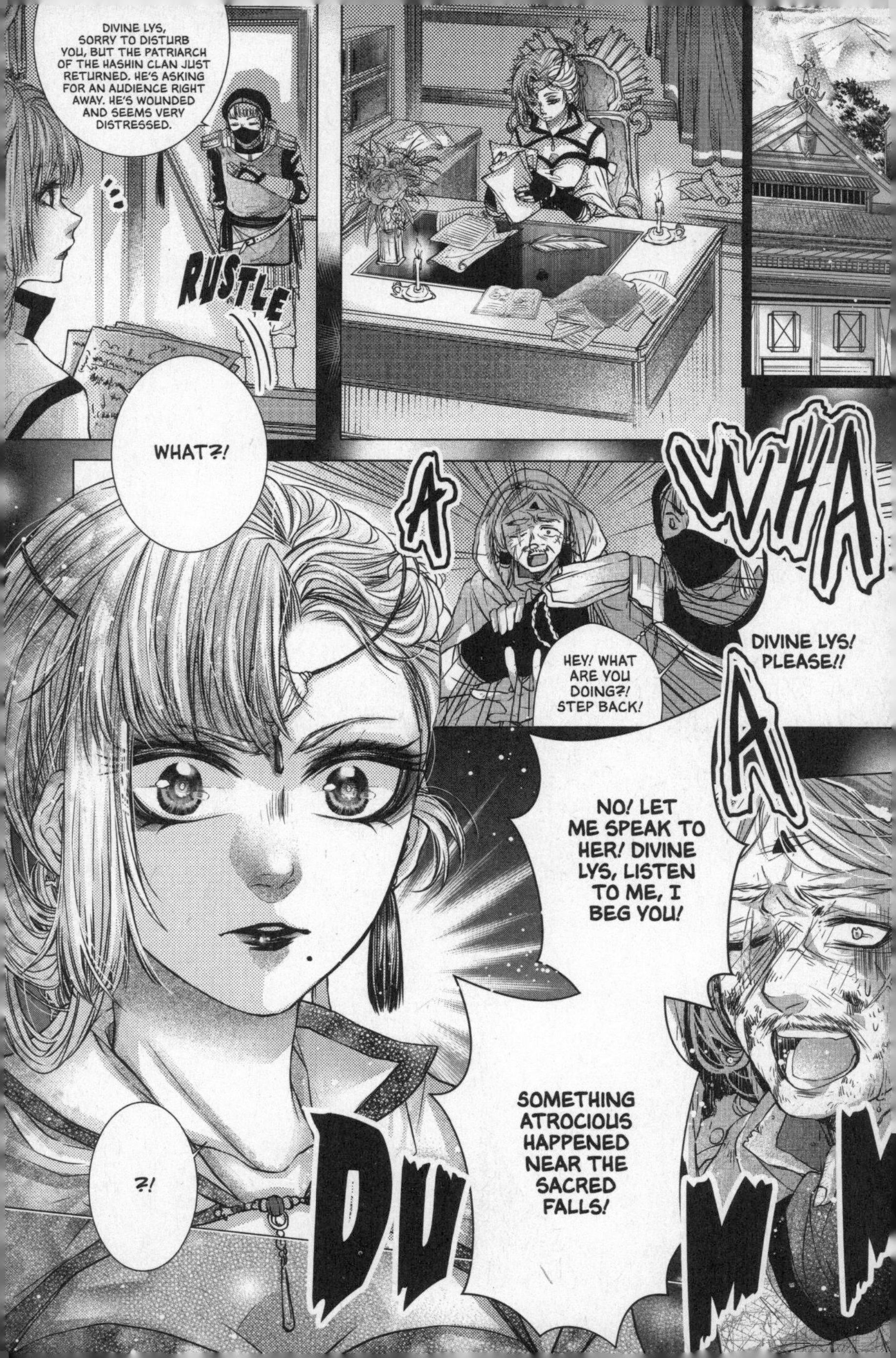
DIVINE LYS, SORRY TO DISTURB YOU, BUT THE PATRIARCH OF THE HASHIN CLAN JUST RETURNED. HE'S ASKING FOR AN AUDIENCE RIGHT AWAY. HE'S WOUNDED AND SEEMS VERY DISTRESSED.
RUSTLE
WHAT?!
WHA
A
A
DIVINE LYS! PLEASE!!
HEY! WHAT ARE YOU DOING?! STEP BACK!
NO! LET ME SPEAK TO HER! DIVINE LYS, LISTEN TO ME, I BEG YOU!
SOMETHING ATROCIOUS HAPPENED NEAR THE SACRED FALLS!
DU
MM
?!

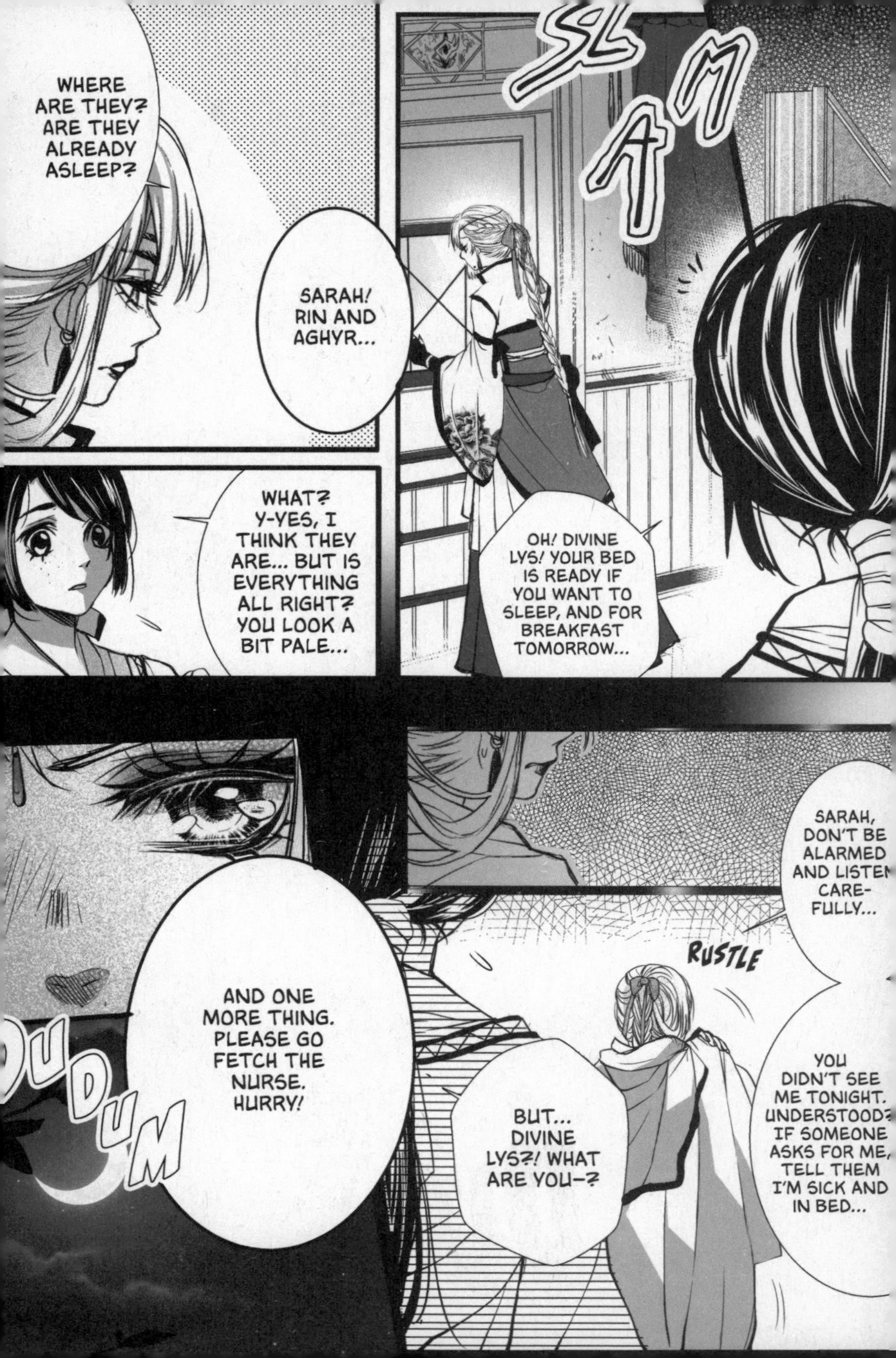
SLAM
OH! DIVINE LYS! YOUR BED IS READY IF YOU WANT TO SLEEP, AND FOR BREAKFAST TOMORROW...
SARAH! RIN AND AGHYR...
WHERE ARE THEY? ARE THEY ALREADY ASLEEP?
WHAT? Y-YES, I THINK THEY ARE... BUT IS EVERYTHING ALL RIGHT? YOU LOOK A BIT PALE...
SARAH, DON'T BE ALARMED AND LISTEN CARE-FULLY...
YOU DIDN'T SEE ME TONIGHT. UNDERSTOOD? IF SOMEONE ASKS FOR ME, TELL THEM I'M SICK AND IN BED...
RUSTLE
BUT... DIVINE LYS?! WHAT ARE YOU—?
AND ONE MORE THING. PLEASE GO FETCH THE NURSE. HURRY!
DUDUM

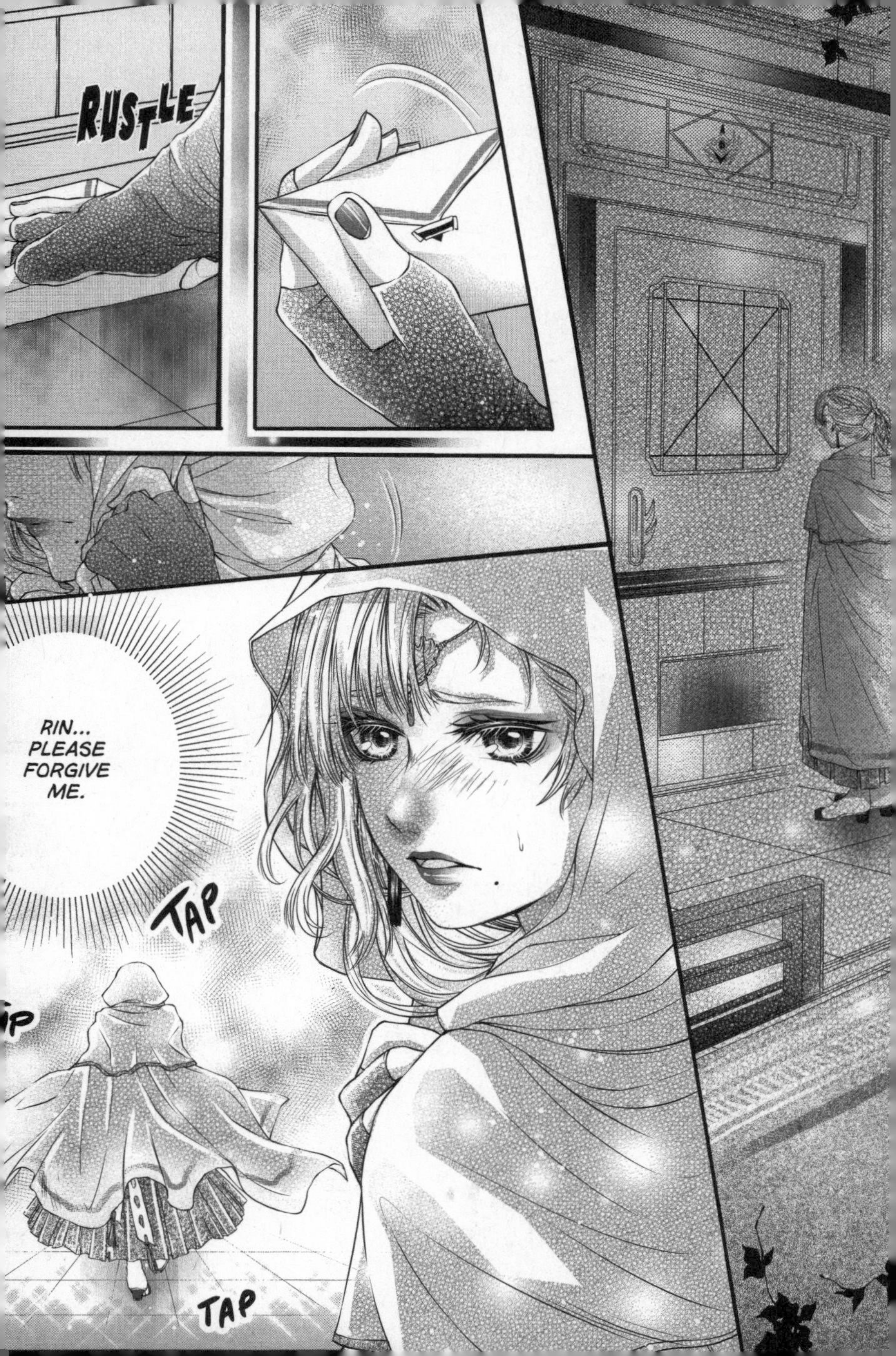
RUSTLE
RIN... PLEASE FORGIVE ME.
TAP
TAP

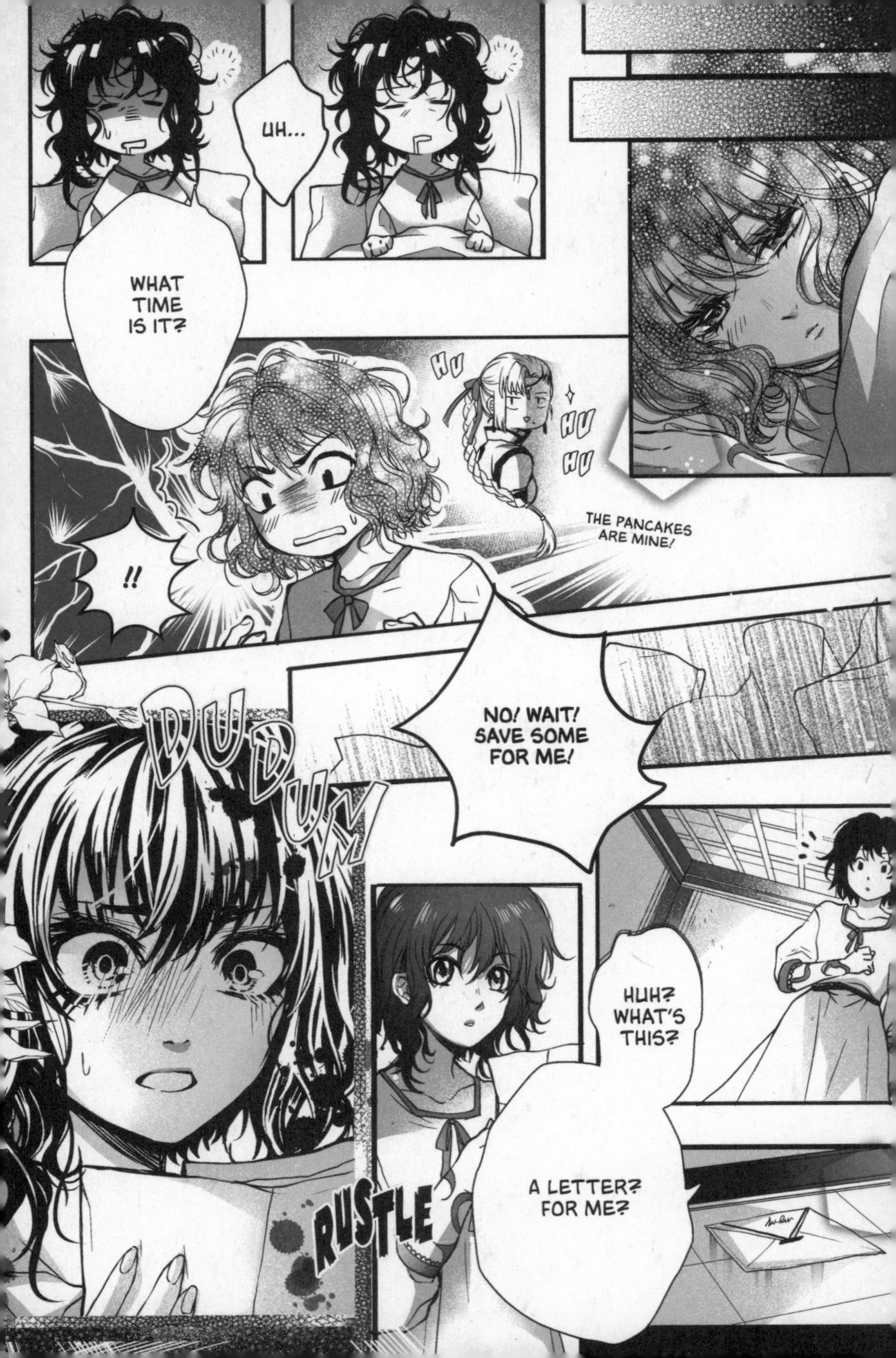
UH...
WHAT TIME IS IT?
HU HU HU HU
THE PANCAKES ARE MINE!
!!
NO! WAIT! SAVE SOME FOR ME!
HUH? WHAT'S THIS?
A LETTER? FOR ME?
RUSTLE
DUDUM

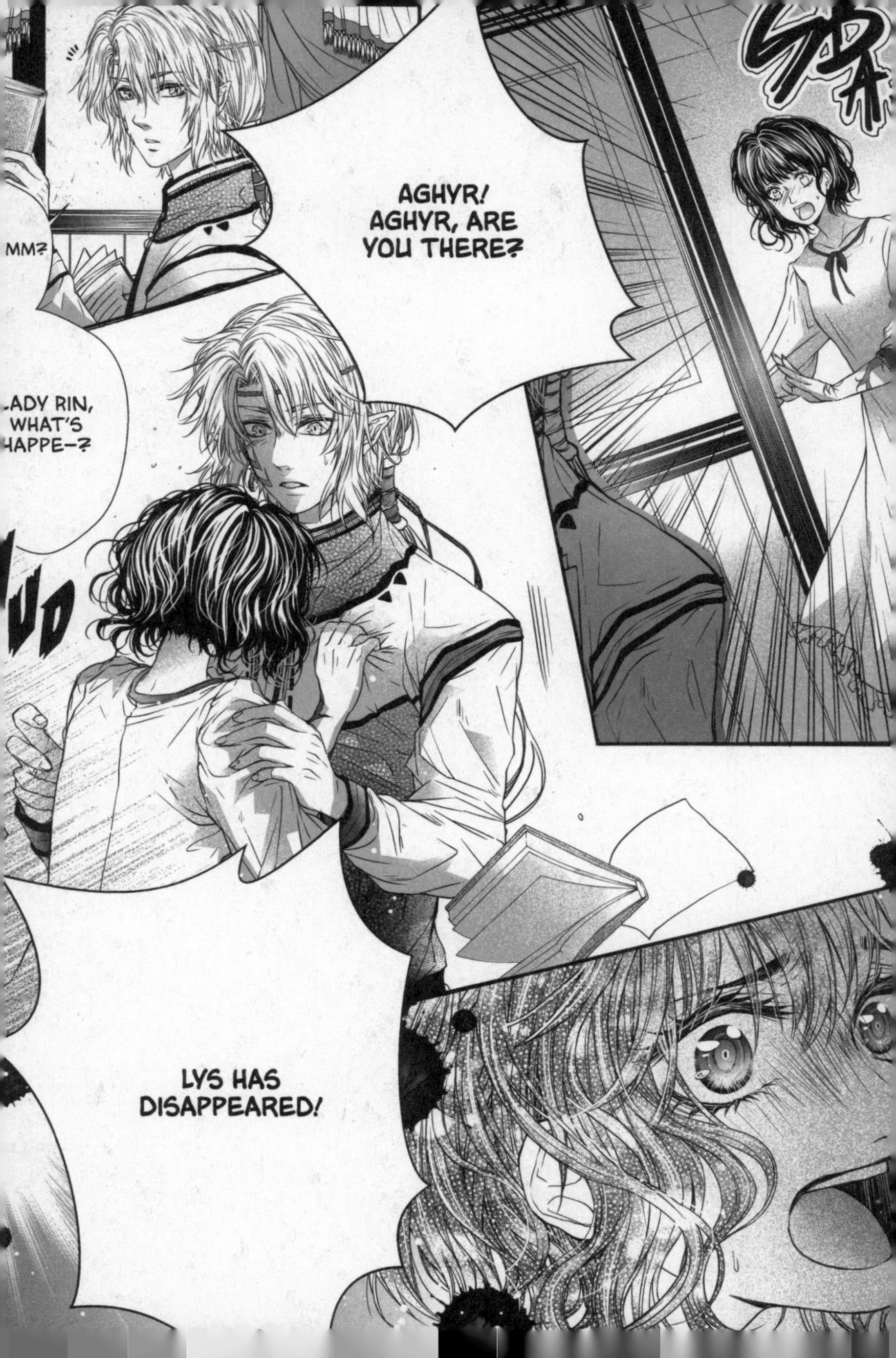
AGHYR! AGHYR, ARE YOU THERE?
MM?
LADY RIN, WHAT'S HAPPE–?
LYS HAS DISAPPEARED!

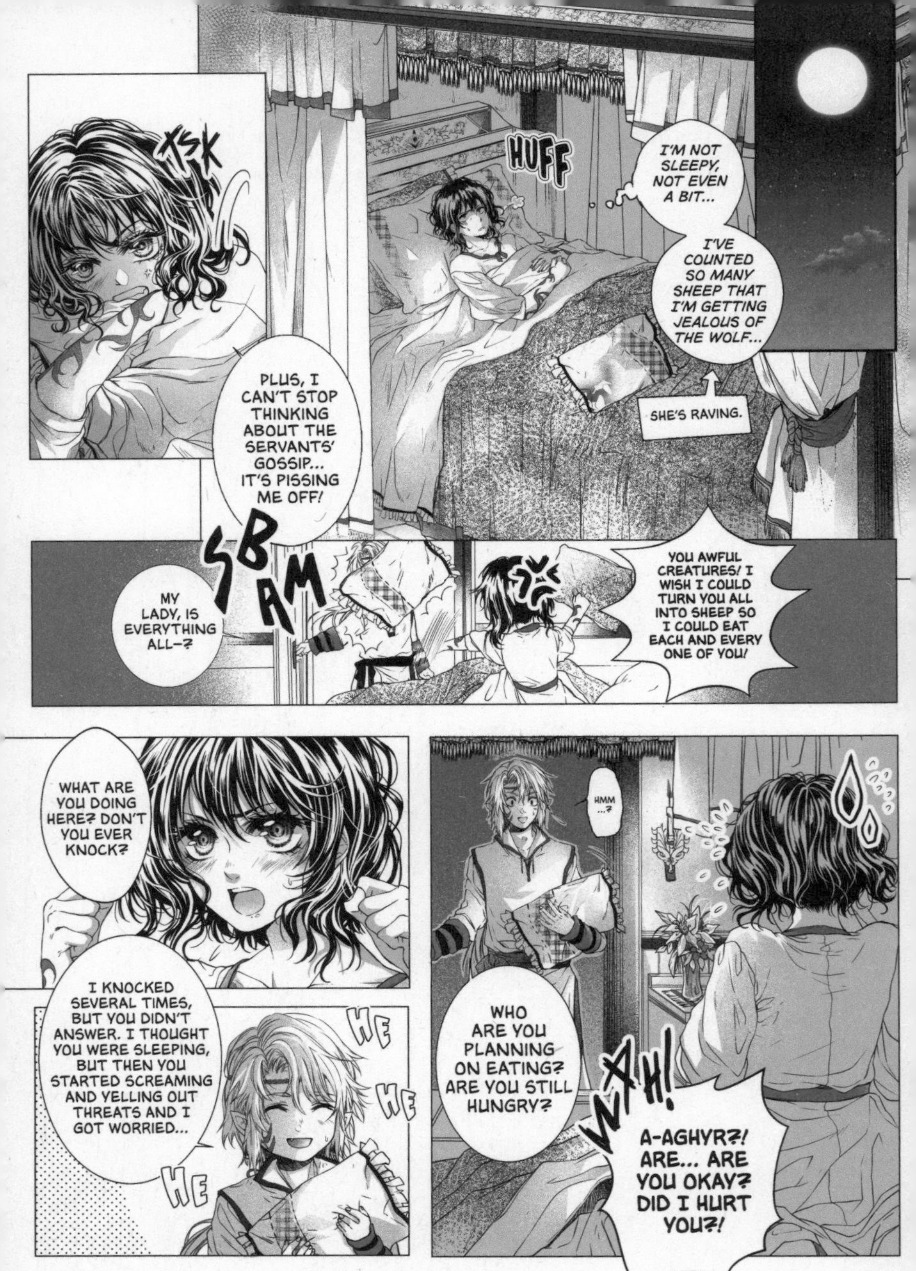
HUFF
I'M NOT SLEEPY, NOT EVEN A BIT...
I'VE COUNTED SO MANY SHEEP THAT I'M GETTING JEALOUS OF THE WOLF...
SHE'S RAVING.
TSK
PLUS, I CAN'T STOP THINKING ABOUT THE SERVANTS' GOSSIP... IT'S PISSING ME OFF!
YOU AWFUL CREATURES! I WISH I COULD TURN YOU ALL INTO SHEEP SO I COULD EAT EACH AND EVERY ONE OF YOU!
SBAM
MY LADY, IS EVERYTHING ALL—?
WAH!
A-AGHYR?! ARE... ARE YOU OKAY? DID I HURT YOU?!
HMM ...?
WHO ARE YOU PLANNING ON EATING? ARE YOU STILL HUNGRY?
WHAT ARE YOU DOING HERE? DON'T YOU EVER KNOCK?
I KNOCKED SEVERAL TIMES, BUT YOU DIDN'T ANSWER. I THOUGHT YOU WERE SLEEPING, BUT THEN YOU STARTED SCREAMING AND YELLING OUT THREATS AND I GOT WORRIED...
HE
HE
HE

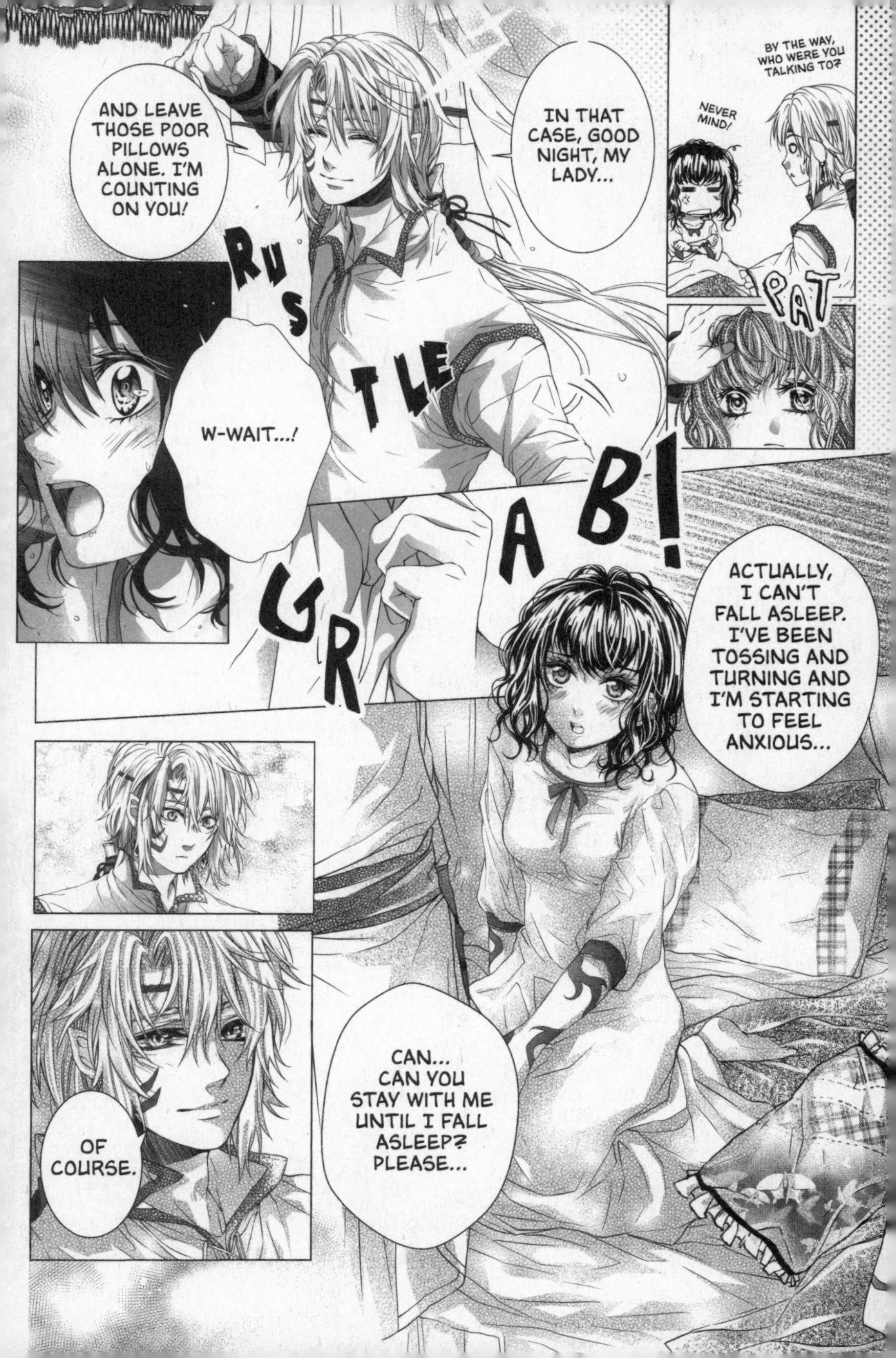
BY THE WAY, WHO WERE YOU TALKING TO?
NEVER MIND!
PAT
AND LEAVE THOSE POOR PILLOWS ALONE. I'M COUNTING ON YOU!
IN THAT CASE, GOOD NIGHT, MY LADY...
RUSTLE
W-WAIT...!
GRAB!
ACTUALLY, I CAN'T FALL ASLEEP. I'VE BEEN TOSSING AND TURNING AND I'M STARTING TO FEEL ANXIOUS...
CAN... CAN YOU STAY WITH ME UNTIL I FALL ASLEEP? PLEASE...
OF COURSE.

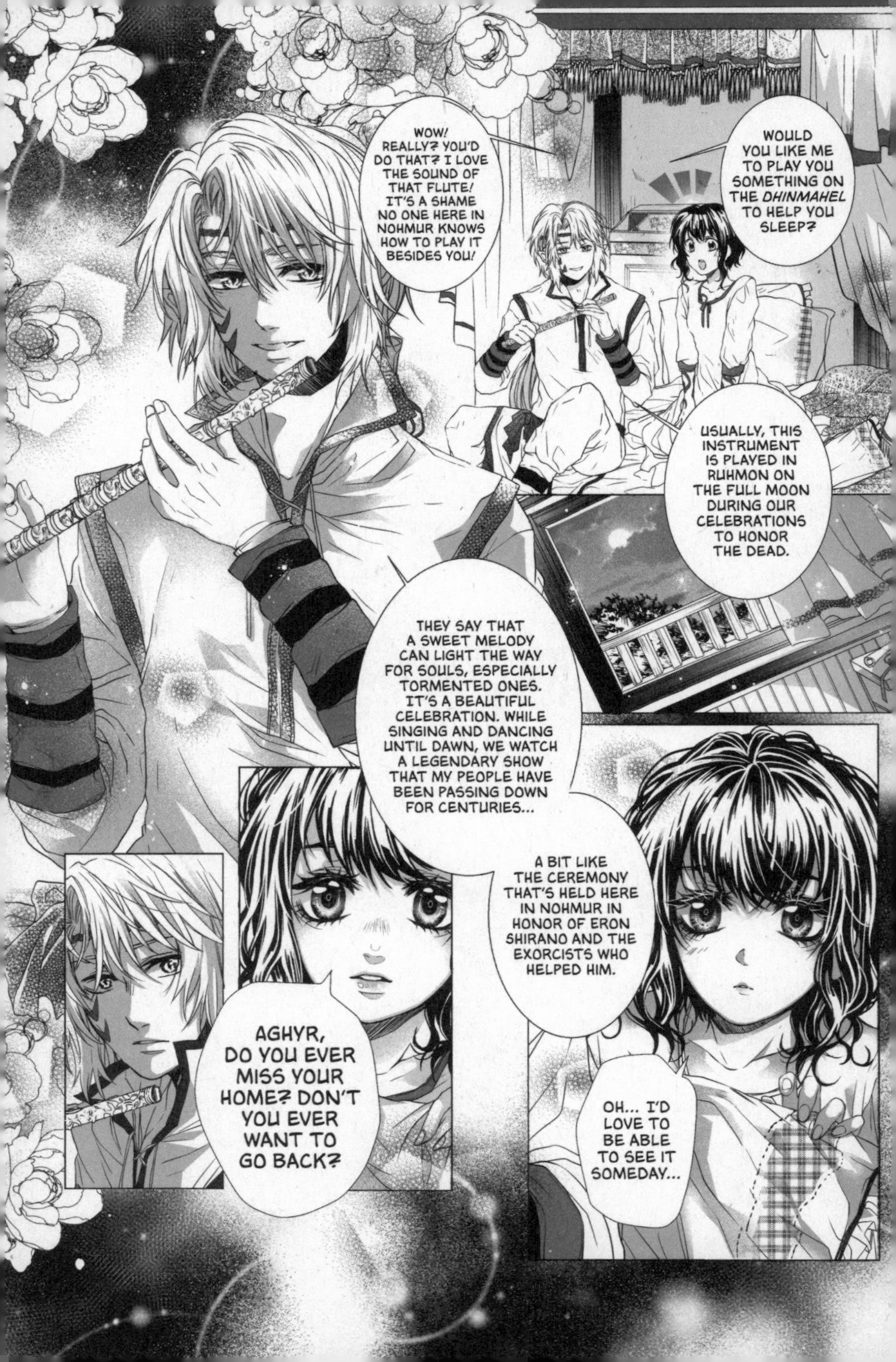
WOULD YOU LIKE ME TO PLAY YOU SOMETHING ON THE *DHINMAHEL* TO HELP YOU SLEEP?
WOW! REALLY? YOU'D DO THAT? I LOVE THE SOUND OF THAT FLUTE! IT'S A SHAME NO ONE HERE IN NOHMUR KNOWS HOW TO PLAY IT BESIDES YOU!
USUALLY, THIS INSTRUMENT IS PLAYED IN RUHMON ON THE FULL MOON DURING OUR CELEBRATIONS TO HONOR THE DEAD.
THEY SAY THAT A SWEET MELODY CAN LIGHT THE WAY FOR SOULS, ESPECIALLY TORMENTED ONES. IT'S A BEAUTIFUL CELEBRATION. WHILE SINGING AND DANCING UNTIL DAWN, WE WATCH A LEGENDARY SHOW THAT MY PEOPLE HAVE BEEN PASSING DOWN FOR CENTURIES...
A BIT LIKE THE CEREMONY THAT'S HELD HERE IN NOHMUR IN HONOR OF ERON SHIRANO AND THE EXORCISTS WHO HELPED HIM.
OH... I'D LOVE TO BE ABLE TO SEE IT SOMEDAY...
AGHYR, DO YOU EVER MISS YOUR HOME? DON'T YOU EVER WANT TO GO BACK?

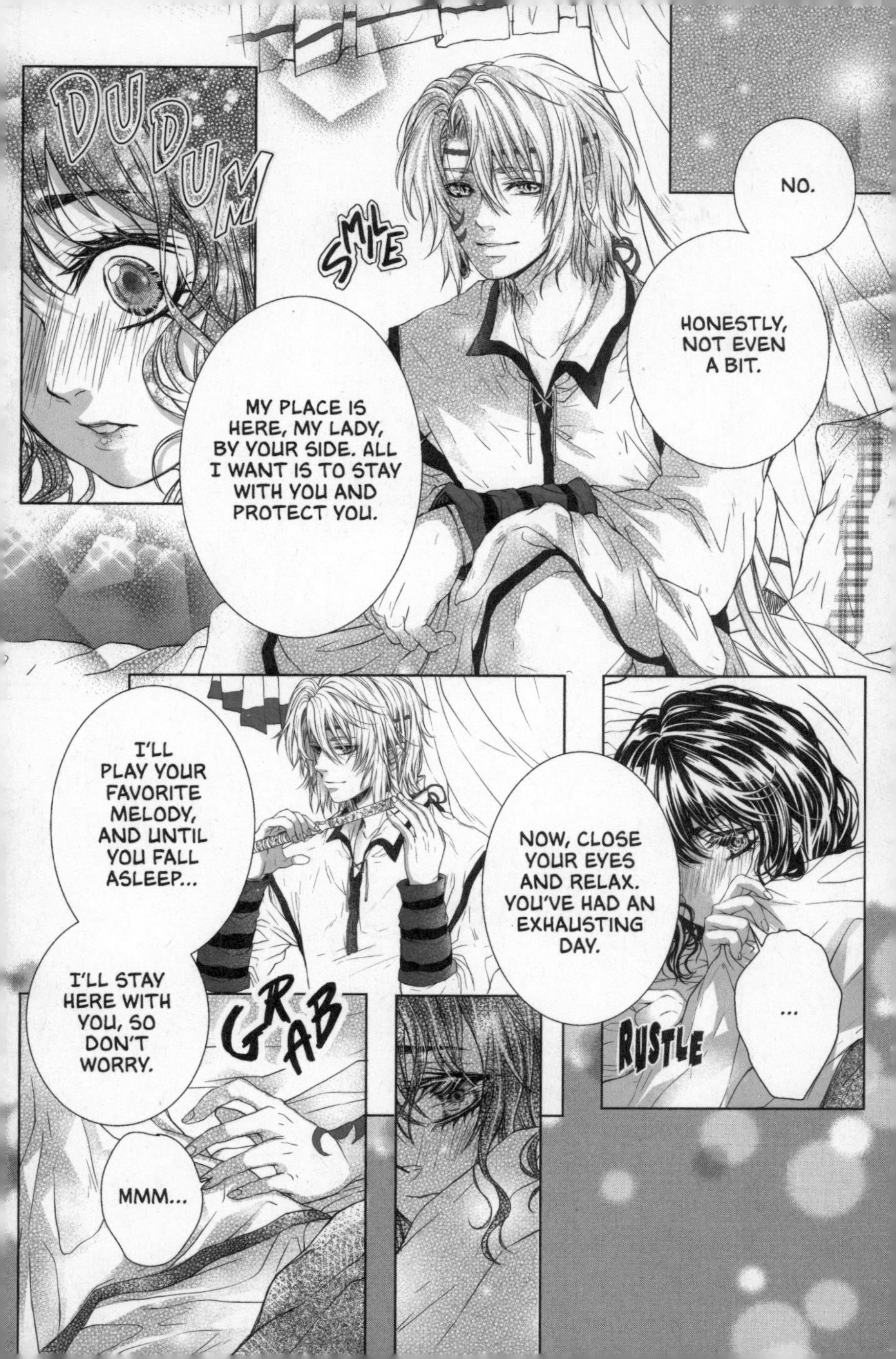
NO.
HONESTLY, NOT EVEN A BIT.
SMILE
MY PLACE IS HERE, MY LADY, BY YOUR SIDE. ALL I WANT IS TO STAY WITH YOU AND PROTECT YOU.
DUDUM
NOW, CLOSE YOUR EYES AND RELAX. YOU'VE HAD AN EXHAUSTING DAY.
...
RUSTLE
I'LL PLAY YOUR FAVORITE MELODY, AND UNTIL YOU FALL ASLEEP...
I'LL STAY HERE WITH YOU, SO DON'T WORRY.
GRAB
MMM...

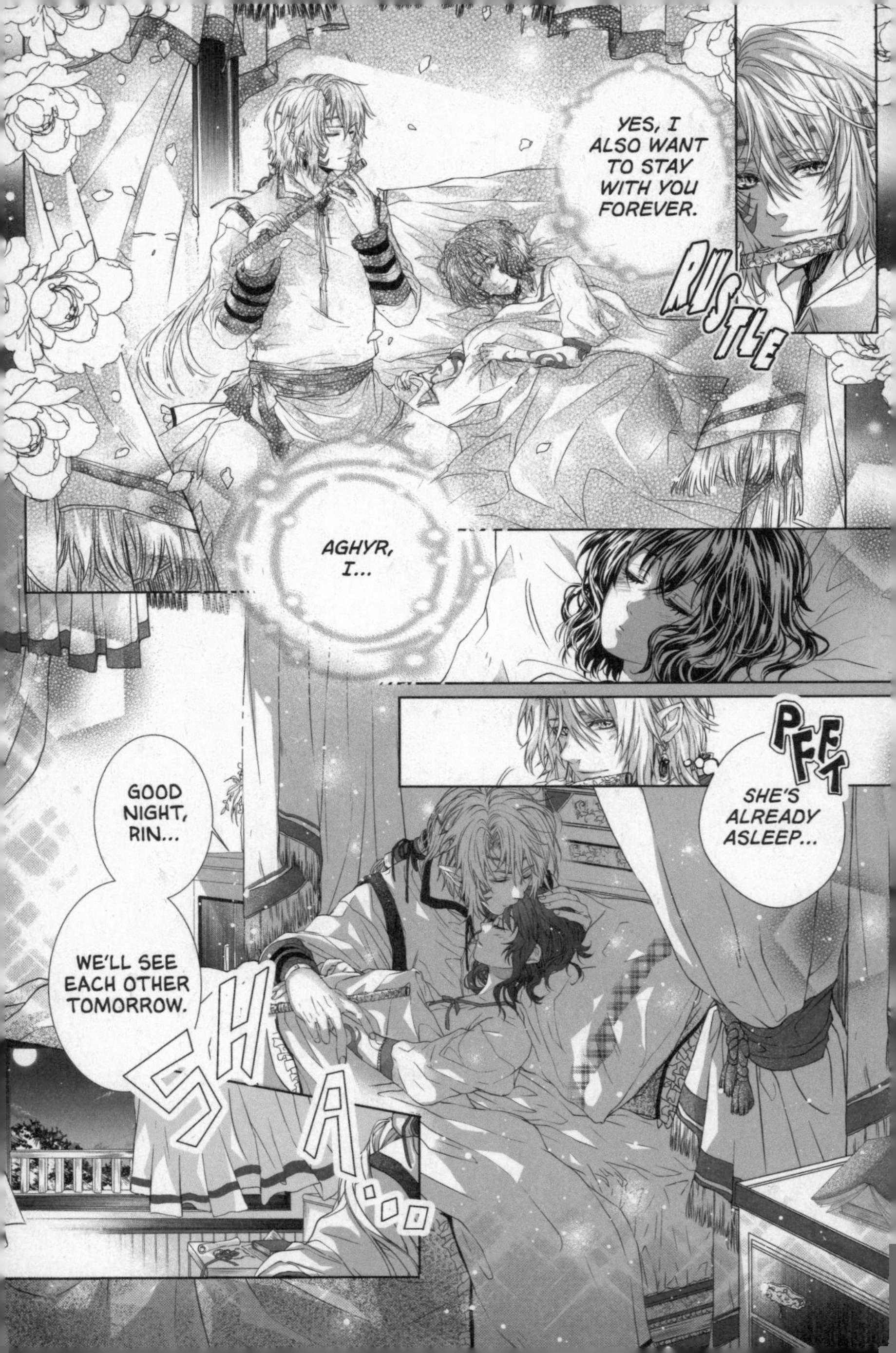
YES, I ALSO WANT TO STAY WITH YOU FOREVER.
RUSTLE
AGHYR, I...
PFFT
SHE'S ALREADY ASLEEP...
GOOD NIGHT, RIN...
WE'LL SEE EACH OTHER TOMORROW.
SHA...

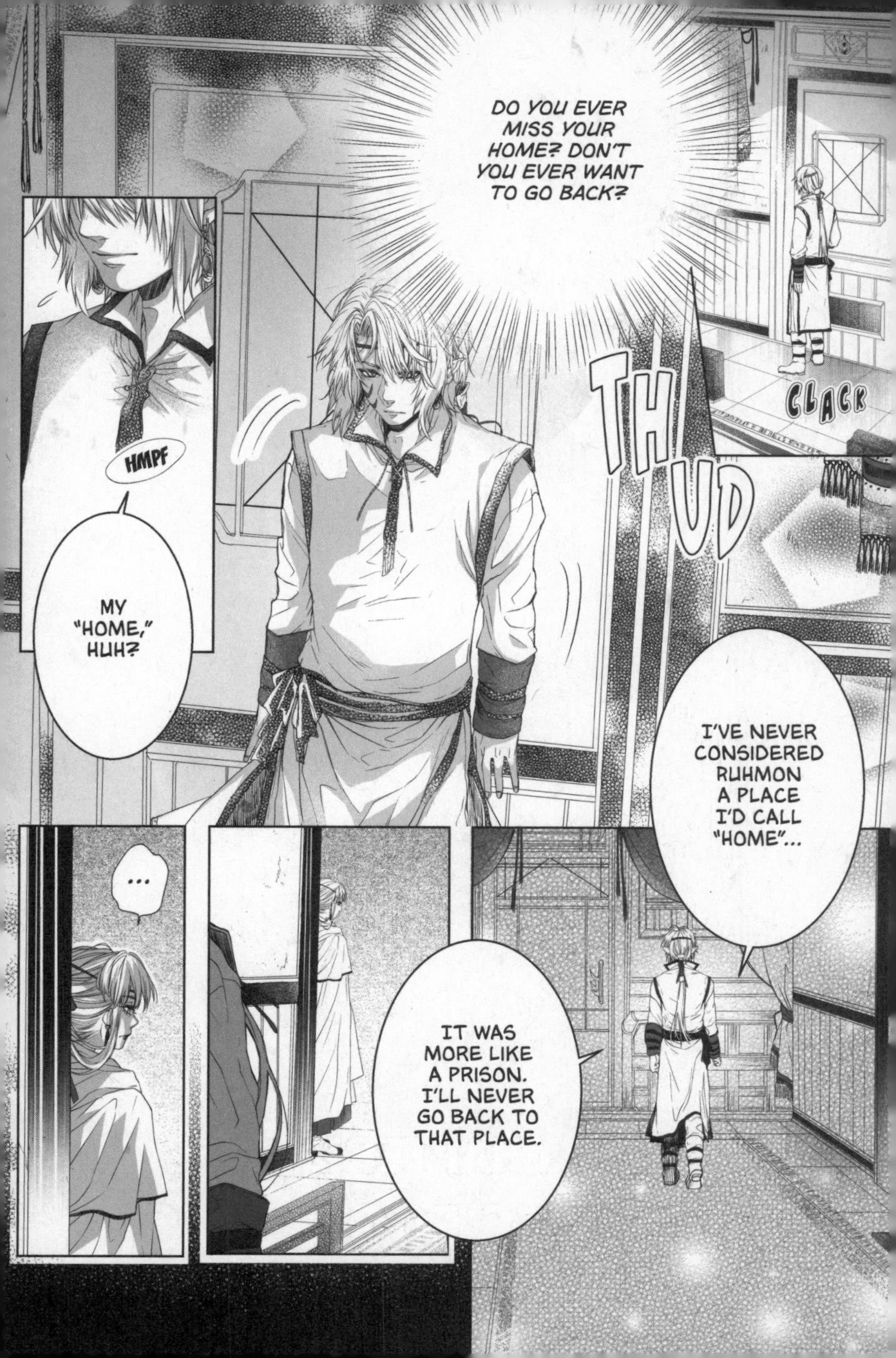
DO YOU EVER MISS YOUR HOME? DON'T YOU EVER WANT TO GO BACK?
CLACK
THUD
HMPF
MY "HOME," HUH?
I'VE NEVER CONSIDERED RUHMON A PLACE I'D CALL "HOME"...
IT WAS MORE LIKE A PRISON. I'LL NEVER GO BACK TO THAT PLACE.
...

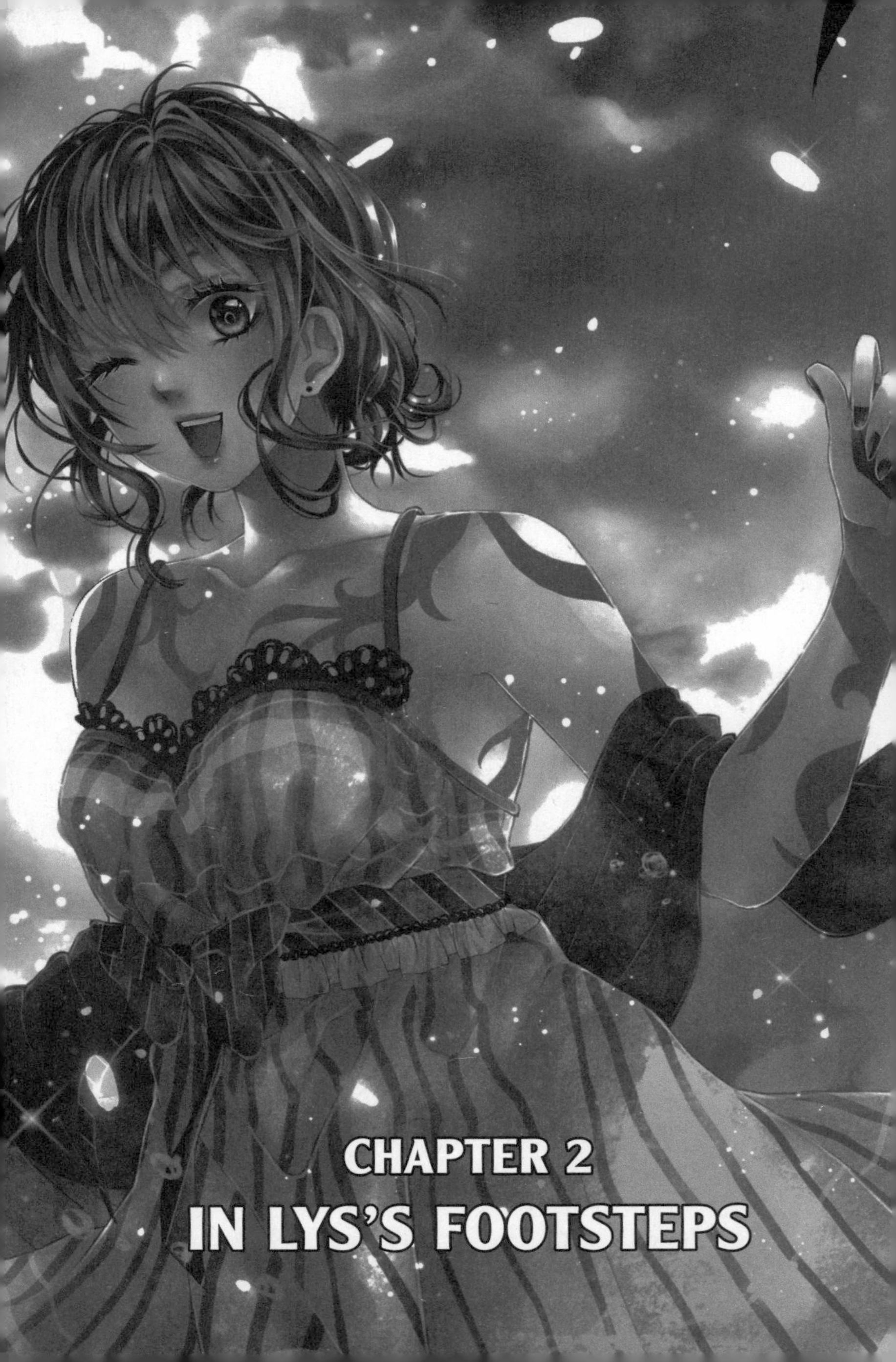

CHAPTER 2
IN LYS'S FOOTSTEPS

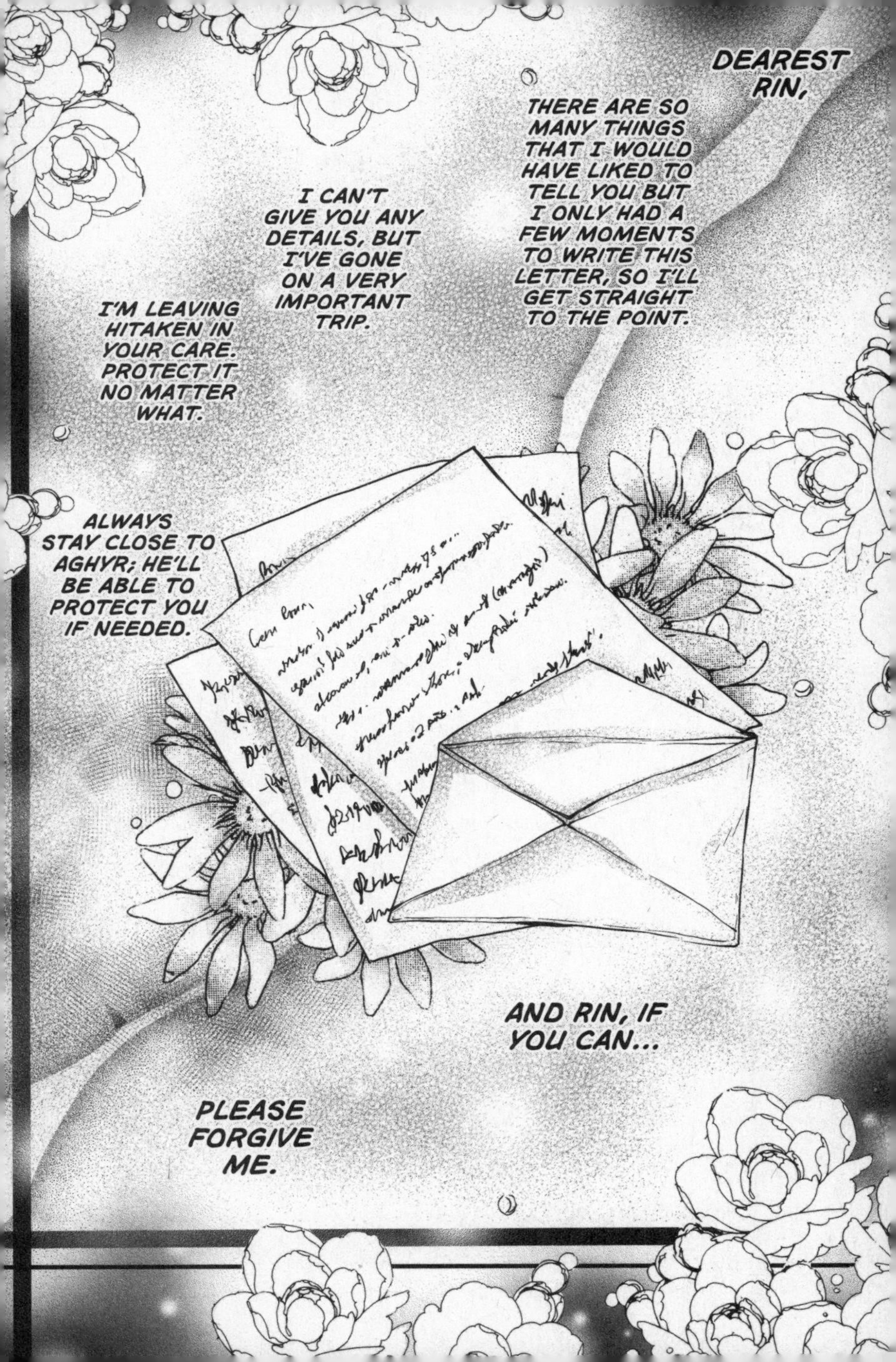
DEAREST RIN,
THERE ARE SO MANY THINGS THAT I WOULD HAVE LIKED TO TELL YOU BUT I ONLY HAD A FEW MOMENTS TO WRITE THIS LETTER, SO I'LL GET STRAIGHT TO THE POINT.
I CAN'T GIVE YOU ANY DETAILS, BUT I'VE GONE ON A VERY IMPORTANT TRIP.
I'M LEAVING HITAKEN IN YOUR CARE. PROTECT IT NO MATTER WHAT.
ALWAYS STAY CLOSE TO AGHYR; HE'LL BE ABLE TO PROTECT YOU IF NEEDED.
AND RIN, IF YOU CAN...
PLEASE FORGIVE ME.

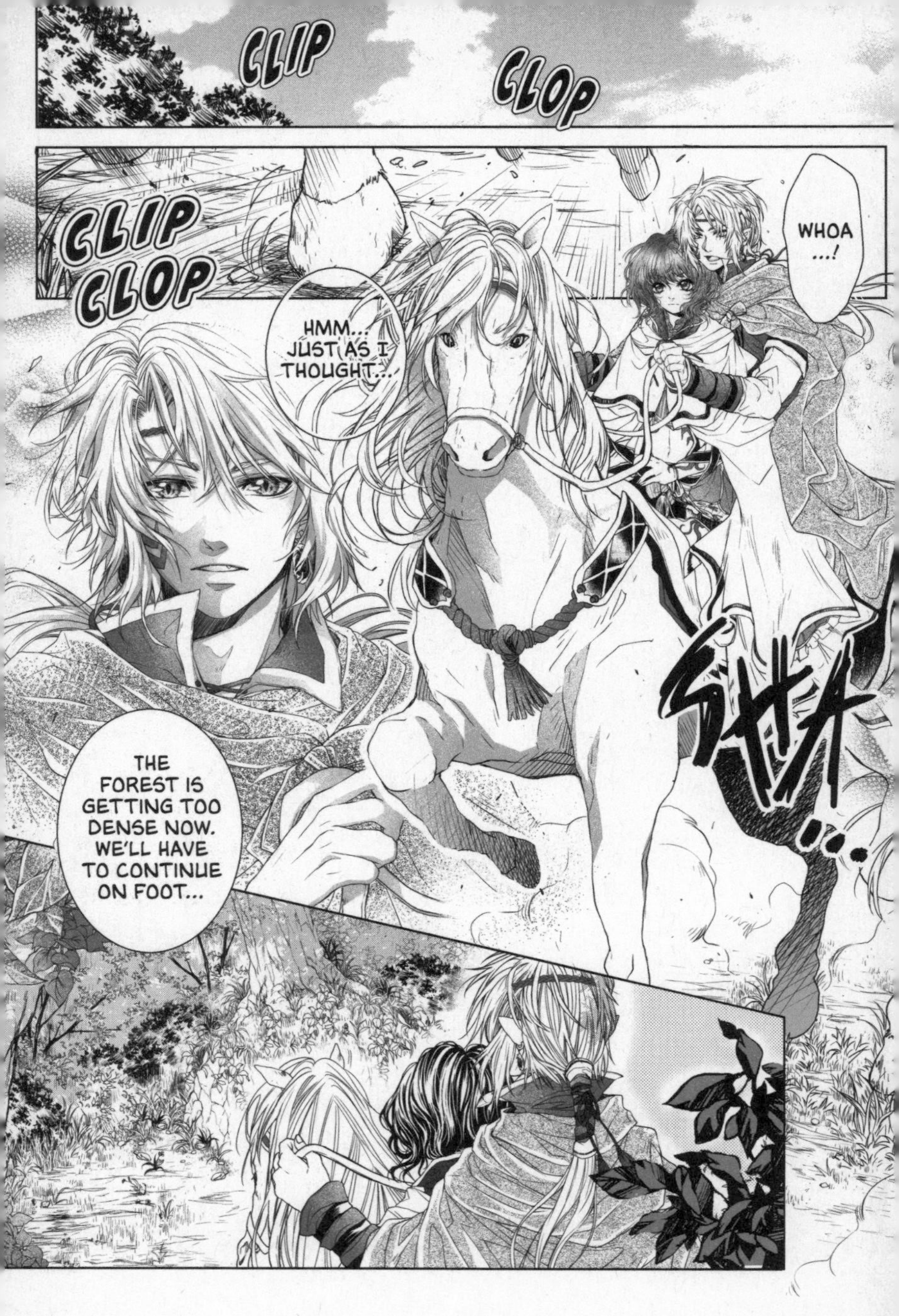
CLIP
CLOP
WHOA ...!
CLIP CLOP
HMM... JUST AS I THOUGHT...
SHA...
THE FOREST IS GETTING TOO DENSE NOW. WE'LL HAVE TO CONTINUE ON FOOT...

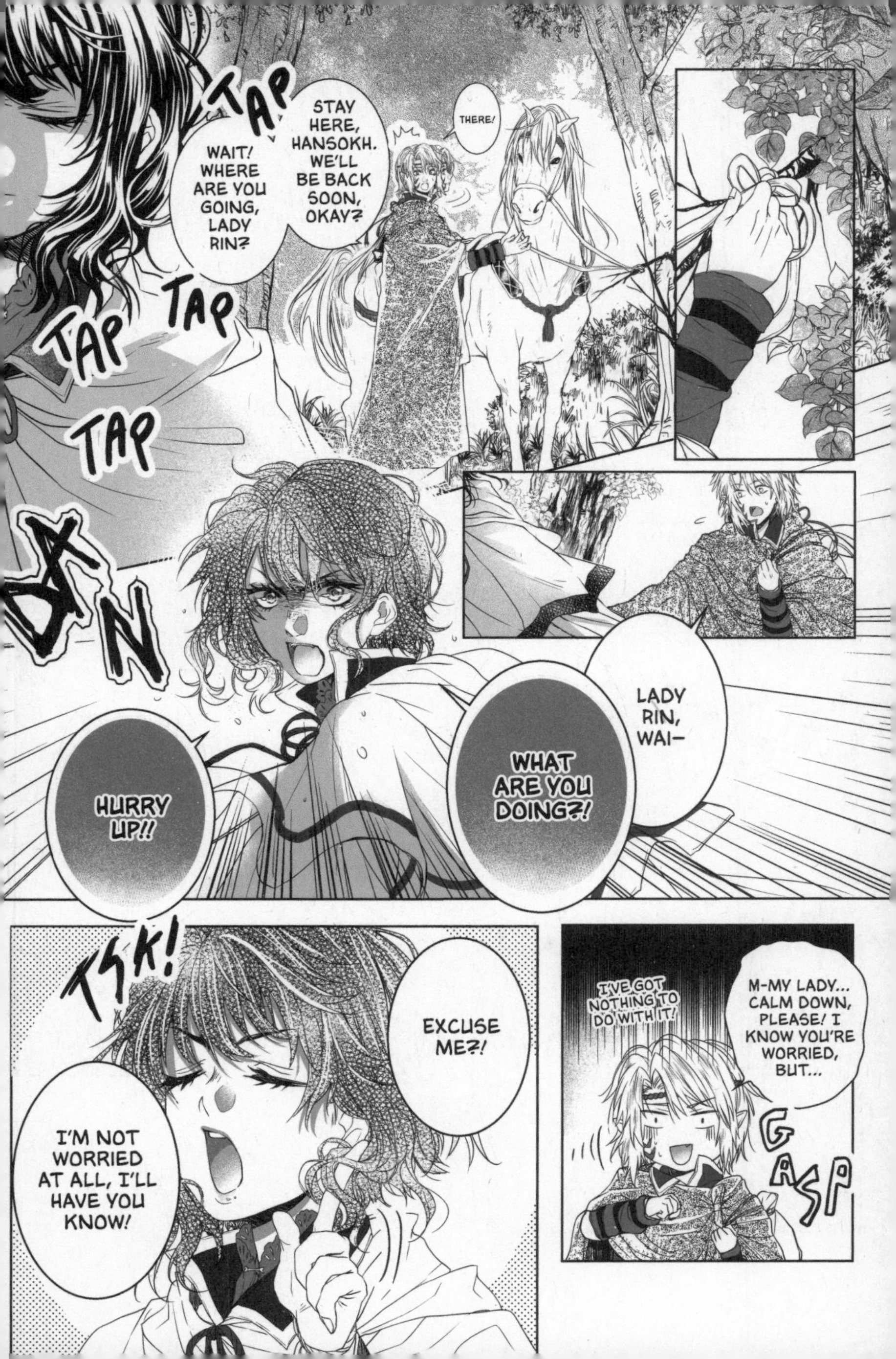
THERE!
STAY HERE, HANSOKH. WE'LL BE BACK SOON, OKAY?
TAP
WAIT! WHERE ARE YOU GOING, LADY RIN?
TAP TAP
TAP
LADY RIN, WAI—
WHAT ARE YOU DOING?!
HURRY UP!!
M-MY LADY... CALM DOWN, PLEASE! I KNOW YOU'RE WORRIED, BUT...
GASP
I'VE GOT NOTHING TO DO WITH IT!
EXCUSE ME?!
TSK!
I'M NOT WORRIED AT ALL, I'LL HAVE YOU KNOW!

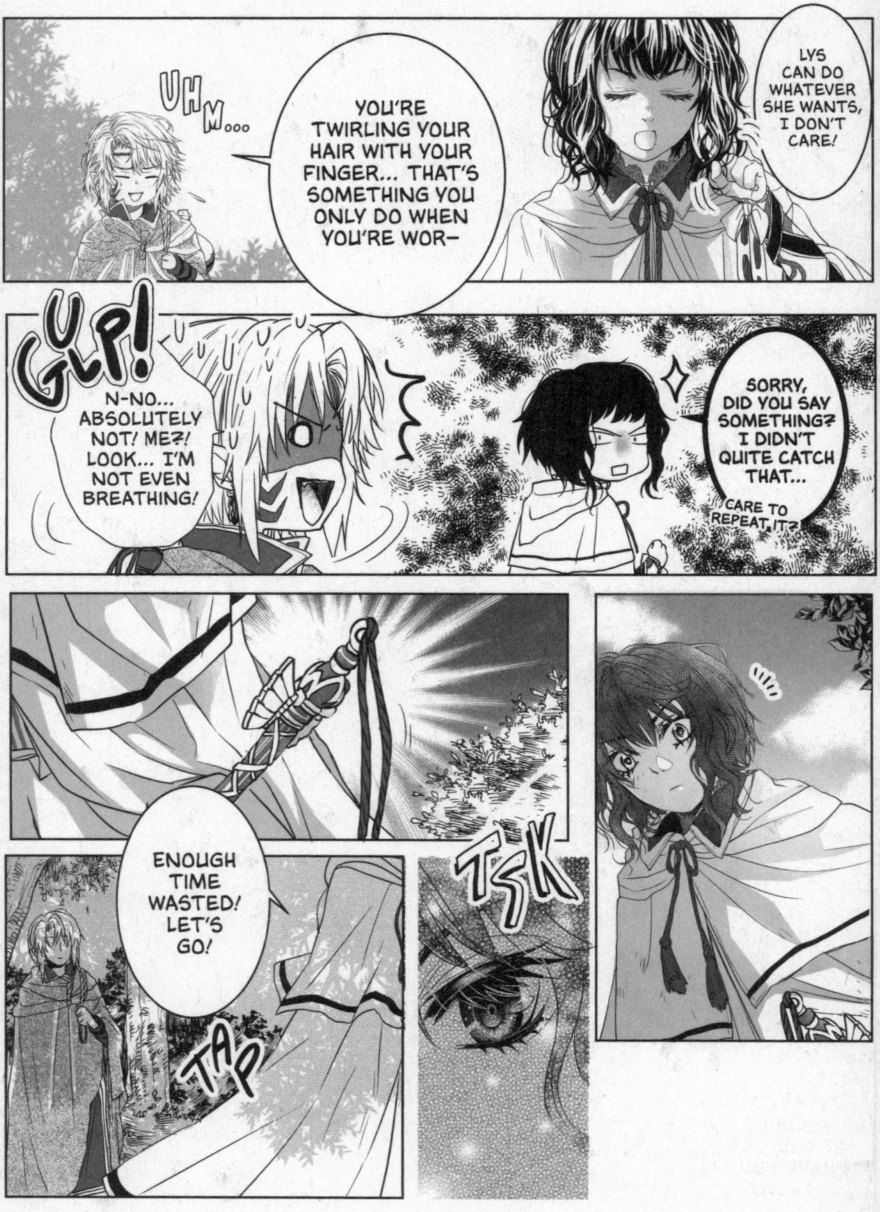
LYS CAN DO WHATEVER SHE WANTS, I DON'T CARE!
UHM...
YOU'RE TWIRLING YOUR HAIR WITH YOUR FINGER... THAT'S SOMETHING YOU ONLY DO WHEN YOU'RE WOR–
SORRY, DID YOU SAY SOMETHING? I DIDN'T QUITE CATCH THAT...
CARE TO REPEAT IT?
GULP!
N-NO... ABSOLUTELY NOT! ME?! LOOK... I'M NOT EVEN BREATHING!
TSK
ENOUGH TIME WASTED! LET'S GO!
TAP

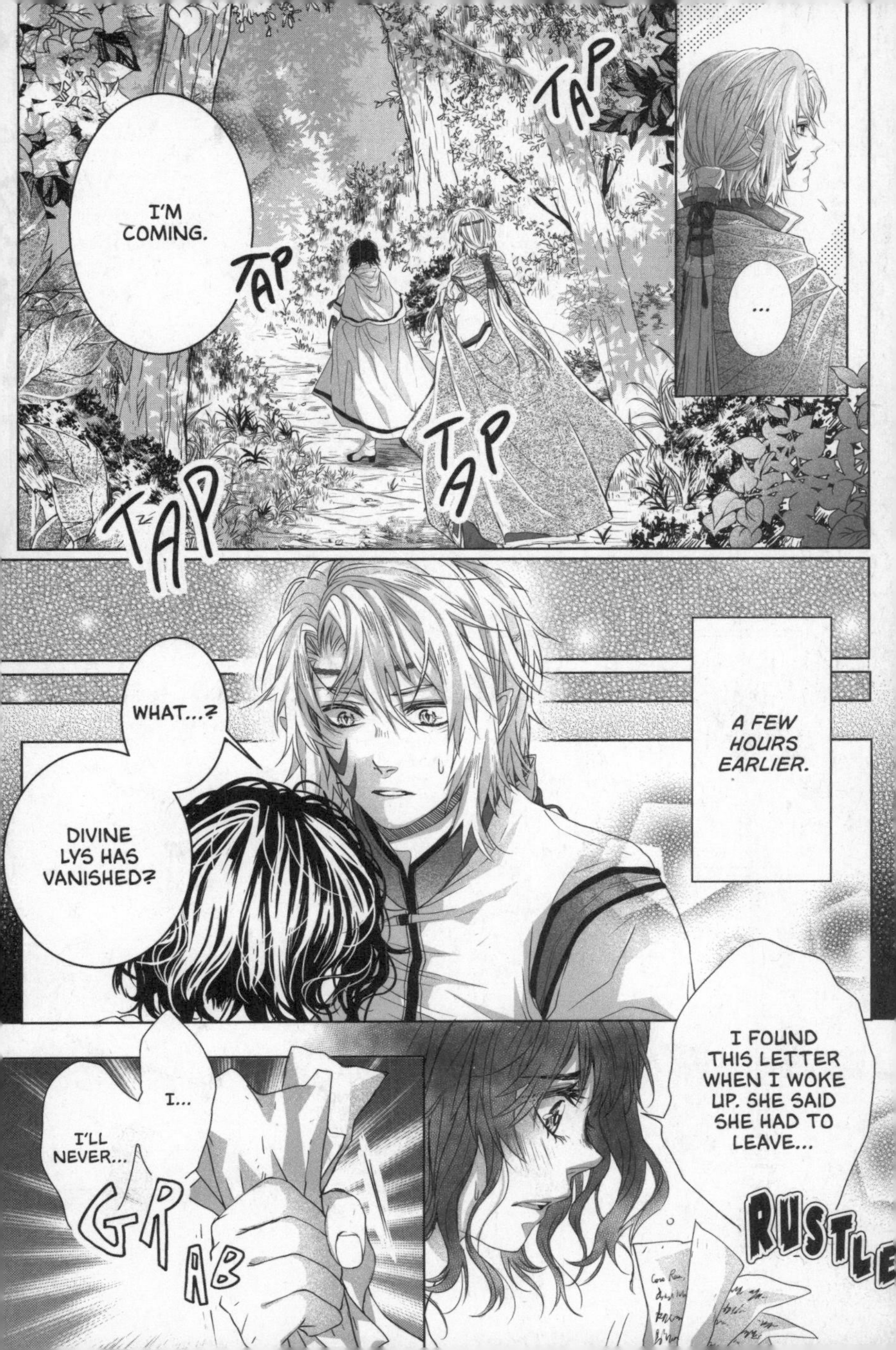
...
TAP
I'M COMING.
TAP
TAP
TAP
A FEW HOURS EARLIER.
WHAT...?
DIVINE LYS HAS VANISHED?
I FOUND THIS LETTER WHEN I WOKE UP. SHE SAID SHE HAD TO LEAVE...
RUSTLE
I...
I'LL NEVER...
GRAB

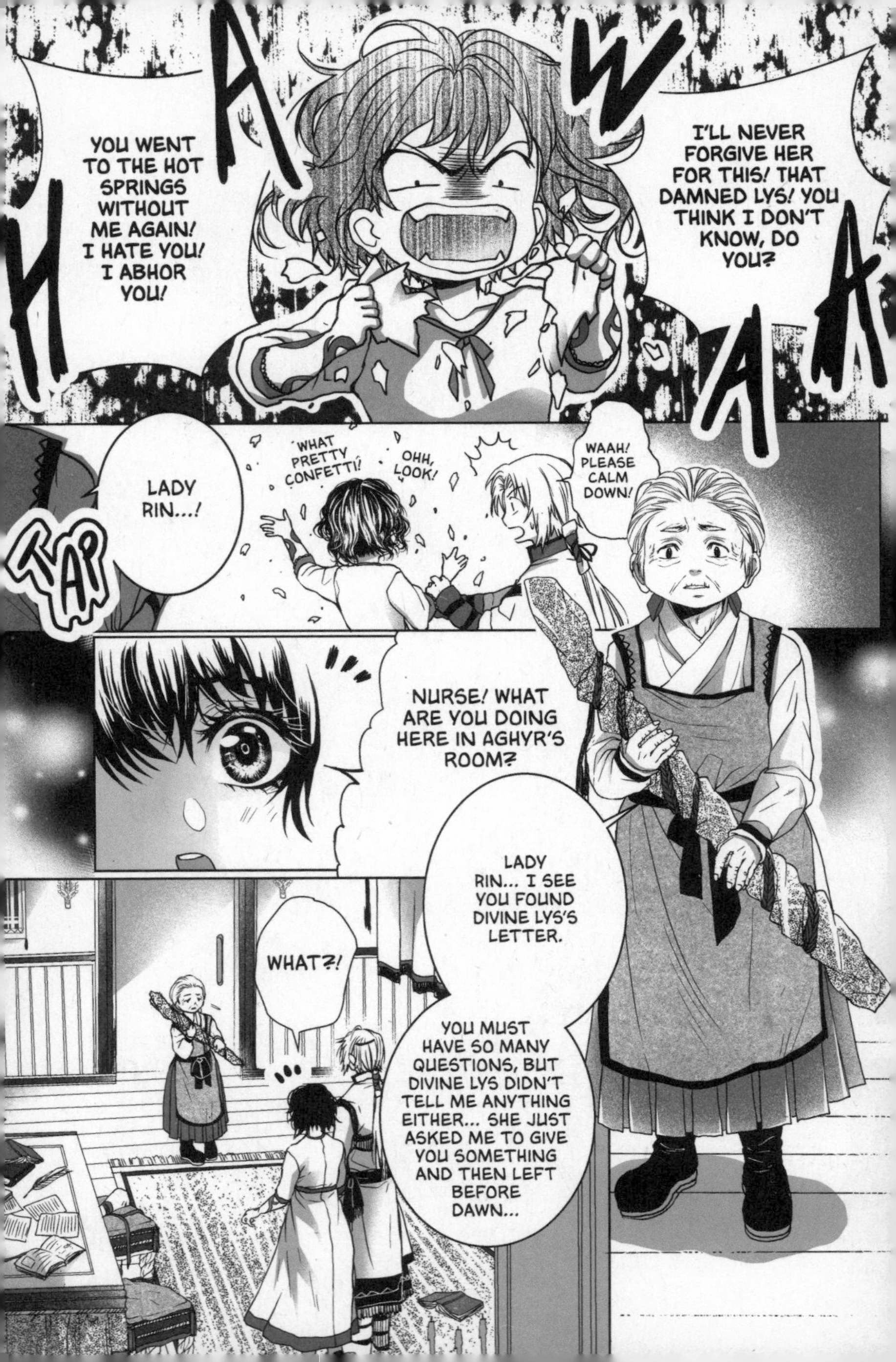
HAWAAA
I'LL NEVER FORGIVE HER FOR THIS! THAT DAMNED LYS! YOU THINK I DON'T KNOW, DO YOU?
YOU WENT TO THE HOT SPRINGS WITHOUT ME AGAIN! I HATE YOU! I ABHOR YOU!
WAAH! PLEASE CALM DOWN!
OHH, LOOK!
WHAT PRETTY CONFETTI!
TAP
LADY RIN...!
NURSE! WHAT ARE YOU DOING HERE IN AGHYR'S ROOM?
LADY RIN... I SEE YOU FOUND DIVINE LYS'S LETTER.
WHAT?!
YOU MUST HAVE SO MANY QUESTIONS, BUT DIVINE LYS DIDN'T TELL ME ANYTHING EITHER... SHE JUST ASKED ME TO GIVE YOU SOMETHING AND THEN LEFT BEFORE DAWN...

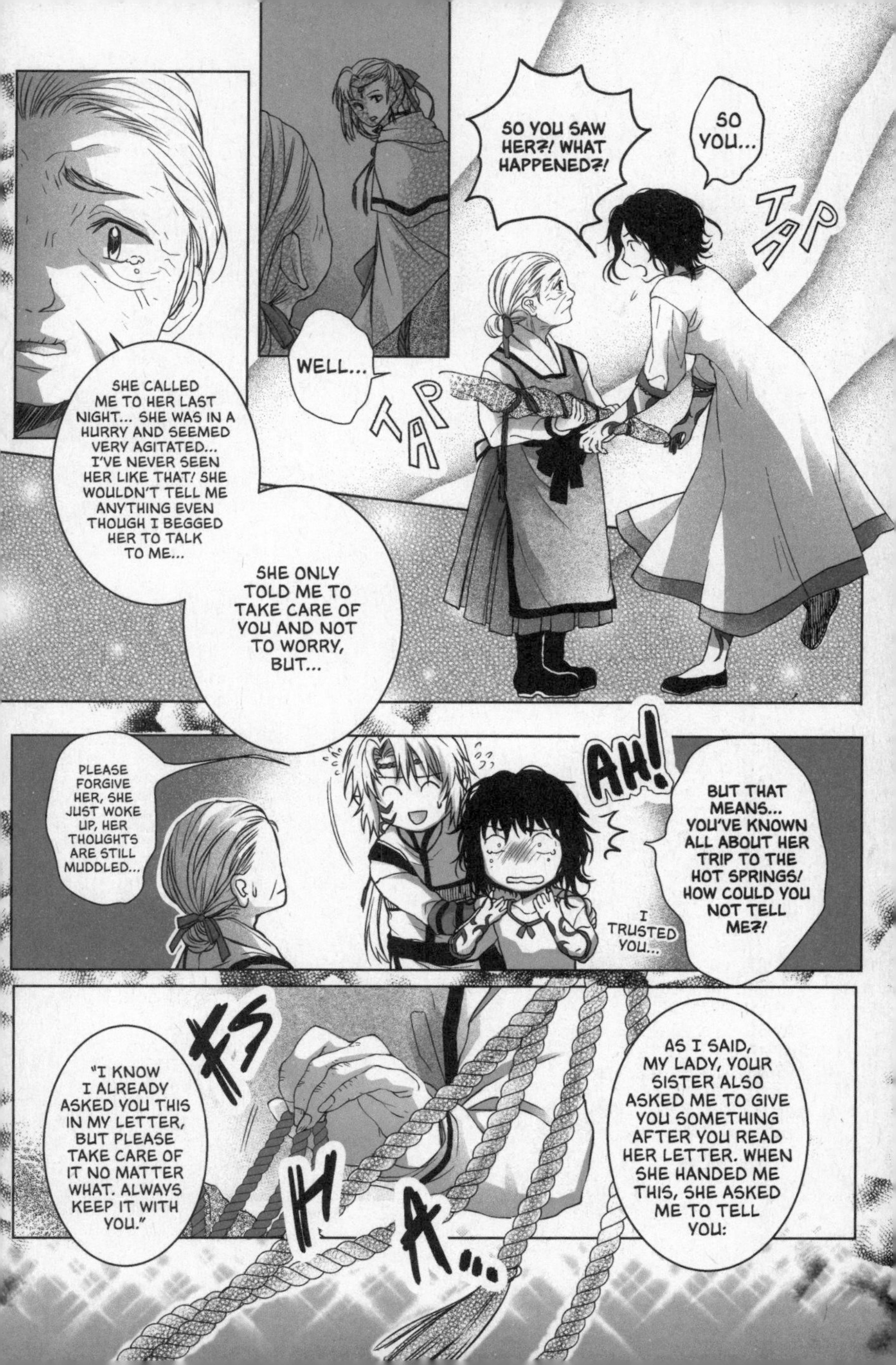
SO YOU...
SO YOU SAW HER?! WHAT HAPPENED?!
TAP
WELL...
TAP
SHE CALLED ME TO HER LAST NIGHT... SHE WAS IN A HURRY AND SEEMED VERY AGITATED... I'VE NEVER SEEN HER LIKE THAT! SHE WOULDN'T TELL ME ANYTHING EVEN THOUGH I BEGGED HER TO TALK TO ME...
SHE ONLY TOLD ME TO TAKE CARE OF YOU AND NOT TO WORRY, BUT...
AH!
BUT THAT MEANS... YOU'VE KNOWN ALL ABOUT HER TRIP TO THE HOT SPRINGS! HOW COULD YOU NOT TELL ME?!
I TRUSTED YOU...
PLEASE FORGIVE HER, SHE JUST WOKE UP, HER THOUGHTS ARE STILL MUDDLED...
AS I SAID, MY LADY, YOUR SISTER ALSO ASKED ME TO GIVE YOU SOMETHING AFTER YOU READ HER LETTER. WHEN SHE HANDED ME THIS, SHE ASKED ME TO TELL YOU:
"I KNOW I ALREADY ASKED YOU THIS IN MY LETTER, BUT PLEASE TAKE CARE OF IT NO MATTER WHAT. ALWAYS KEEP IT WITH YOU."
FS
HA...

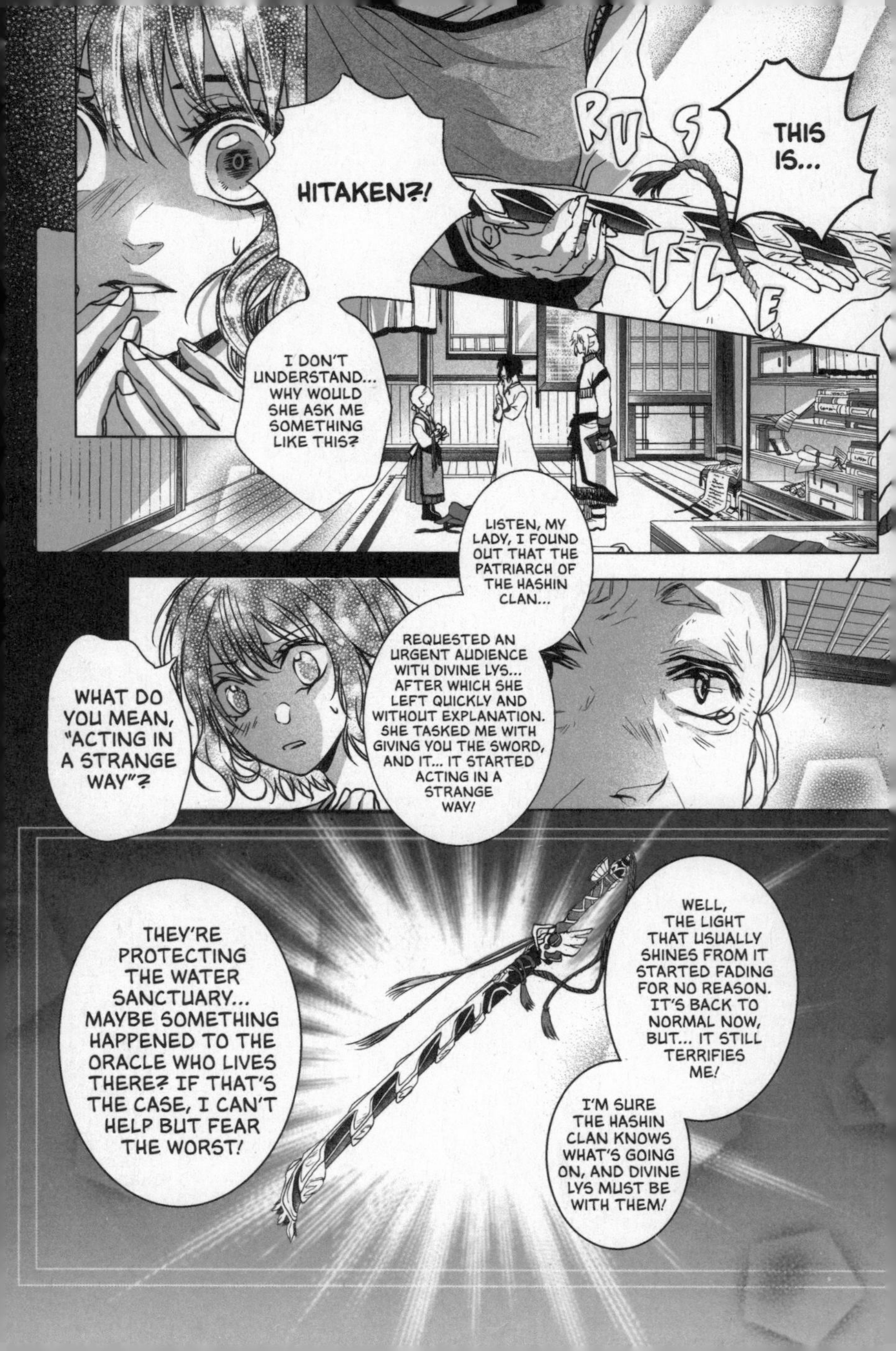
THIS IS...
RUSTLE
HITAKEN?!
I DON'T UNDERSTAND... WHY WOULD SHE ASK ME SOMETHING LIKE THIS?
LISTEN, MY LADY, I FOUND OUT THAT THE PATRIARCH OF THE HASHIN CLAN...
REQUESTED AN URGENT AUDIENCE WITH DIVINE LYS... AFTER WHICH SHE LEFT QUICKLY AND WITHOUT EXPLANATION. SHE TASKED ME WITH GIVING YOU THE SWORD, AND IT... IT STARTED ACTING IN A STRANGE WAY!
WHAT DO YOU MEAN, "ACTING IN A STRANGE WAY"?
WELL, THE LIGHT THAT USUALLY SHINES FROM IT STARTED FADING FOR NO REASON. IT'S BACK TO NORMAL NOW, BUT... IT STILL TERRIFIES ME!
THEY'RE PROTECTING THE WATER SANCTUARY... MAYBE SOMETHING HAPPENED TO THE ORACLE WHO LIVES THERE? IF THAT'S THE CASE, I CAN'T HELP BUT FEAR THE WORST!
I'M SURE THE HASHIN CLAN KNOWS WHAT'S GOING ON, AND DIVINE LYS MUST BE WITH THEM!

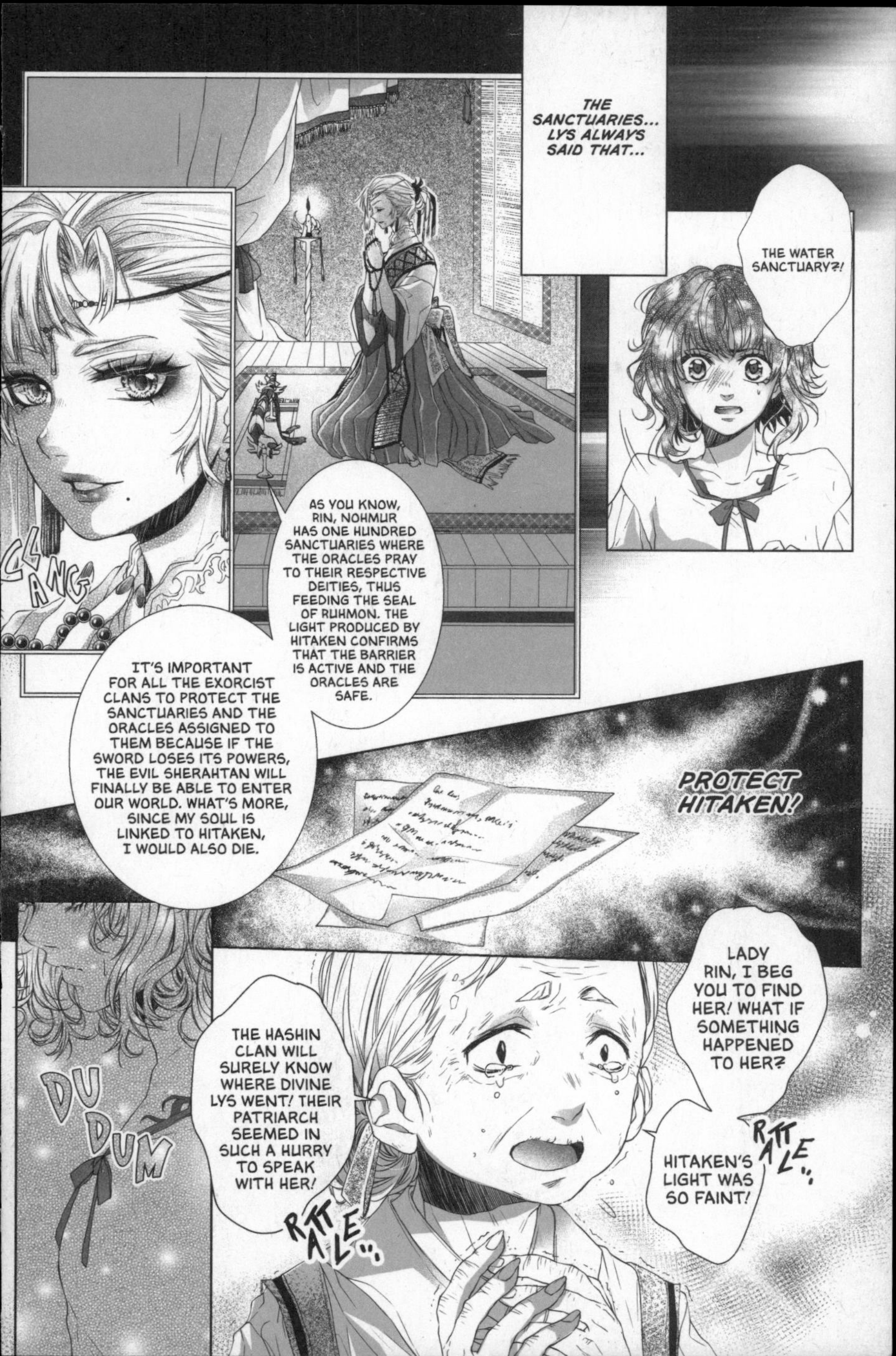
THE SANCTUARIES... LYS ALWAYS SAID THAT...
THE WATER SANCTUARY?!
AS YOU KNOW, RIN, NOHMUR HAS ONE HUNDRED SANCTUARIES WHERE THE ORACLES PRAY TO THEIR RESPECTIVE DEITIES, THUS FEEDING THE SEAL OF RUHMON. THE LIGHT PRODUCED BY HITAKEN CONFIRMS THAT THE BARRIER IS ACTIVE AND THE ORACLES ARE SAFE.
IT'S IMPORTANT FOR ALL THE EXORCIST CLANS TO PROTECT THE SANCTUARIES AND THE ORACLES ASSIGNED TO THEM BECAUSE IF THE SWORD LOSES ITS POWERS, THE EVIL SHERAHTAN WILL FINALLY BE ABLE TO ENTER OUR WORLD. WHAT'S MORE, SINCE MY SOUL IS LINKED TO HITAKEN, I WOULD ALSO DIE.
CLANG
PROTECT HITAKEN!
LADY RIN, I BEG YOU TO FIND HER! WHAT IF SOMETHING HAPPENED TO HER?
RATTLE..
HITAKEN'S LIGHT WAS SO FAINT!
THE HASHIN CLAN WILL SURELY KNOW WHERE DIVINE LYS WENT! THEIR PATRIARCH SEEMED IN SUCH A HURRY TO SPEAK WITH HER!
RATTLE..
DU DUM

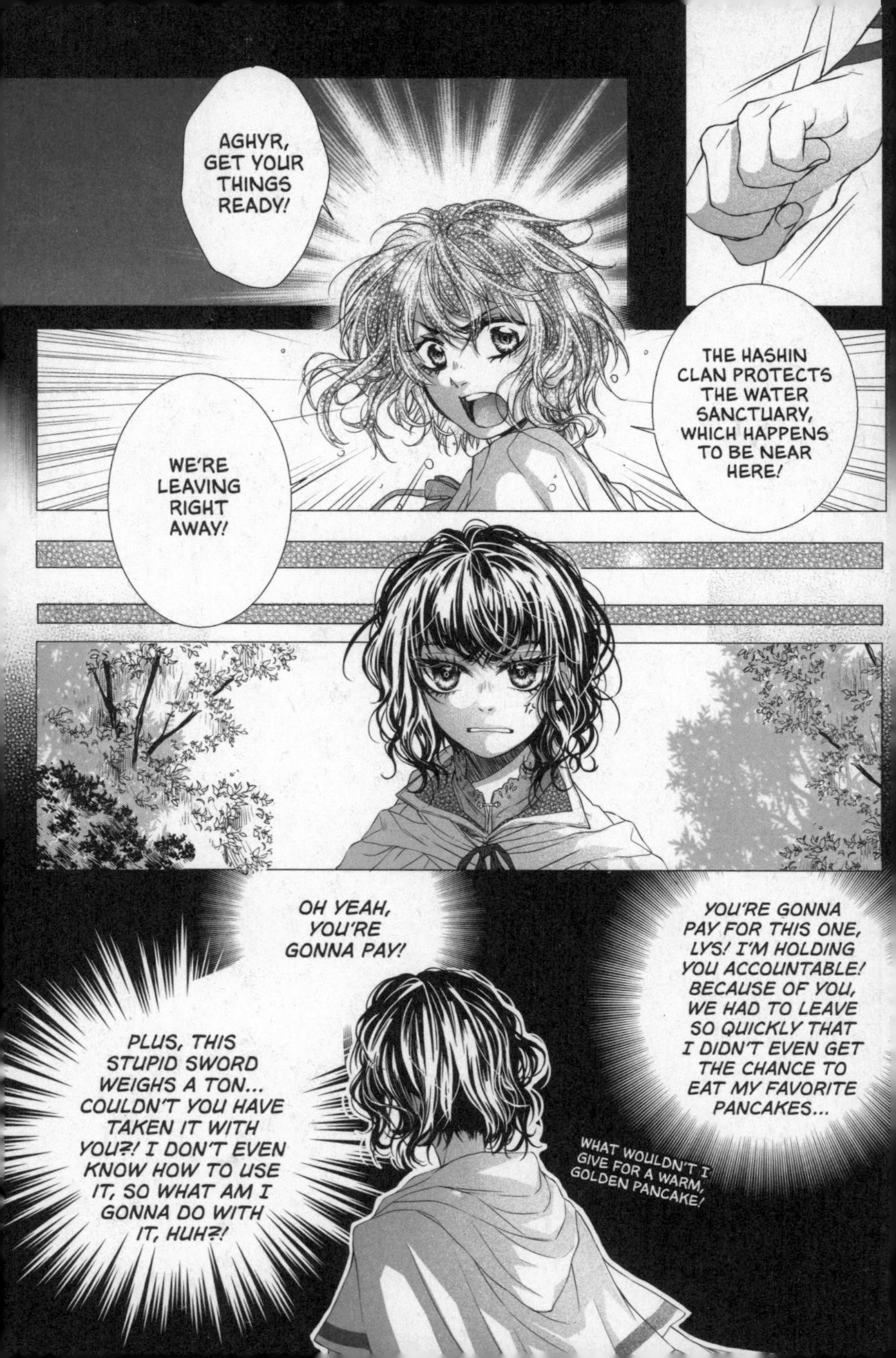
THE HASHIN CLAN PROTECTS THE WATER SANCTUARY, WHICH HAPPENS TO BE NEAR HERE!
AGHYR, GET YOUR THINGS READY!
WE'RE LEAVING RIGHT AWAY!
YOU'RE GONNA PAY FOR THIS ONE, LYS! I'M HOLDING YOU ACCOUNTABLE! BECAUSE OF YOU, WE HAD TO LEAVE SO QUICKLY THAT I DIDN'T EVEN GET THE CHANCE TO EAT MY FAVORITE PANCAKES...
WHAT WOULDN'T I GIVE FOR A WARM, GOLDEN PANCAKE!
OH YEAH, YOU'RE GONNA PAY!
PLUS, THIS STUPID SWORD WEIGHS A TON... COULDN'T YOU HAVE TAKEN IT WITH YOU?! I DON'T EVEN KNOW HOW TO USE IT, SO WHAT AM I GONNA DO WITH IT, HUH?!

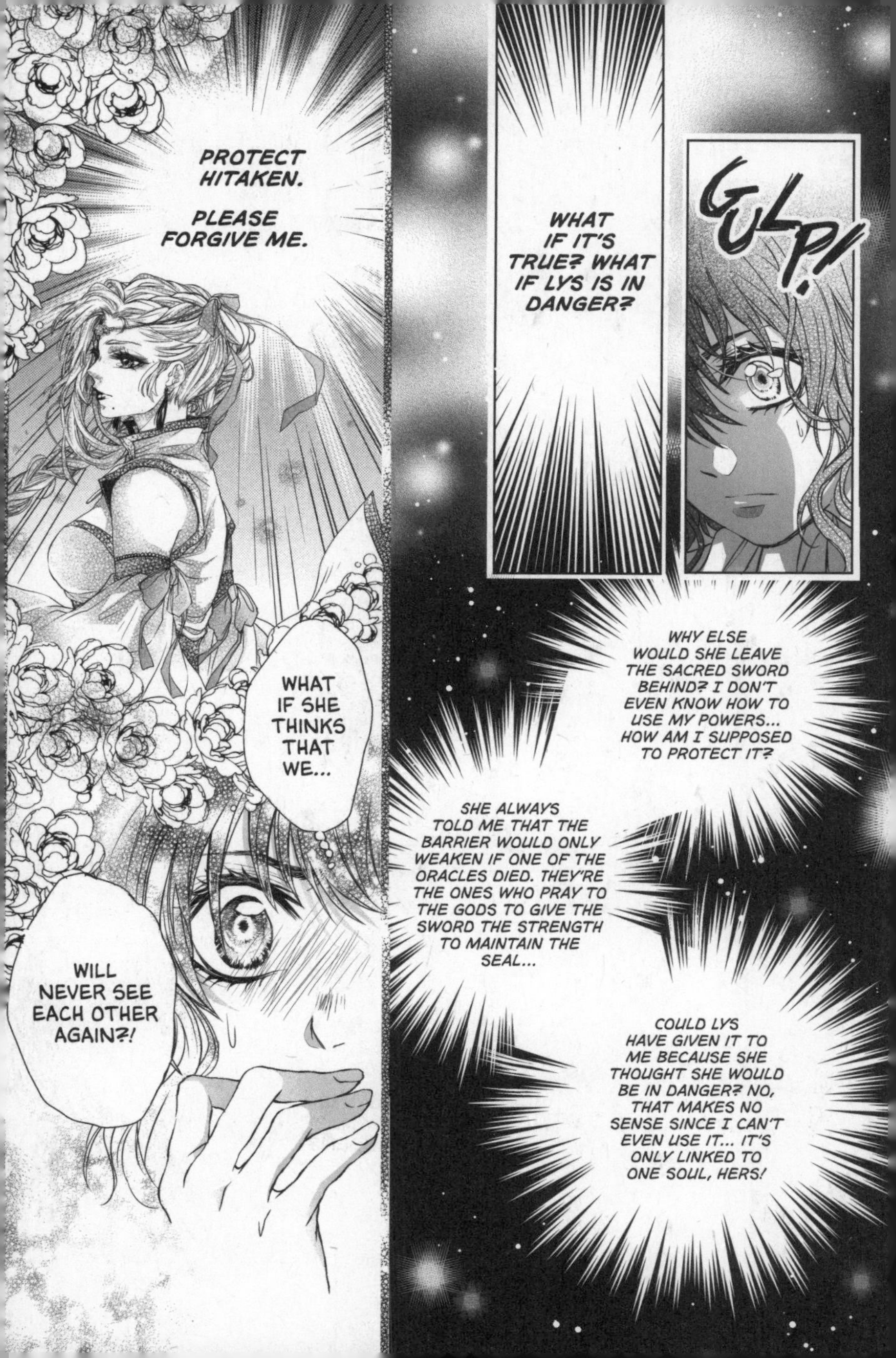
GULP!
WHAT IF IT'S TRUE? WHAT IF LYS IS IN DANGER?
WHY ELSE WOULD SHE LEAVE THE SACRED SWORD BEHIND? I DON'T EVEN KNOW HOW TO USE MY POWERS... HOW AM I SUPPOSED TO PROTECT IT?
SHE ALWAYS TOLD ME THAT THE BARRIER WOULD ONLY WEAKEN IF ONE OF THE ORACLES DIED. THEY'RE THE ONES WHO PRAY TO THE GODS TO GIVE THE SWORD THE STRENGTH TO MAINTAIN THE SEAL...
COULD LYS HAVE GIVEN IT TO ME BECAUSE SHE THOUGHT SHE WOULD BE IN DANGER? NO, THAT MAKES NO SENSE SINCE I CAN'T EVEN USE IT... IT'S ONLY LINKED TO ONE SOUL, HERS!
PROTECT HITAKEN.
PLEASE FORGIVE ME.
WHAT IF SHE THINKS THAT WE...
WILL NEVER SEE EACH OTHER AGAIN?!

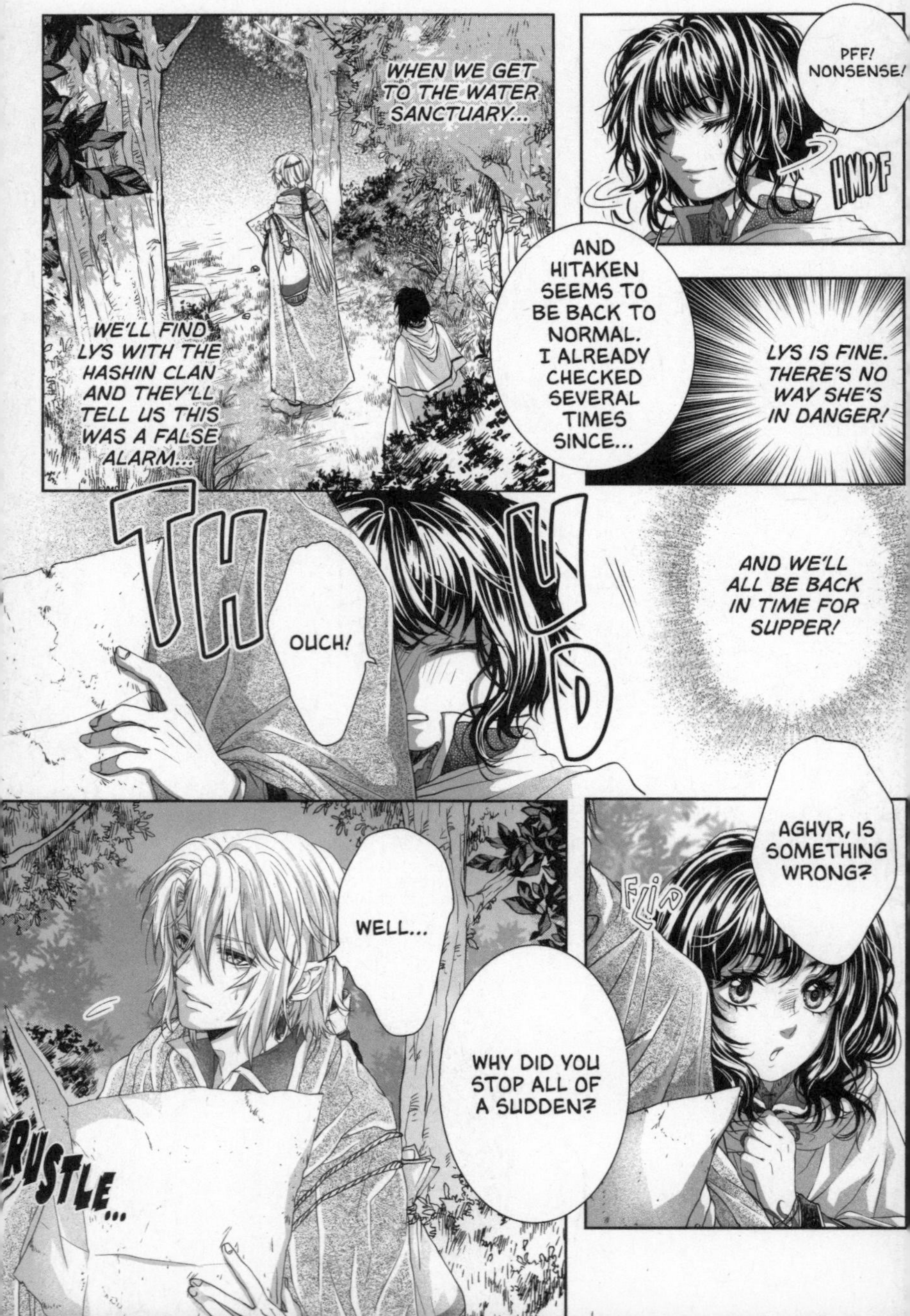
PFF! NONSENSE!
HMPF
AND HITAKEN SEEMS TO BE BACK TO NORMAL. I ALREADY CHECKED SEVERAL TIMES SINCE...
LYS IS FINE. THERE'S NO WAY SHE'S IN DANGER!
WHEN WE GET TO THE WATER SANCTUARY...
WE'LL FIND LYS WITH THE HASHIN CLAN AND THEY'LL TELL US THIS WAS A FALSE ALARM...
AND WE'LL ALL BE BACK IN TIME FOR SUPPER!
THUD
OUCH!
AGHYR, IS SOMETHING WRONG?
FLIP
WHY DID YOU STOP ALL OF A SUDDEN?
WELL...
RUSTLE...

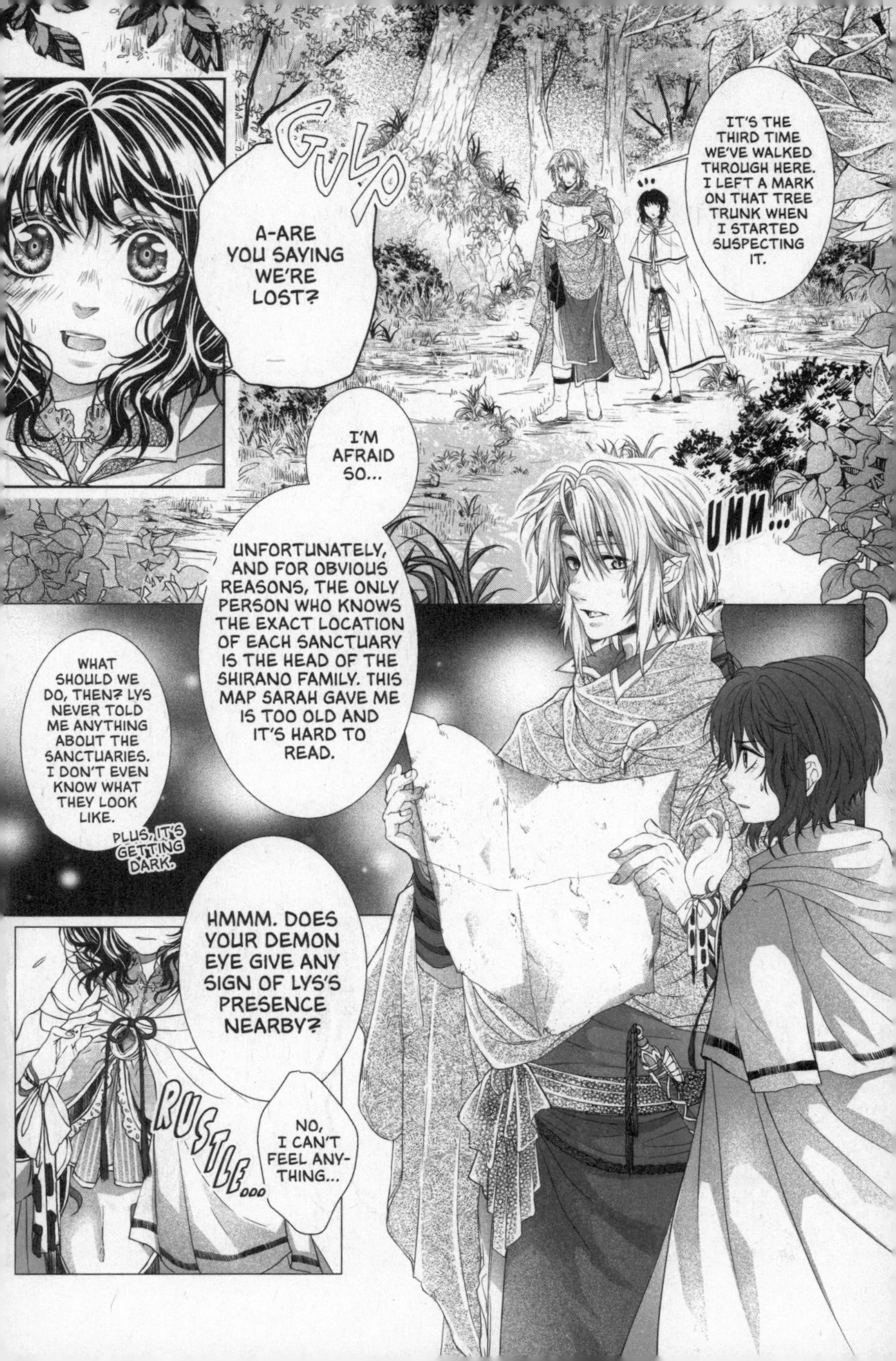
IT'S THE THIRD TIME WE'VE WALKED THROUGH HERE. I LEFT A MARK ON THAT TREE TRUNK WHEN I STARTED SUSPECTING IT.
GULP
A-ARE YOU SAYING WE'RE LOST?
I'M AFRAID SO...
UNFORTUNATELY, AND FOR OBVIOUS REASONS, THE ONLY PERSON WHO KNOWS THE EXACT LOCATION OF EACH SANCTUARY IS THE HEAD OF THE SHIRANO FAMILY. THIS MAP SARAH GAVE ME IS TOO OLD AND IT'S HARD TO READ.
UMM...
WHAT SHOULD WE DO, THEN? LYS NEVER TOLD ME ANYTHING ABOUT THE SANCTUARIES. I DON'T EVEN KNOW WHAT THEY LOOK LIKE.
PLUS, IT'S GETTING DARK.
HMMM. DOES YOUR DEMON EYE GIVE ANY SIGN OF LYS'S PRESENCE NEARBY?
RUSTLE...
NO, I CAN'T FEEL ANY-THING...

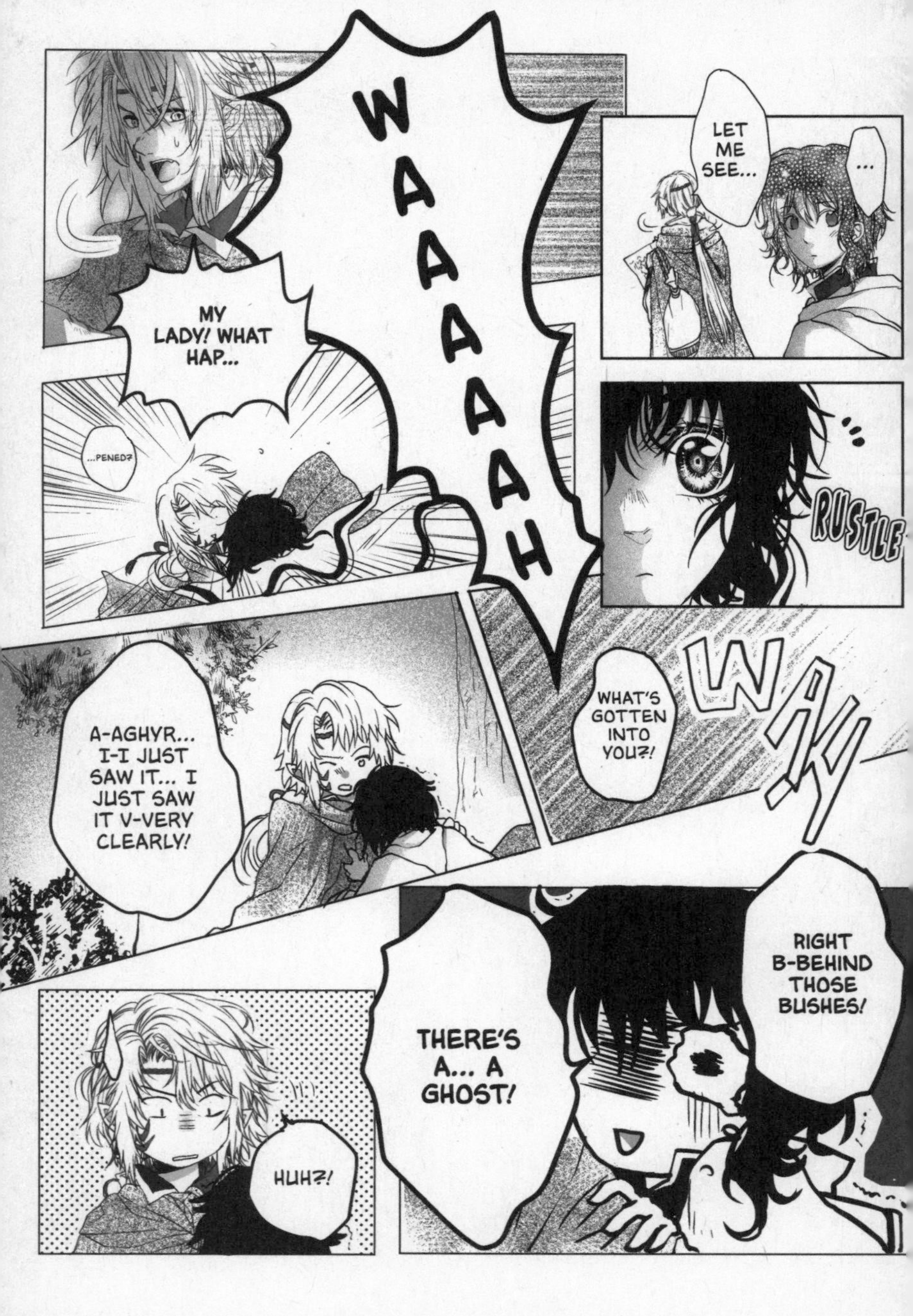
LET ME SEE...
...
RUSTLE
WAAAAAAH
MY LADY! WHAT HAP...
...PENED?
WHAT'S GOTTEN INTO YOU?!
A-AGHYR... I-I JUST SAW IT... I JUST SAW IT V-VERY CLEARLY!
RIGHT B-BEHIND THOSE BUSHES!
THERE'S A... A GHOST!
HUH?!

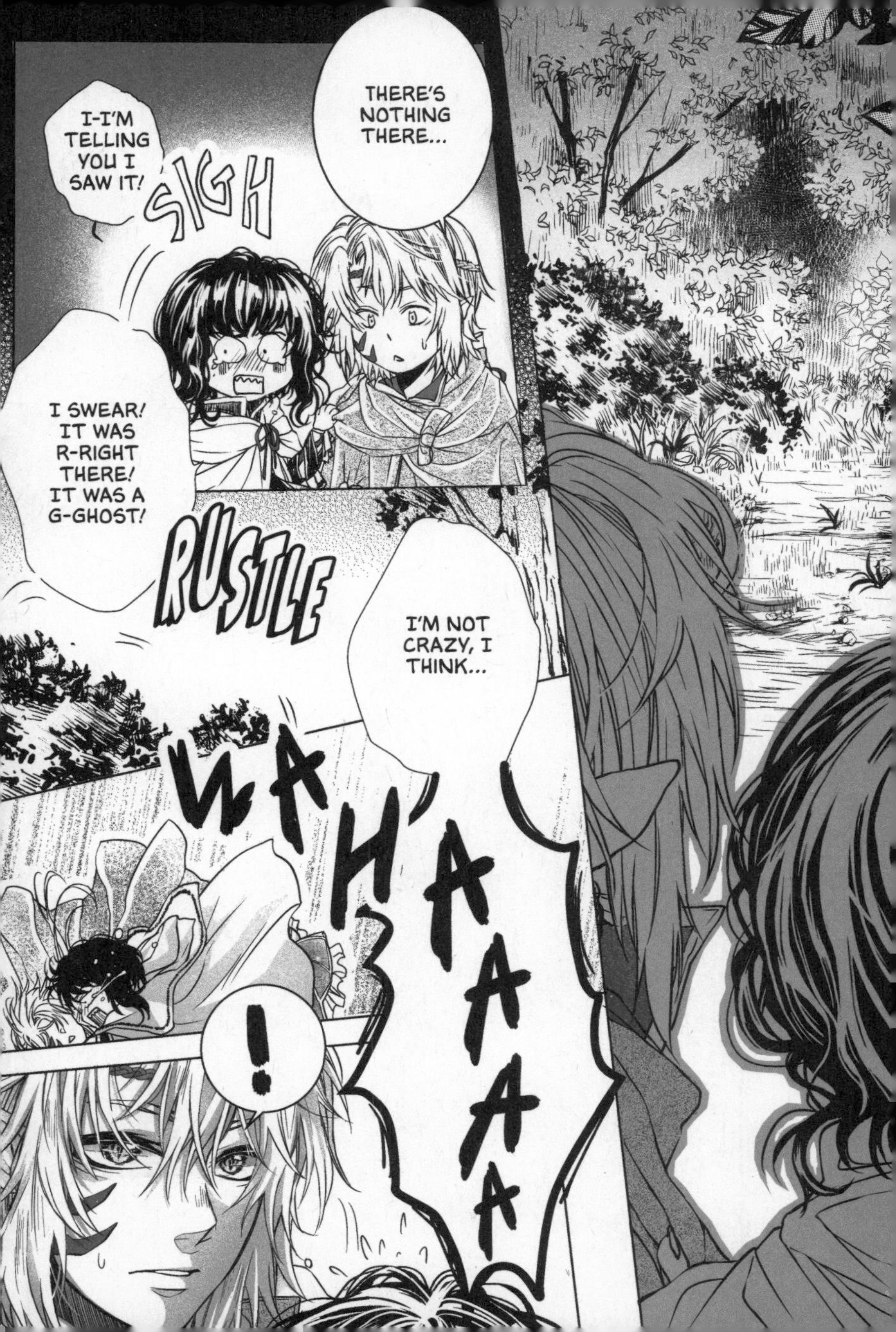
THERE'S NOTHING THERE...
I-I'M TELLING YOU I SAW IT!
SIGH
I SWEAR! IT WAS R-RIGHT THERE! IT WAS A G-GHOST!
RUSTLE
I'M NOT CRAZY, I THINK...
WAHAAAAAA
!

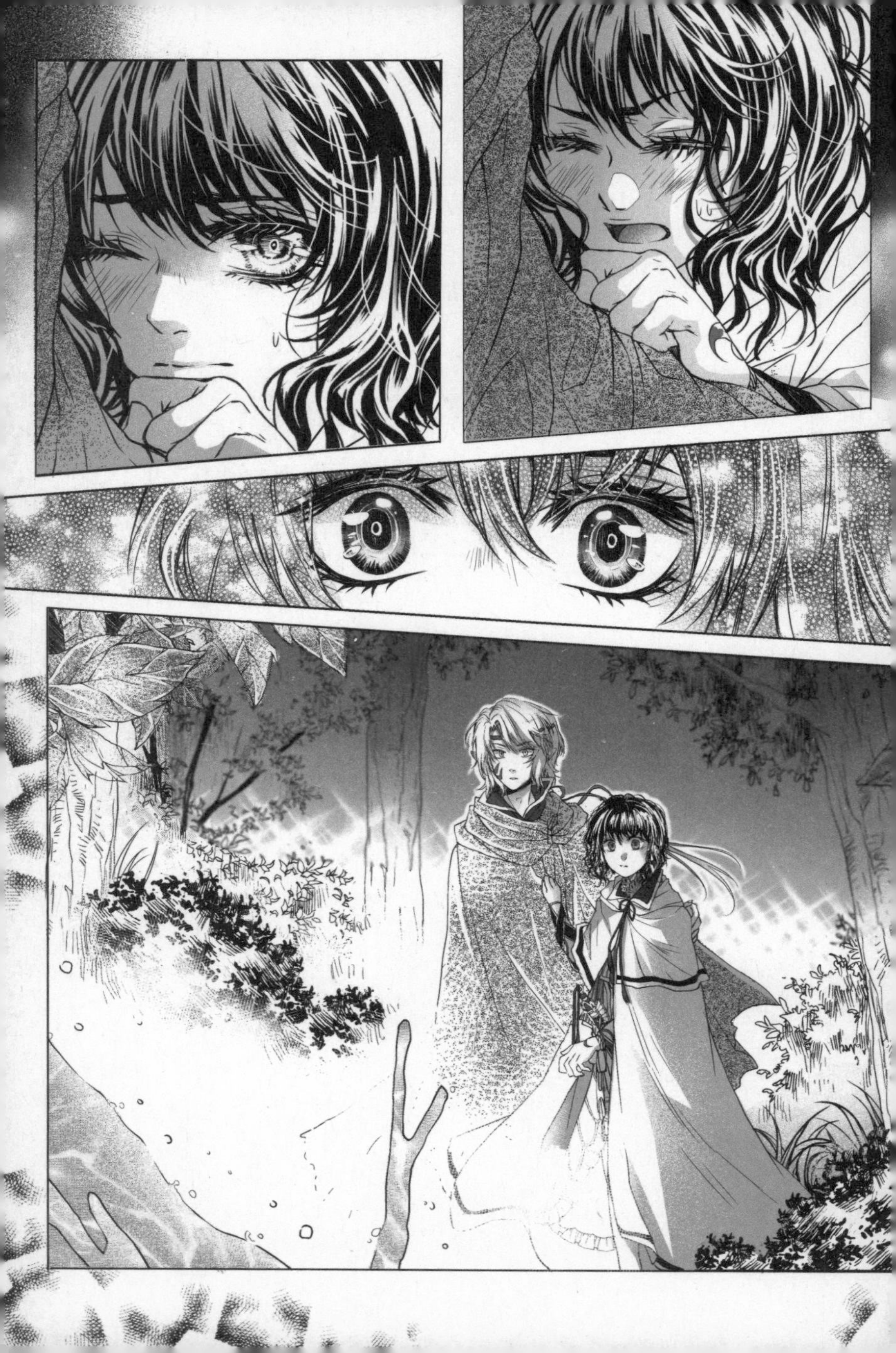

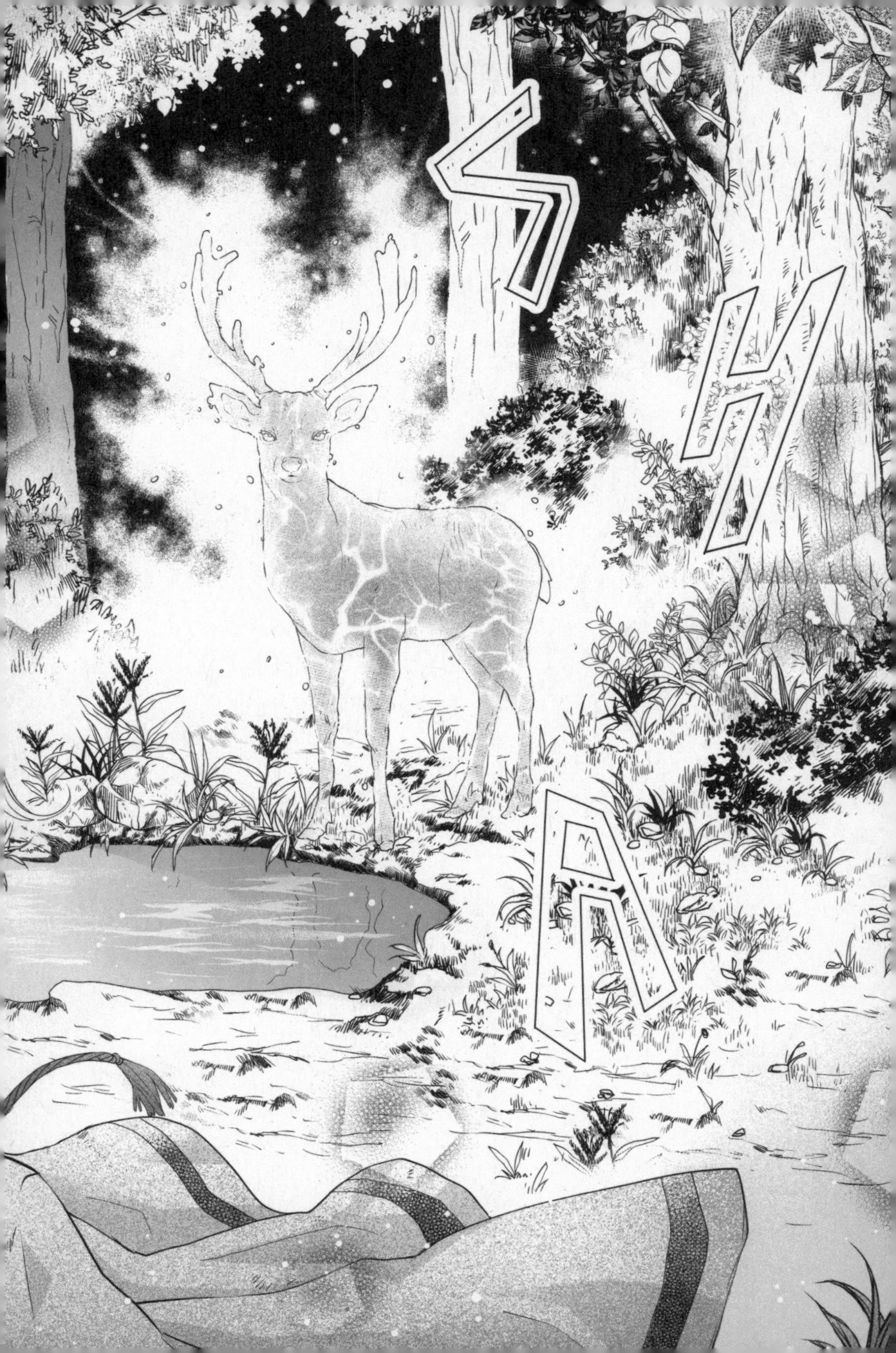
SHA

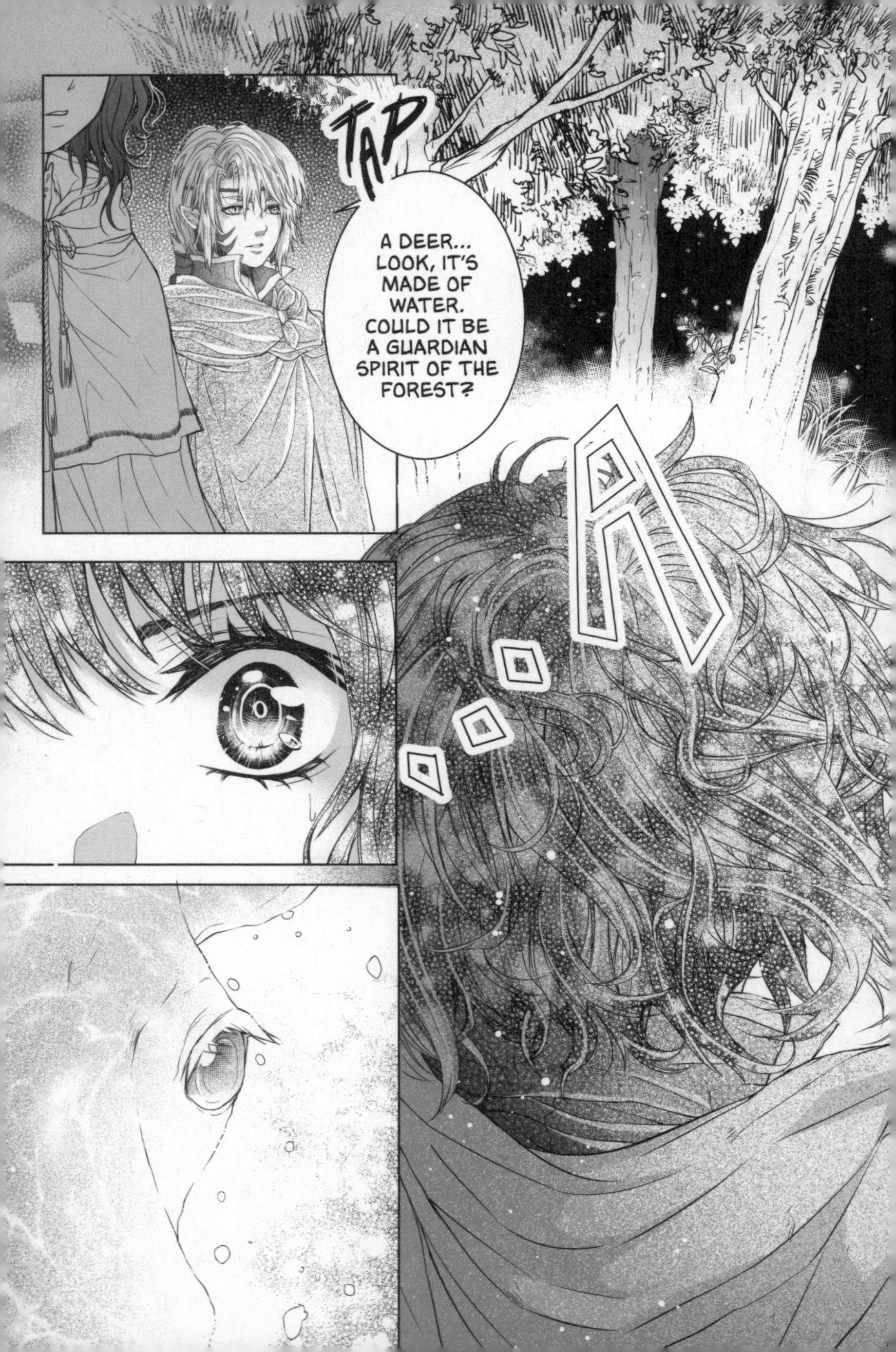
TAP
A DEER... LOOK, IT'S MADE OF WATER. COULD IT BE A GUARDIAN SPIRIT OF THE FOREST?

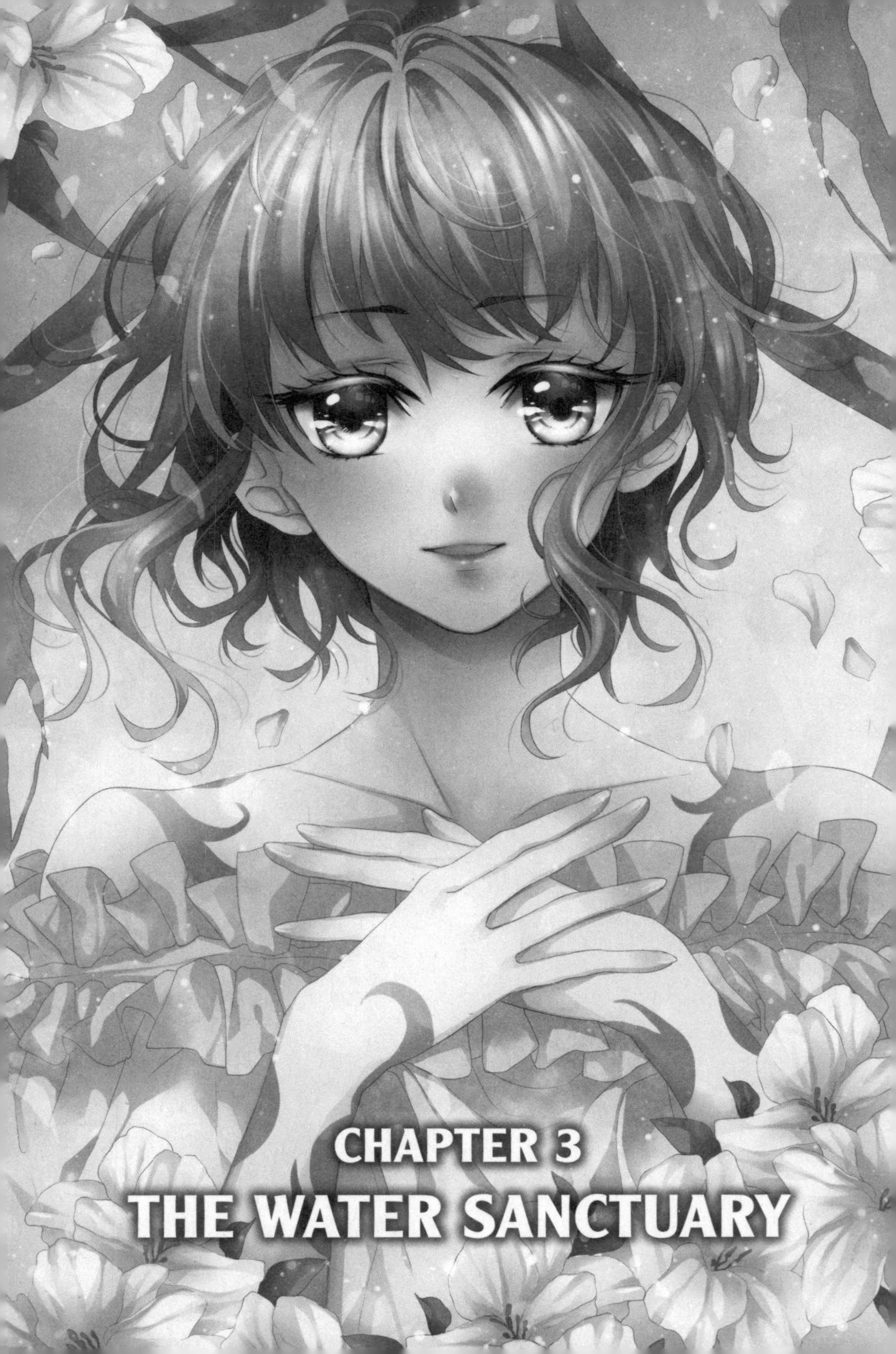

CHAPTER 3
THE WATER SANCTUARY

Scarlet Soul

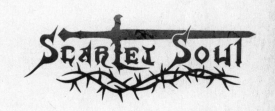

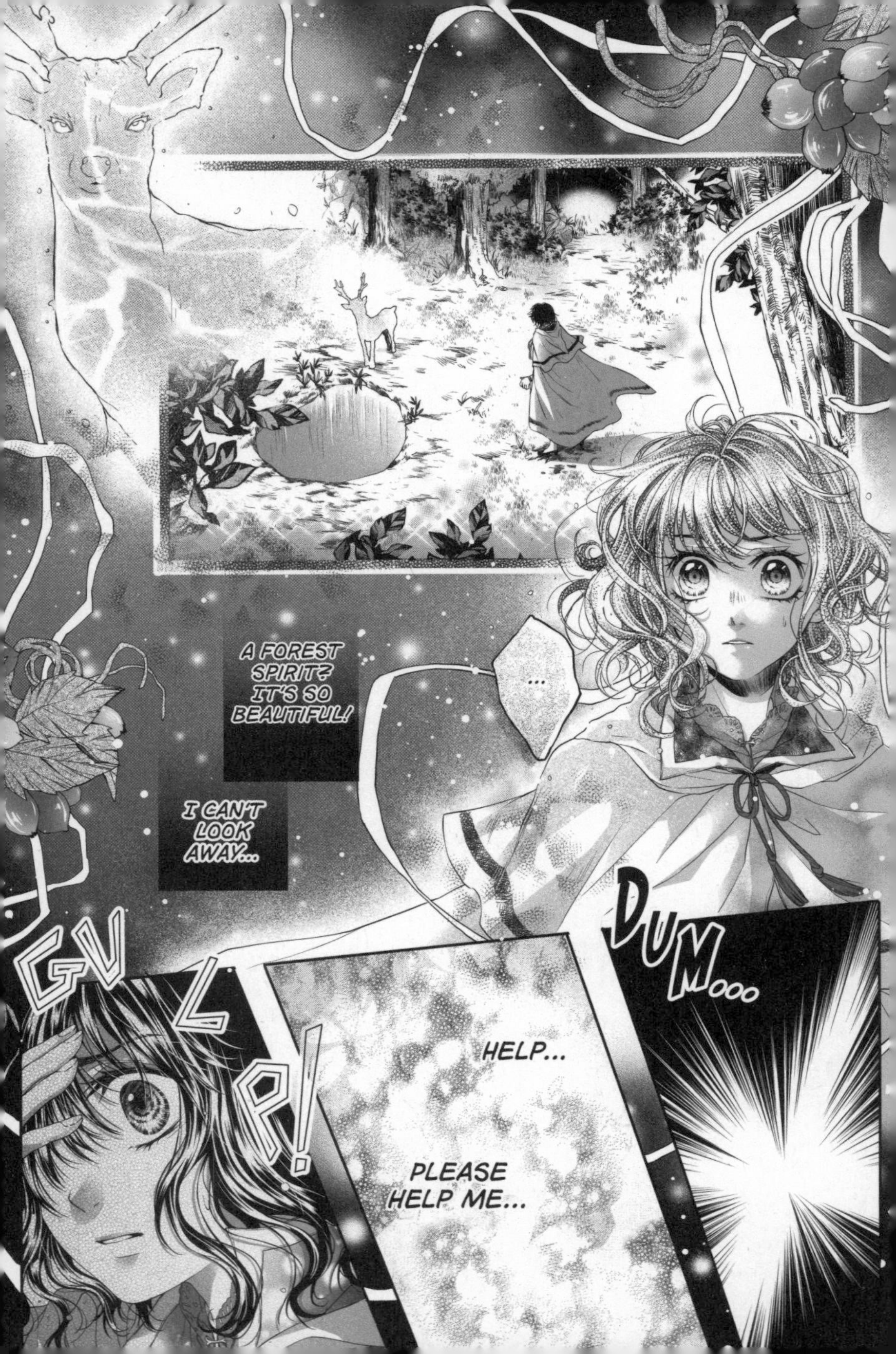
...
A FOREST SPIRIT? IT'S SO BEAUTIFUL!
I CAN'T LOOK AWAY...
DUM...
HELP...
PLEASE HELP ME...
GULP!

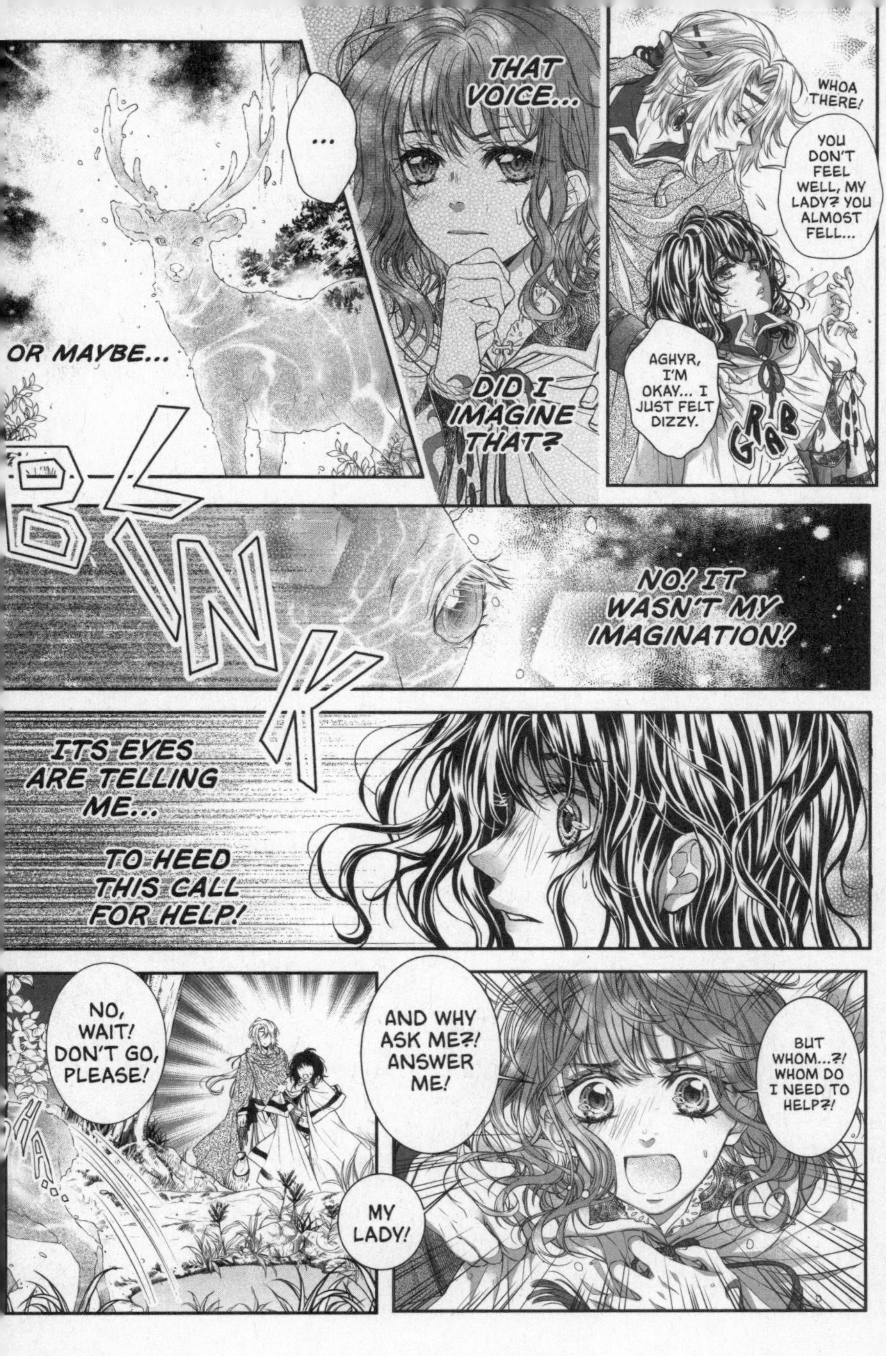
WHOA THERE!
YOU DON'T FEEL WELL, MY LADY? YOU ALMOST FELL...
AGHYR, I'M OKAY... I JUST FELT DIZZY.
GRAB
THAT VOICE...
DID I IMAGINE THAT?
...
OR MAYBE...
BLINK
NO! IT WASN'T MY IMAGINATION!
ITS EYES ARE TELLING ME...
TO HEED THIS CALL FOR HELP!
BUT WHOM...?! WHOM DO I NEED TO HELP?!
AND WHY ASK ME?! ANSWER ME!
MY LADY!
NO, WAIT! DON'T GO, PLEASE!
HA...

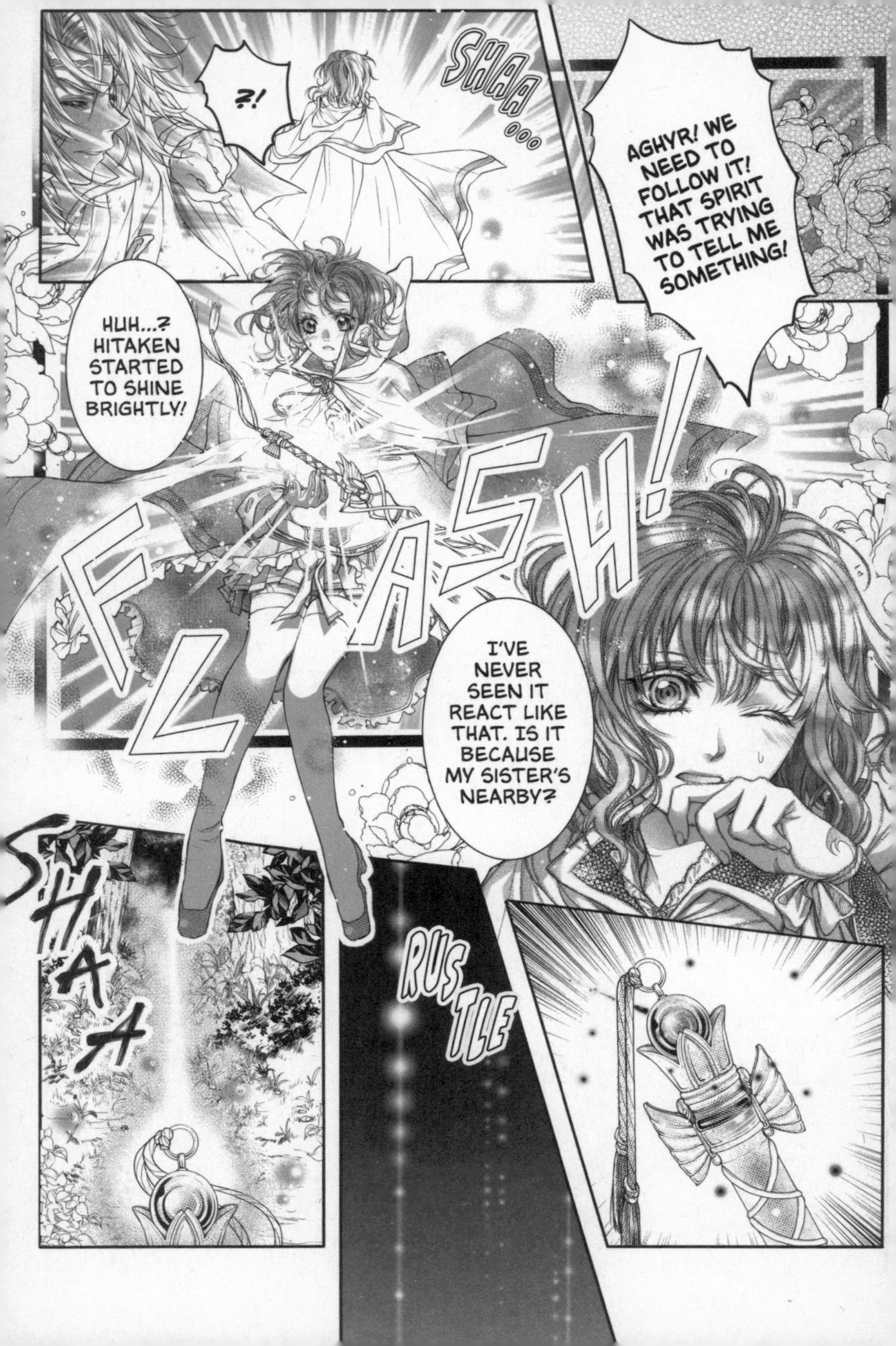
?!
SHAA...
AGHYR! WE NEED TO FOLLOW IT! THAT SPIRIT WAS TRYING TO TELL ME SOMETHING!
HUH...? HITAKEN STARTED TO SHINE BRIGHTLY!
FLASH!
I'VE NEVER SEEN IT REACT LIKE THAT. IS IT BECAUSE MY SISTER'S NEARBY?
SHAA
RUSTLE

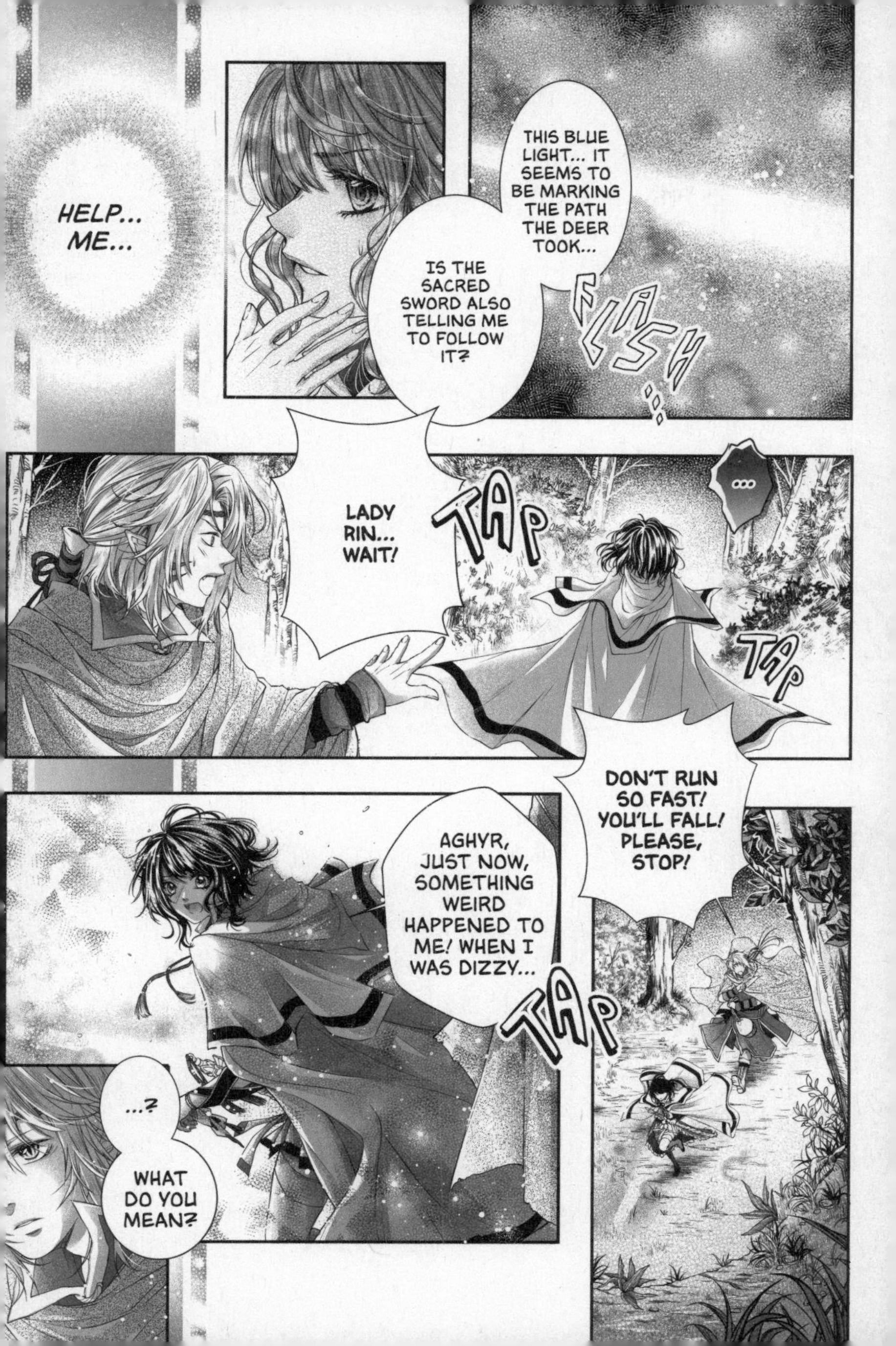
THIS BLUE LIGHT... IT SEEMS TO BE MARKING THE PATH THE DEER TOOK...
IS THE SACRED SWORD ALSO TELLING ME TO FOLLOW IT?
FLASH
HELP... ME...
...
LADY RIN... WAIT!
TAP
TAP
DON'T RUN SO FAST! YOU'LL FALL! PLEASE, STOP!
TAP
AGHYR, JUST NOW, SOMETHING WEIRD HAPPENED TO ME! WHEN I WAS DIZZY...
...?
WHAT DO YOU MEAN?

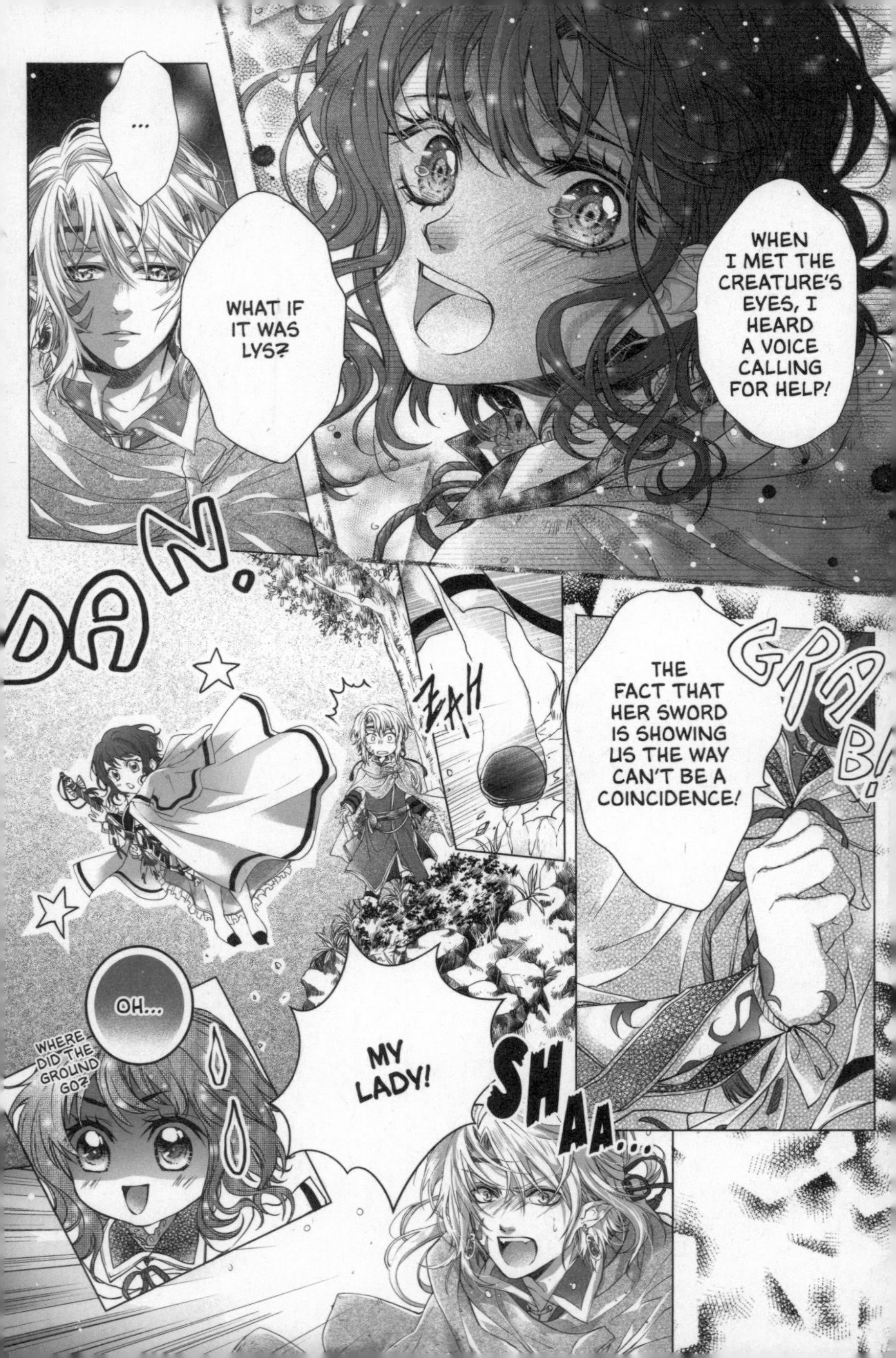
WHEN I MET THE CREATURE'S EYES, I HEARD A VOICE CALLING FOR HELP!
...
WHAT IF IT WAS LYS?
GRAB!
THE FACT THAT HER SWORD IS SHOWING US THE WAY CAN'T BE A COINCIDENCE!
ZAH
DAN.
SHAA...
MY LADY!
OH...
WHERE DID THE GROUND GO?

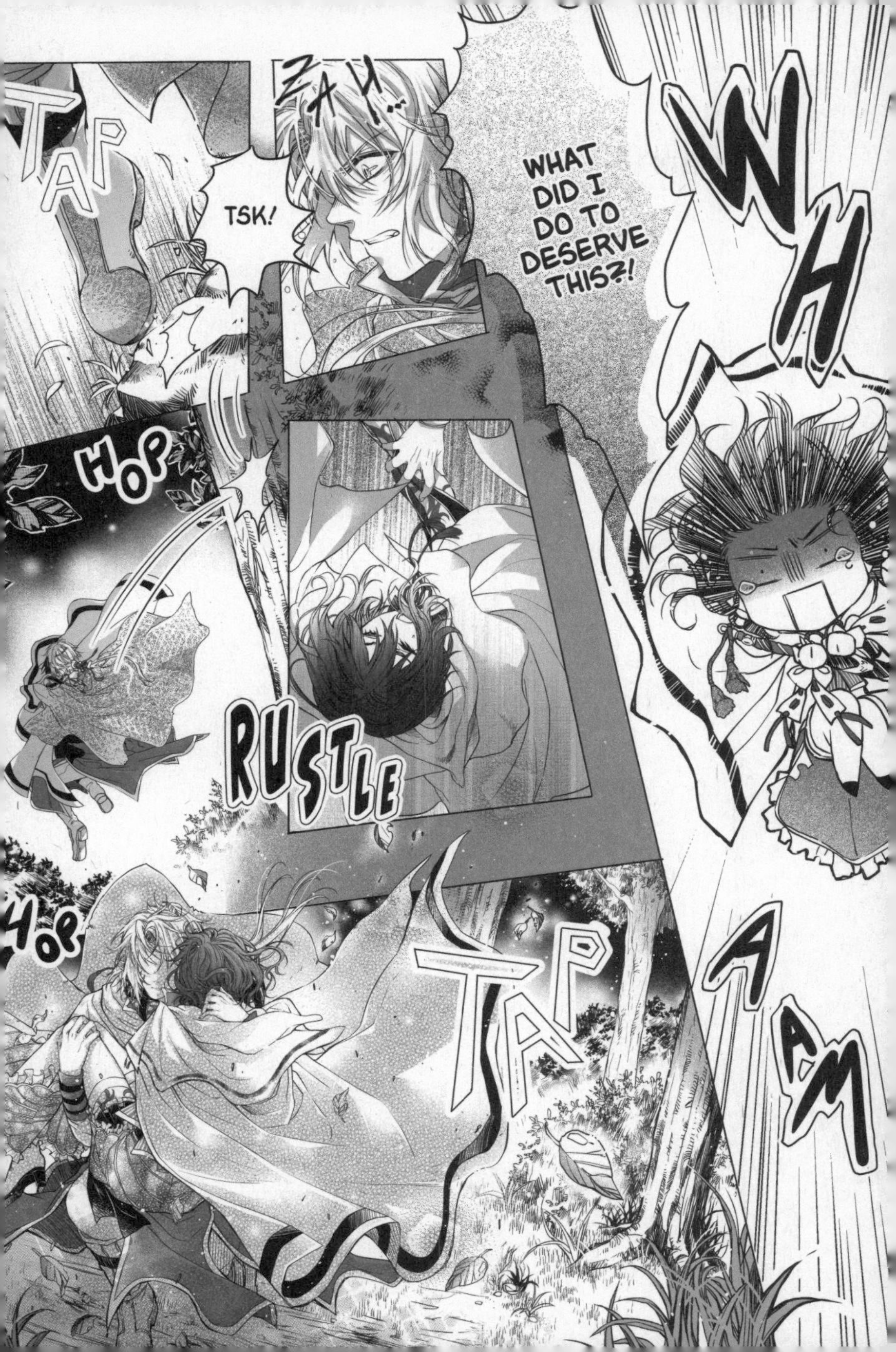
WAH
WHAT DID I DO TO DESERVE THIS?!
ZAY..
TSK!
TAP
HOP
RUSTLE
TAP TAP
HOP

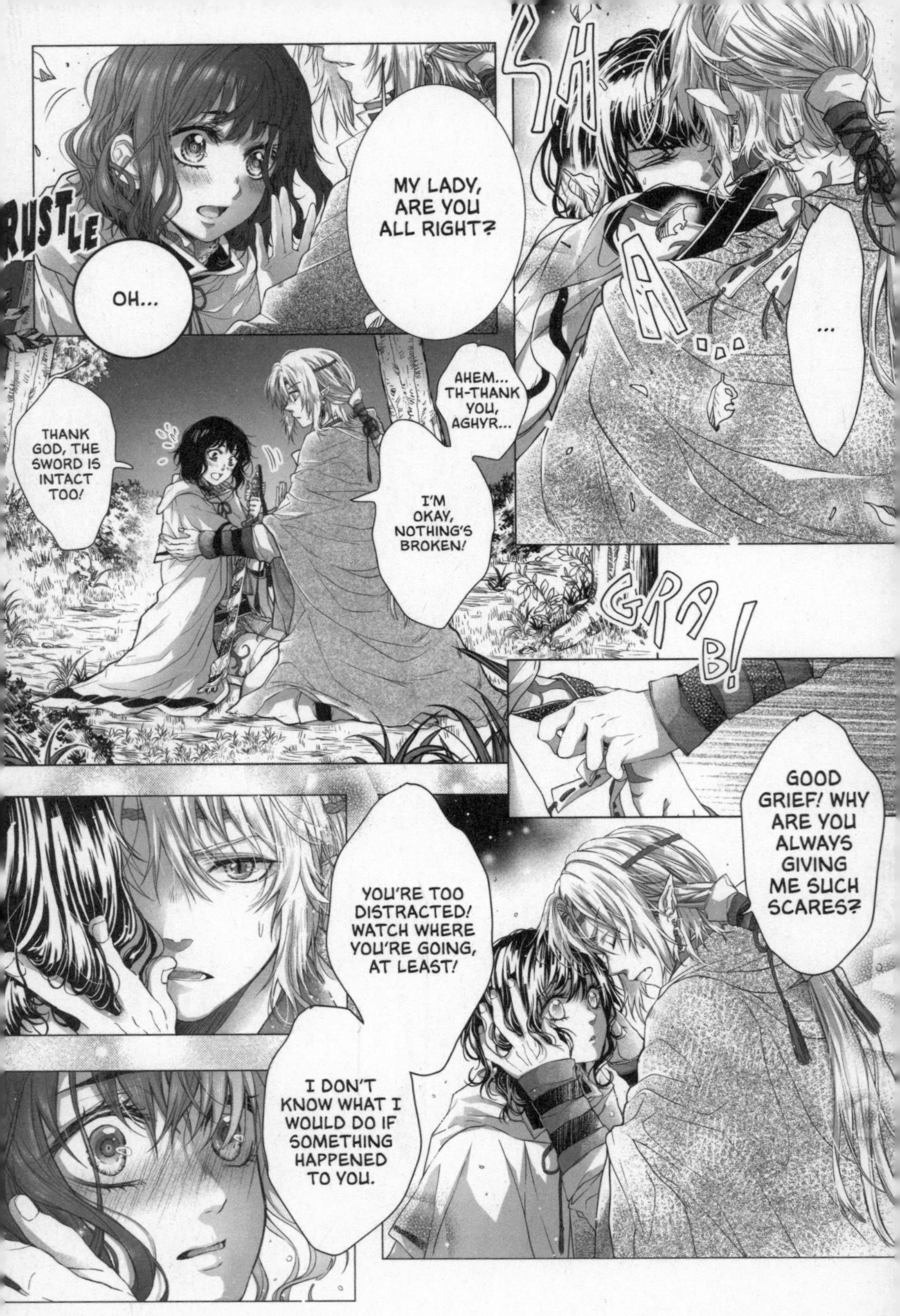
SHAA...
...
RUSTLE
MY LADY, ARE YOU ALL RIGHT?
OH...
AHEM... TH-THANK YOU, AGHYR...
I'M OKAY, NOTHING'S BROKEN!
THANK GOD, THE SWORD IS INTACT TOO!
GRAB!
GOOD GRIEF! WHY ARE YOU ALWAYS GIVING ME SUCH SCARES?
YOU'RE TOO DISTRACTED! WATCH WHERE YOU'RE GOING, AT LEAST!
I DON'T KNOW WHAT I WOULD DO IF SOMETHING HAPPENED TO YOU.

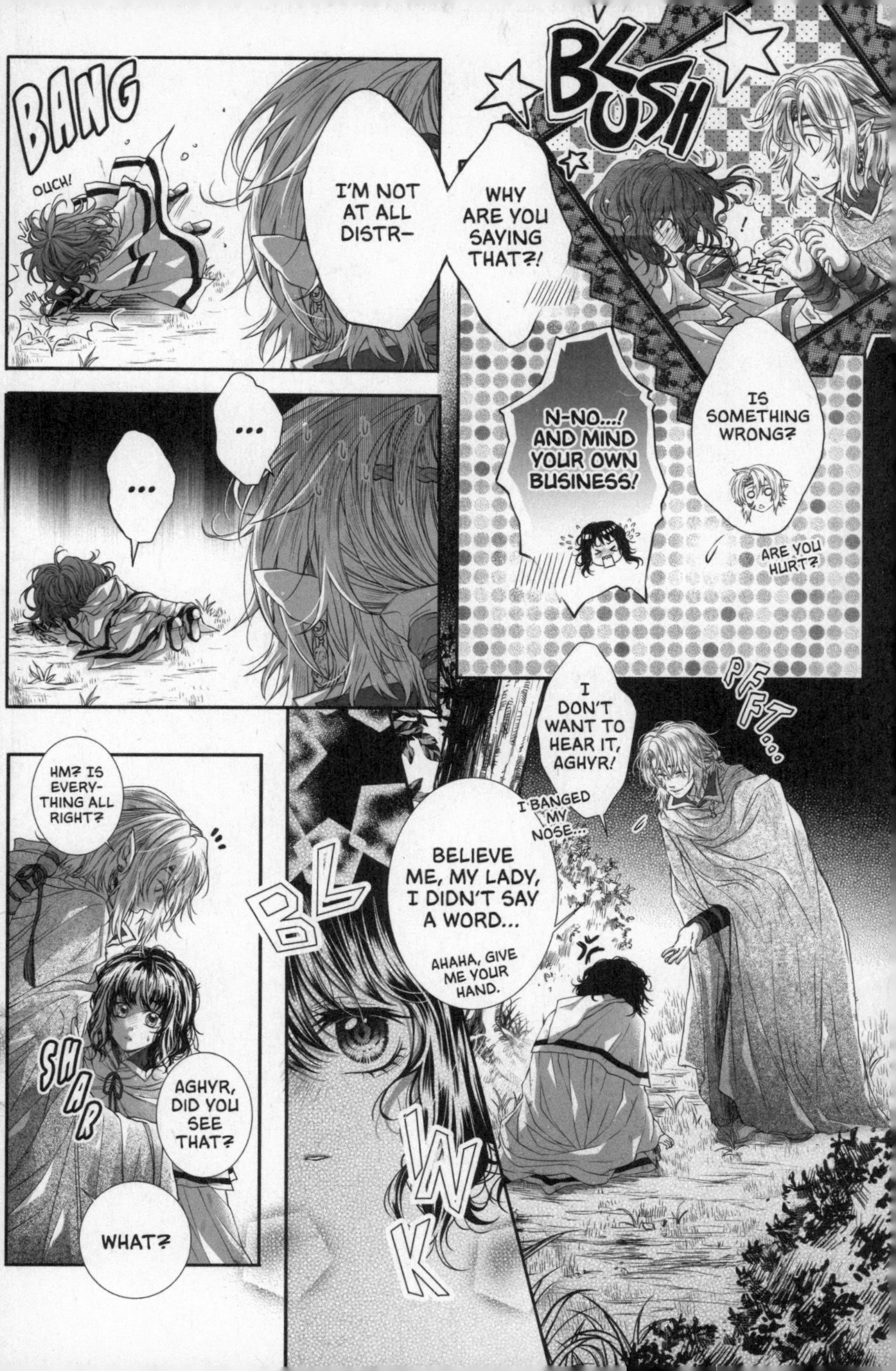
WHY ARE YOU SAYING THAT?!
I'M NOT AT ALL DISTR-
BANG
OUCH!
...
...
BLUSH
IS SOMETHING WRONG?
ARE YOU HURT?
N-NO...! AND MIND YOUR OWN BUSINESS!
I DON'T WANT TO HEAR IT, AGHYR!
PFFT...
I BANGED MY NOSE...
BELIEVE ME, MY LADY, I DIDN'T SAY A WORD...
AHAHA, GIVE ME YOUR HAND.
BLINK
HM? IS EVERYTHING ALL RIGHT?
SHAR
AGHYR, DID YOU SEE THAT?
WHAT?

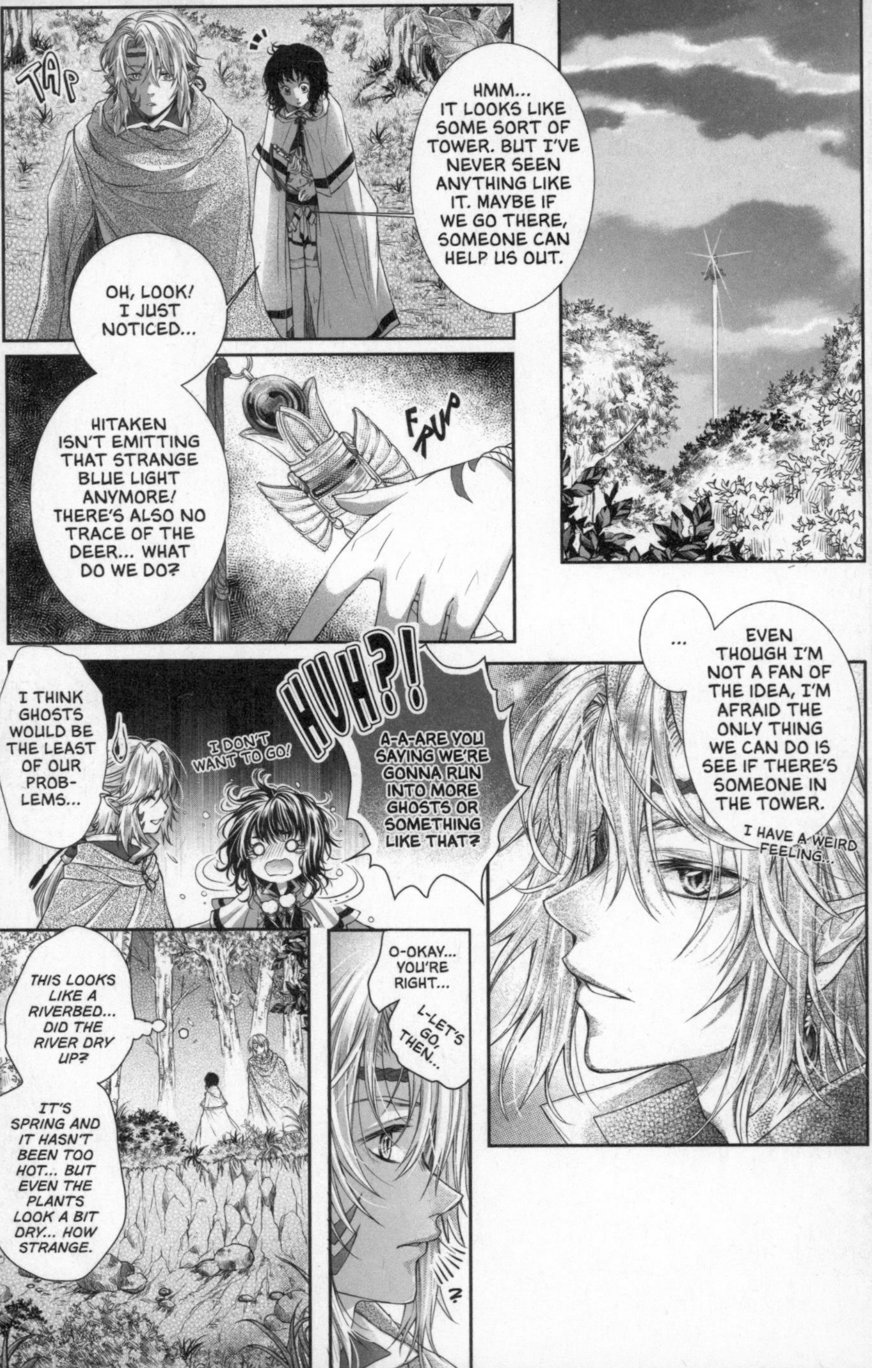
TAP
HMM... IT LOOKS LIKE SOME SORT OF TOWER. BUT I'VE NEVER SEEN ANYTHING LIKE IT. MAYBE IF WE GO THERE, SOMEONE CAN HELP US OUT.
OH, LOOK! I JUST NOTICED...
HITAKEN ISN'T EMITTING THAT STRANGE BLUE LIGHT ANYMORE! THERE'S ALSO NO TRACE OF THE DEER... WHAT DO WE DO?
FRUP
...
EVEN THOUGH I'M NOT A FAN OF THE IDEA, I'M AFRAID THE ONLY THING WE CAN DO IS SEE IF THERE'S SOMEONE IN THE TOWER.
I HAVE A WEIRD FEELING...
HUH?!
A-A-ARE YOU SAYING WE'RE GONNA RUN INTO MORE GHOSTS OR SOMETHING LIKE THAT?
I DON'T WANT TO GO!
I THINK GHOSTS WOULD BE THE LEAST OF OUR PROB-LEMS...
O-OKAY... YOU'RE RIGHT...
L-LET'S GO, THEN...
THIS LOOKS LIKE A RIVERBED... DID THE RIVER DRY UP?
IT'S SPRING AND IT HASN'T BEEN TOO HOT... BUT EVEN THE PLANTS LOOK A BIT DRY... HOW STRANGE.

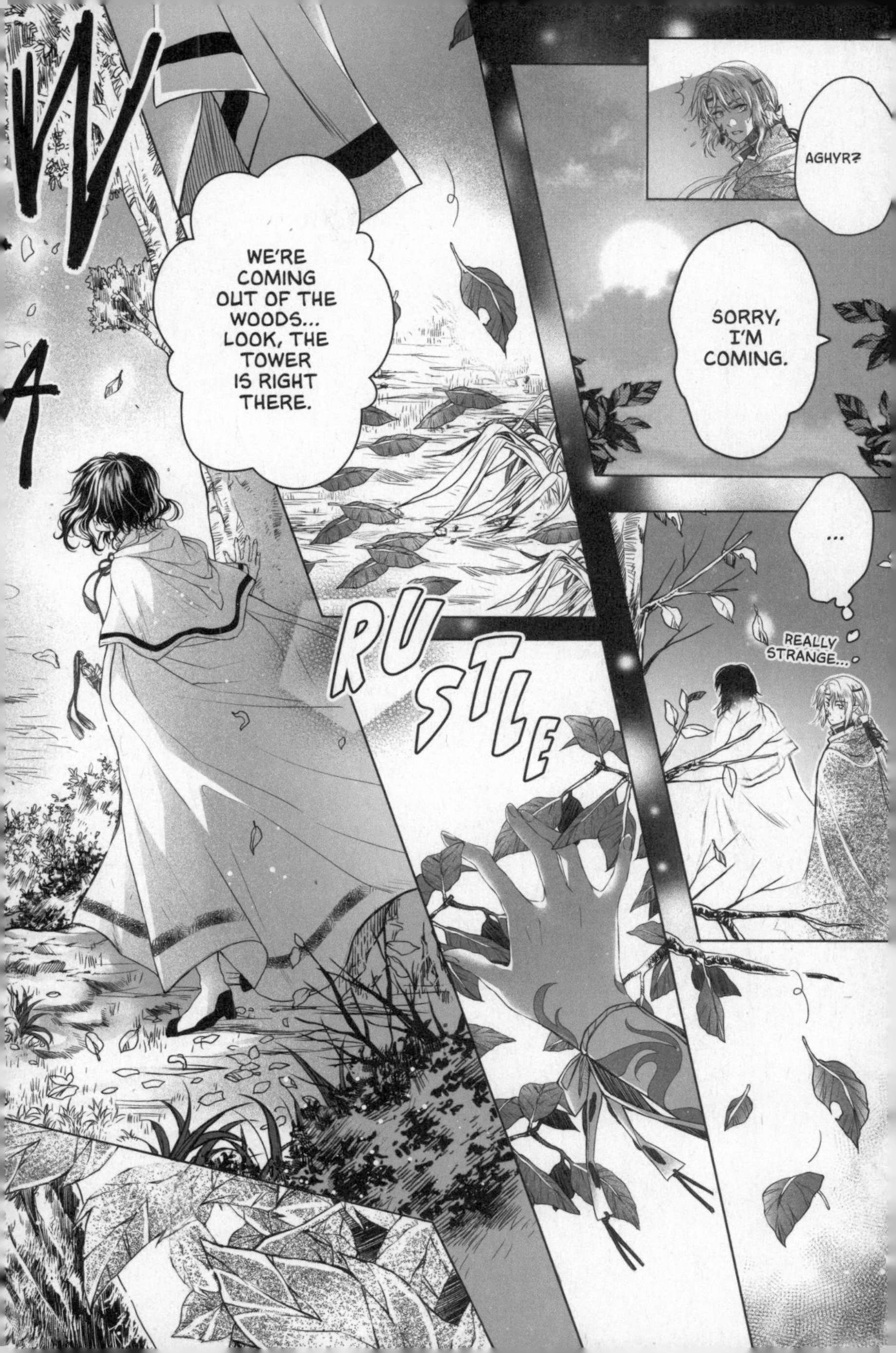
AGHYR?
SORRY, I'M COMING.
...
REALLY STRANGE...
WE'RE COMING OUT OF THE WOODS... LOOK, THE TOWER IS RIGHT THERE.
WA
RUSTLE

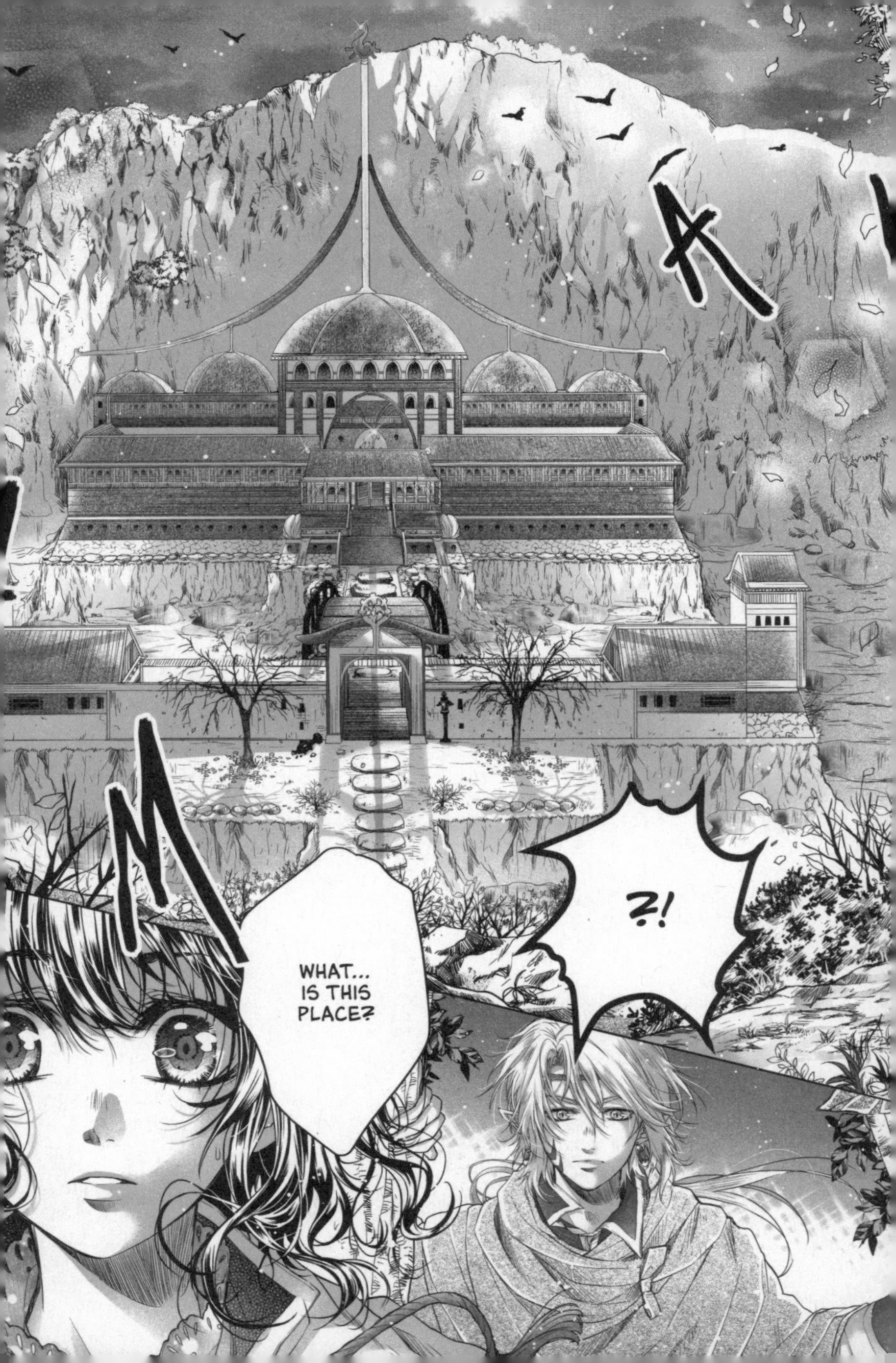
A
M
?!
WHAT... IS THIS PLACE?

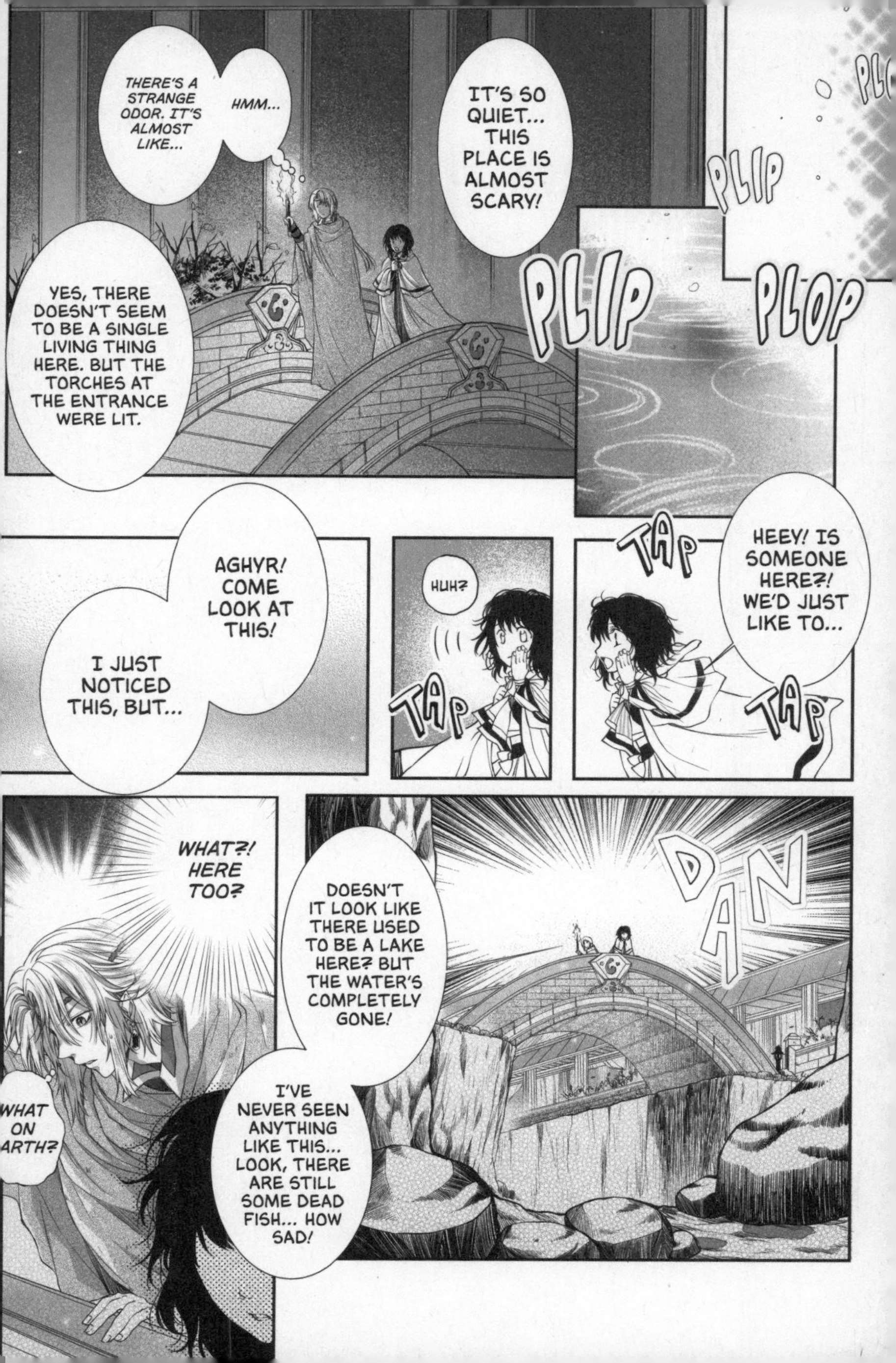
PLIP
PLOP
PLIP
PLIP PLOP
IT'S SO QUIET... THIS PLACE IS ALMOST SCARY!
HMM...
THERE'S A STRANGE ODOR. IT'S ALMOST LIKE...
YES, THERE DOESN'T SEEM TO BE A SINGLE LIVING THING HERE. BUT THE TORCHES AT THE ENTRANCE WERE LIT.
TAP
HEEY! IS SOMEONE HERE?! WE'D JUST LIKE TO...
TAP
HUH?
TAP
AGHYR! COME LOOK AT THIS!
I JUST NOTICED THIS, BUT...
DAN
DOESN'T IT LOOK LIKE THERE USED TO BE A LAKE HERE? BUT THE WATER'S COMPLETELY GONE!
I'VE NEVER SEEN ANYTHING LIKE THIS... LOOK, THERE ARE STILL SOME DEAD FISH... HOW SAD!
WHAT?! HERE TOO?
WHAT ON ARTH?

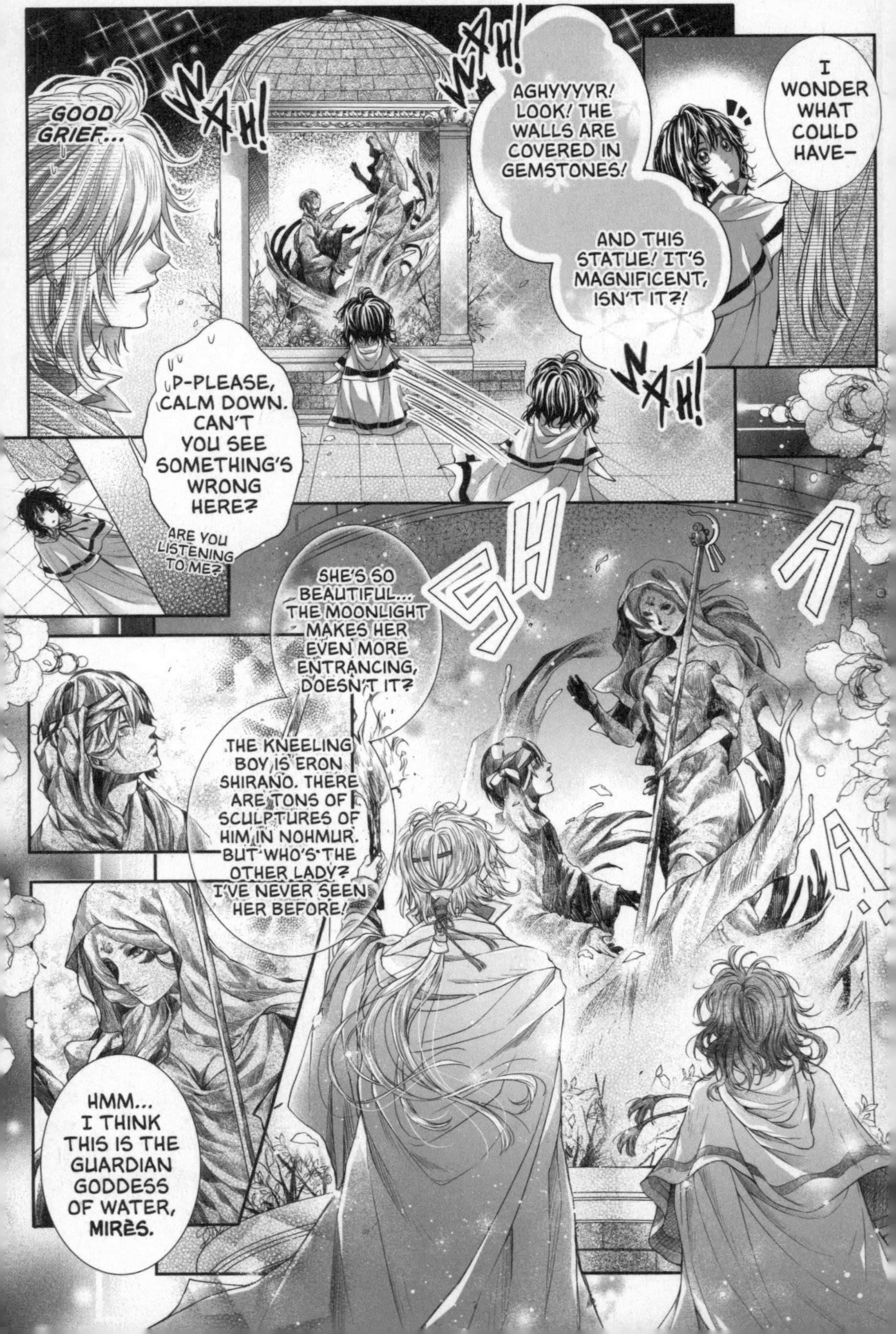
I WONDER WHAT COULD HAVE–
WAH!
AGHYYYR! LOOK! THE WALLS ARE COVERED IN GEMSTONES!
AND THIS STATUE! IT'S MAGNIFICENT, ISN'T IT?!
WAH!
WAH!
GOOD GRIEF...
P-PLEASE, CALM DOWN. CAN'T YOU SEE SOMETHING'S WRONG HERE?
ARE YOU LISTENING TO ME?
SHAA...
SHE'S SO BEAUTIFUL... THE MOONLIGHT MAKES HER EVEN MORE ENTRANCING, DOESN'T IT?
THE KNEELING BOY IS ERON SHIRANO. THERE ARE TONS OF SCULPTURES OF HIM IN NOHMUR. BUT WHO'S THE OTHER LADY? I'VE NEVER SEEN HER BEFORE!
HMM... I THINK THIS IS THE GUARDIAN GODDESS OF WATER, MIRÈS.

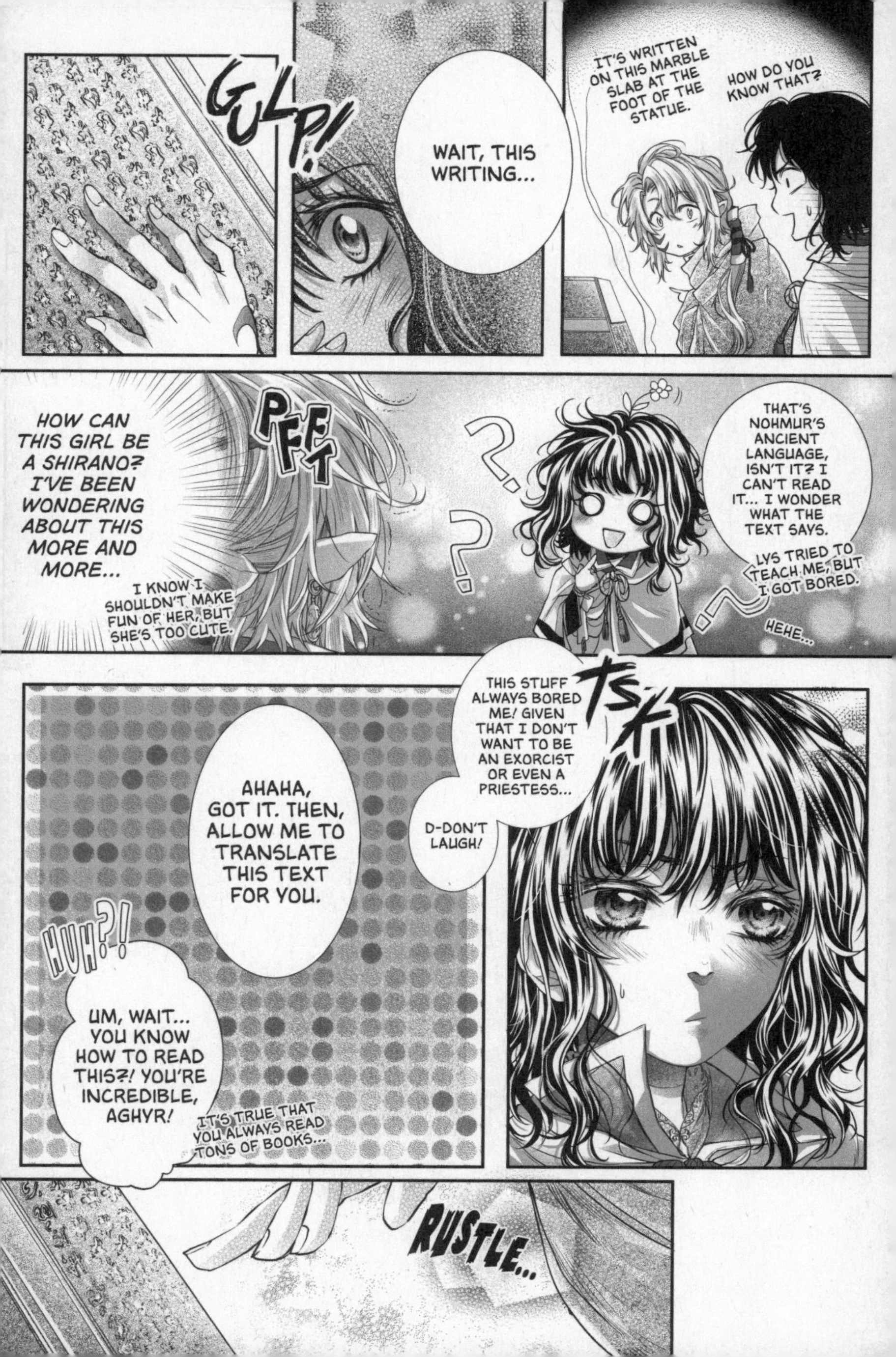
IT'S WRITTEN ON THIS MARBLE SLAB AT THE FOOT OF THE STATUE.
HOW DO YOU KNOW THAT?
WAIT, THIS WRITING...
GULP!
THAT'S NOHMUR'S ANCIENT LANGUAGE, ISN'T IT? I CAN'T READ IT... I WONDER WHAT THE TEXT SAYS.
LYS TRIED TO TEACH ME, BUT I GOT BORED.
HEHE...
PFFT
HOW CAN THIS GIRL BE A SHIRANO? I'VE BEEN WONDERING ABOUT THIS MORE AND MORE...
I KNOW I SHOULDN'T MAKE FUN OF HER, BUT SHE'S TOO CUTE.
TSK
THIS STUFF ALWAYS BORED ME! GIVEN THAT I DON'T WANT TO BE AN EXORCIST OR EVEN A PRIESTESS...
D-DON'T LAUGH!
AHAHA, GOT IT. THEN, ALLOW ME TO TRANSLATE THIS TEXT FOR YOU.
HUH?!
UM, WAIT... YOU KNOW HOW TO READ THIS?! YOU'RE INCREDIBLE, AGHYR!
IT'S TRUE THAT YOU ALWAYS READ TONS OF BOOKS...
RUSTLE...

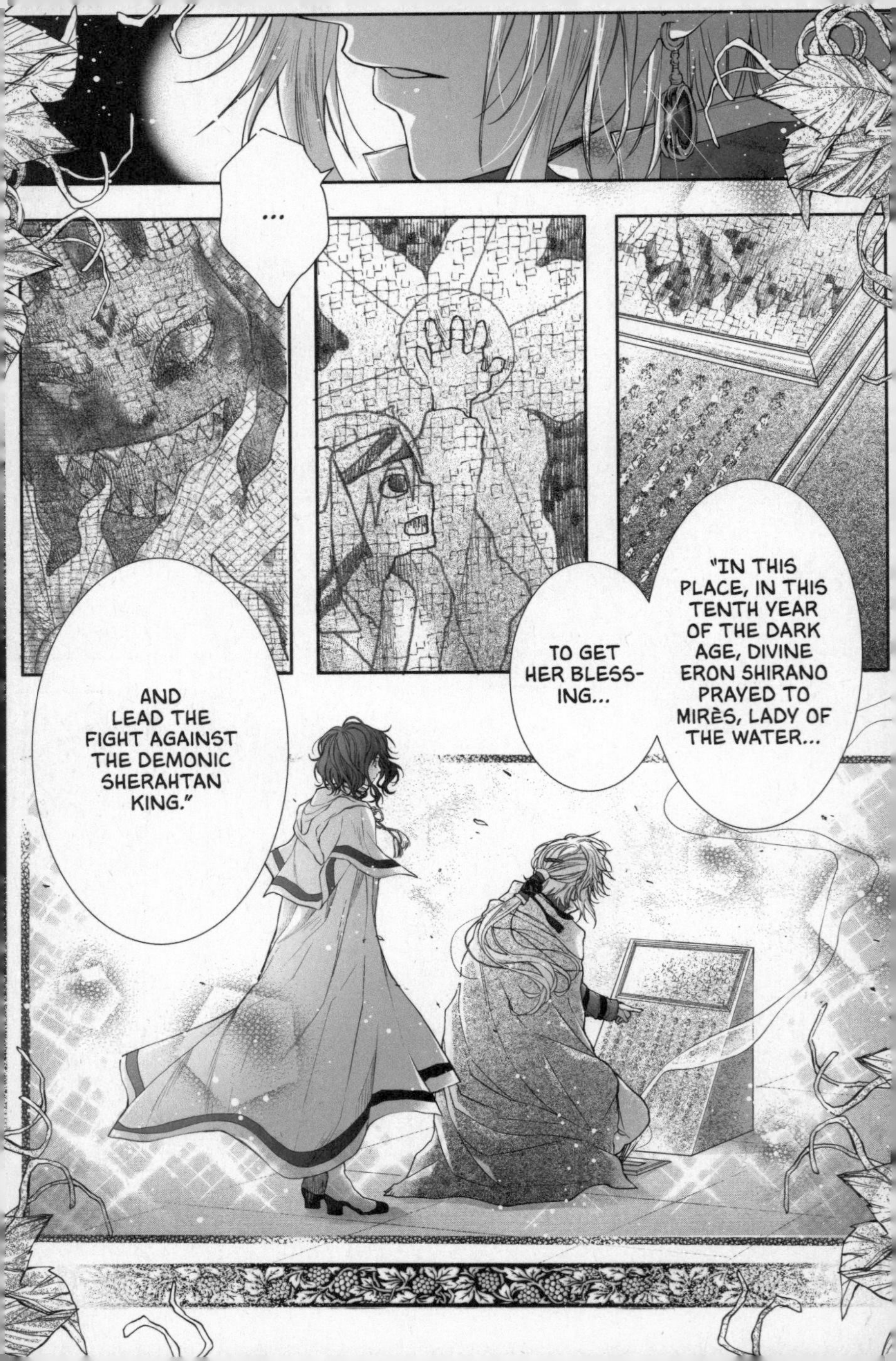
...
"IN THIS PLACE, IN THIS TENTH YEAR OF THE DARK AGE, DIVINE ERON SHIRANO PRAYED TO MIRÈS, LADY OF THE WATER...
TO GET HER BLESS-ING...
AND LEAD THE FIGHT AGAINST THE DEMONIC SHERAHTAN KING."

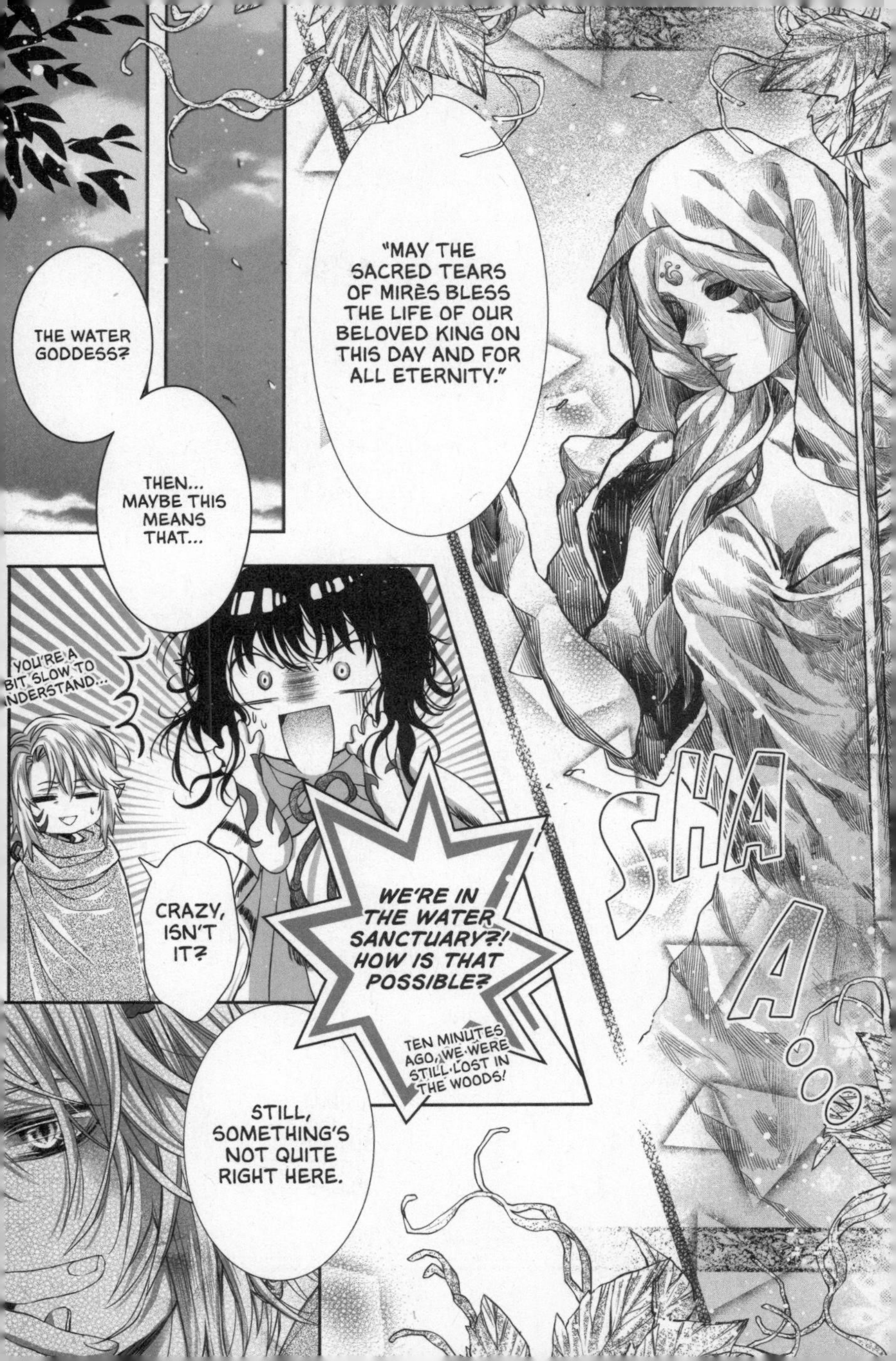
"MAY THE SACRED TEARS OF MIRÈS BLESS THE LIFE OF OUR BELOVED KING ON THIS DAY AND FOR ALL ETERNITY."
THE WATER GODDESS?
THEN... MAYBE THIS MEANS THAT...
SHAAOOO
WE'RE IN THE WATER SANCTUARY?! HOW IS THAT POSSIBLE?
TEN MINUTES AGO, WE WERE STILL LOST IN THE WOODS!
YOU'RE A BIT SLOW TO NDERSTAND...
CRAZY, ISN'T IT?
STILL, SOMETHING'S NOT QUITE RIGHT HERE.

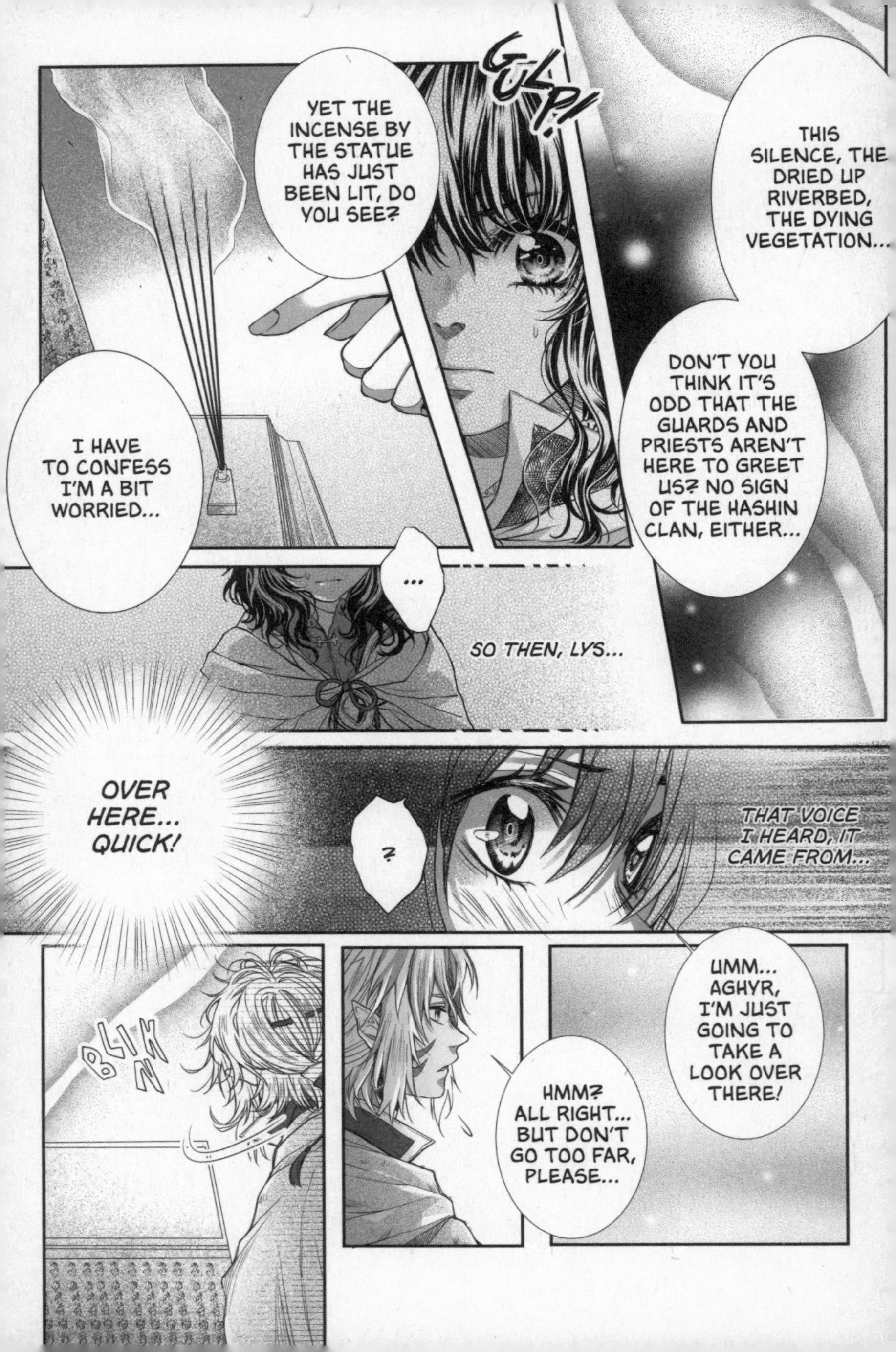
THIS SILENCE, THE DRIED UP RIVERBED, THE DYING VEGETATION...
DON'T YOU THINK IT'S ODD THAT THE GUARDS AND PRIESTS AREN'T HERE TO GREET US? NO SIGN OF THE HASHIN CLAN, EITHER...
GULP!
YET THE INCENSE BY THE STATUE HAS JUST BEEN LIT, DO YOU SEE?
I HAVE TO CONFESS I'M A BIT WORRIED...
...
SO THEN, LYS...
THAT VOICE I HEARD, IT CAME FROM...
?
OVER HERE... QUICK!
UMM... AGHYR, I'M JUST GOING TO TAKE A LOOK OVER THERE!
HMM? ALL RIGHT... BUT DON'T GO TOO FAR, PLEASE...
BLINK

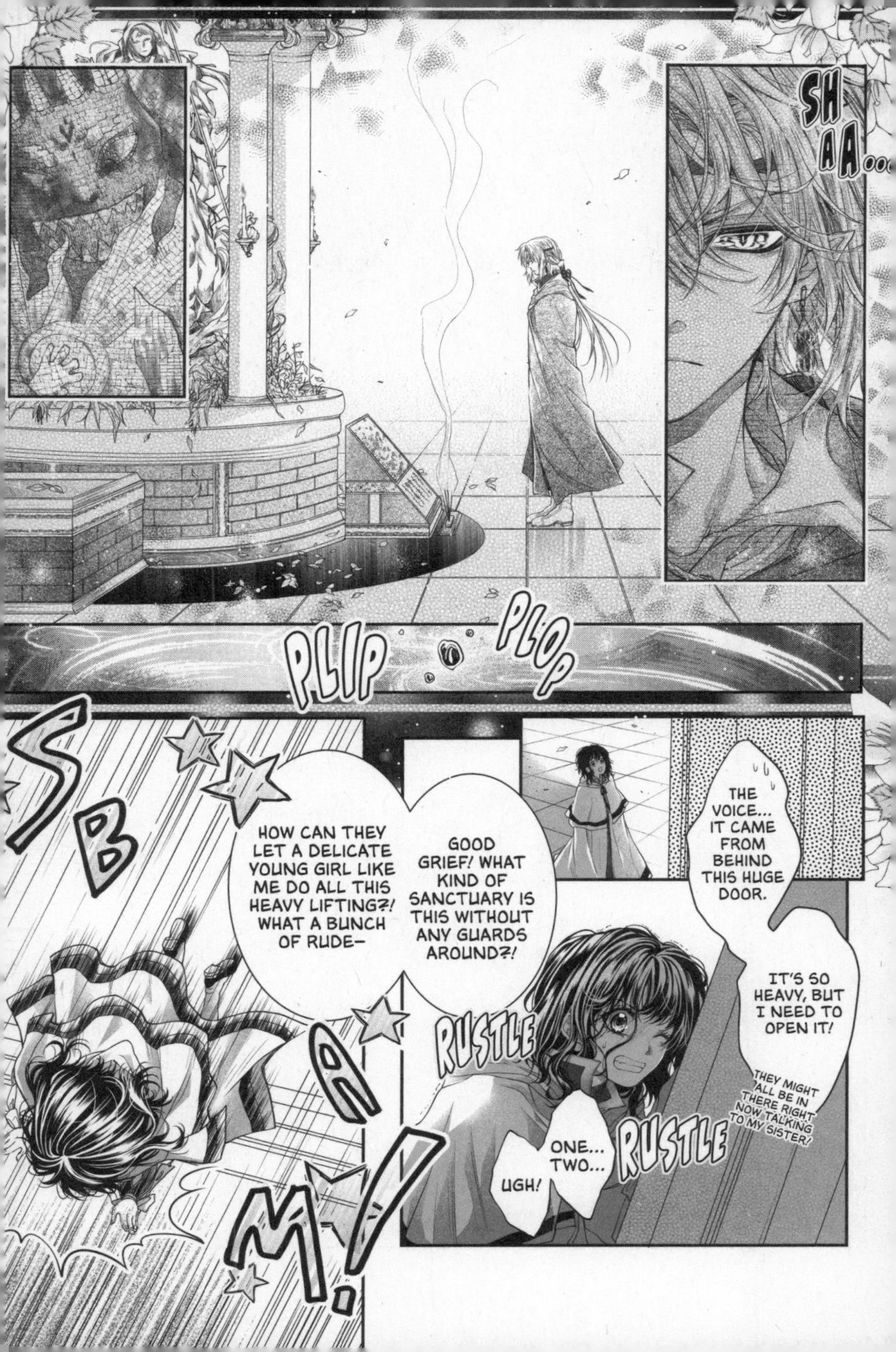
SHAA...
PLIP
PLOP
THE VOICE... IT CAME FROM BEHIND THIS HUGE DOOR.
IT'S SO HEAVY, BUT I NEED TO OPEN IT!
THEY MIGHT ALL BE IN THERE RIGHT NOW TALKING TO MY SISTER!
RUSTLE
RUSTLE
ONE... TWO...
UGH!
GOOD GRIEF! WHAT KIND OF SANCTUARY IS THIS WITHOUT ANY GUARDS AROUND?!
HOW CAN THEY LET A DELICATE YOUNG GIRL LIKE ME DO ALL THIS HEAVY LIFTING?! WHAT A BUNCH OF RUDE–
SBAM!

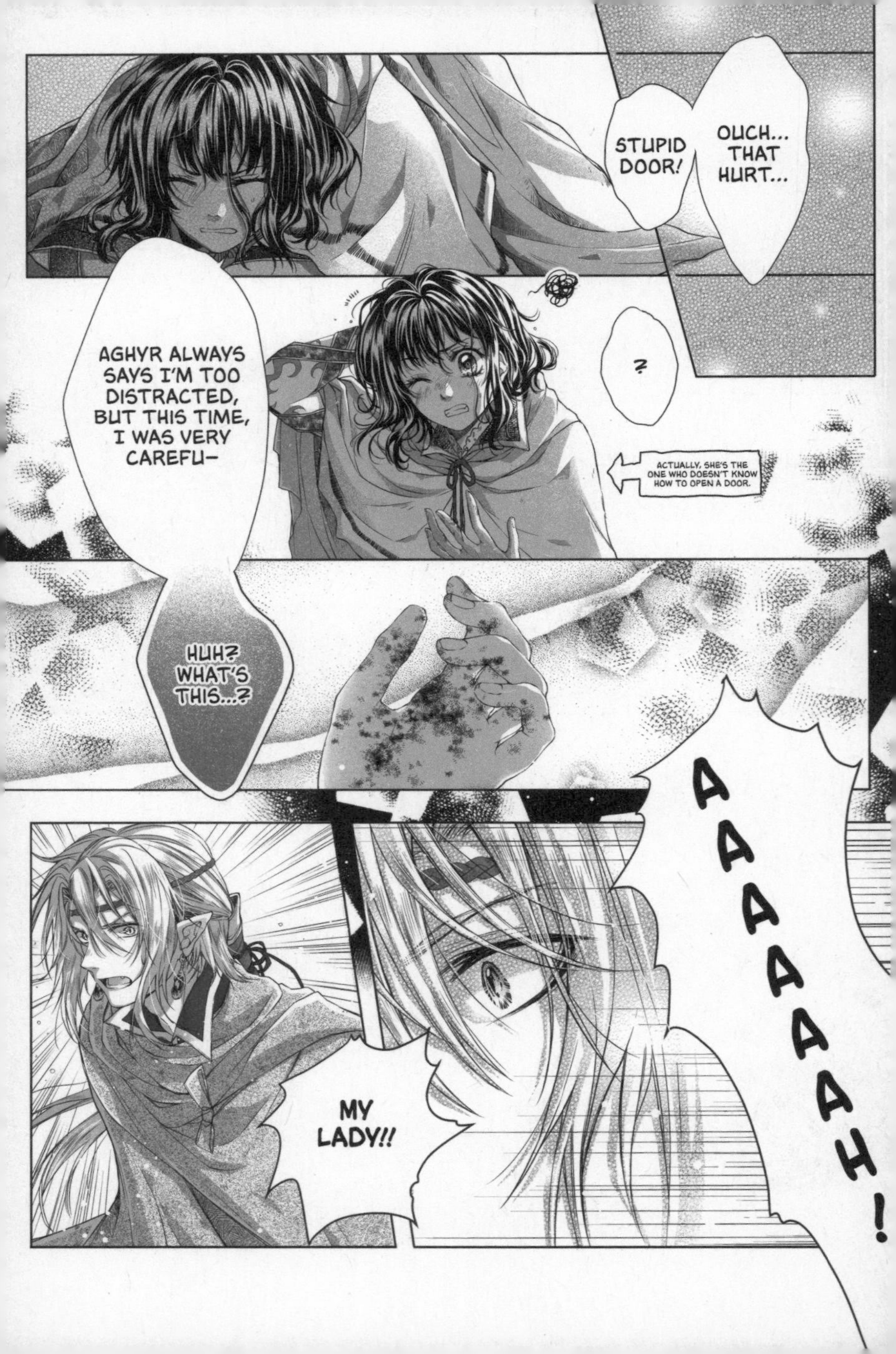
OUCH... THAT HURT...
STUPID DOOR!
?
AGHYR ALWAYS SAYS I'M TOO DISTRACTED, BUT THIS TIME, I WAS VERY CAREFU—
ACTUALLY, SHE'S THE ONE WHO DOESN'T KNOW HOW TO OPEN A DOOR.
HUH? WHAT'S THIS...?
AAAAAAH!
MY LADY!!

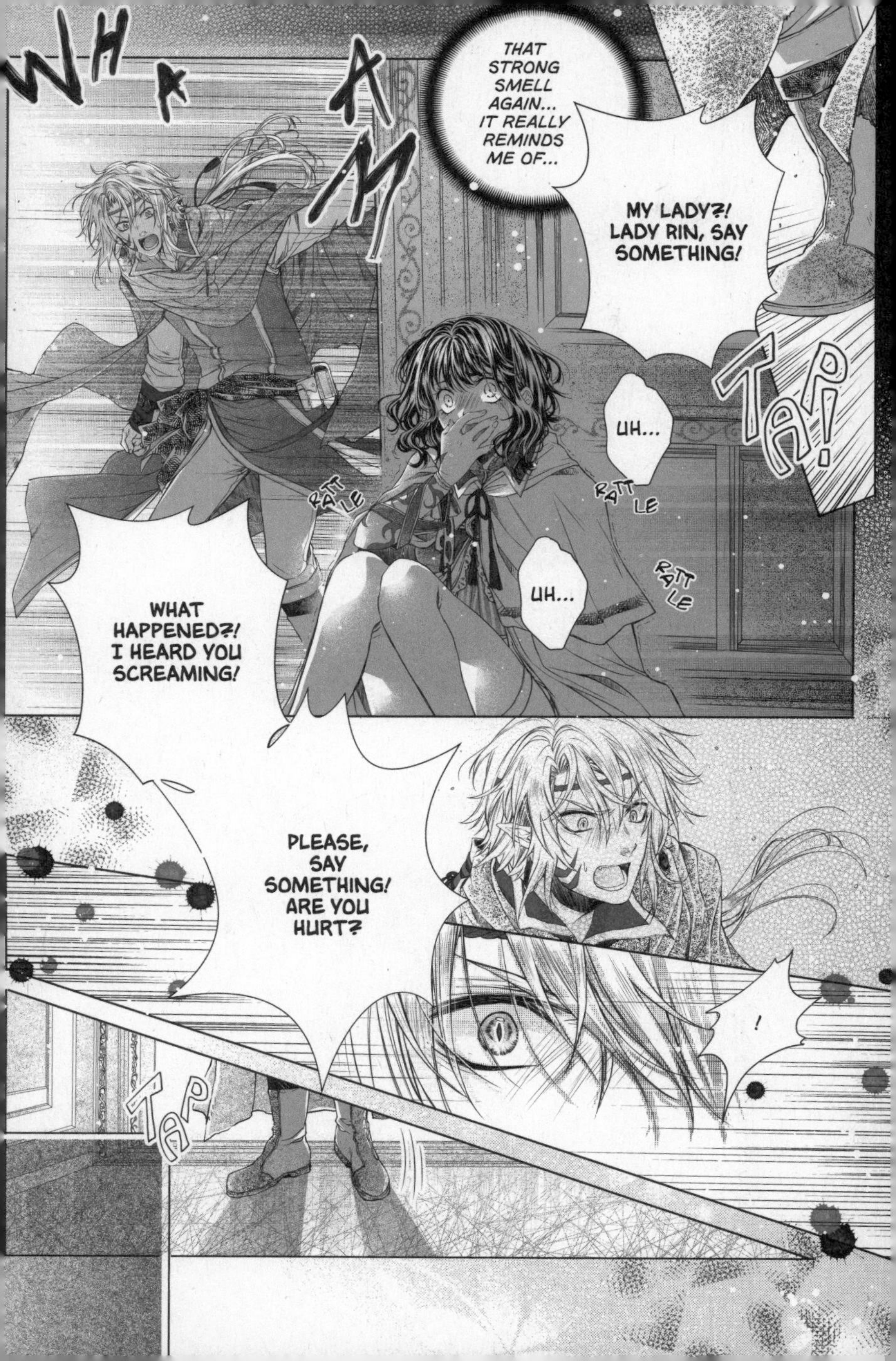
THAT STRONG SMELL AGAIN... IT REALLY REMINDS ME OF...
MY LADY?! LADY RIN, SAY SOMETHING!
TAP!
WHAM
UH...
RATTLE
UH...
RATTLE
RATTLE
WHAT HAPPENED?! I HEARD YOU SCREAMING!
PLEASE, SAY SOMETHING! ARE YOU HURT?
!
TAP TAP

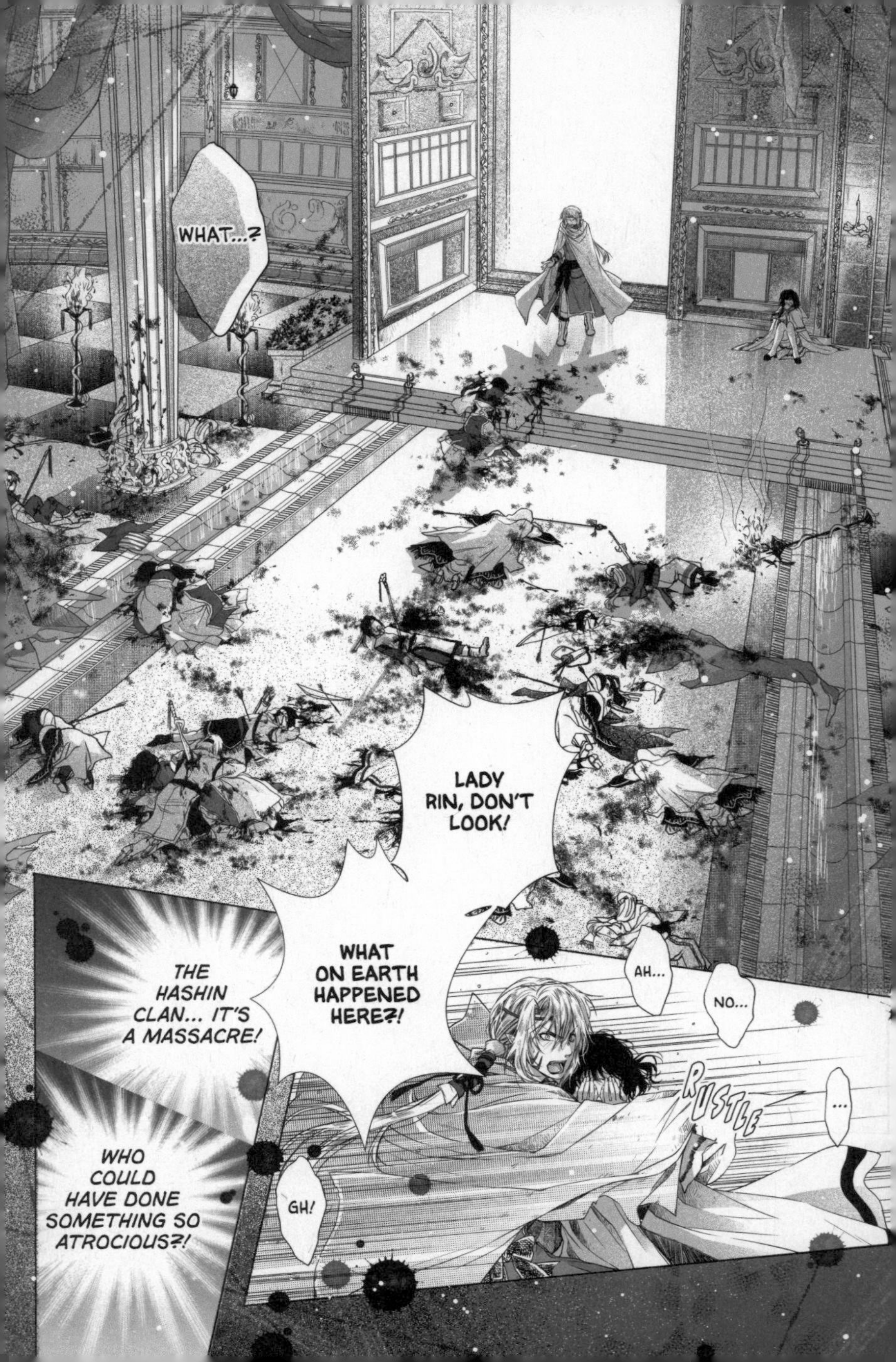
WHAT...?
LADY RIN, DON'T LOOK!
AH...
NO...
...
RUSTLE
GH!
WHAT ON EARTH HAPPENED HERE?!
THE HASHIN CLAN... IT'S A MASSACRE!
WHO COULD HAVE DONE SOMETHING SO ATROCIOUS?!

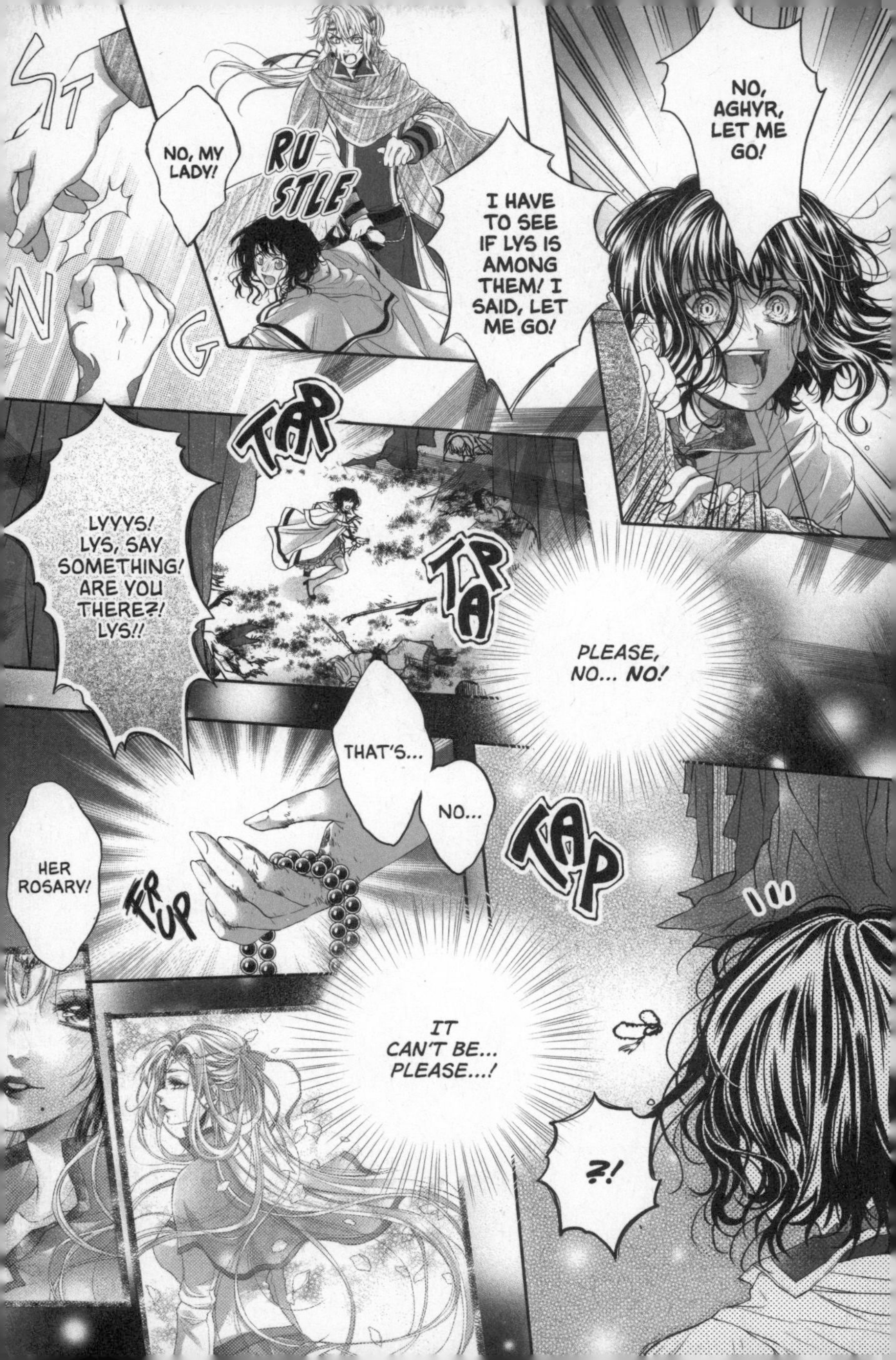
NO, AGHYR, LET ME GO!
RUSTLE
NO, MY LADY!
I HAVE TO SEE IF LYS IS AMONG THEM! I SAID, LET ME GO!
STING
TAR
TRA
LYYYS! LYS, SAY SOMETHING! ARE YOU THERE?! LYS!!
PLEASE, NO... NO!
TAP
?!
THAT'S...
NO...
FRUP
HER ROSARY!
IT CAN'T BE... PLEASE...!

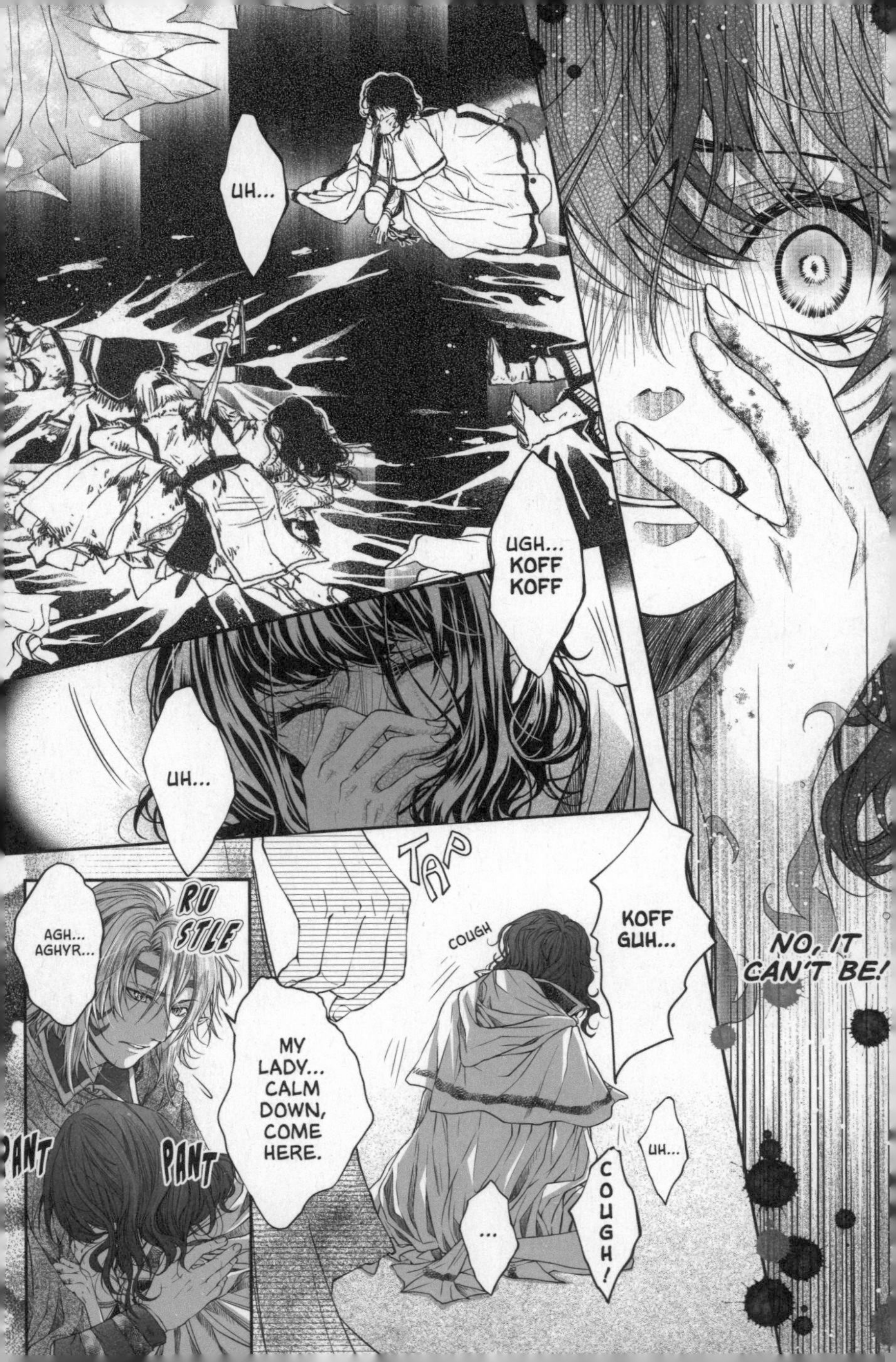
NO, IT CAN'T BE!
UH...
UGH... KOFF KOFF
UH...
KOFF GUH...
UH...
COUGH!
TAP
COUGH
...
MY LADY... CALM DOWN, COME HERE.
RUSTLE
AGH... AGHYR...
PANT
PANT

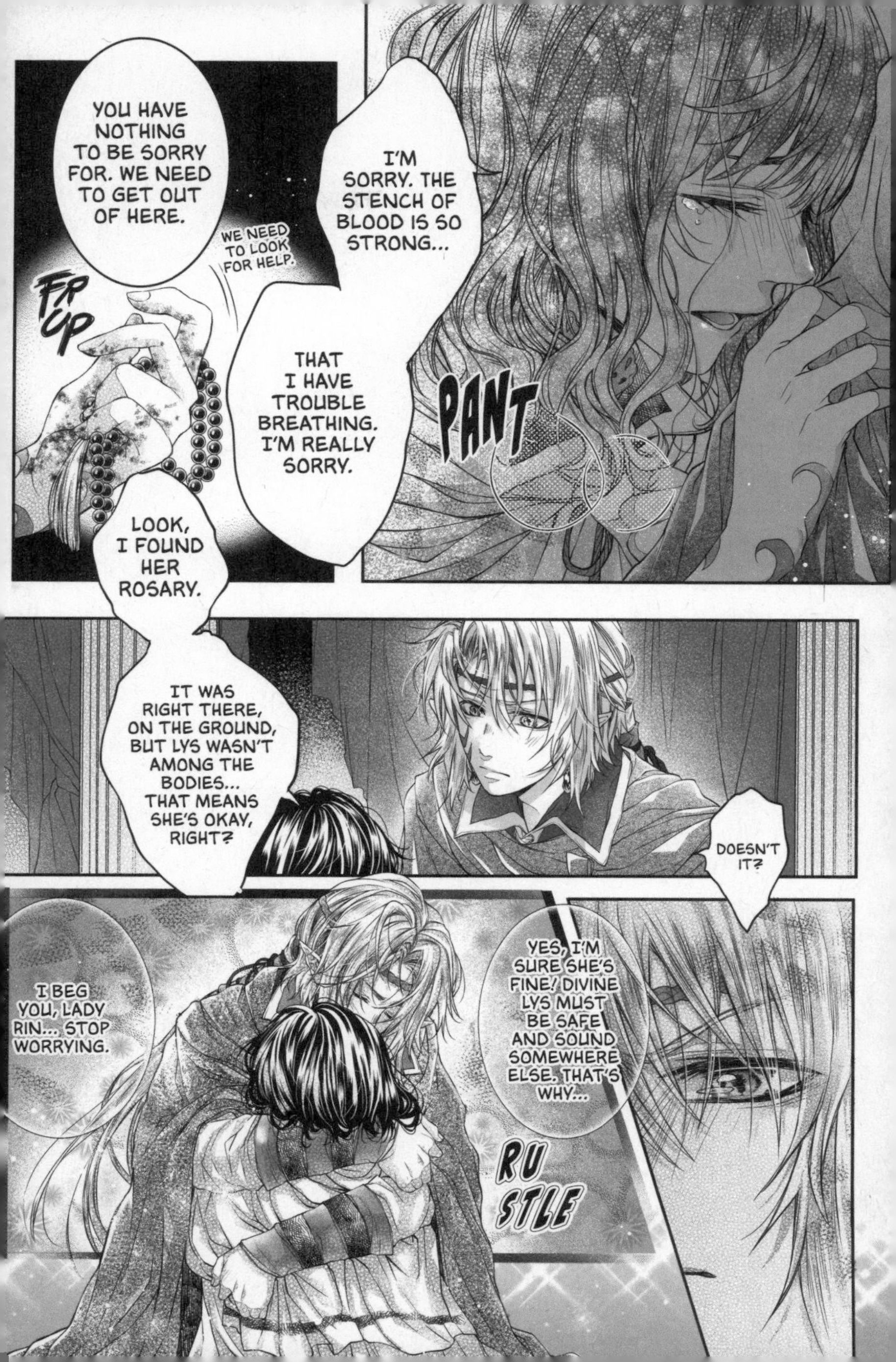
I'M SORRY. THE STENCH OF BLOOD IS SO STRONG...
THAT I HAVE TROUBLE BREATHING. I'M REALLY SORRY.
PANT
YOU HAVE NOTHING TO BE SORRY FOR. WE NEED TO GET OUT OF HERE.
WE NEED TO LOOK FOR HELP.
LOOK, I FOUND HER ROSARY.
IT WAS RIGHT THERE, ON THE GROUND, BUT LYS WASN'T AMONG THE BODIES... THAT MEANS SHE'S OKAY, RIGHT?
DOESN'T IT?
YES, I'M SURE SHE'S FINE! DIVINE LYS MUST BE SAFE AND SOUND SOMEWHERE ELSE. THAT'S WHY...
RU STLE
I BEG YOU, LADY RIN... STOP WORRYING.

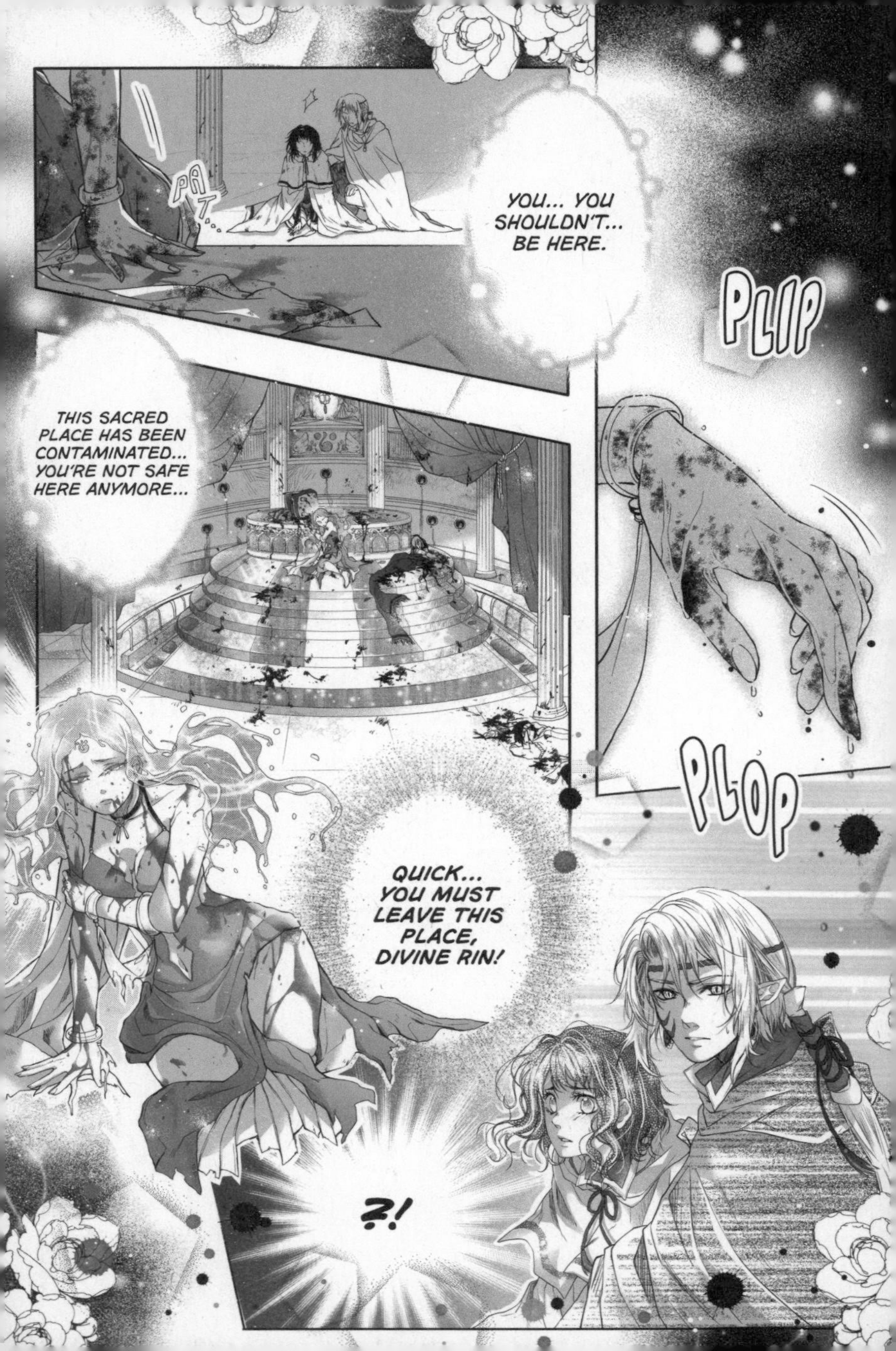
YOU... YOU SHOULDN'T... BE HERE.
PLIP
PLOP
!
PAT...
THIS SACRED PLACE HAS BEEN CONTAMINATED... YOU'RE NOT SAFE HERE ANYMORE...
QUICK... YOU MUST LEAVE THIS PLACE, DIVINE RIN!
?!

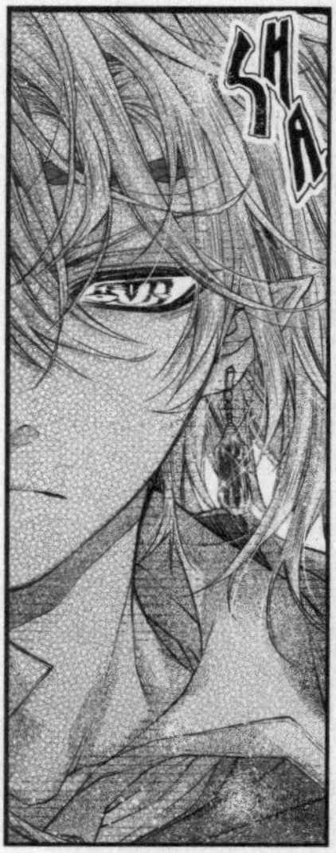
SHA

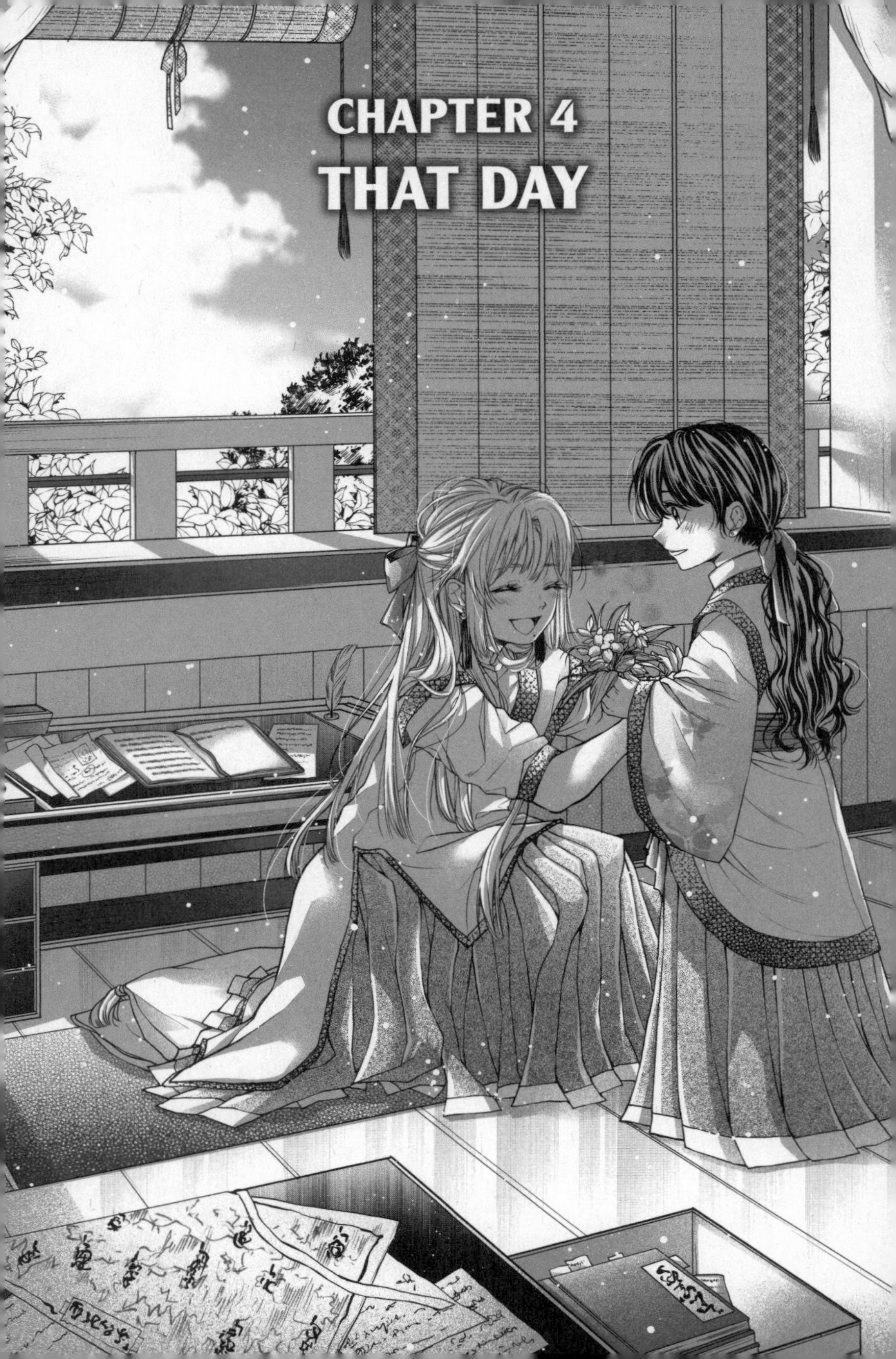
CHAPTER 4
THAT DAY

Scarlet Soul

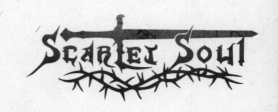

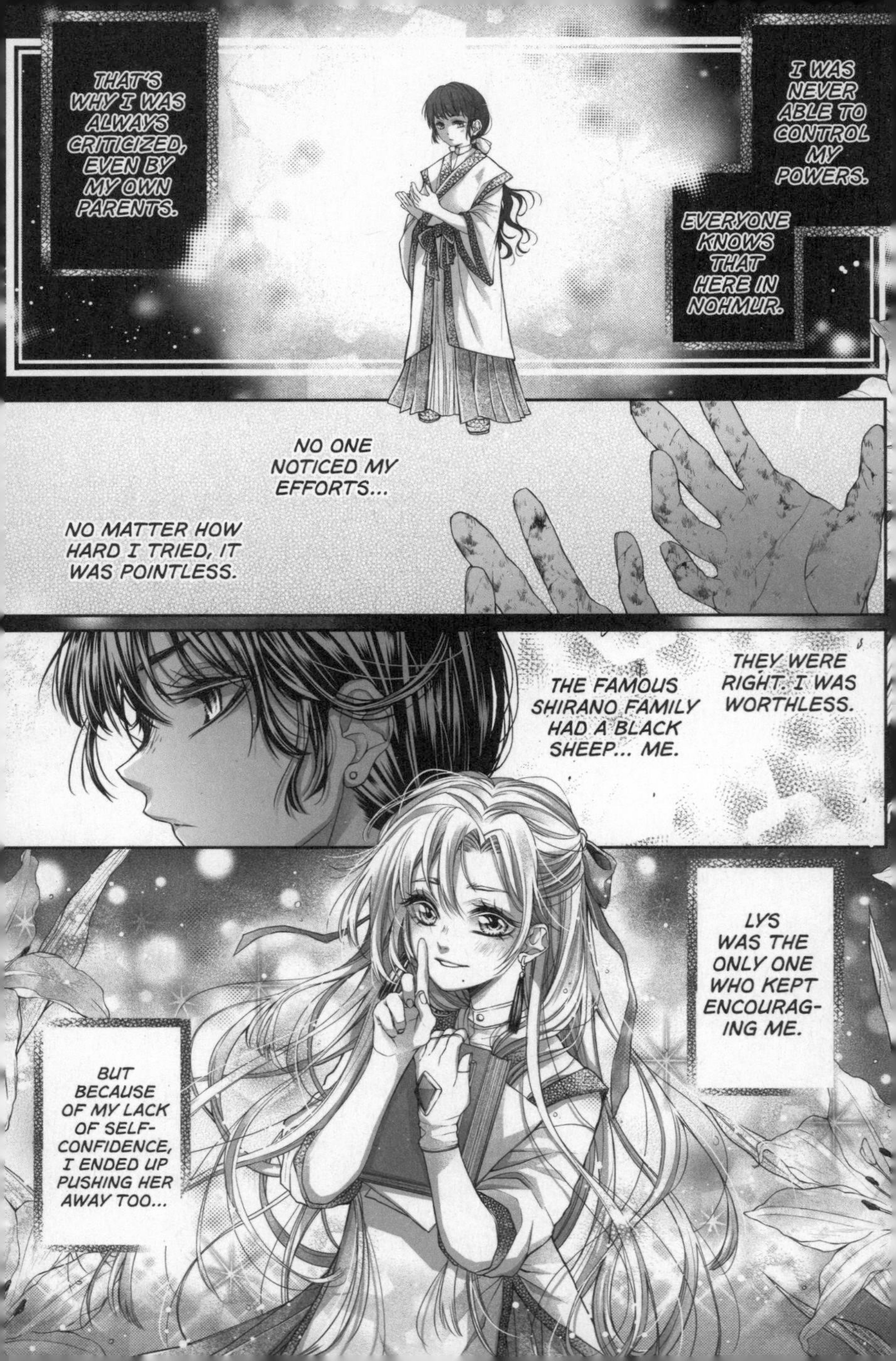
I WAS NEVER ABLE TO CONTROL MY POWERS.
EVERYONE KNOWS THAT HERE IN NOHMUR.
THAT'S WHY I WAS ALWAYS CRITICIZED, EVEN BY MY OWN PARENTS.
NO ONE NOTICED MY EFFORTS...
NO MATTER HOW HARD I TRIED, IT WAS POINTLESS.
THEY WERE RIGHT. I WAS WORTHLESS.
THE FAMOUS SHIRANO FAMILY HAD A BLACK SHEEP... ME.
LYS WAS THE ONLY ONE WHO KEPT ENCOURAG-ING ME.
BUT BECAUSE OF MY LACK OF SELF-CONFIDENCE, I ENDED UP PUSHING HER AWAY TOO...

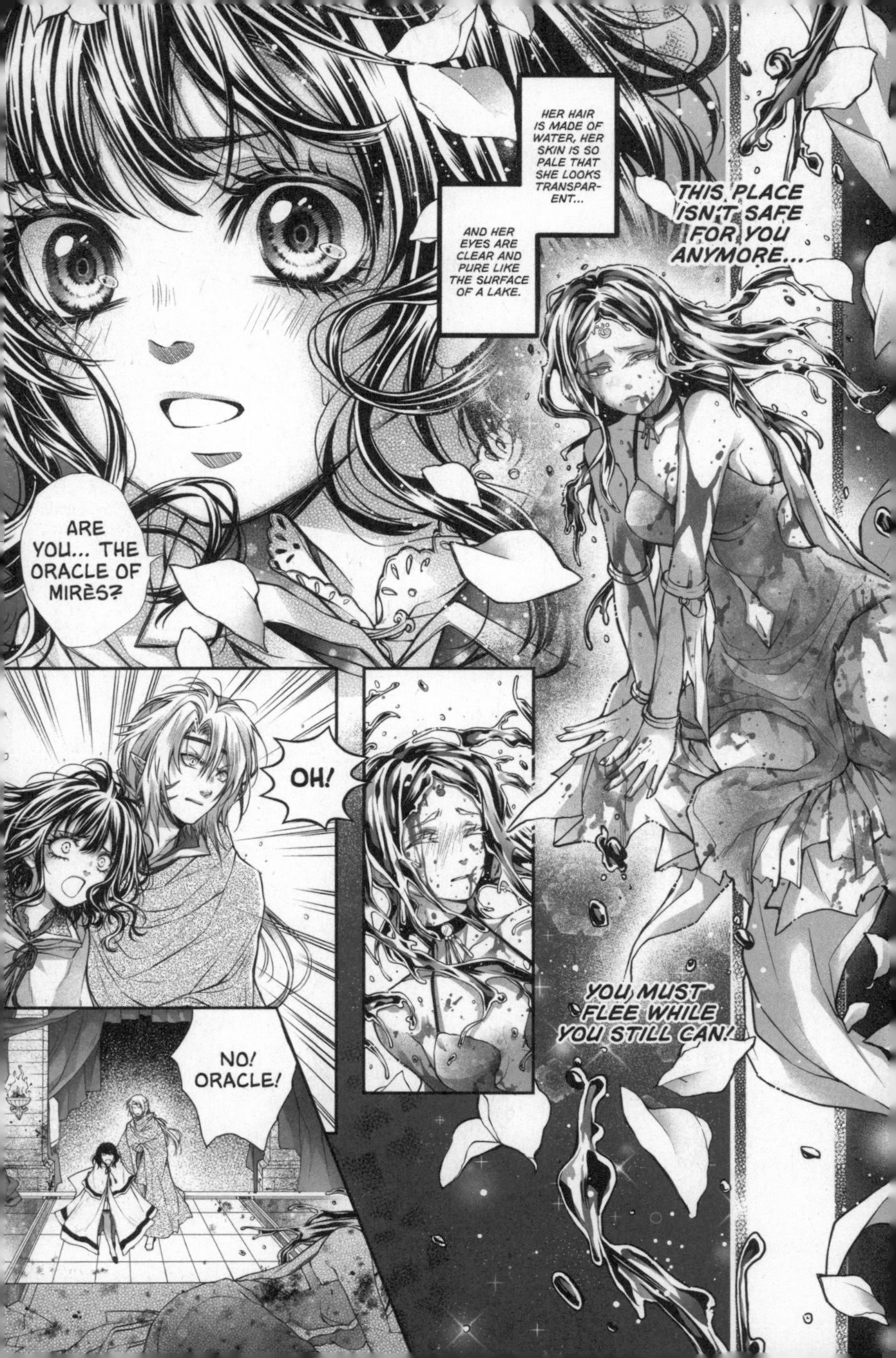
HER HAIR IS MADE OF WATER, HER SKIN IS SO PALE THAT SHE LOOKS TRANSPARENT...
AND HER EYES ARE CLEAR AND PURE LIKE THE SURFACE OF A LAKE.
ARE YOU... THE ORACLE OF MIRÈS?
THIS PLACE ISN'T SAFE FOR YOU ANYMORE...
OH!
YOU MUST FLEE WHILE YOU STILL CAN!
NO! ORACLE!

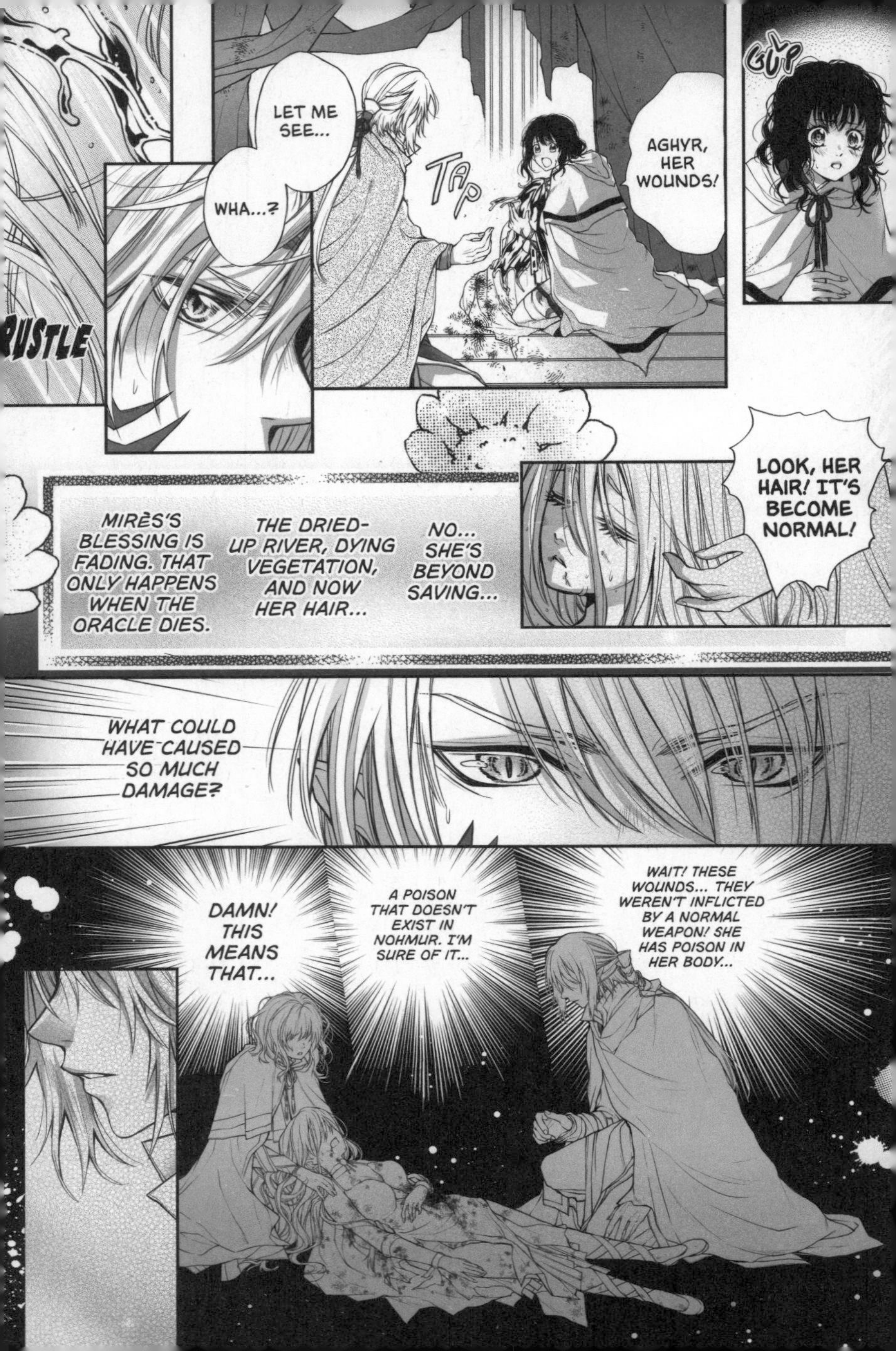
GULP
AGHYR, HER WOUNDS!
TAP
LET ME SEE...
WHA...?
RUSTLE
LOOK, HER HAIR! IT'S BECOME NORMAL!
MIRÈS'S BLESSING IS FADING. THAT ONLY HAPPENS WHEN THE ORACLE DIES.
THE DRIED-UP RIVER, DYING VEGETATION, AND NOW HER HAIR...
NO... SHE'S BEYOND SAVING...
WHAT COULD HAVE CAUSED SO MUCH DAMAGE?
WAIT! THESE WOUNDS... THEY WEREN'T INFLICTED BY A NORMAL WEAPON! SHE HAS POISON IN HER BODY...
A POISON THAT DOESN'T EXIST IN NOHMUR. I'M SURE OF IT...
DAMN! THIS MEANS THAT...

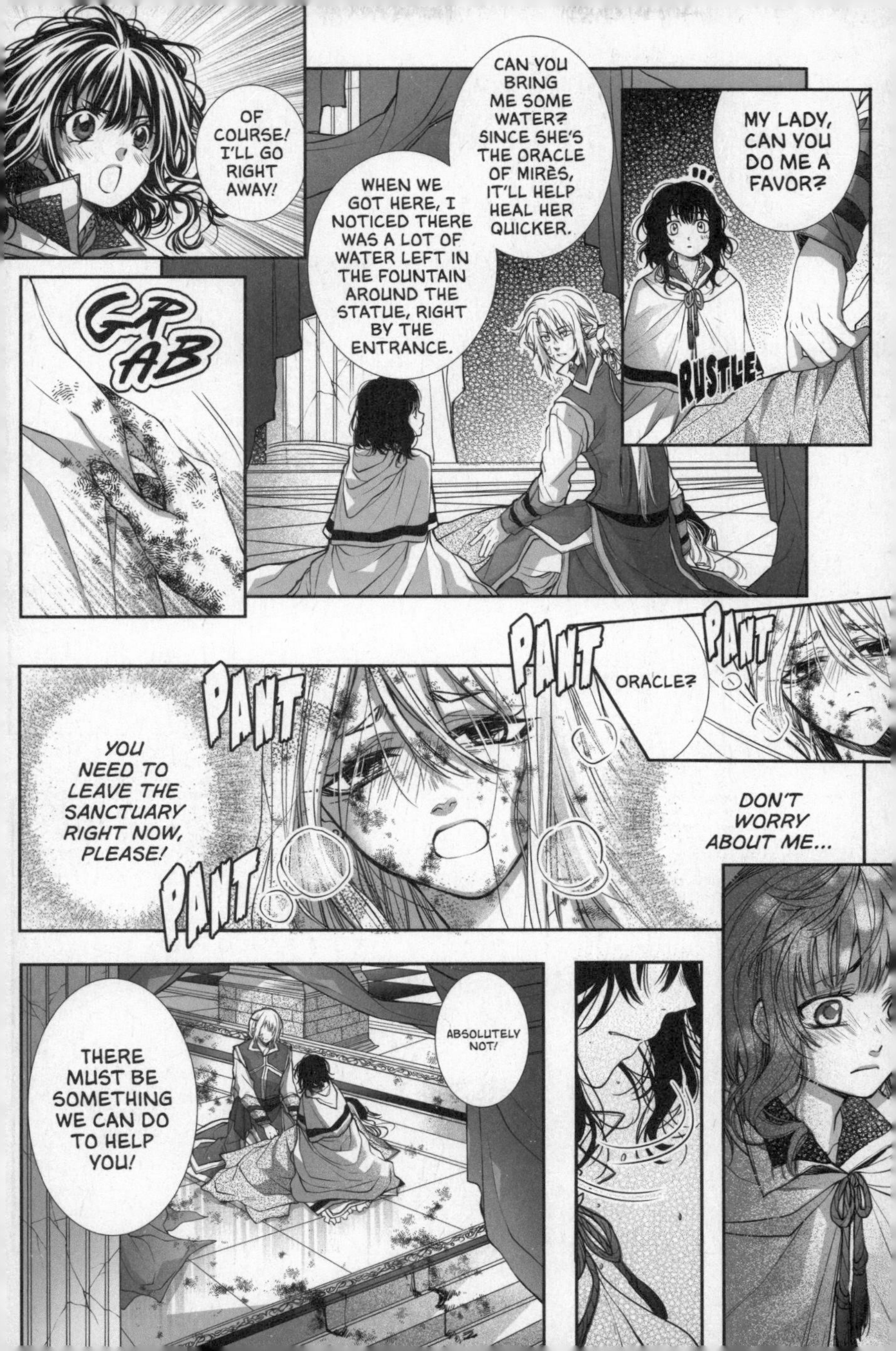
MY LADY, CAN YOU DO ME A FAVOR?
RUSTLE
CAN YOU BRING ME SOME WATER? SINCE SHE'S THE ORACLE OF MIRÈS, IT'LL HELP HEAL HER QUICKER.
WHEN WE GOT HERE, I NOTICED THERE WAS A LOT OF WATER LEFT IN THE FOUNTAIN AROUND THE STATUE, RIGHT BY THE ENTRANCE.
OF COURSE! I'LL GO RIGHT AWAY!
GRAB
PANT
ORACLE?
PANT
PANT
YOU NEED TO LEAVE THE SANCTUARY RIGHT NOW, PLEASE!
PANT
DON'T WORRY ABOUT ME...
ABSOLUTELY NOT!
THERE MUST BE SOMETHING WE CAN DO TO HELP YOU!

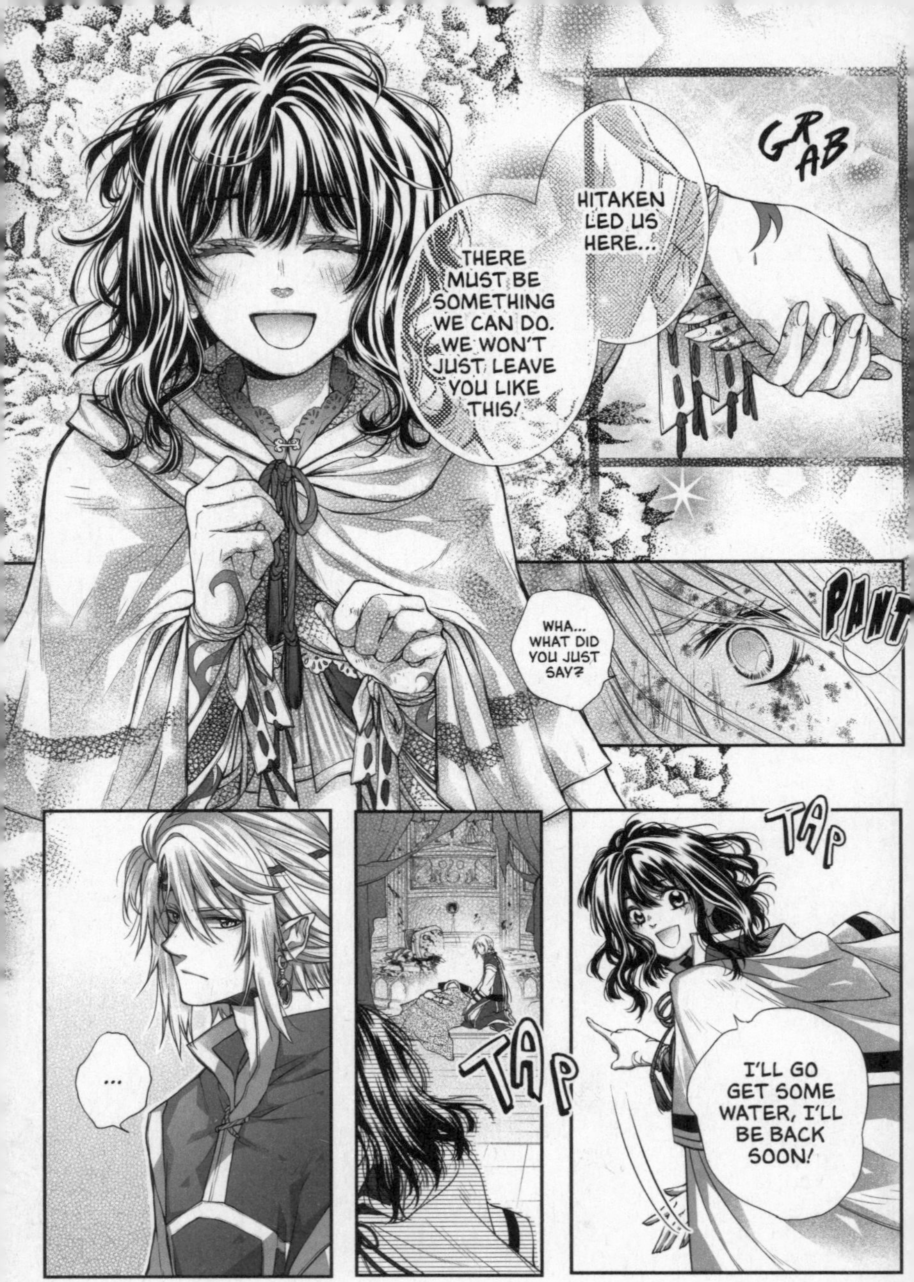
GRAB
HITAKEN LED US HERE...
THERE MUST BE SOMETHING WE CAN DO. WE WON'T JUST LEAVE YOU LIKE THIS!
PANT
WHA... WHAT DID YOU JUST SAY?
TAP
I'LL GO GET SOME WATER, I'LL BE BACK SOON!
TAP
...

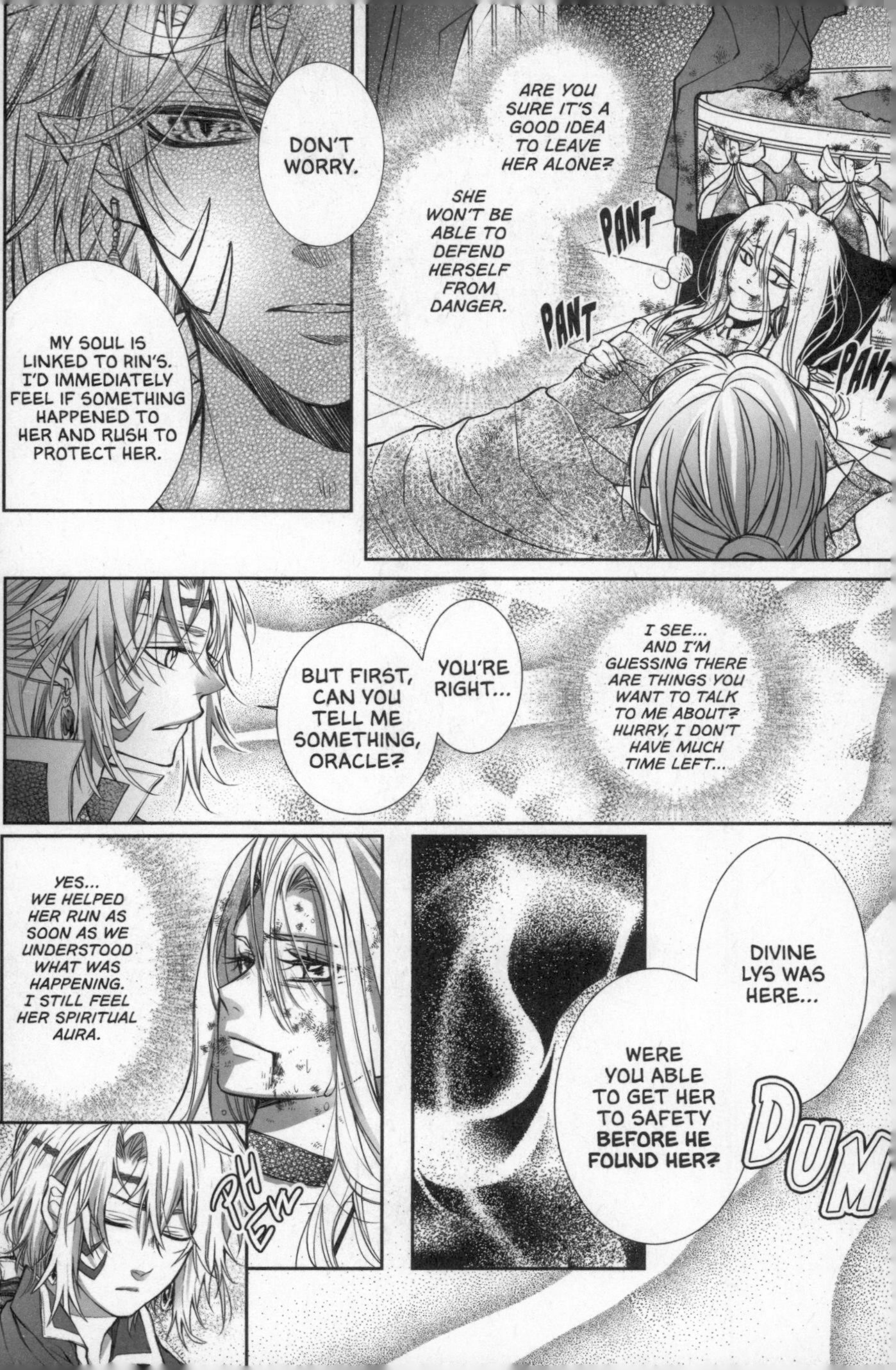
ARE YOU SURE IT'S A GOOD IDEA TO LEAVE HER ALONE?
SHE WON'T BE ABLE TO DEFEND HERSELF FROM DANGER.
PANT
PANT
PANT
DON'T WORRY.
MY SOUL IS LINKED TO RIN'S. I'D IMMEDIATELY FEEL IF SOMETHING HAPPENED TO HER AND RUSH TO PROTECT HER.
I SEE... AND I'M GUESSING THERE ARE THINGS YOU WANT TO TALK TO ME ABOUT? HURRY, I DON'T HAVE MUCH TIME LEFT...
YOU'RE RIGHT...
BUT FIRST, CAN YOU TELL ME SOMETHING, ORACLE?
DIVINE LYS WAS HERE...
WERE YOU ABLE TO GET HER TO SAFETY BEFORE HE FOUND HER?
DUM
YES... WE HELPED HER RUN AS SOON AS WE UNDERSTOOD WHAT WAS HAPPENING. I STILL FEEL HER SPIRITUAL AURA.
PHEW

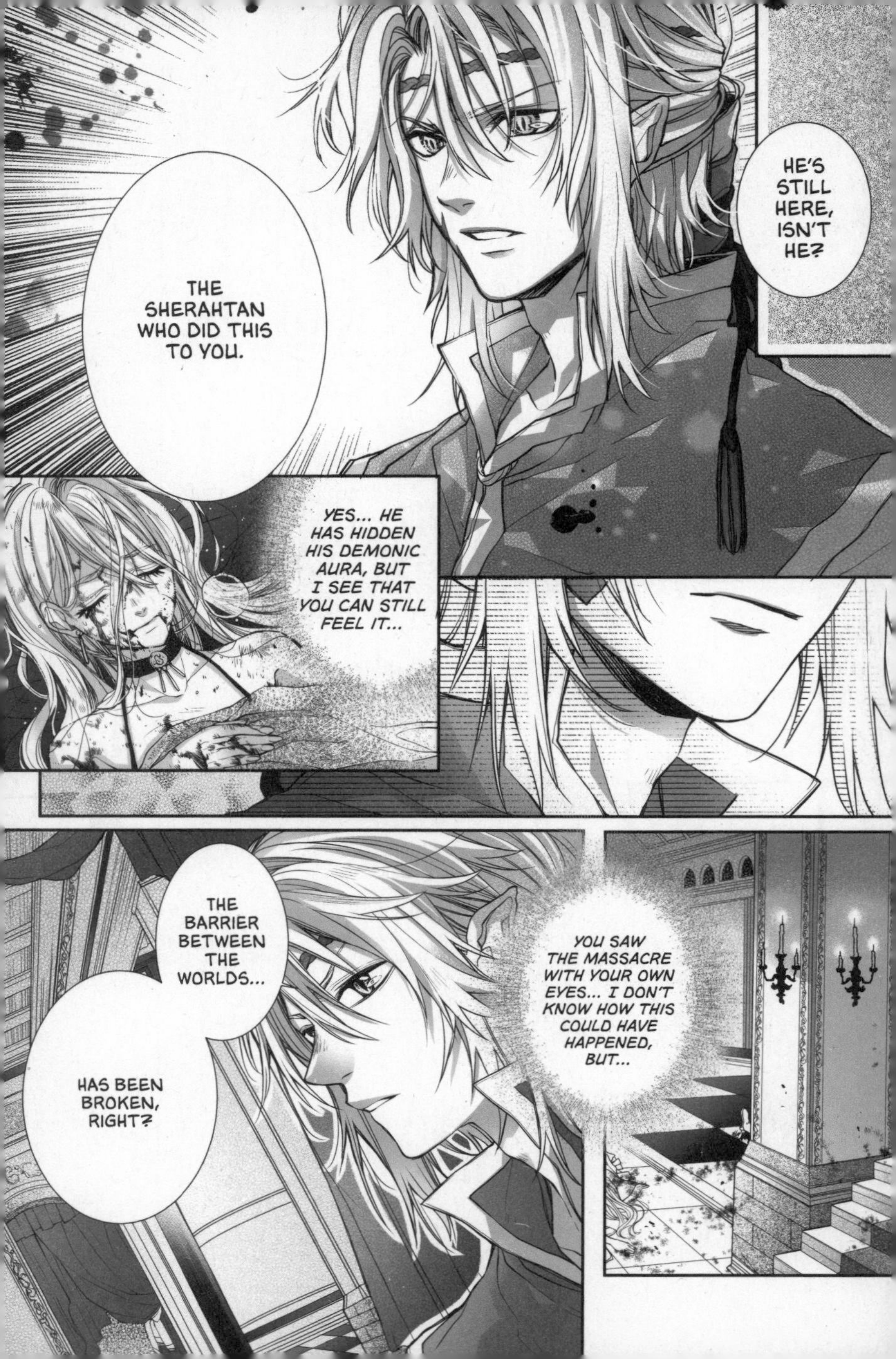
HE'S STILL HERE, ISN'T HE?
THE SHERAHTAN WHO DID THIS TO YOU.
YES... HE HAS HIDDEN HIS DEMONIC AURA, BUT I SEE THAT YOU CAN STILL FEEL IT...
YOU SAW THE MASSACRE WITH YOUR OWN EYES... I DON'T KNOW HOW THIS COULD HAVE HAPPENED, BUT...
THE BARRIER BETWEEN THE WORLDS...
HAS BEEN BROKEN, RIGHT?

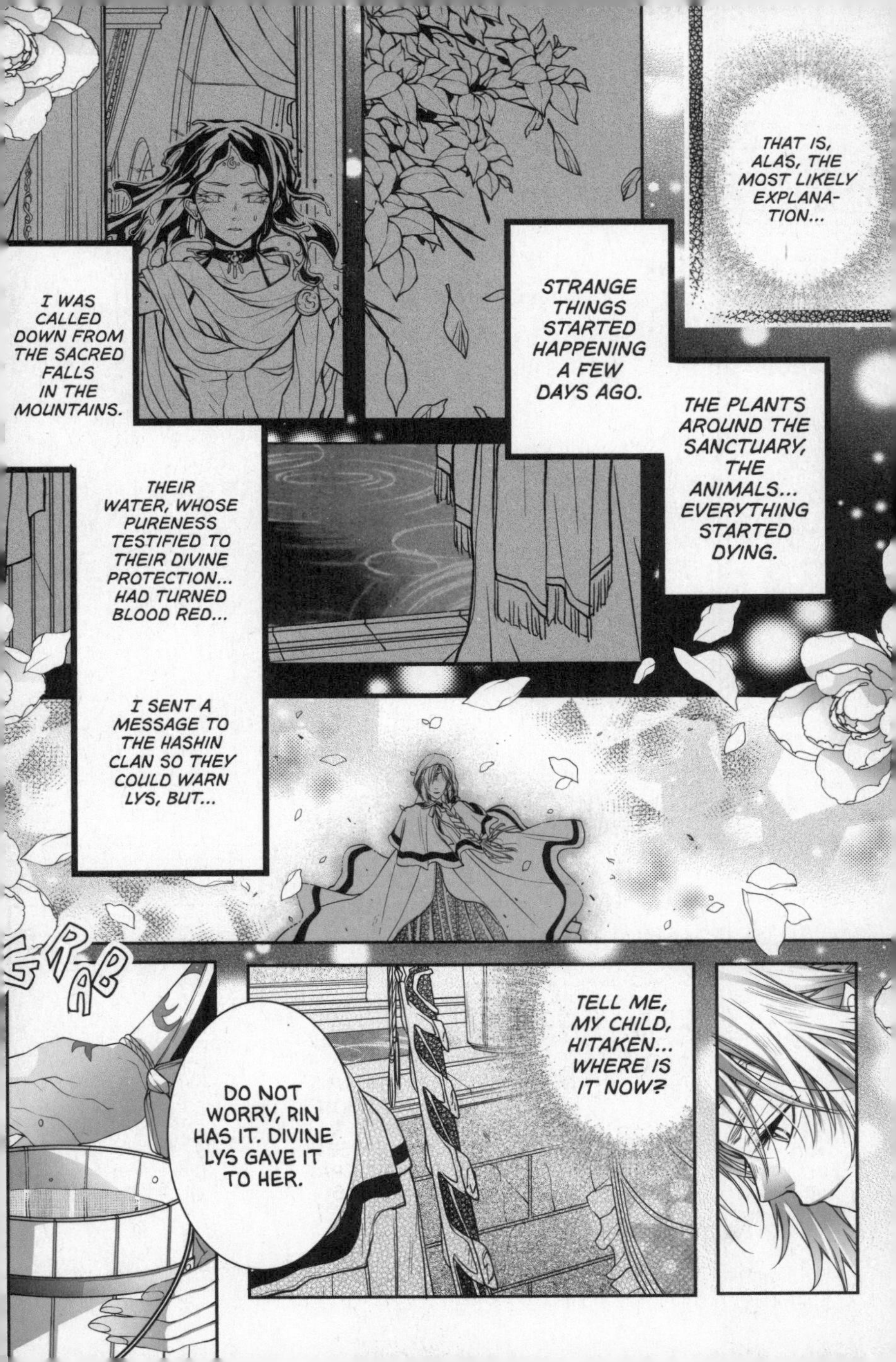
THAT IS, ALAS, THE MOST LIKELY EXPLANATION...
STRANGE THINGS STARTED HAPPENING A FEW DAYS AGO.
I WAS CALLED DOWN FROM THE SACRED FALLS IN THE MOUNTAINS.
THE PLANTS AROUND THE SANCTUARY, THE ANIMALS... EVERYTHING STARTED DYING.
THEIR WATER, WHOSE PURENESS TESTIFIED TO THEIR DIVINE PROTECTION... HAD TURNED BLOOD RED...
I SENT A MESSAGE TO THE HASHIN CLAN SO THEY COULD WARN LYS, BUT...
TELL ME, MY CHILD, HITAKEN... WHERE IS IT NOW?
DO NOT WORRY, RIN HAS IT. DIVINE LYS GAVE IT TO HER.
GRAB

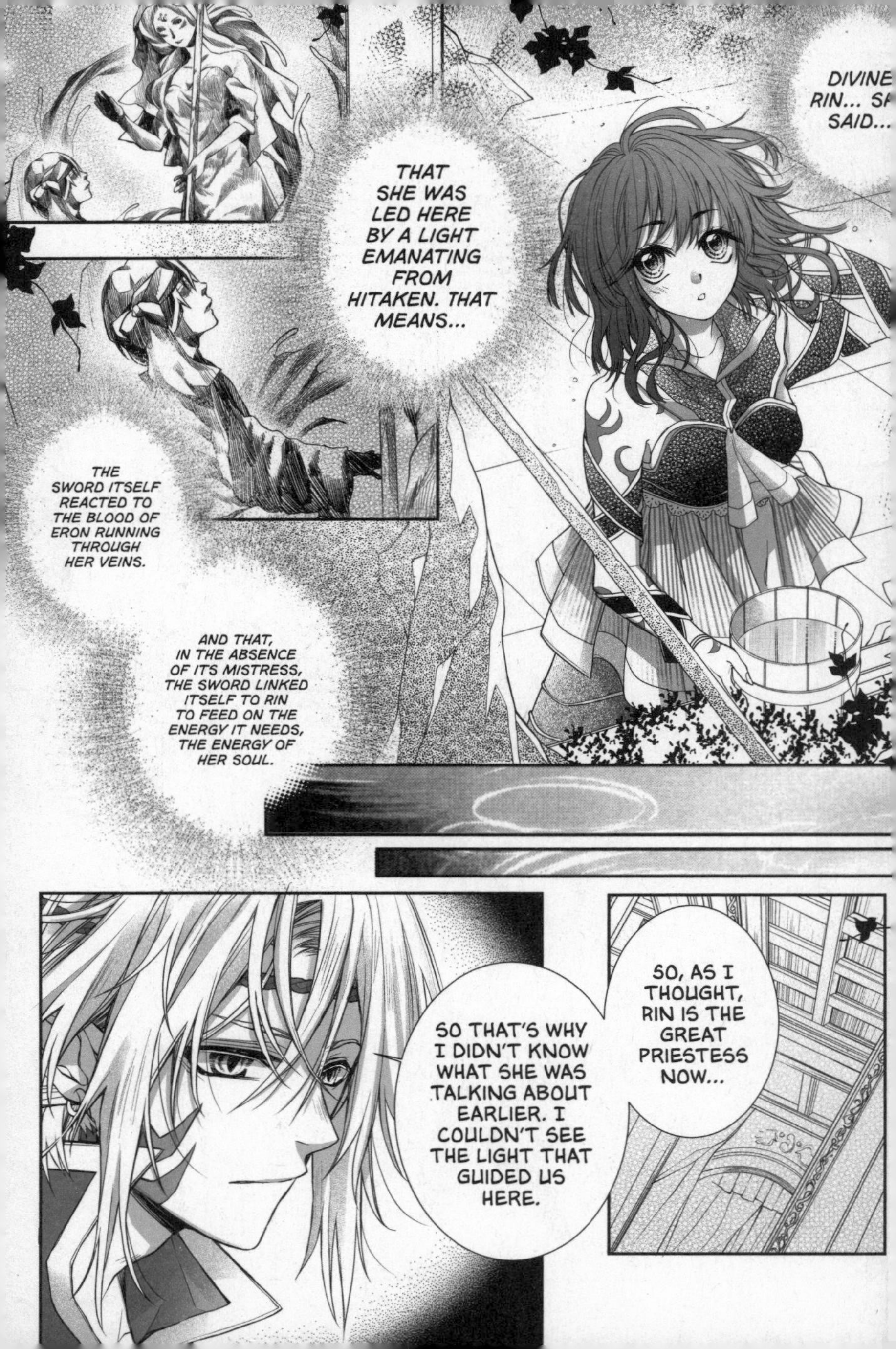
DIVINE RIN... S SAID...
THAT SHE WAS LED HERE BY A LIGHT EMANATING FROM HITAKEN. THAT MEANS...
THE SWORD ITSELF REACTED TO THE BLOOD OF ERON RUNNING THROUGH HER VEINS.
AND THAT, IN THE ABSENCE OF ITS MISTRESS, THE SWORD LINKED ITSELF TO RIN TO FEED ON THE ENERGY IT NEEDS, THE ENERGY OF HER SOUL.
SO, AS I THOUGHT, RIN IS THE GREAT PRIESTESS NOW...
SO THAT'S WHY I DIDN'T KNOW WHAT SHE WAS TALKING ABOUT EARLIER. I COULDN'T SEE THE LIGHT THAT GUIDED US HERE.

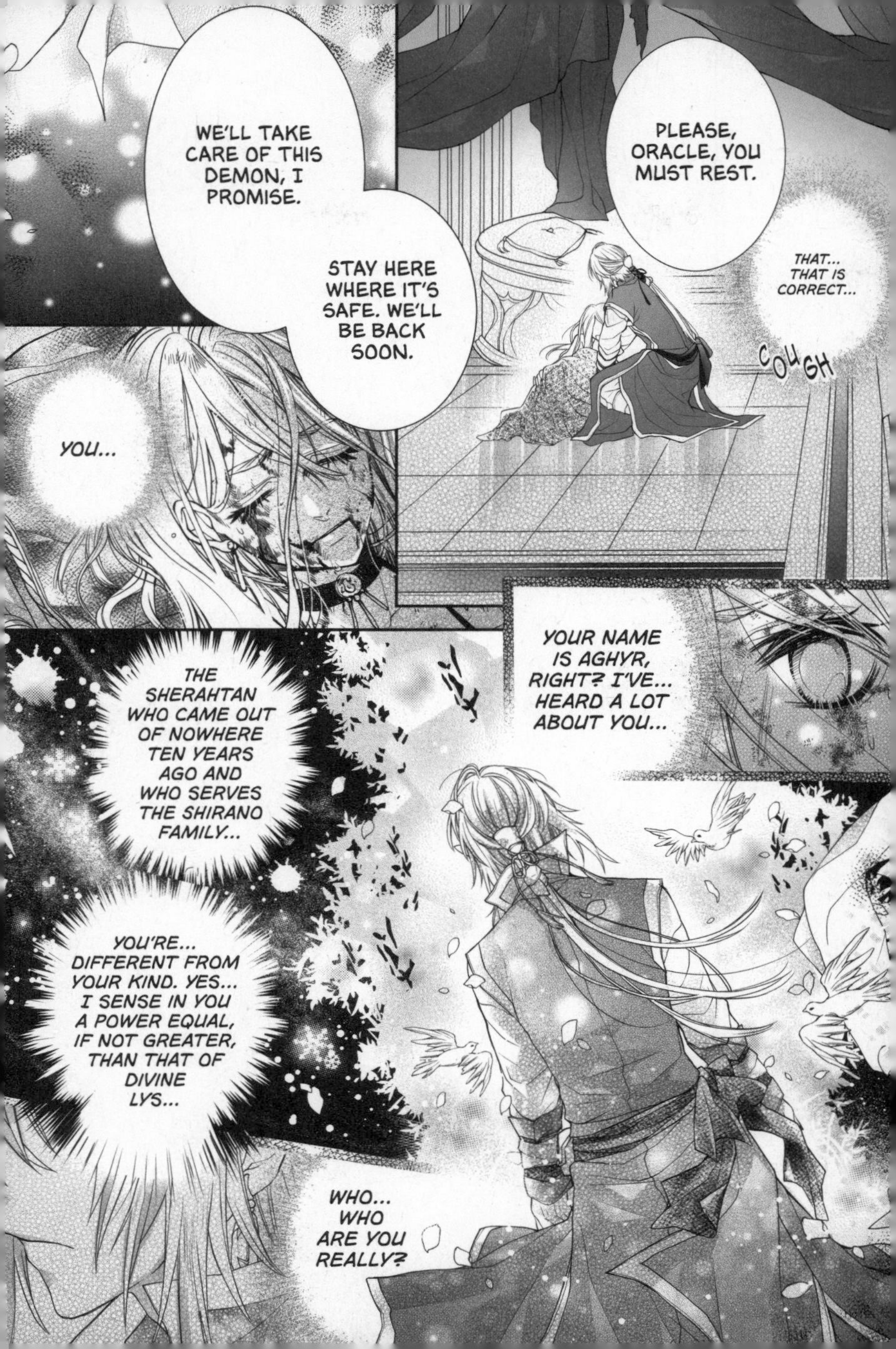
PLEASE, ORACLE, YOU MUST REST.
THAT... THAT IS CORRECT...
COUGH
WE'LL TAKE CARE OF THIS DEMON, I PROMISE.
STAY HERE WHERE IT'S SAFE. WE'LL BE BACK SOON.
YOU...
YOUR NAME IS AGHYR, RIGHT? I'VE... HEARD A LOT ABOUT YOU...
THE SHERAHTAN WHO CAME OUT OF NOWHERE TEN YEARS AGO AND WHO SERVES THE SHIRANO FAMILY...
YOU'RE... DIFFERENT FROM YOUR KIND. YES... I SENSE IN YOU A POWER EQUAL, IF NOT GREATER, THAN THAT OF DIVINE LYS...
WHO... WHO ARE YOU REALLY?

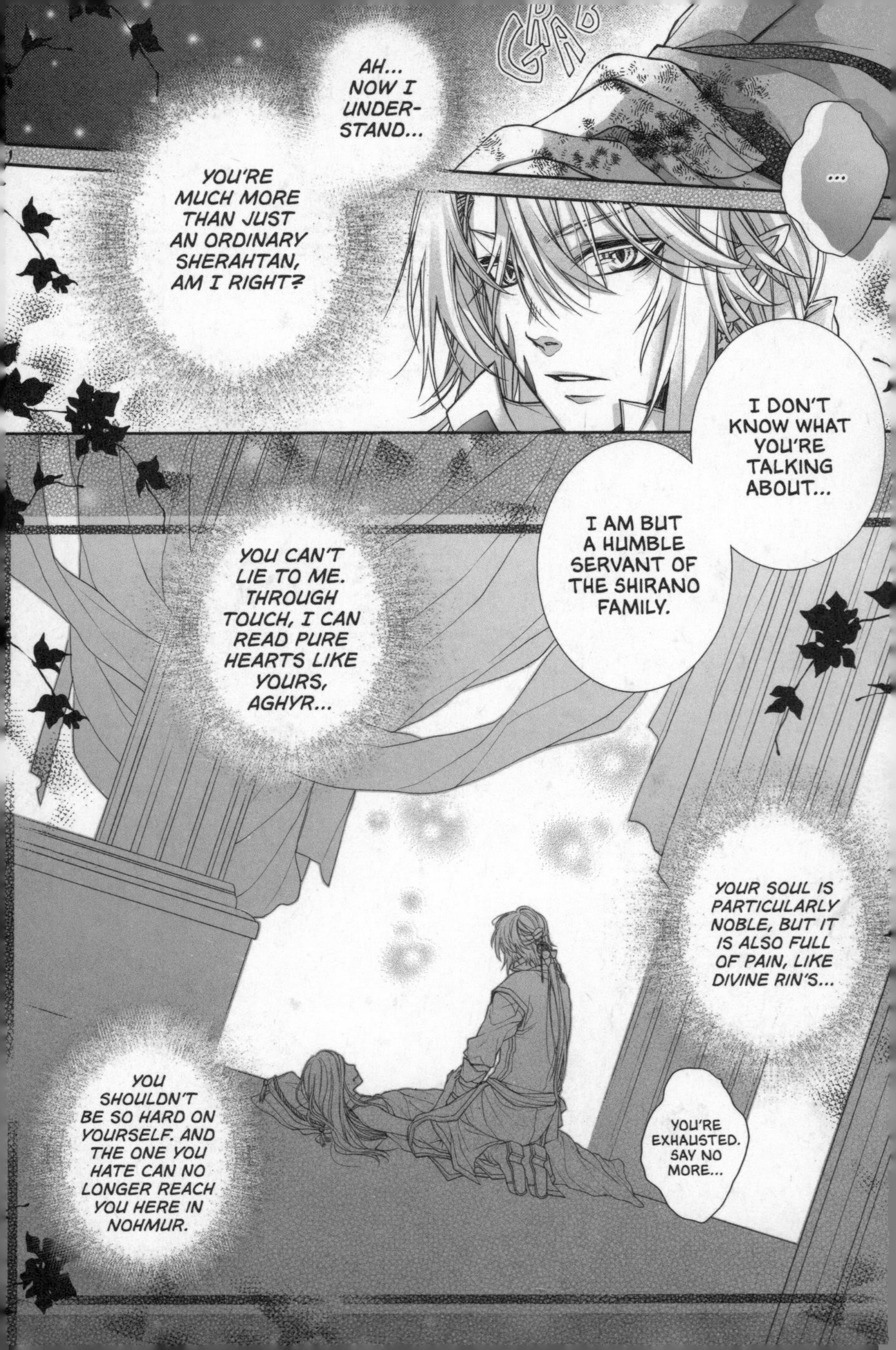
GRAB
...
AH... NOW I UNDER-STAND...
YOU'RE MUCH MORE THAN JUST AN ORDINARY SHERAHTAN, AM I RIGHT?
I DON'T KNOW WHAT YOU'RE TALKING ABOUT...
I AM BUT A HUMBLE SERVANT OF THE SHIRANO FAMILY.
YOU CAN'T LIE TO ME. THROUGH TOUCH, I CAN READ PURE HEARTS LIKE YOURS, AGHYR...
YOUR SOUL IS PARTICULARLY NOBLE, BUT IT IS ALSO FULL OF PAIN, LIKE DIVINE RIN'S...
YOU'RE EXHAUSTED. SAY NO MORE...
YOU SHOULDN'T BE SO HARD ON YOURSELF. AND THE ONE YOU HATE CAN NO LONGER REACH YOU HERE IN NOHMUR.

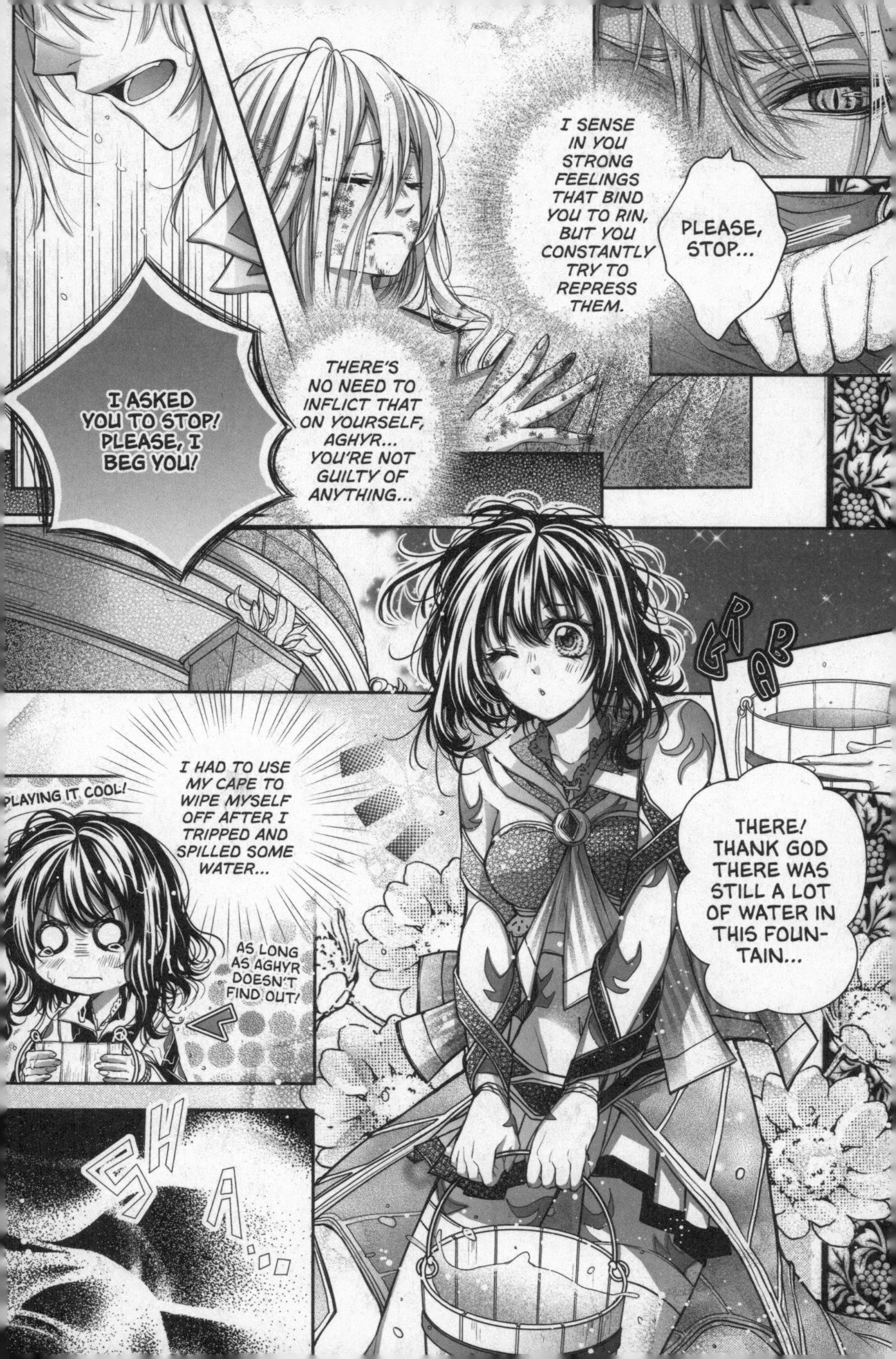
I SENSE IN YOU STRONG FEELINGS THAT BIND YOU TO RIN, BUT YOU CONSTANTLY TRY TO REPRESS THEM.
PLEASE, STOP...
THERE'S NO NEED TO INFLICT THAT ON YOURSELF, AGHYR... YOU'RE NOT GUILTY OF ANYTHING...
I ASKED YOU TO STOP! PLEASE, I BEG YOU!
GRAB
THERE! THANK GOD THERE WAS STILL A LOT OF WATER IN THIS FOUN-TAIN...
I HAD TO USE MY CAPE TO WIPE MYSELF OFF AFTER I TRIPPED AND SPILLED SOME WATER...
PLAYING IT COOL!
AS LONG AS AGHYR DOESN'T FIND OUT!
SHA...

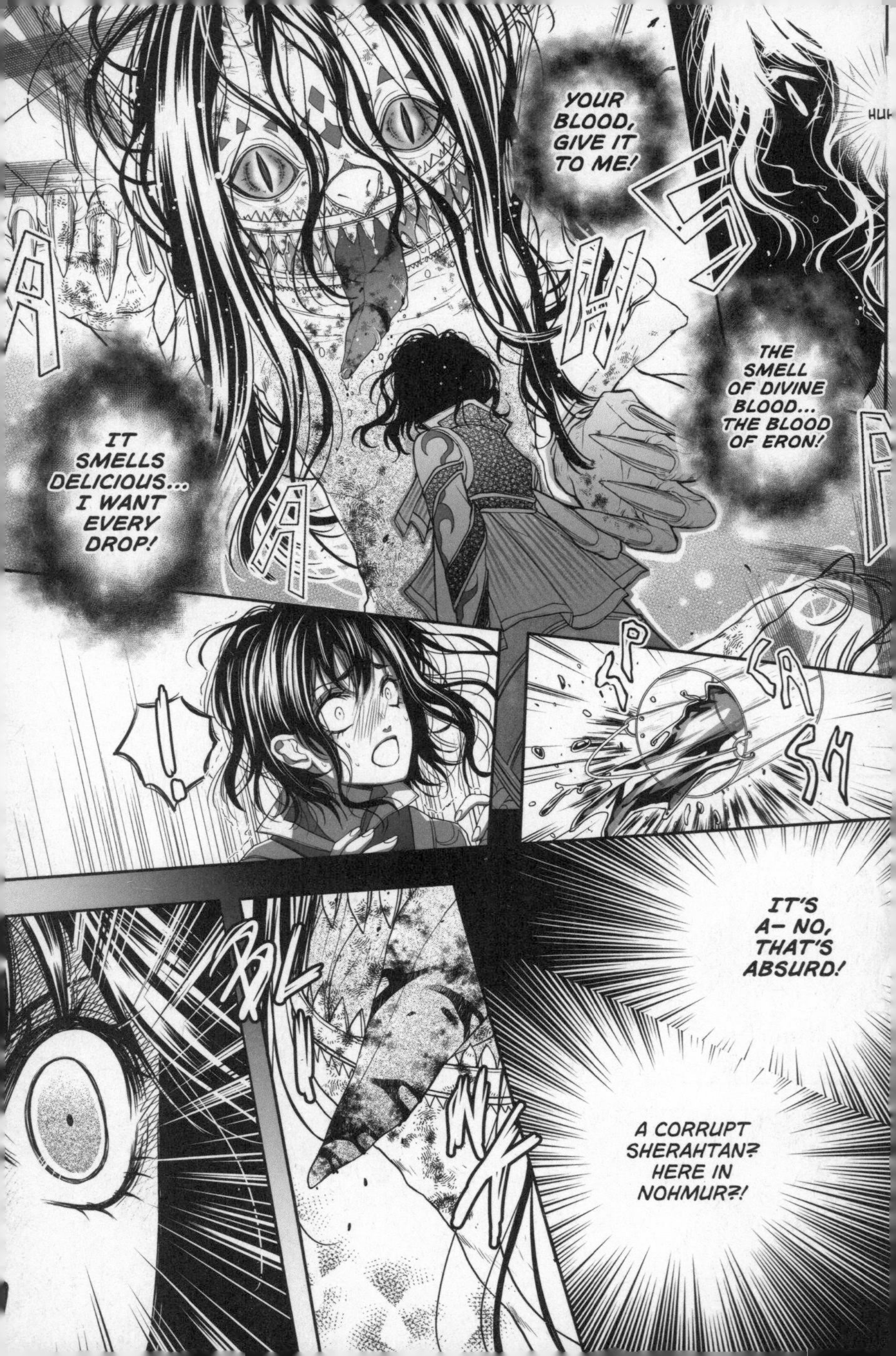
YOUR BLOOD, GIVE IT TO ME!
THE SMELL OF DIVINE BLOOD... THE BLOOD OF ERON!
IT SMELLS DELICIOUS... I WANT EVERY DROP!
SPLASH
!
IT'S A— NO, THAT'S ABSURD!
A CORRUPT SHERAHTAN? HERE IN NOHMUR?!

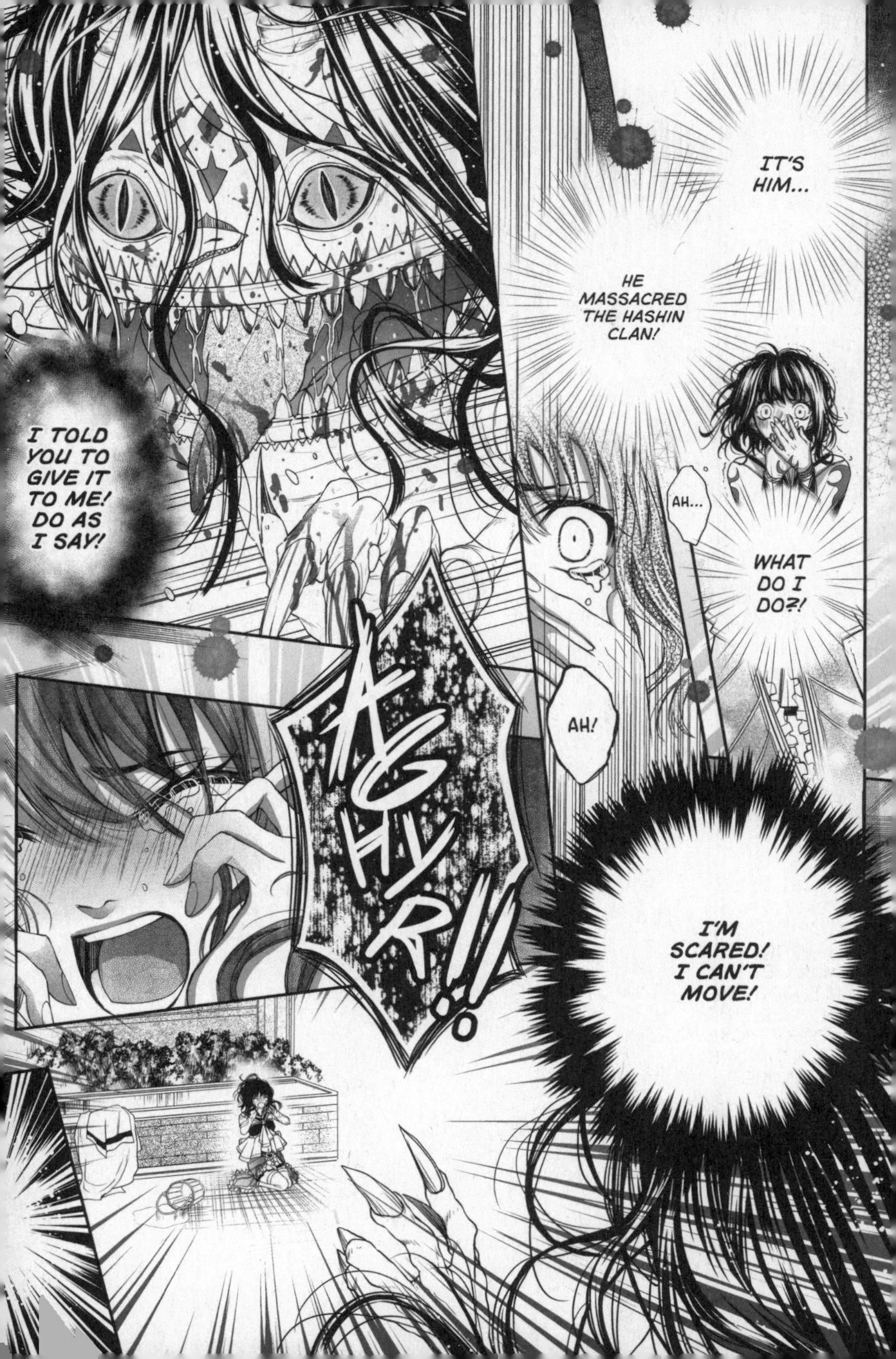
IT'S HIM...
HE MASSACRED THE HASHIN CLAN!
AH...
WHAT DO I DO?!
AH!
I'M SCARED! I CAN'T MOVE!
I TOLD YOU TO GIVE IT TO ME! DO AS I SAY!
AGHYR!!

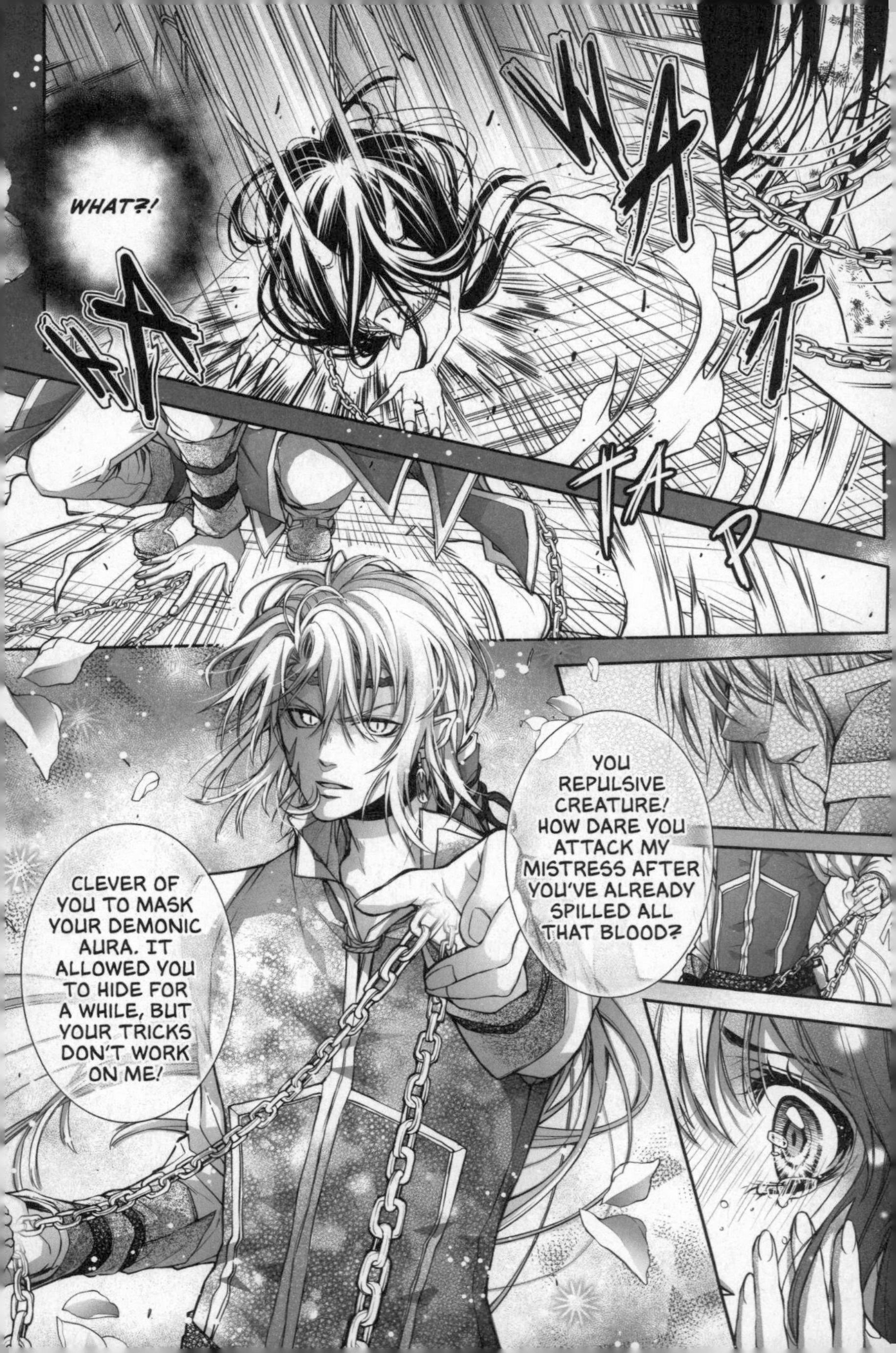
WAAA
WHAT?!
HA
TAP
YOU REPULSIVE CREATURE! HOW DARE YOU ATTACK MY MISTRESS AFTER YOU'VE ALREADY SPILLED ALL THAT BLOOD?
CLEVER OF YOU TO MASK YOUR DEMONIC AURA. IT ALLOWED YOU TO HIDE FOR A WHILE, BUT YOUR TRICKS DON'T WORK ON ME!

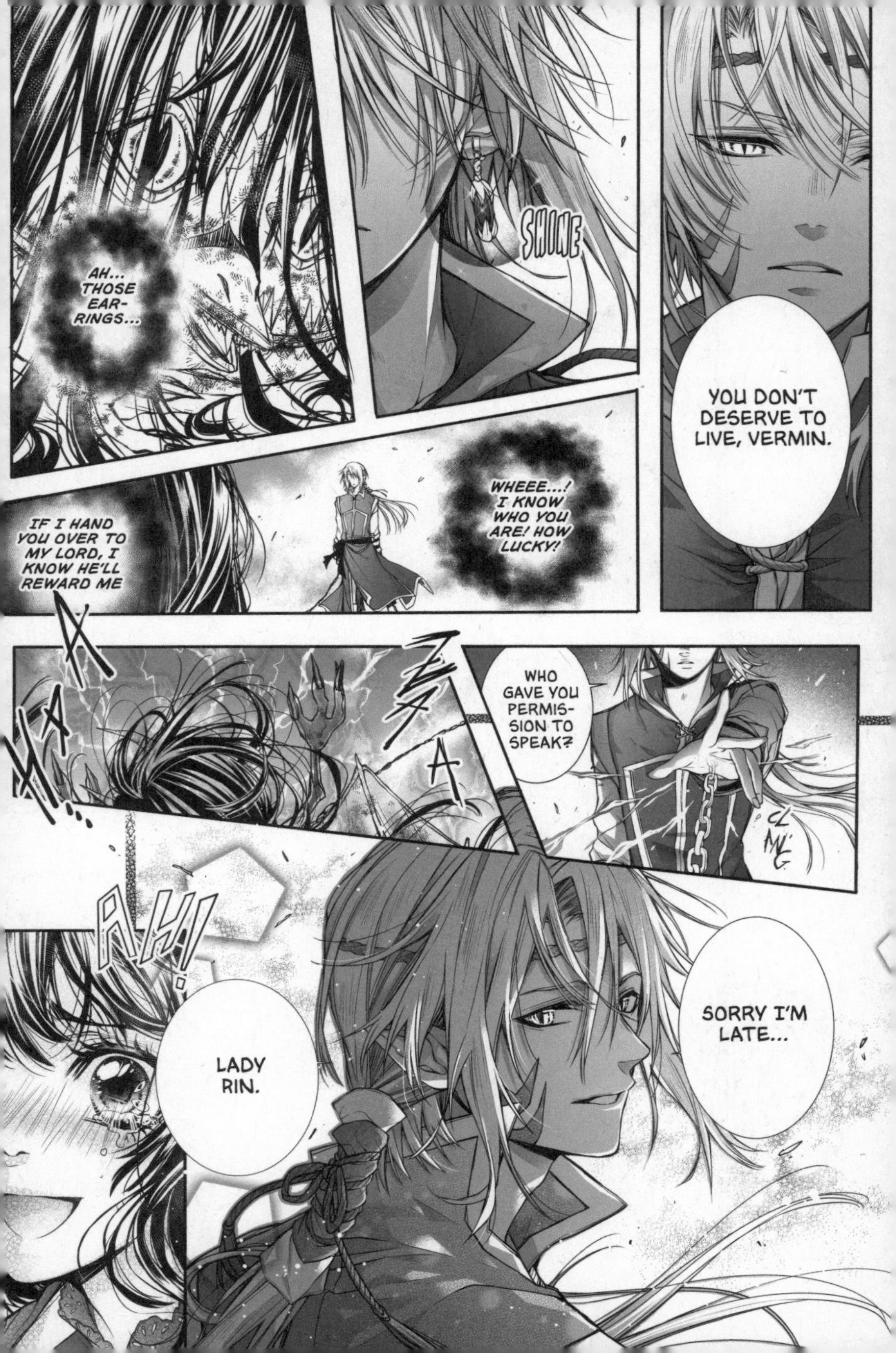

YOU DON'T DESERVE TO LIVE, VERMIN.
SHINE
AH... THOSE EAR-RINGS...
WHEEE...! I KNOW WHO YOU ARE! HOW LUCKY!
IF I HAND YOU OVER TO MY LORD, I KNOW HE'LL REWARD ME
WHO GAVE YOU PERMIS-SION TO SPEAK?
CLANG
ZZA A
HA HA...
SORRY I'M LATE...
LADY RIN.
AH!

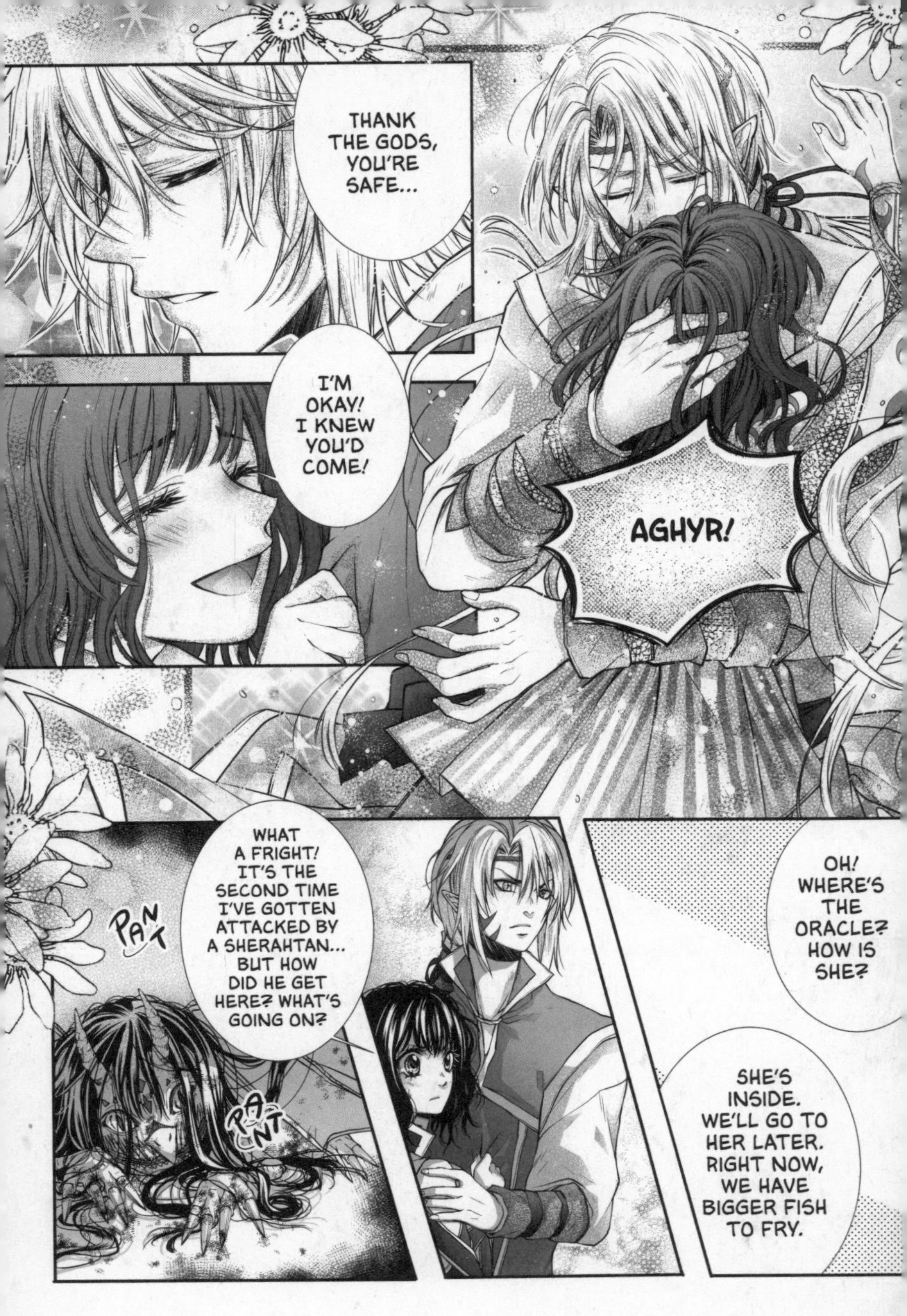
AGHYR!
THANK THE GODS, YOU'RE SAFE...
I'M OKAY! I KNEW YOU'D COME!
OH! WHERE'S THE ORACLE? HOW IS SHE?
SHE'S INSIDE. WE'LL GO TO HER LATER. RIGHT NOW, WE HAVE BIGGER FISH TO FRY.
WHAT A FRIGHT! IT'S THE SECOND TIME I'VE GOTTEN ATTACKED BY A SHERAHTAN... BUT HOW DID HE GET HERE? WHAT'S GOING ON?
PANT
PANT

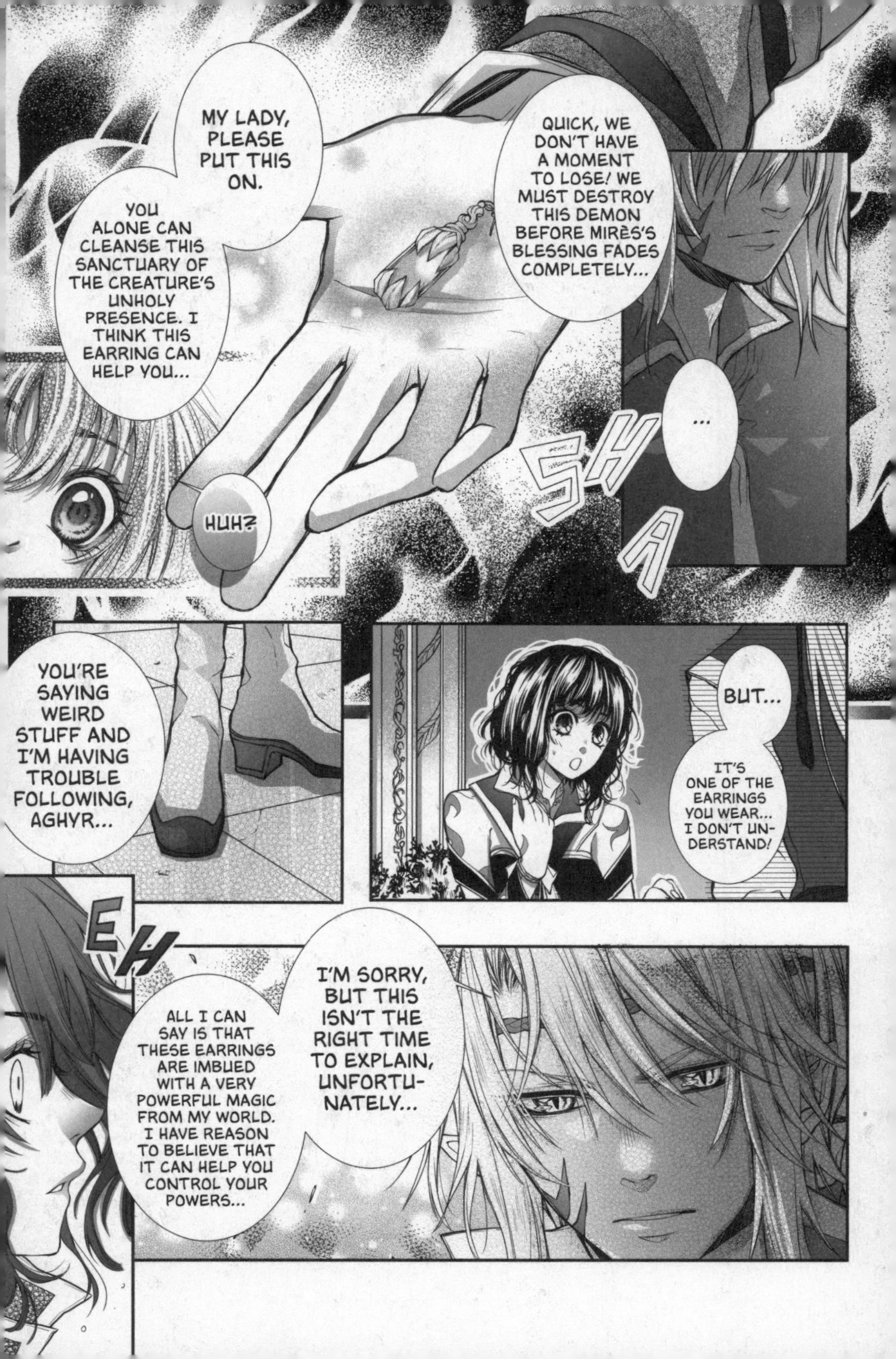
QUICK, WE DON'T HAVE A MOMENT TO LOSE! WE MUST DESTROY THIS DEMON BEFORE MIRÈS'S BLESSING FADES COMPLETELY...
MY LADY, PLEASE PUT THIS ON.
YOU ALONE CAN CLEANSE THIS SANCTUARY OF THE CREATURE'S UNHOLY PRESENCE. I THINK THIS EARRING CAN HELP YOU...
...
SHA
HUH?
BUT...
IT'S ONE OF THE EARRINGS YOU WEAR... I DON'T UNDERSTAND!
YOU'RE SAYING WEIRD STUFF AND I'M HAVING TROUBLE FOLLOWING, AGHYR...
EH
I'M SORRY, BUT THIS ISN'T THE RIGHT TIME TO EXPLAIN, UNFORTUNATELY...
ALL I CAN SAY IS THAT THESE EARRINGS ARE IMBUED WITH A VERY POWERFUL MAGIC FROM MY WORLD. I HAVE REASON TO BELIEVE THAT IT CAN HELP YOU CONTROL YOUR POWERS...

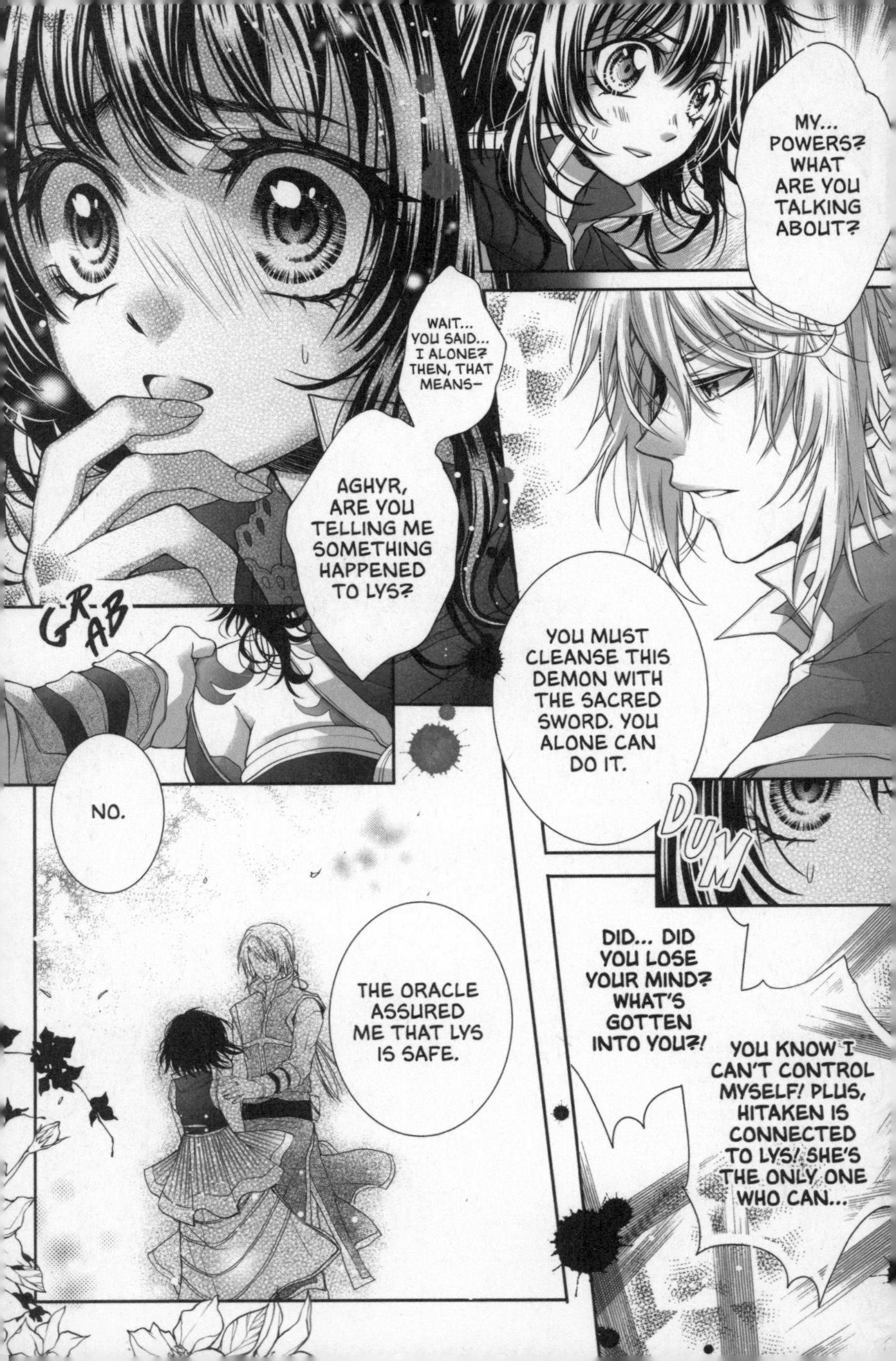
MY... POWERS? WHAT ARE YOU TALKING ABOUT?
YOU MUST CLEANSE THIS DEMON WITH THE SACRED SWORD. YOU ALONE CAN DO IT.
WAIT... YOU SAID... I ALONE? THEN, THAT MEANS—
AGHYR, ARE YOU TELLING ME SOMETHING HAPPENED TO LYS?
GR-AB
NO.
THE ORACLE ASSURED ME THAT LYS IS SAFE.
DUM
DID... DID YOU LOSE YOUR MIND? WHAT'S GOTTEN INTO YOU?!
YOU KNOW I CAN'T CONTROL MYSELF! PLUS, HITAKEN IS CONNECTED TO LYS! SHE'S THE ONLY ONE WHO CAN...

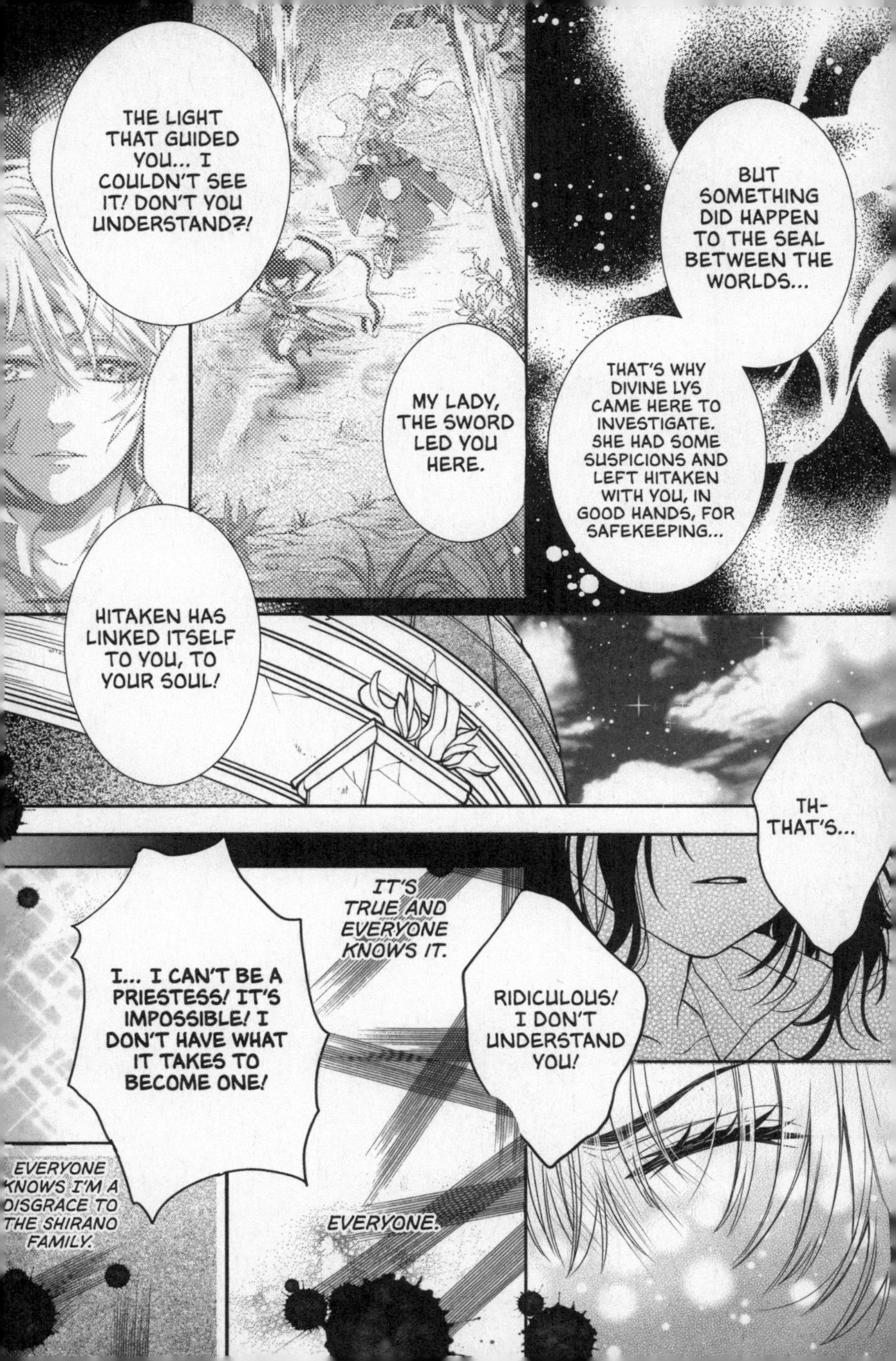
BUT SOMETHING DID HAPPEN TO THE SEAL BETWEEN THE WORLDS...
THAT'S WHY DIVINE LYS CAME HERE TO INVESTIGATE. SHE HAD SOME SUSPICIONS AND LEFT HITAKEN WITH YOU, IN GOOD HANDS, FOR SAFEKEEPING...
MY LADY, THE SWORD LED YOU HERE.
THE LIGHT THAT GUIDED YOU... I COULDN'T SEE IT! DON'T YOU UNDERSTAND?!
HITAKEN HAS LINKED ITSELF TO YOU, TO YOUR SOUL!
TH-THAT'S...
RIDICULOUS! I DON'T UNDERSTAND YOU!
IT'S TRUE AND EVERYONE KNOWS IT.
I... I CAN'T BE A PRIESTESS! IT'S IMPOSSIBLE! I DON'T HAVE WHAT IT TAKES TO BECOME ONE!
EVERYONE.
EVERYONE KNOWS I'M A DISGRACE TO THE SHIRANO FAMILY.

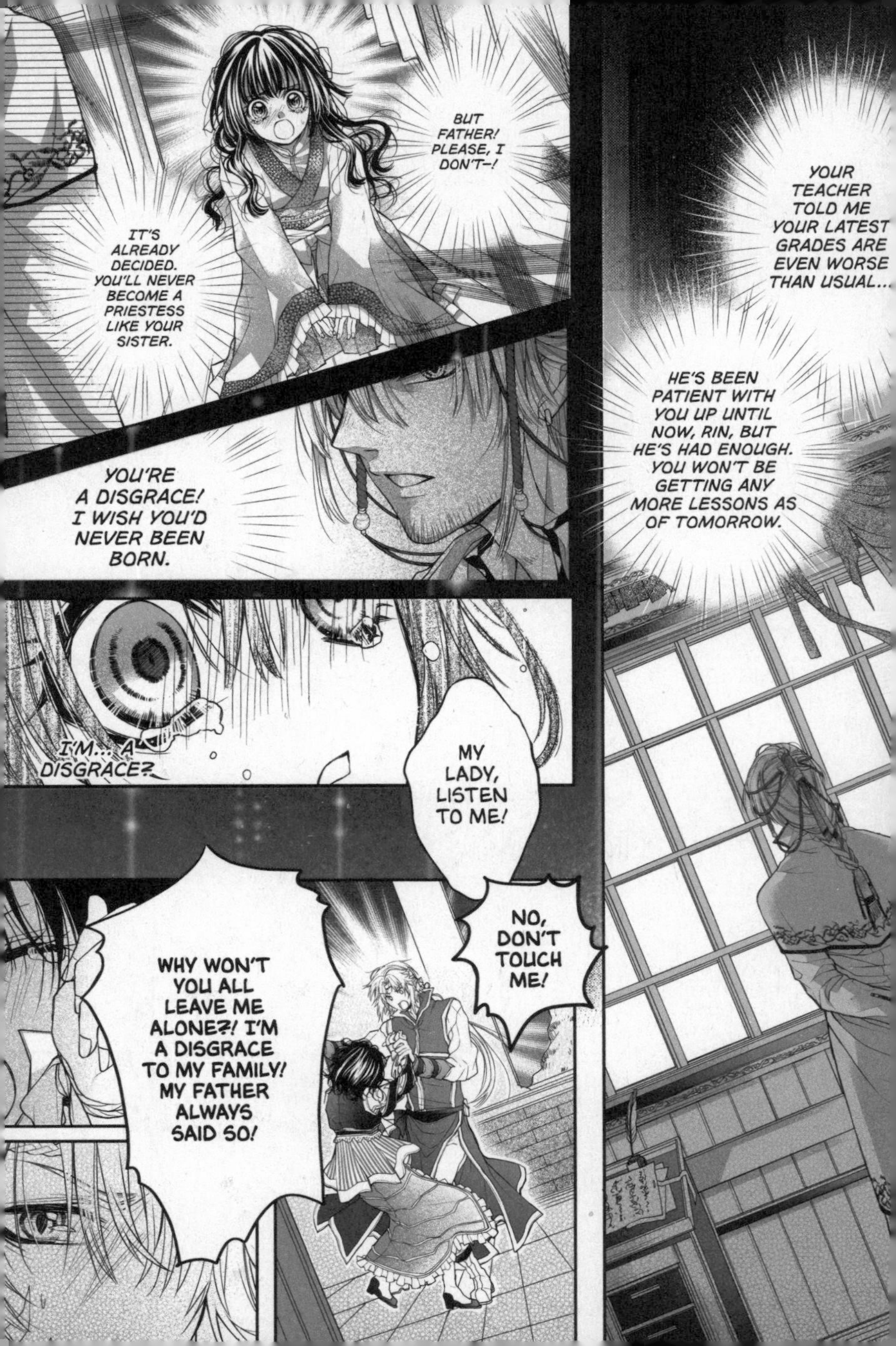
YOUR TEACHER TOLD ME YOUR LATEST GRADES ARE EVEN WORSE THAN USUAL...
HE'S BEEN PATIENT WITH YOU UP UNTIL NOW, RIN, BUT HE'S HAD ENOUGH. YOU WON'T BE GETTING ANY MORE LESSONS AS OF TOMORROW.
BUT FATHER! PLEASE, I DON'T–!
IT'S ALREADY DECIDED. YOU'LL NEVER BECOME A PRIESTESS LIKE YOUR SISTER.
YOU'RE A DISGRACE! I WISH YOU'D NEVER BEEN BORN.
I'M... A DISGRACE?
MY LADY, LISTEN TO ME!
NO, DON'T TOUCH ME!
WHY WON'T YOU ALL LEAVE ME ALONE?! I'M A DISGRACE TO MY FAMILY! MY FATHER ALWAYS SAID SO!

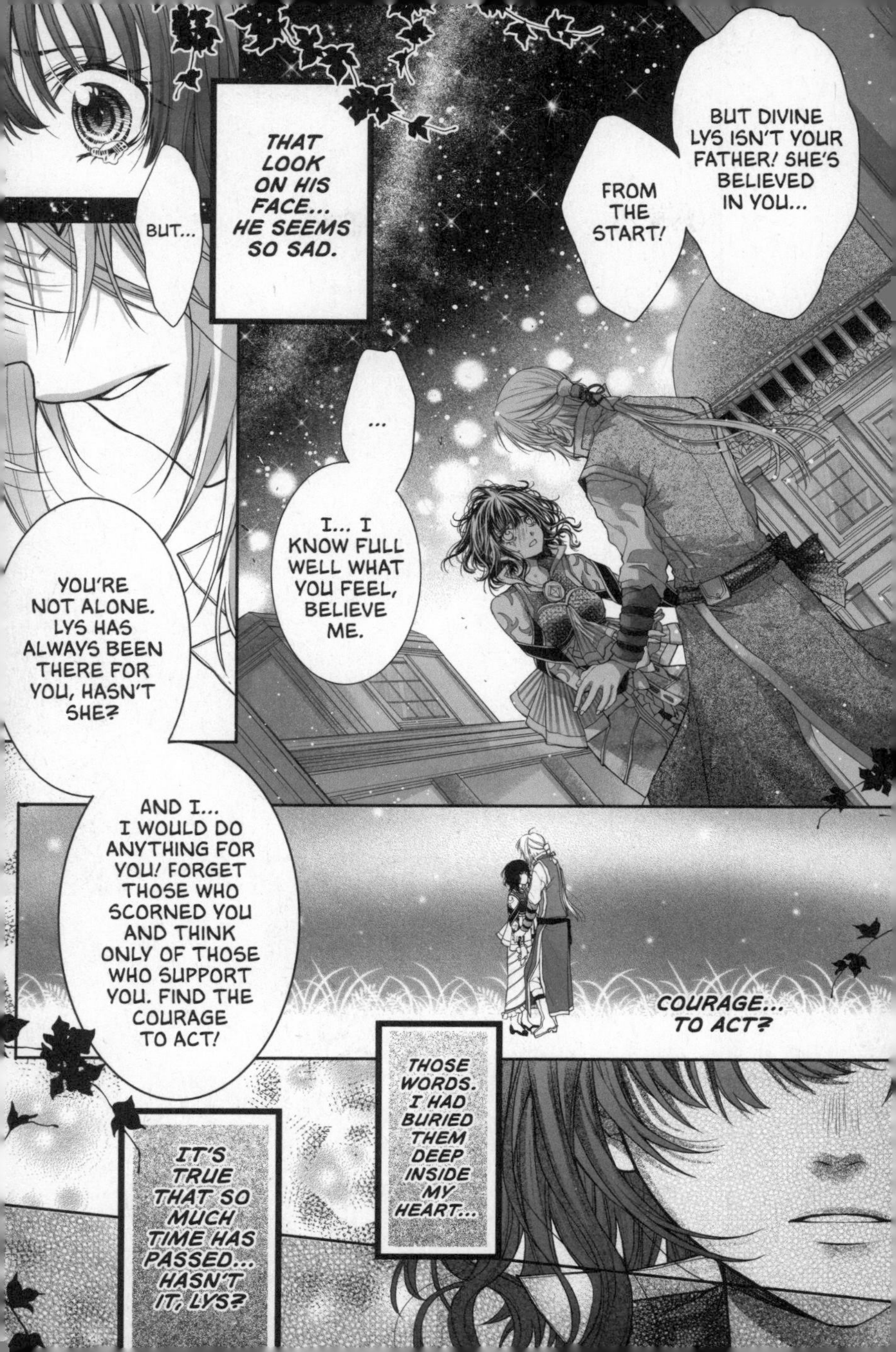
BUT DIVINE LYS ISN'T YOUR FATHER! SHE'S BELIEVED IN YOU...
FROM THE START!
...
I... I KNOW FULL WELL WHAT YOU FEEL, BELIEVE ME.
THAT LOOK ON HIS FACE... HE SEEMS SO SAD.
BUT...
YOU'RE NOT ALONE. LYS HAS ALWAYS BEEN THERE FOR YOU, HASN'T SHE?
AND I... I WOULD DO ANYTHING FOR YOU! FORGET THOSE WHO SCORNED YOU AND THINK ONLY OF THOSE WHO SUPPORT YOU. FIND THE COURAGE TO ACT!
COURAGE... TO ACT?
THOSE WORDS. I HAD BURIED THEM DEEP INSIDE MY HEART...
IT'S TRUE THAT SO MUCH TIME HAS PASSED... HASN'T IT, LYS?

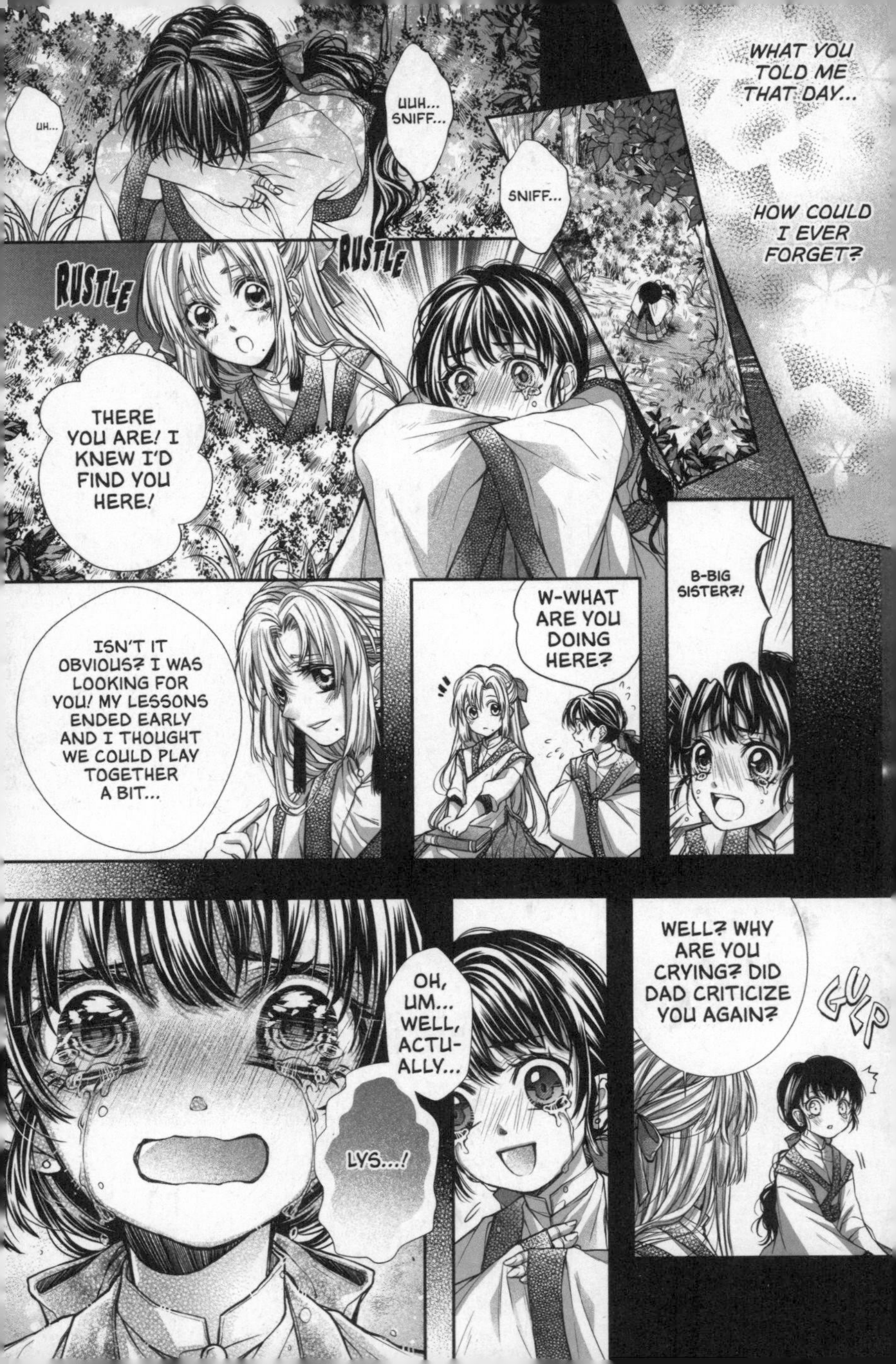
WHAT YOU TOLD ME THAT DAY...
HOW COULD I EVER FORGET?
SNIFF...
UUH... SNIFF...
UH...
RUSTLE
RUSTLE
THERE YOU ARE! I KNEW I'D FIND YOU HERE!
B-BIG SISTER?!
W-WHAT ARE YOU DOING HERE?
ISN'T IT OBVIOUS? I WAS LOOKING FOR YOU! MY LESSONS ENDED EARLY AND I THOUGHT WE COULD PLAY TOGETHER A BIT...
WELL? WHY ARE YOU CRYING? DID DAD CRITICIZE YOU AGAIN?
GULP
OH, UM... WELL, ACTU-ALLY...
LYS...!

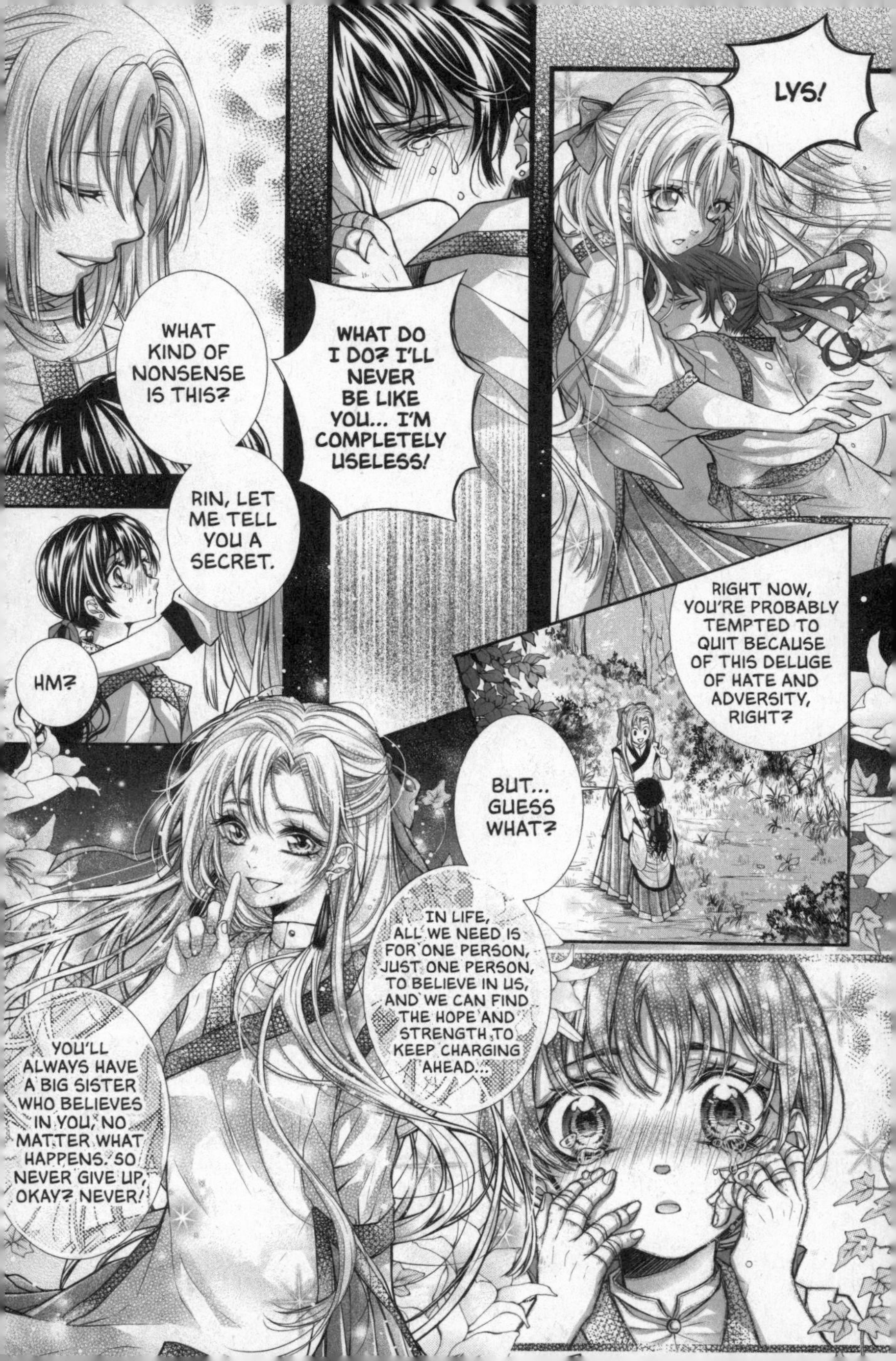
LYS!
WHAT DO I DO? I'LL NEVER BE LIKE YOU... I'M COMPLETELY USELESS!
WHAT KIND OF NONSENSE IS THIS?
RIN, LET ME TELL YOU A SECRET.
HM?
RIGHT NOW, YOU'RE PROBABLY TEMPTED TO QUIT BECAUSE OF THIS DELUGE OF HATE AND ADVERSITY, RIGHT?
BUT... GUESS WHAT?
IN LIFE, ALL WE NEED IS FOR ONE PERSON, JUST ONE PERSON, TO BELIEVE IN US, AND WE CAN FIND THE HOPE AND STRENGTH TO KEEP CHARGING AHEAD...
YOU'LL ALWAYS HAVE A BIG SISTER WHO BELIEVES IN YOU, NO MATTER WHAT HAPPENS. SO NEVER GIVE UP, OKAY? NEVER!

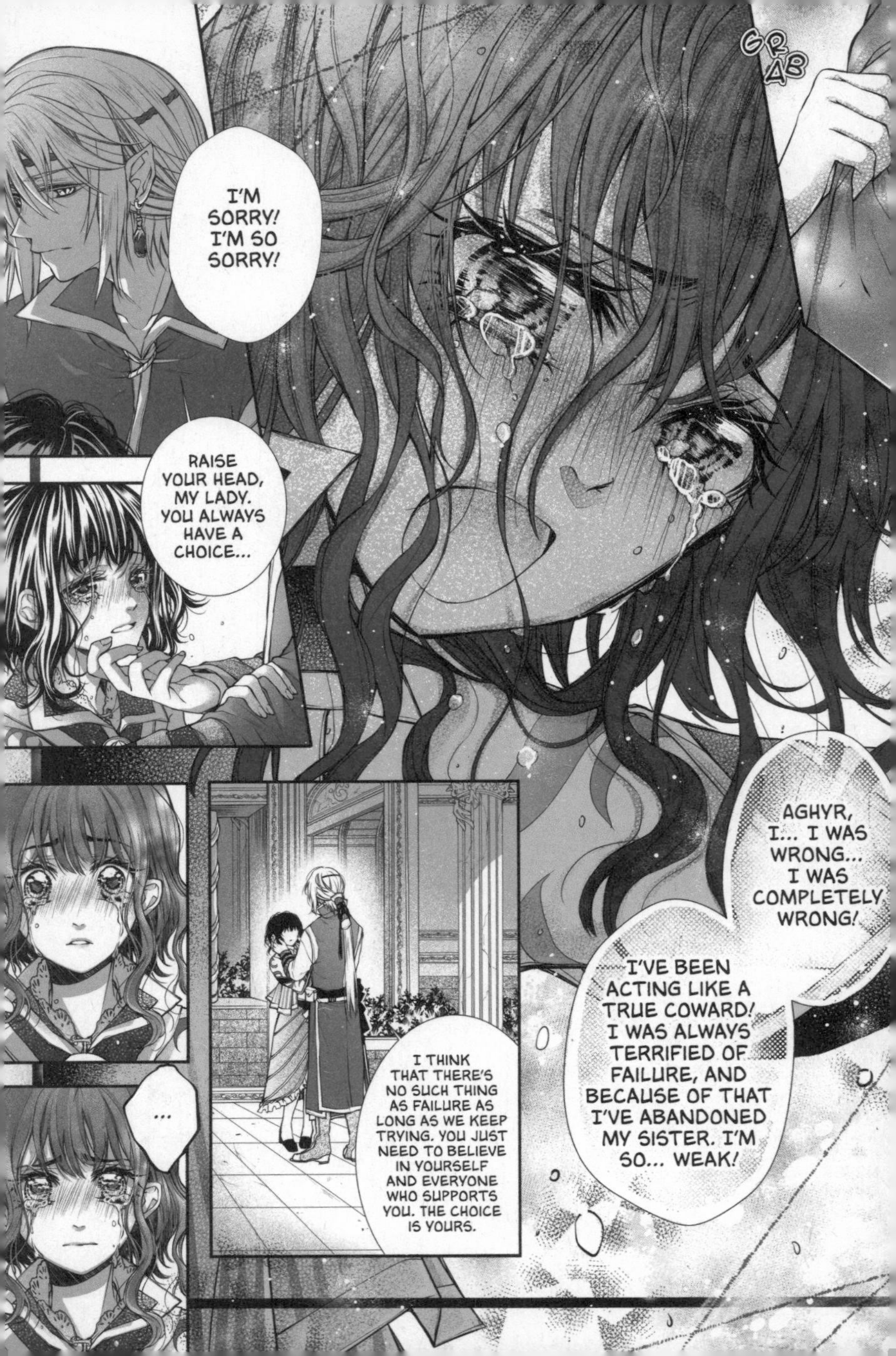
GRAB
AGHYR, I... I WAS WRONG... I WAS COMPLETELY WRONG!
I'VE BEEN ACTING LIKE A TRUE COWARD! I WAS ALWAYS TERRIFIED OF FAILURE, AND BECAUSE OF THAT I'VE ABANDONED MY SISTER. I'M SO... WEAK!
I'M SORRY! I'M SO SORRY!
RAISE YOUR HEAD, MY LADY. YOU ALWAYS HAVE A CHOICE...
I THINK THAT THERE'S NO SUCH THING AS FAILURE AS LONG AS WE KEEP TRYING. YOU JUST NEED TO BELIEVE IN YOURSELF AND EVERYONE WHO SUPPORTS YOU. THE CHOICE IS YOURS.
...

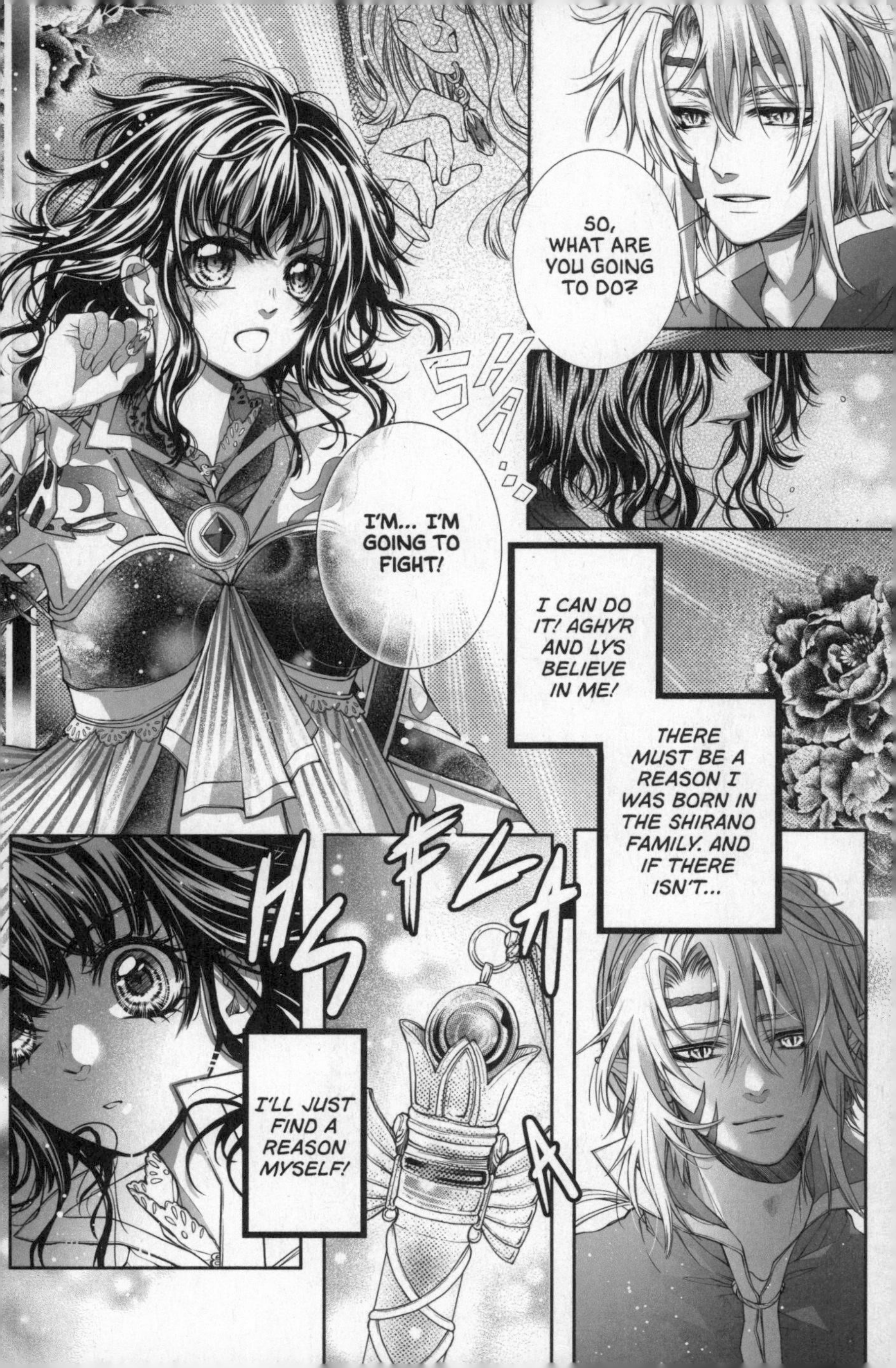
SO, WHAT ARE YOU GOING TO DO?
SHA...
I'M... I'M GOING TO FIGHT!
I CAN DO IT! AGHYR AND LYS BELIEVE IN ME!
THERE MUST BE A REASON I WAS BORN IN THE SHIRANO FAMILY. AND IF THERE ISN'T...
FLA
A
HS
I'LL JUST FIND A REASON MYSELF!

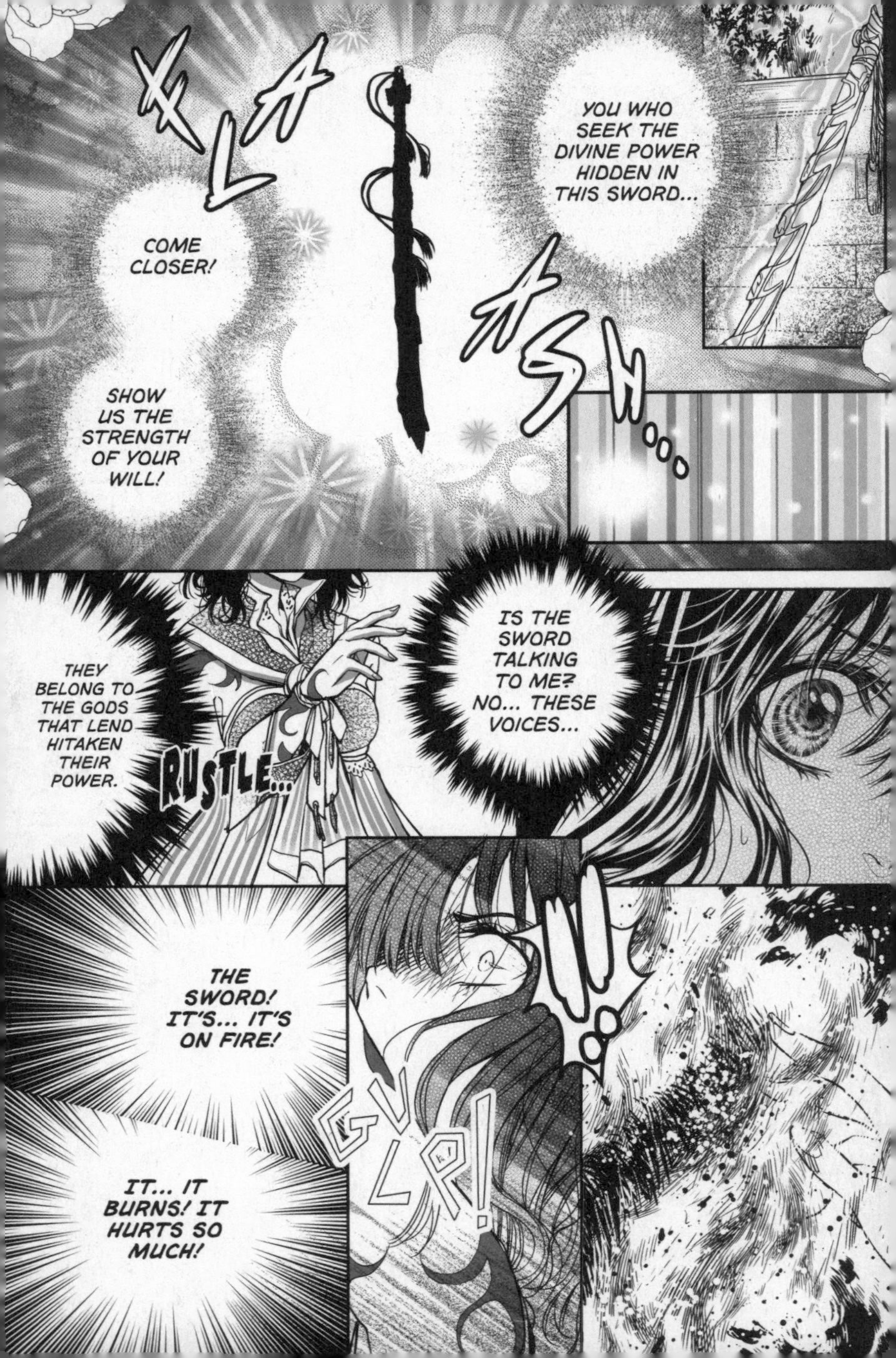
YOU WHO SEEK THE DIVINE POWER HIDDEN IN THIS SWORD...
FLASH...
COME CLOSER!
SHOW US THE STRENGTH OF YOUR WILL!
IS THE SWORD TALKING TO ME? NO... THESE VOICES...
THEY BELONG TO THE GODS THAT LEND HITAKEN THEIR POWER.
RUSTLE...
!!...
GULP!
THE SWORD! IT'S... IT'S ON FIRE!
IT... IT BURNS! IT HURTS SO MUCH!

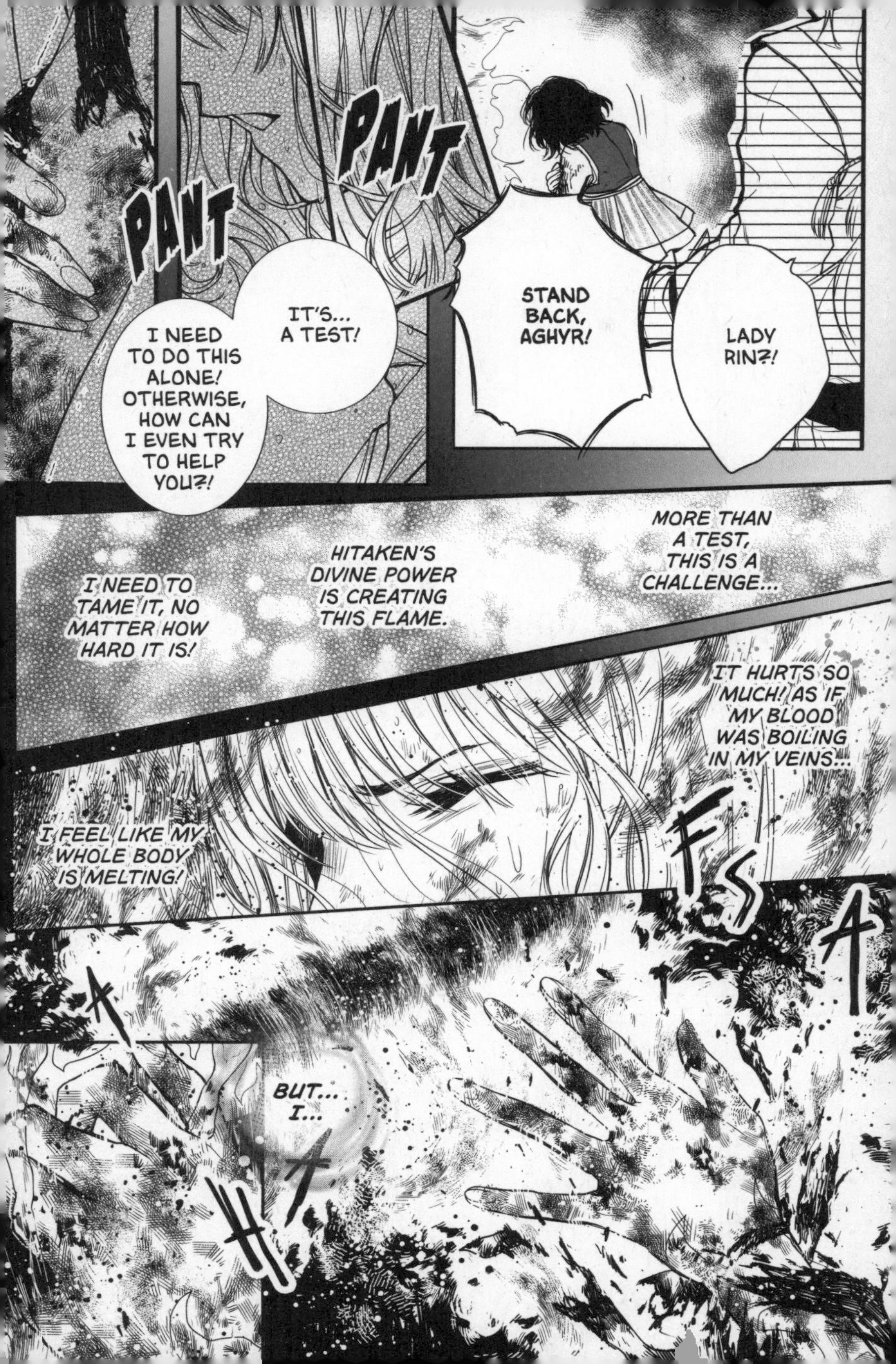
LADY RIN?!
STAND BACK, AGHYR!
PANT PANT
PANT
IT'S... A TEST!
I NEED TO DO THIS ALONE! OTHERWISE, HOW CAN I EVEN TRY TO HELP YOU?!
MORE THAN A TEST, THIS IS A CHALLENGE...
HITAKEN'S DIVINE POWER IS CREATING THIS FLAME.
I NEED TO TAME IT, NO MATTER HOW HARD IT IS!
IT HURTS SO MUCH! AS IF MY BLOOD WAS BOILING IN MY VEINS...
I FEEL LIKE MY WHOLE BODY IS MELTING!
FSA
BUT... I...

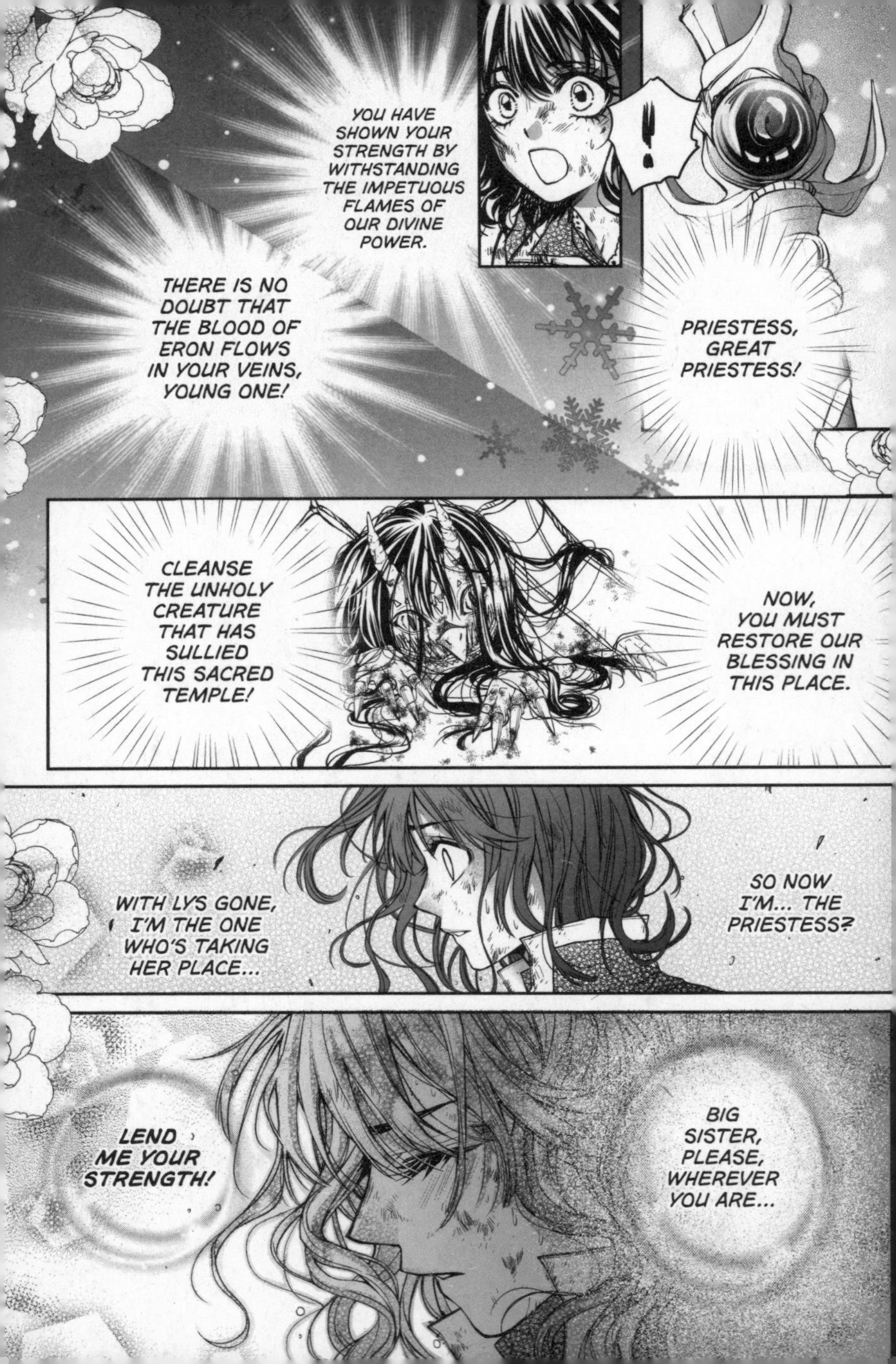
!
YOU HAVE SHOWN YOUR STRENGTH BY WITHSTANDING THE IMPETUOUS FLAMES OF OUR DIVINE POWER.
PRIESTESS, GREAT PRIESTESS!
THERE IS NO DOUBT THAT THE BLOOD OF ERON FLOWS IN YOUR VEINS, YOUNG ONE!
NOW, YOU MUST RESTORE OUR BLESSING IN THIS PLACE.
CLEANSE THE UNHOLY CREATURE THAT HAS SULLIED THIS SACRED TEMPLE!
SO NOW I'M... THE PRIESTESS?
WITH LYS GONE, I'M THE ONE WHO'S TAKING HER PLACE...
BIG SISTER, PLEASE, WHEREVER YOU ARE...
LEND ME YOUR STRENGTH!

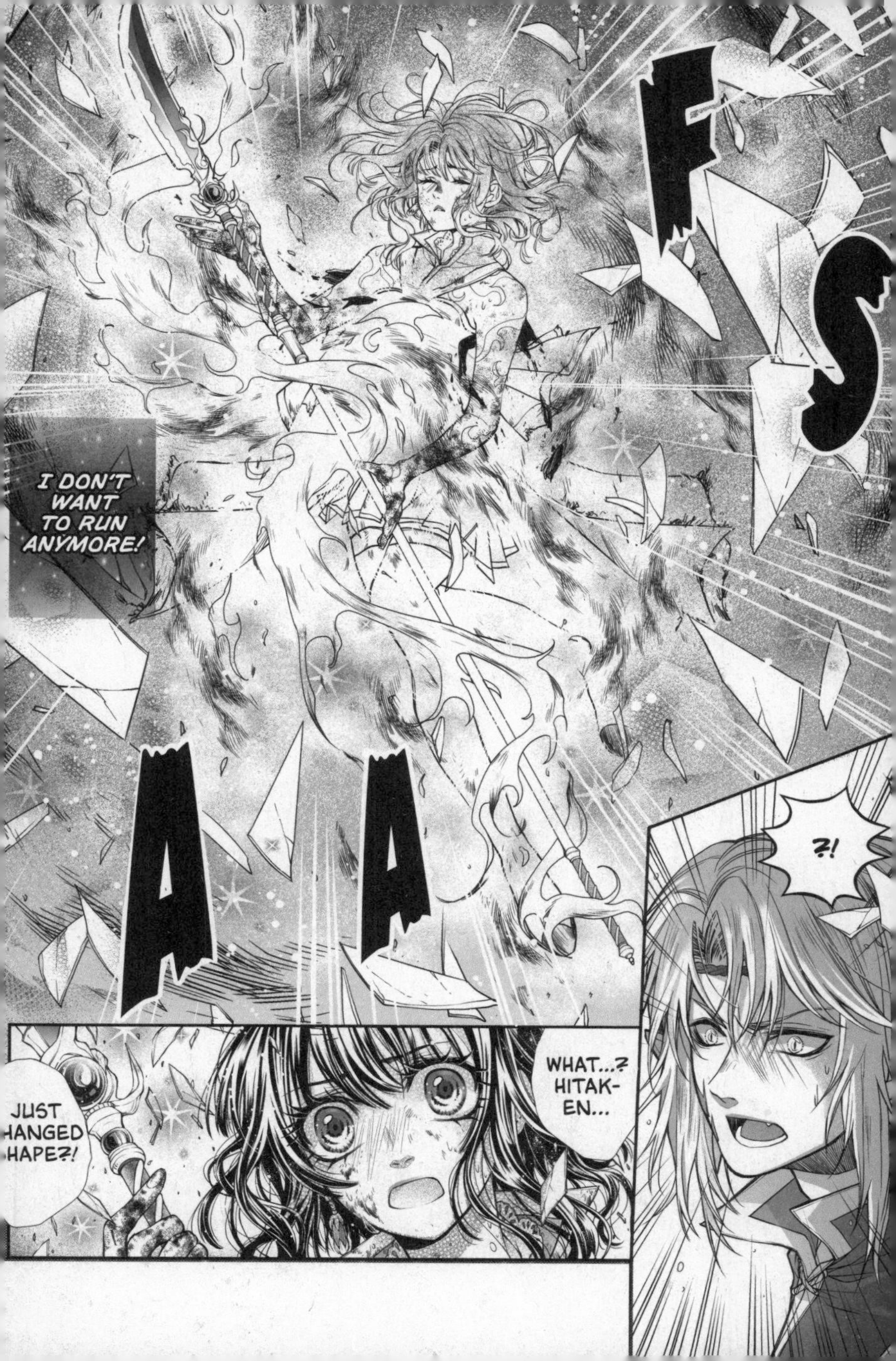
FSSH
I DON'T WANT TO RUN ANYMORE!
AA
?!
WHAT...? HITAK-EN...
JUST HANGED HAPE?!

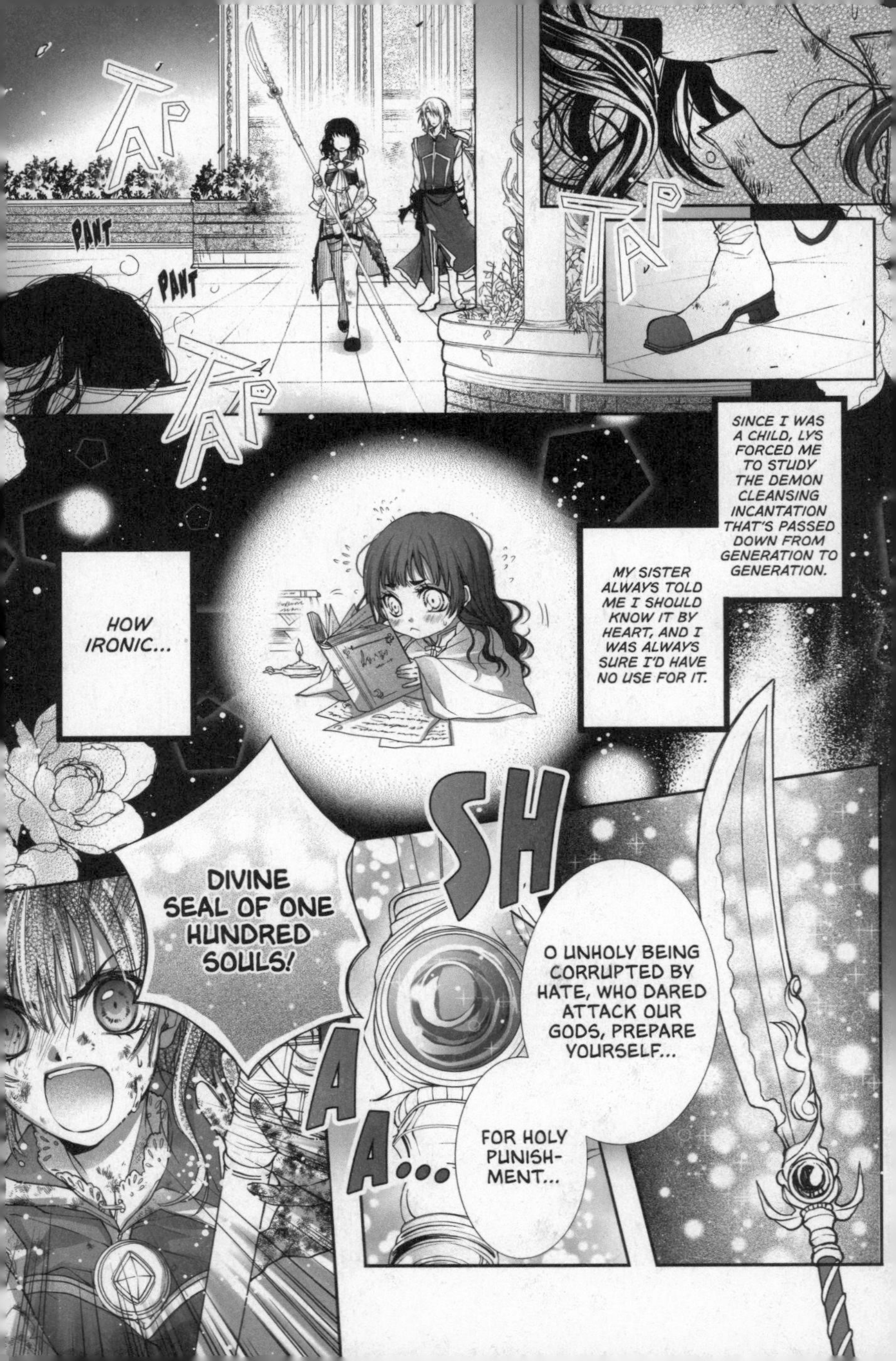
TAP
TAP
PANT
PANT
TAP
SINCE I WAS A CHILD, LYS FORCED ME TO STUDY THE DEMON CLEANSING INCANTATION THAT'S PASSED DOWN FROM GENERATION TO GENERATION.
MY SISTER ALWAYS TOLD ME I SHOULD KNOW IT BY HEART, AND I WAS ALWAYS SURE I'D HAVE NO USE FOR IT.
HOW IRONIC...
O UNHOLY BEING CORRUPTED BY HATE, WHO DARED ATTACK OUR GODS, PREPARE YOURSELF...
FOR HOLY PUNISH-MENT...
SHAA...
DIVINE SEAL OF ONE HUNDRED SOULS!

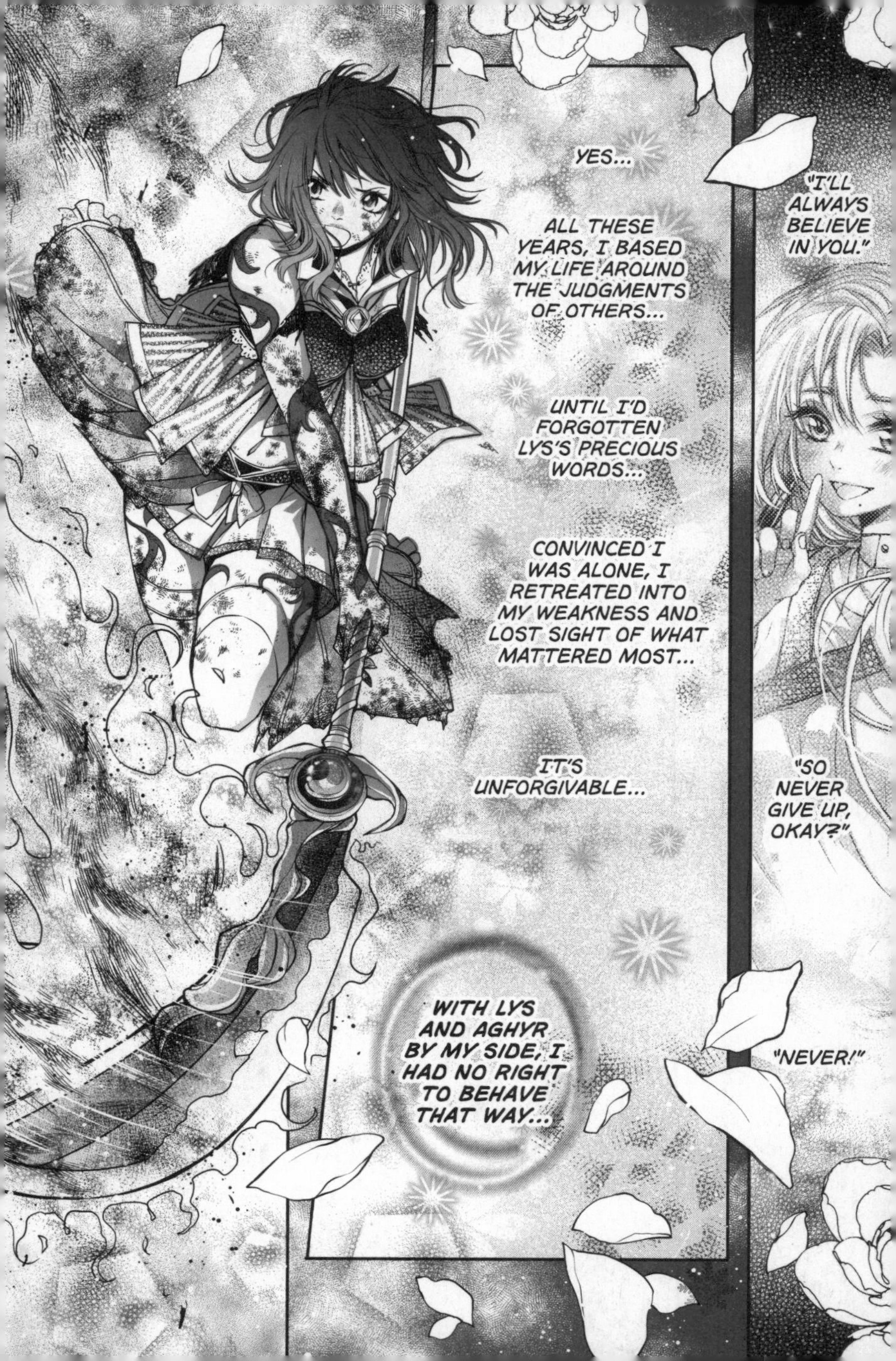
"I'LL ALWAYS BELIEVE IN YOU."
"SO NEVER GIVE UP, OKAY?"
"NEVER!"
YES...
ALL THESE YEARS, I BASED MY LIFE AROUND THE JUDGMENTS OF OTHERS...
UNTIL I'D FORGOTTEN LYS'S PRECIOUS WORDS...
CONVINCED I WAS ALONE, I RETREATED INTO MY WEAKNESS AND LOST SIGHT OF WHAT MATTERED MOST...
IT'S UNFORGIVABLE...
WITH LYS AND AGHYR BY MY SIDE, I HAD NO RIGHT TO BEHAVE THAT WAY...

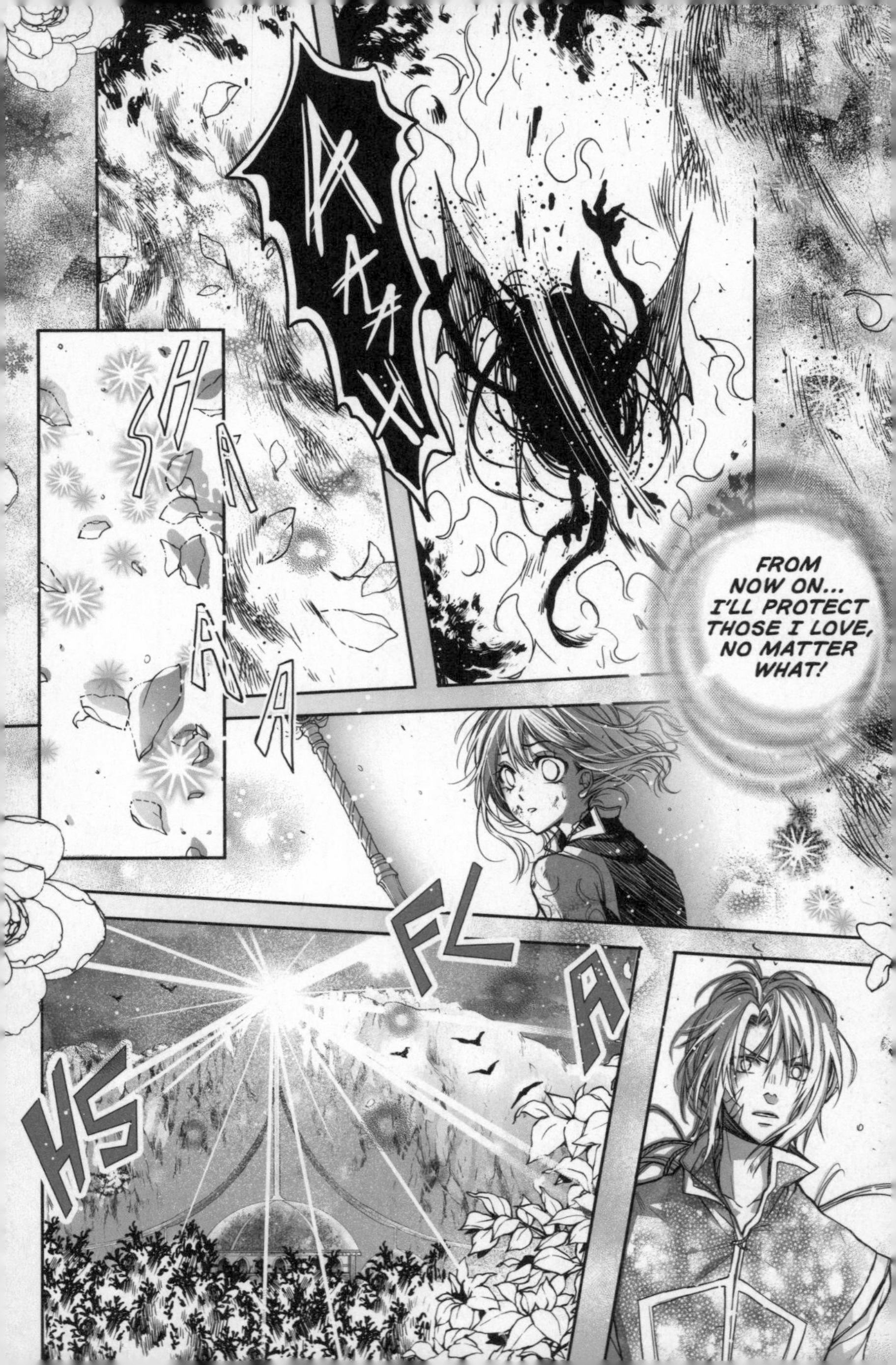
AAAAA
SHAAAA
FROM NOW ON... I'LL PROTECT THOSE I LOVE, NO MATTER WHAT!
FLA
HS

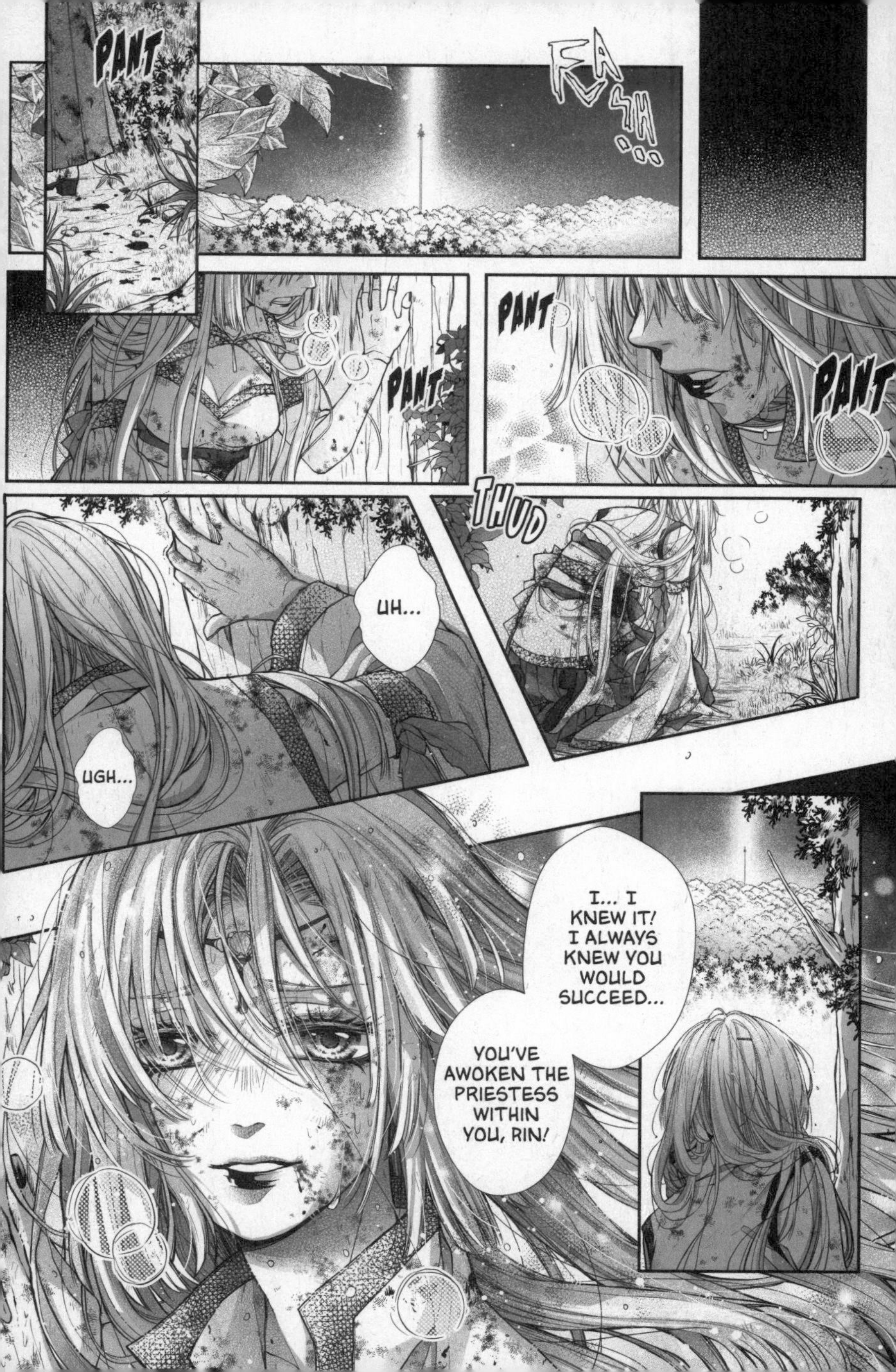
FLASH...
PANT
PANT
PANT
PANT
THUD
UH...
UGH...
I... I KNEW IT! I ALWAYS KNEW YOU WOULD SUCCEED...
YOU'VE AWOKEN THE PRIESTESS WITHIN YOU, RIN!

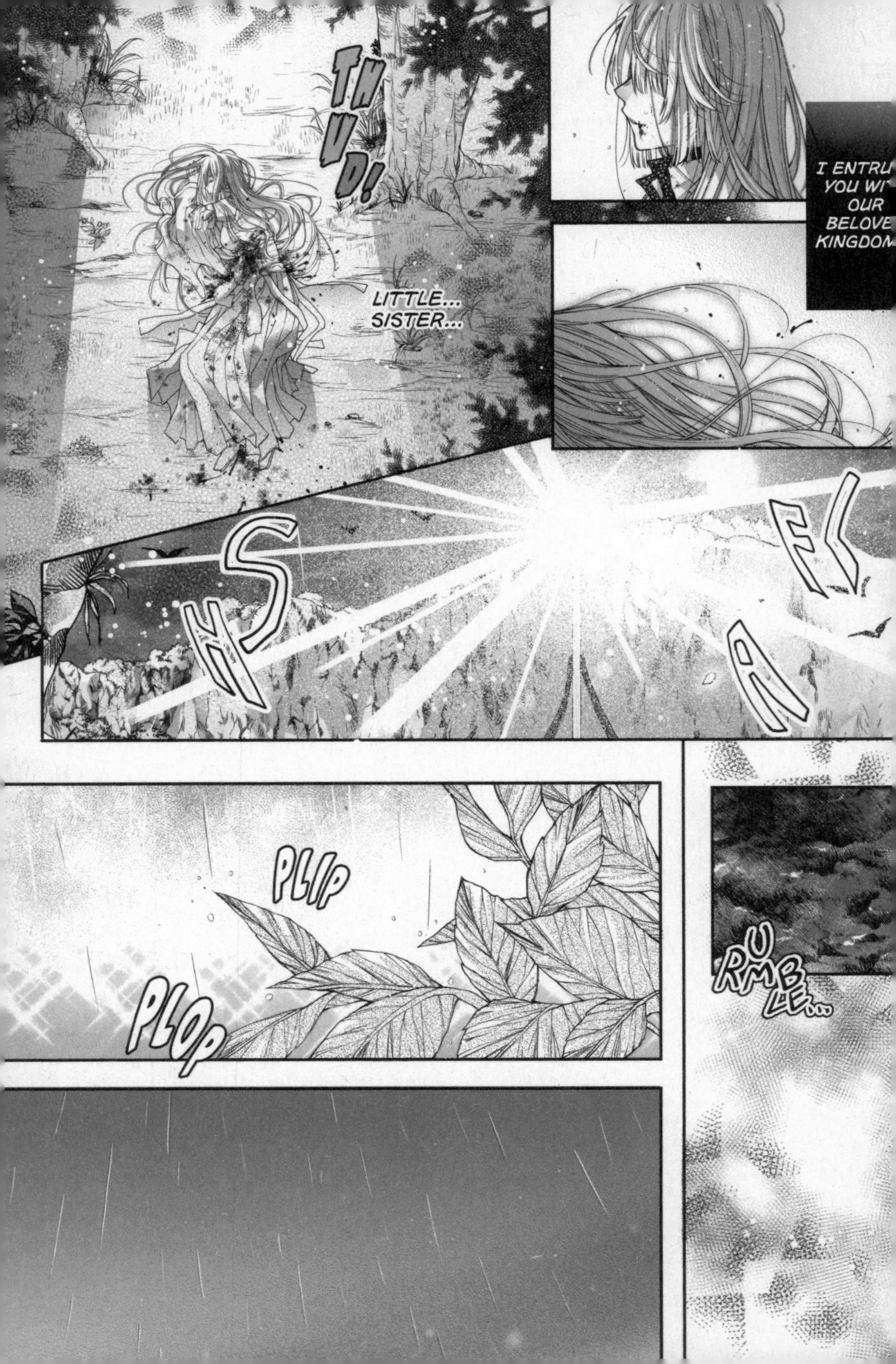
I ENTRU YOU WI OUR BELOVE KINGDOM
THUD!
LITTLE... SISTER...
FLASH
RUMBLE...
PLIP
PLOP

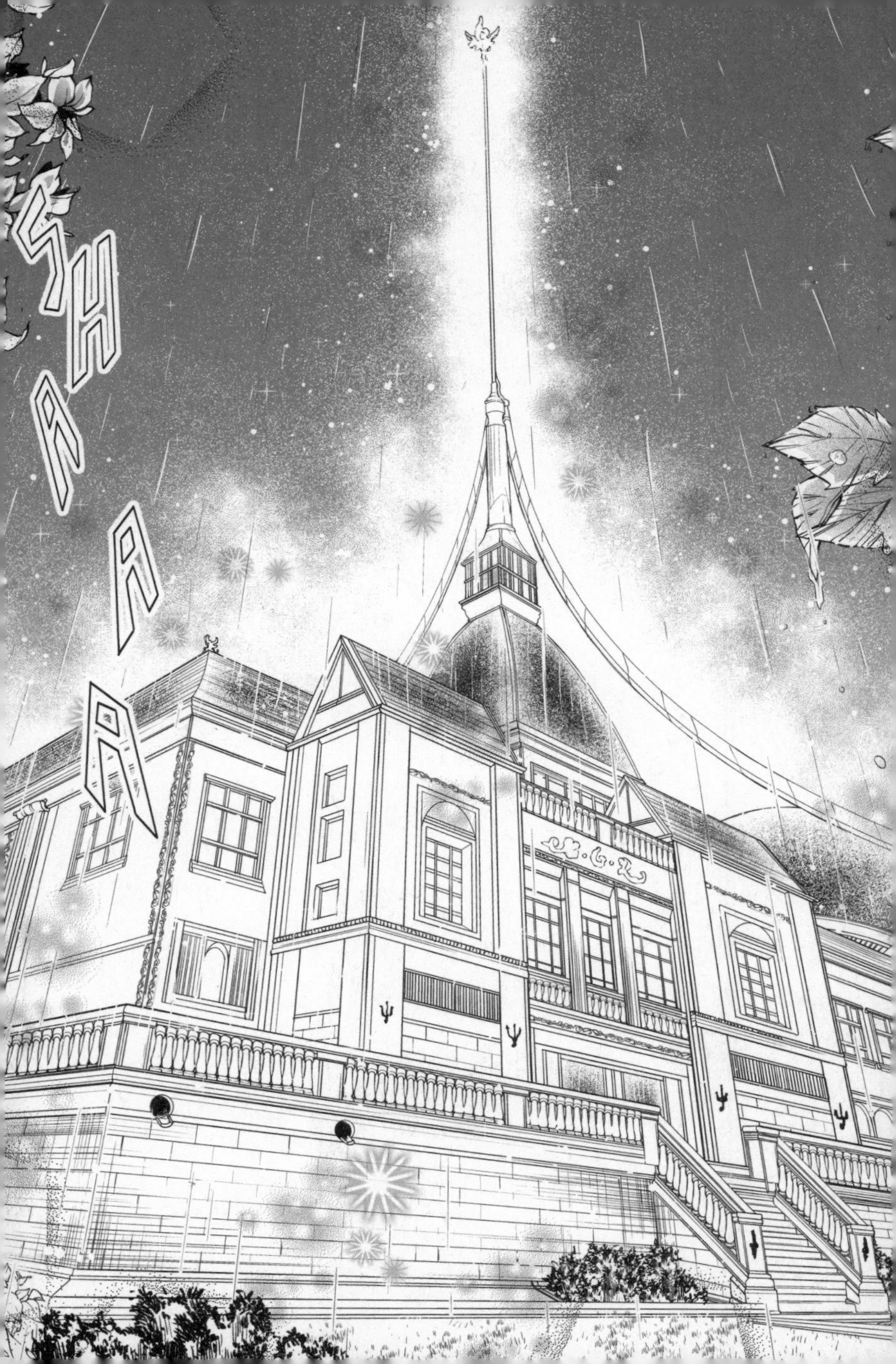
SHAAA

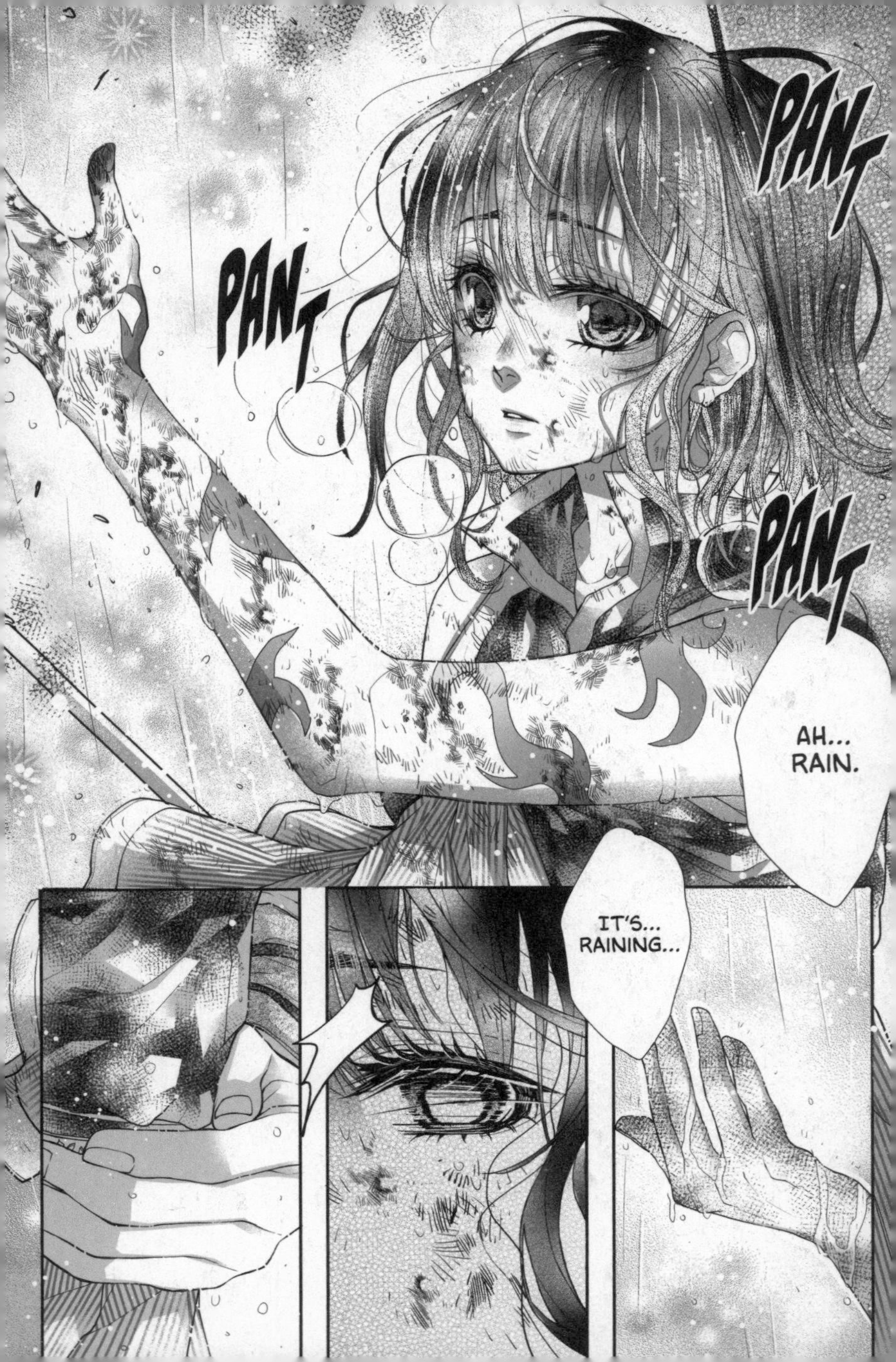
PANT
PANT
PANT
AH... RAIN.
IT'S... RAINING...

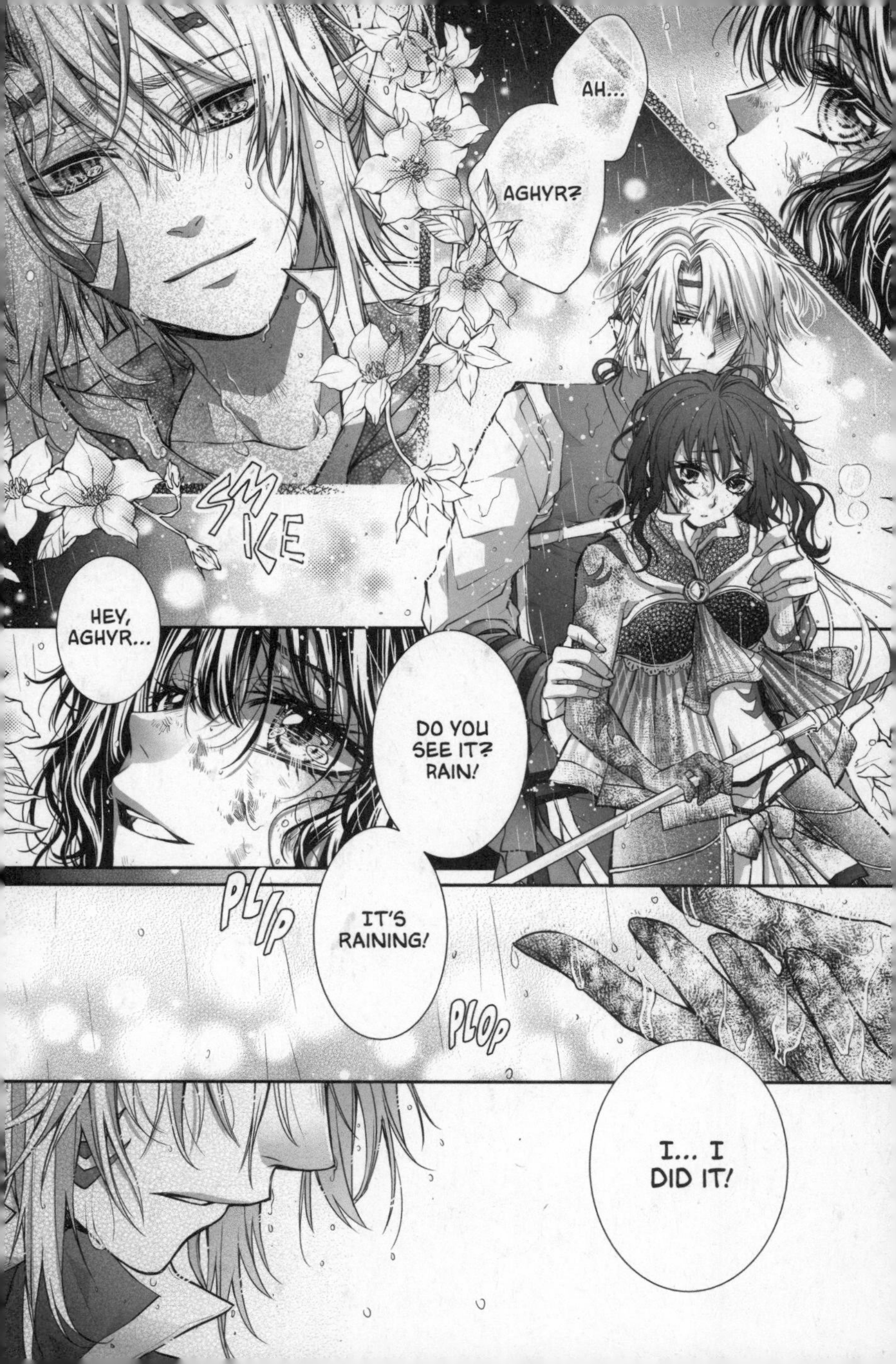
AH...
AGHYR?
SMIKE
HEY, AGHYR...
DO YOU SEE IT? RAIN!
IT'S RAINING!
PLIP
PLOP
I... I DID IT!

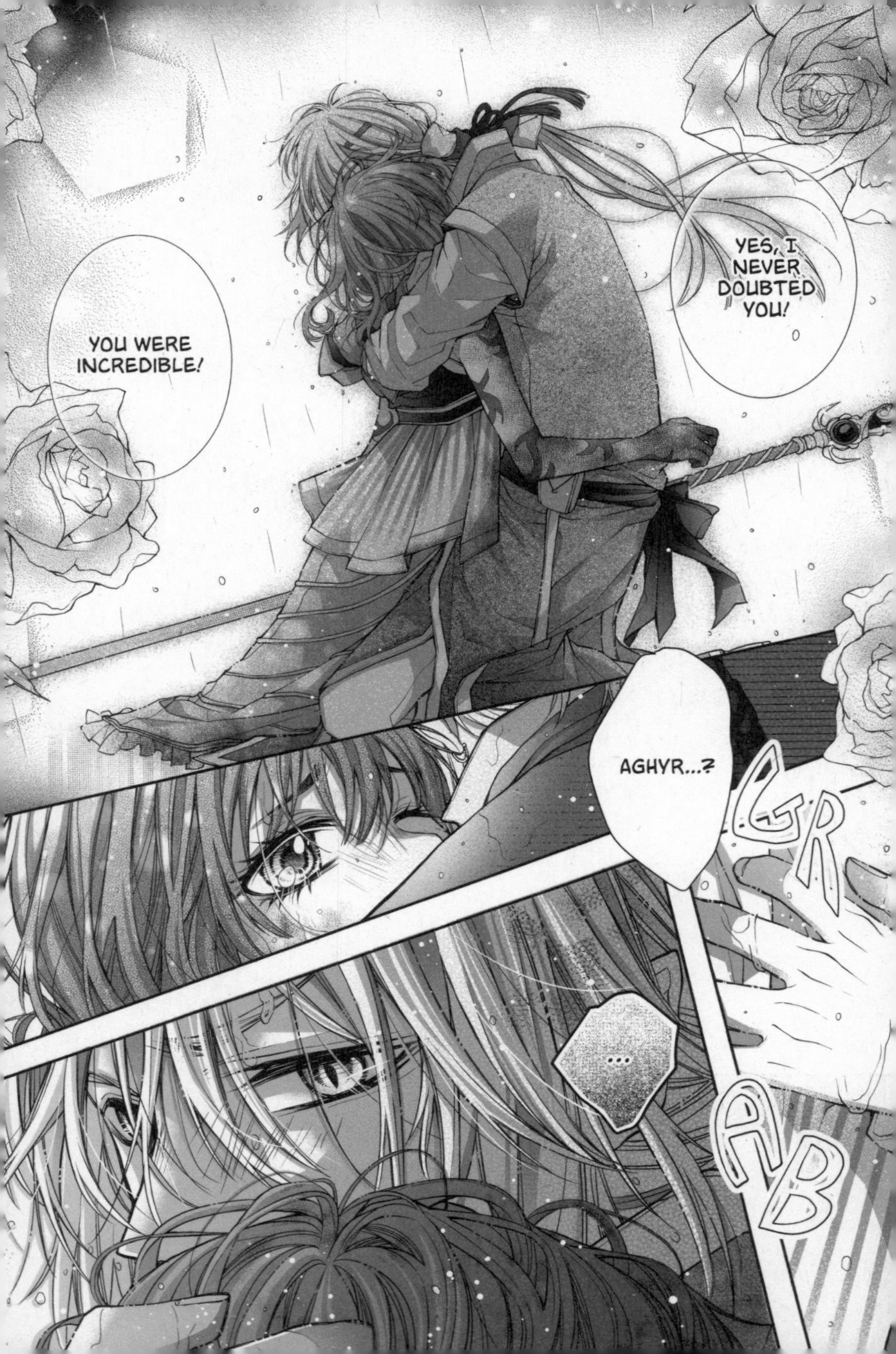
YES, I NEVER DOUBTED YOU!
YOU WERE INCREDIBLE!
AGHYR...?
...
GR
AB

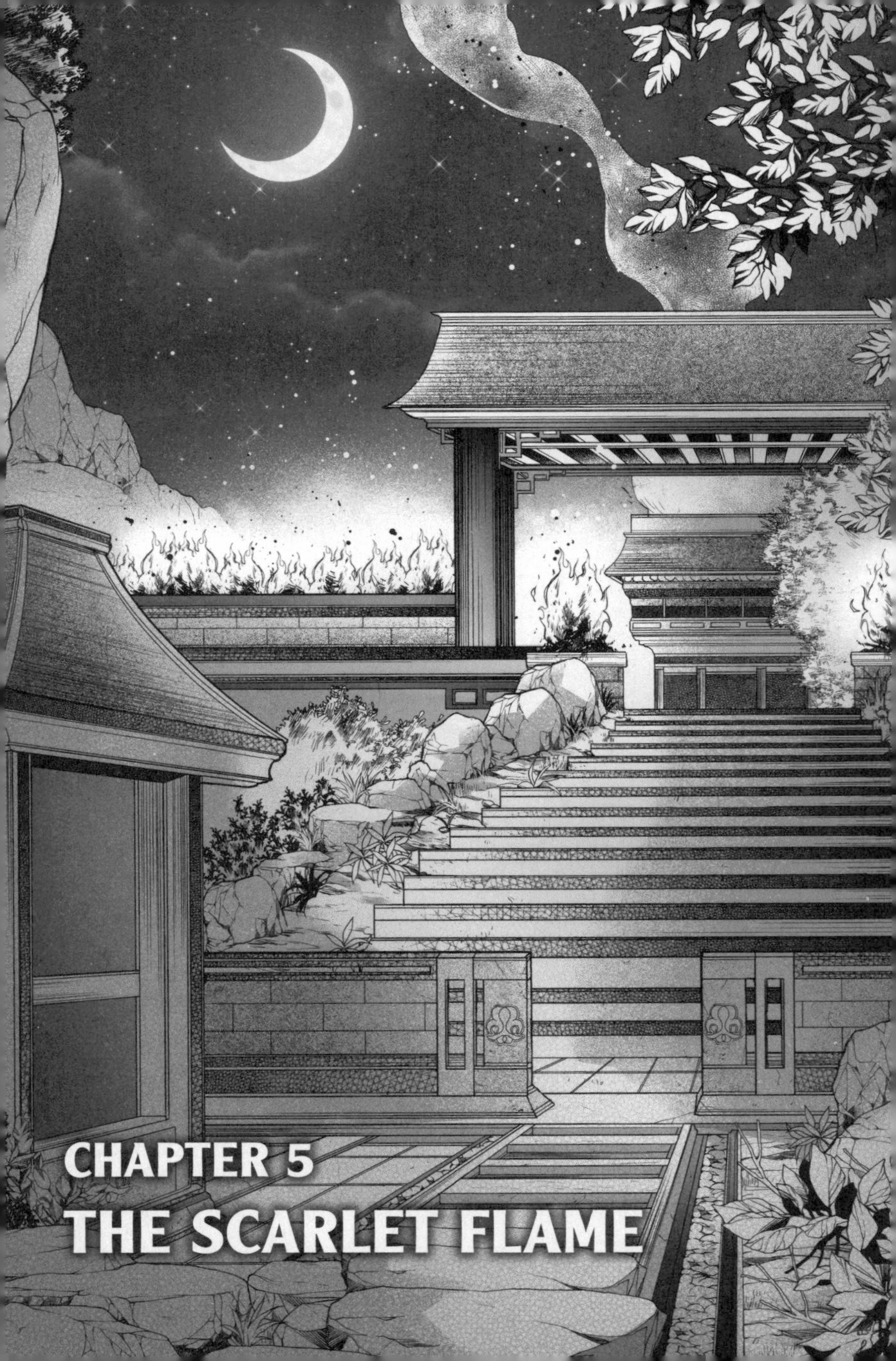
CHAPTER 5
THE SCARLET FLAME

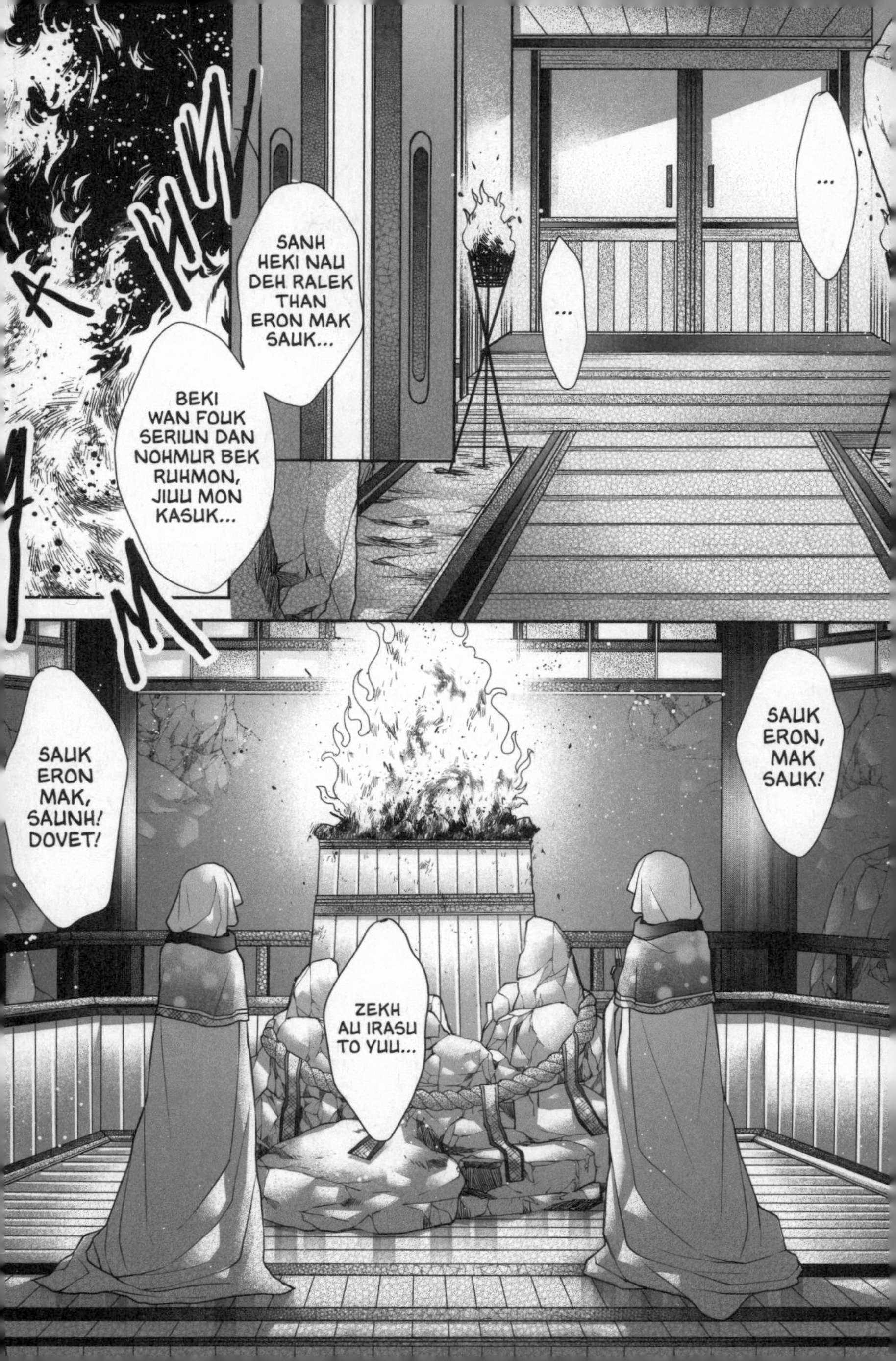
...
...
SANH HEKI NAU DEH RALEK THAN ERON MAK SAUK...
BEKI WAN FOUK SERIUN DAN NOHMUR BEK RUHMON, JIUU MON KASUK...
SAUK ERON, MAK SAUK!
SAUK ERON MAK, SAUNH! DOVET!
ZEKH AU IRASU TO YUU...

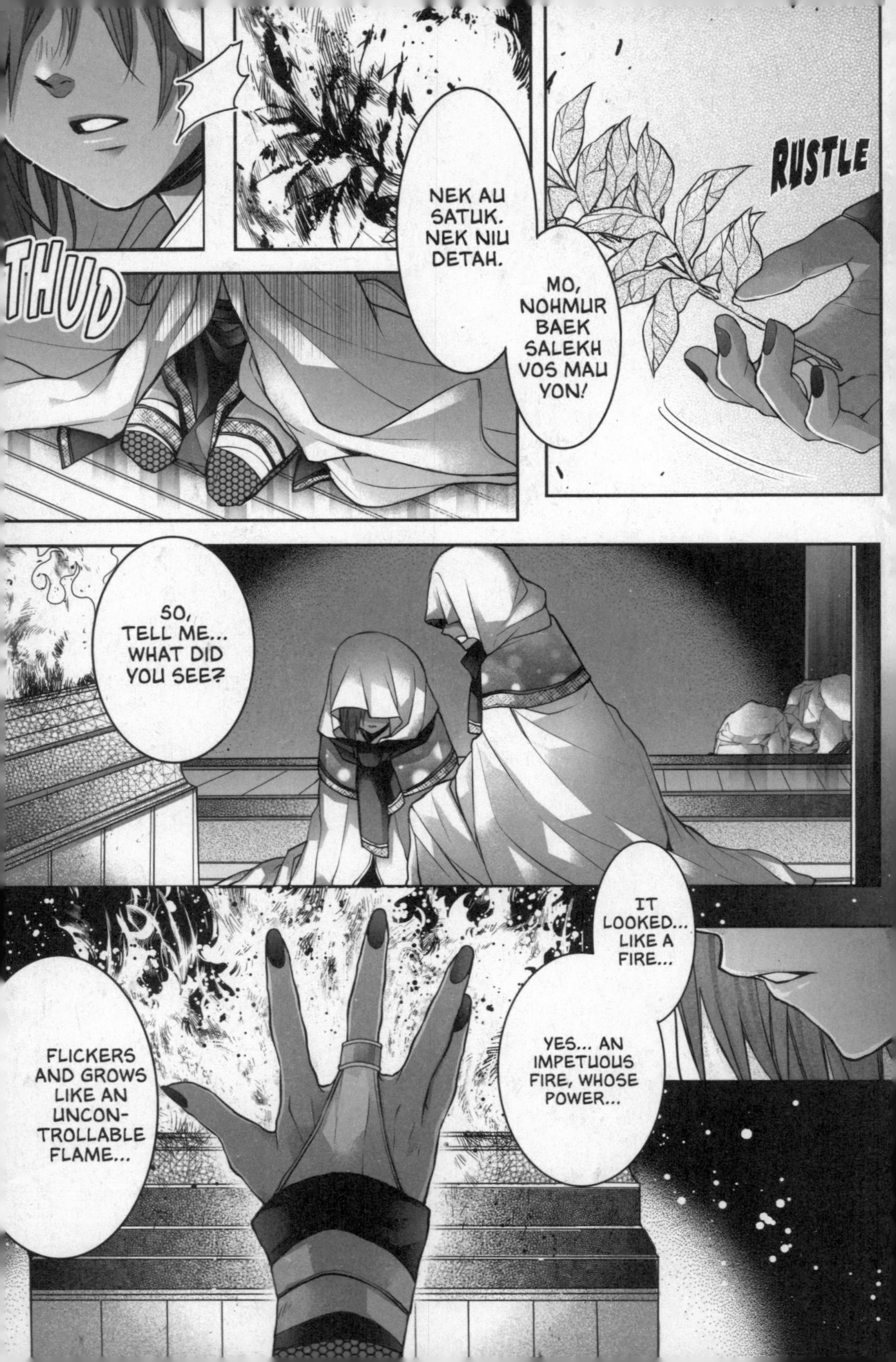
RUSTLE
NEK AU SATUK. NEK NIU DETAH.
MO, NOHMUR BAEK SALEKH VOS MAU YON!
THUD
SO, TELL ME... WHAT DID YOU SEE?
IT LOOKED... LIKE A FIRE...
YES... AN IMPETUOUS FIRE, WHOSE POWER...
FLICKERS AND GROWS LIKE AN UNCON-TROLLABLE FLAME...

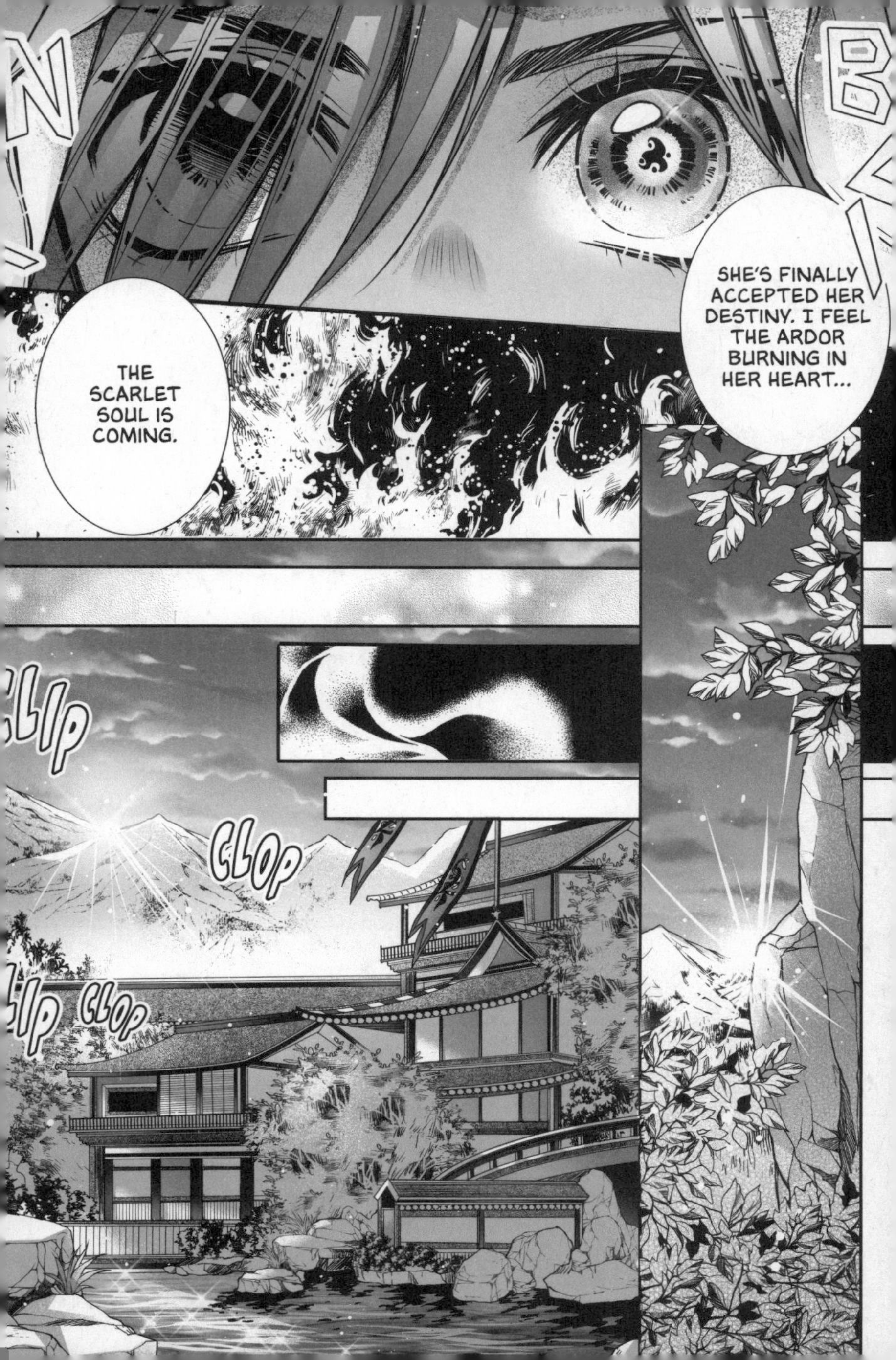
B
N
SHE'S FINALLY ACCEPTED HER DESTINY. I FEEL THE ARDOR BURNING IN HER HEART...
THE SCARLET SOUL IS COMING.
CLOP
CLIP
CLIP CLOP

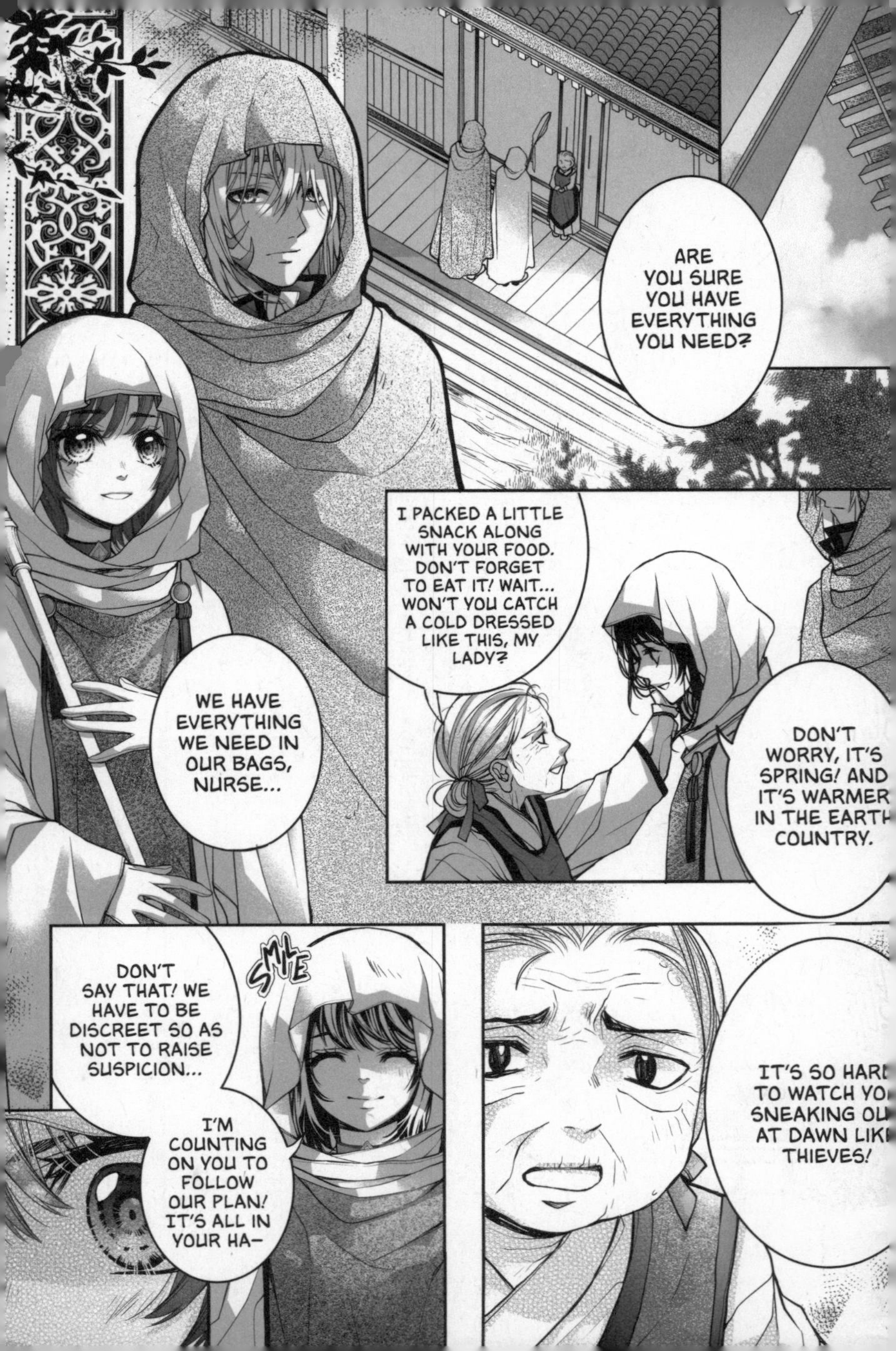
ARE YOU SURE YOU HAVE EVERYTHING YOU NEED?
WE HAVE EVERYTHING WE NEED IN OUR BAGS, NURSE...
I PACKED A LITTLE SNACK ALONG WITH YOUR FOOD. DON'T FORGET TO EAT IT! WAIT... WON'T YOU CATCH A COLD DRESSED LIKE THIS, MY LADY?
DON'T WORRY, IT'S SPRING! AND IT'S WARMER IN THE EARTH COUNTRY.
IT'S SO HARD TO WATCH YOU SNEAKING OUT AT DAWN LIKE THIEVES!
SMILE
DON'T SAY THAT! WE HAVE TO BE DISCREET SO AS NOT TO RAISE SUSPICION...
I'M COUNTING ON YOU TO FOLLOW OUR PLAN! IT'S ALL IN YOUR HA–

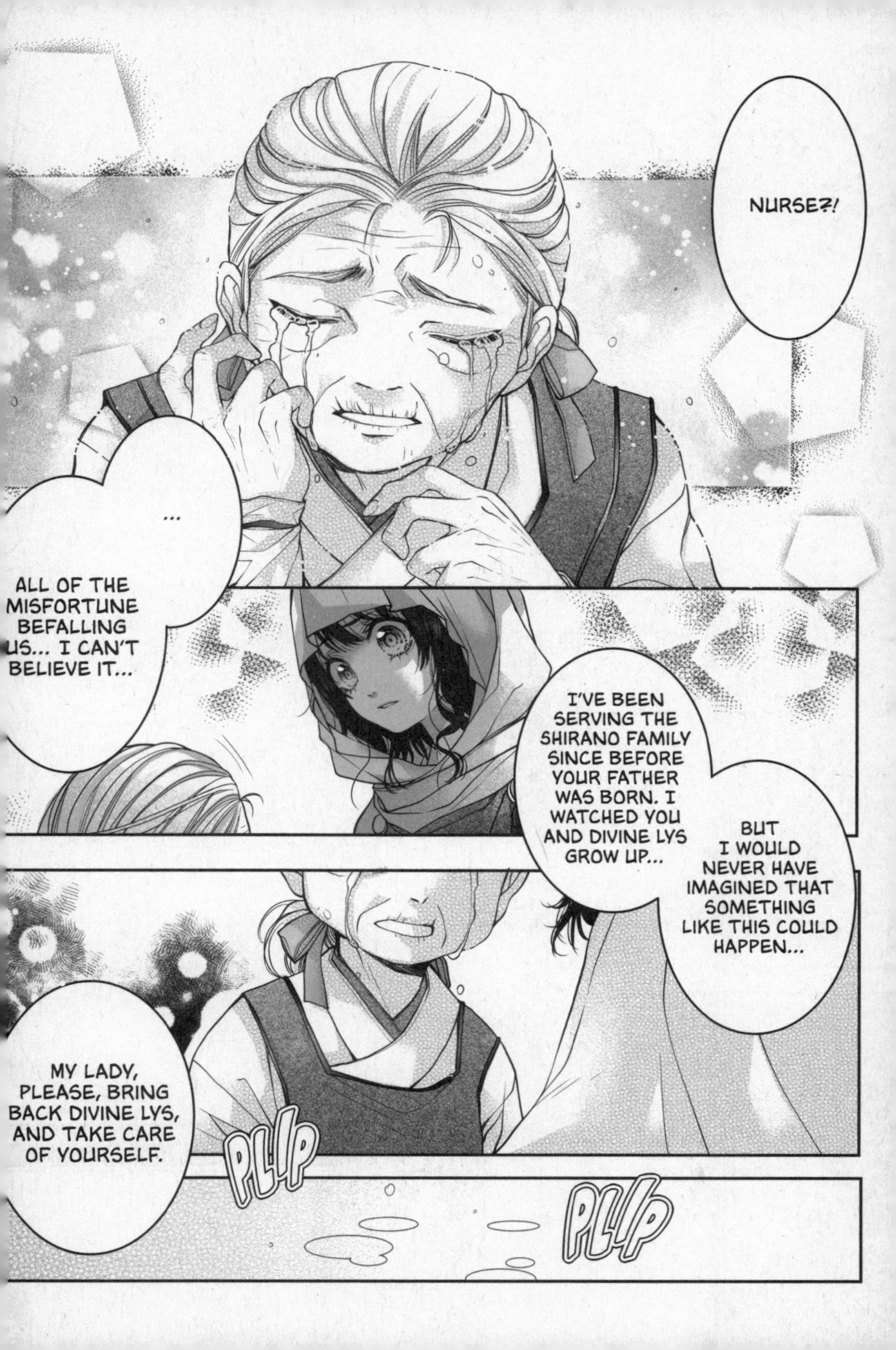
NURSE?!
...
ALL OF THE MISFORTUNE BEFALLING US... I CAN'T BELIEVE IT...
I'VE BEEN SERVING THE SHIRANO FAMILY SINCE BEFORE YOUR FATHER WAS BORN. I WATCHED YOU AND DIVINE LYS GROW UP...
BUT I WOULD NEVER HAVE IMAGINED THAT SOMETHING LIKE THIS COULD HAPPEN...
MY LADY, PLEASE, BRING BACK DIVINE LYS, AND TAKE CARE OF YOURSELF.
PLIP
PLIP

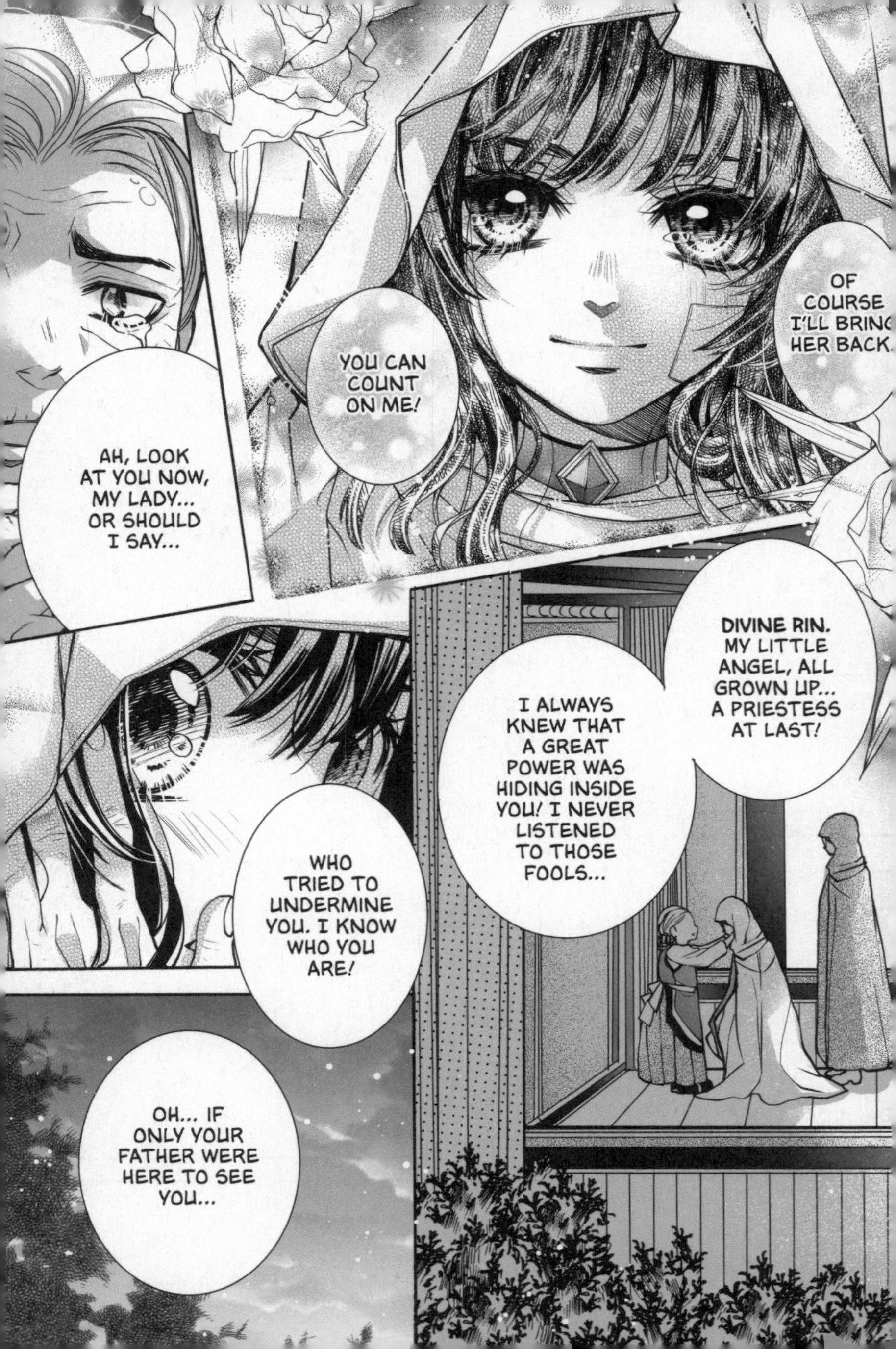
OF COURSE I'LL BRING HER BACK.
YOU CAN COUNT ON ME!
AH, LOOK AT YOU NOW, MY LADY... OR SHOULD I SAY...
DIVINE RIN. MY LITTLE ANGEL, ALL GROWN UP... A PRIESTESS AT LAST!
I ALWAYS KNEW THAT A GREAT POWER WAS HIDING INSIDE YOU! I NEVER LISTENED TO THOSE FOOLS...
WHO TRIED TO UNDERMINE YOU. I KNOW WHO YOU ARE!
OH... IF ONLY YOUR FATHER WERE HERE TO SEE YOU...

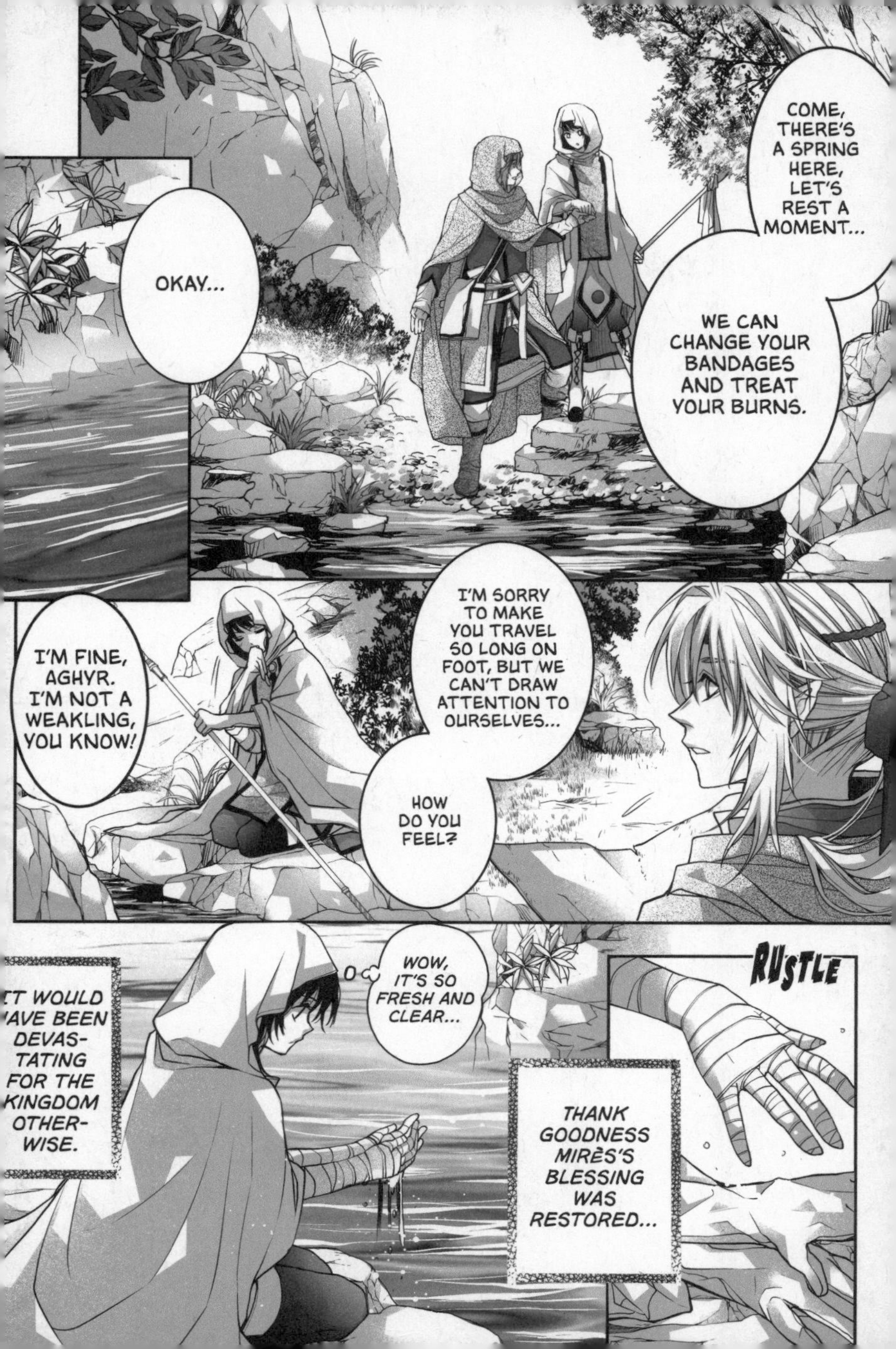
COME, THERE'S A SPRING HERE, LET'S REST A MOMENT...
WE CAN CHANGE YOUR BANDAGES AND TREAT YOUR BURNS.
OKAY...
I'M SORRY TO MAKE YOU TRAVEL SO LONG ON FOOT, BUT WE CAN'T DRAW ATTENTION TO OURSELVES...
HOW DO YOU FEEL?
I'M FINE, AGHYR. I'M NOT A WEAKLING, YOU KNOW!
RUSTLE
THANK GOODNESS MIRÈS'S BLESSING WAS RESTORED...
WOW, IT'S SO FRESH AND CLEAR...
T WOULD AVE BEEN DEVAS-TATING FOR THE KINGDOM OTHER-WISE.

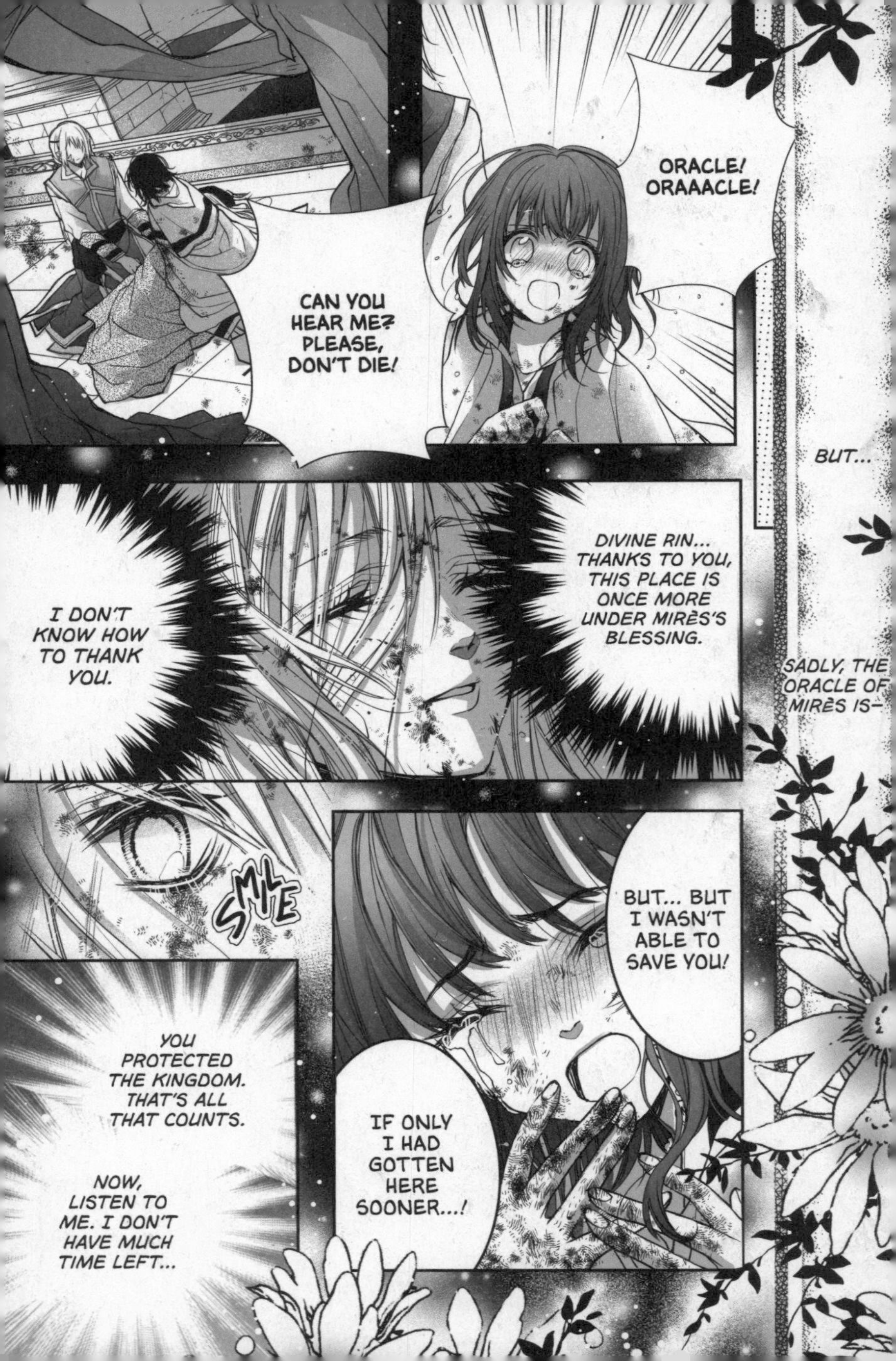

ORACLE! ORAAACLE!
CAN YOU HEAR ME? PLEASE, DON'T DIE!
BUT...
SADLY, THE ORACLE OF MIRÈS IS—
DIVINE RIN... THANKS TO YOU, THIS PLACE IS ONCE MORE UNDER MIRÈS'S BLESSING.
I DON'T KNOW HOW TO THANK YOU.
SMILE
BUT... BUT I WASN'T ABLE TO SAVE YOU!
IF ONLY I HAD GOTTEN HERE SOONER...!
YOU PROTECTED THE KINGDOM. THAT'S ALL THAT COUNTS.
NOW, LISTEN TO ME. I DON'T HAVE MUCH TIME LEFT...

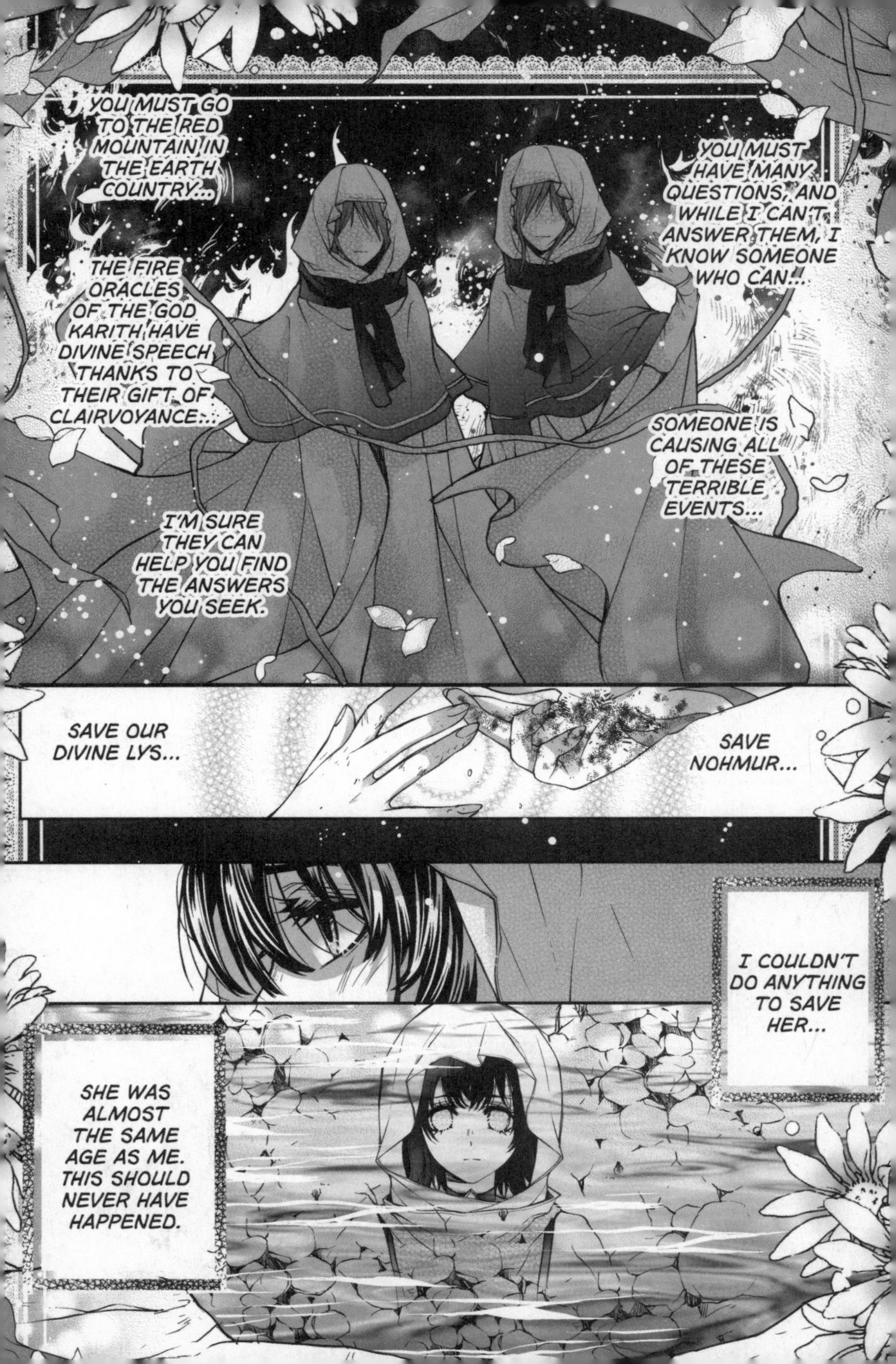
YOU MUST HAVE MANY QUESTIONS, AND WHILE I CAN'T ANSWER THEM, I KNOW SOMEONE WHO CAN...
SOMEONE IS CAUSING ALL OF THESE TERRIBLE EVENTS...
YOU MUST GO TO THE RED MOUNTAIN IN THE EARTH COUNTRY...
THE FIRE ORACLES OF THE GOD KARITH HAVE DIVINE SPEECH THANKS TO THEIR GIFT OF CLAIRVOYANCE...
I'M SURE THEY CAN HELP YOU FIND THE ANSWERS YOU SEEK.
SAVE NOHMUR...
SAVE OUR DIVINE LYS...
I COULDN'T DO ANYTHING TO SAVE HER...
SHE WAS ALMOST THE SAME AGE AS ME. THIS SHOULD NEVER HAVE HAPPENED.

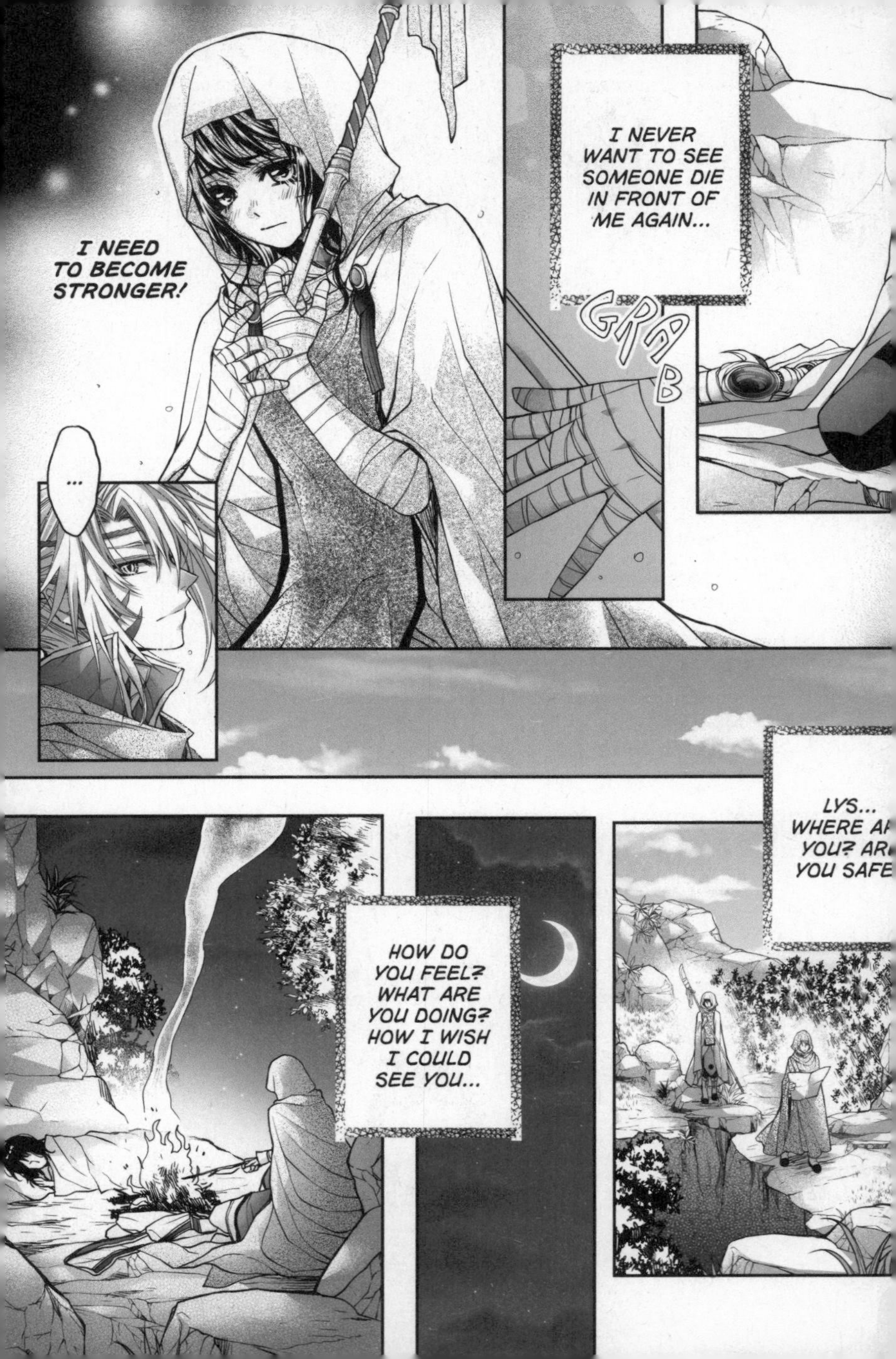
I NEVER WANT TO SEE SOMEONE DIE IN FRONT OF ME AGAIN...
GRAB
I NEED TO BECOME STRONGER!
...
LYS... WHERE AR YOU? AR YOU SAFE
HOW DO YOU FEEL? WHAT ARE YOU DOING? HOW I WISH I COULD SEE YOU...

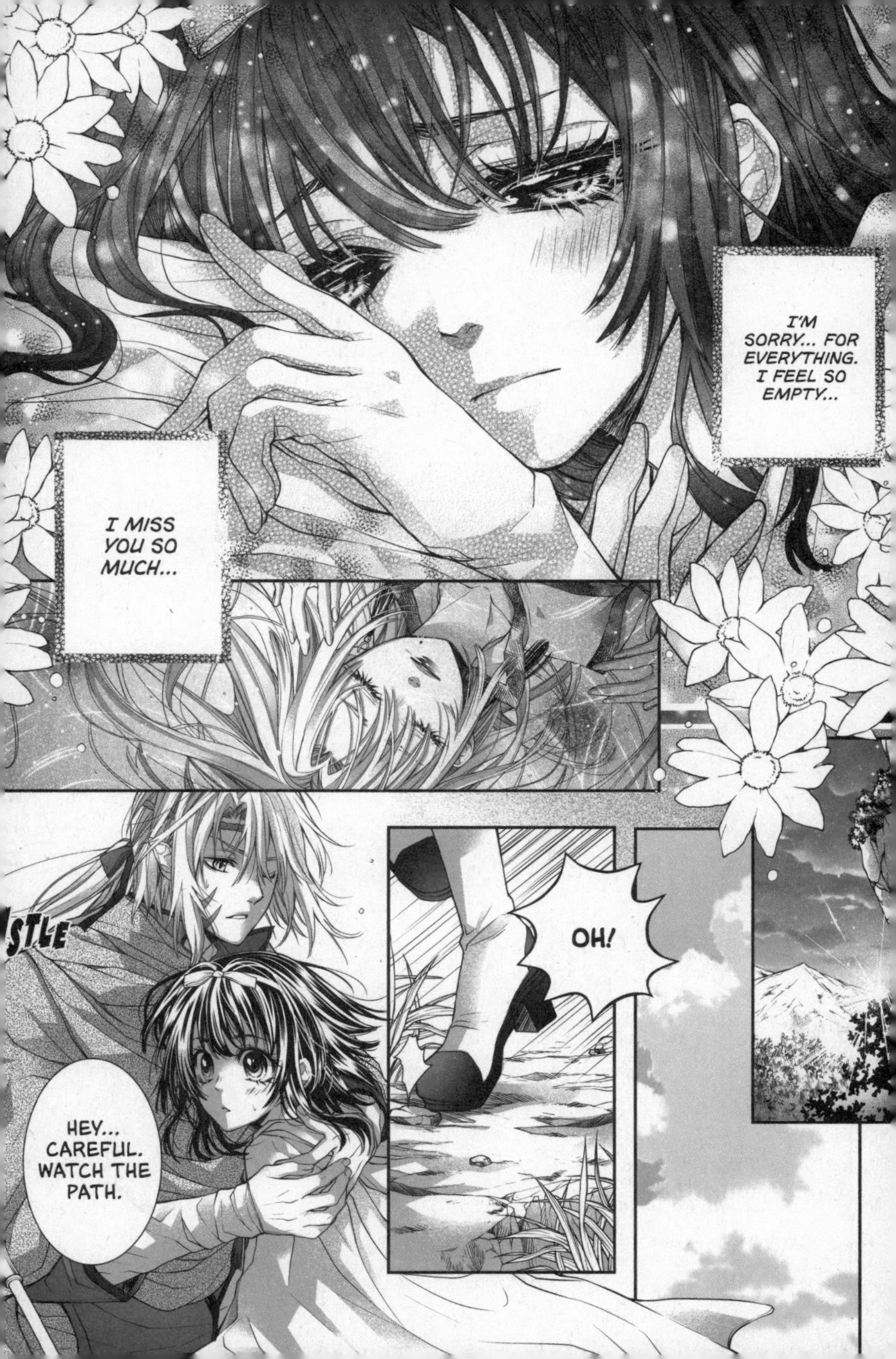
I'M SORRY... FOR EVERYTHING. I FEEL SO EMPTY...
I MISS YOU SO MUCH...
OH!
STLE
HEY... CAREFUL. WATCH THE PATH.

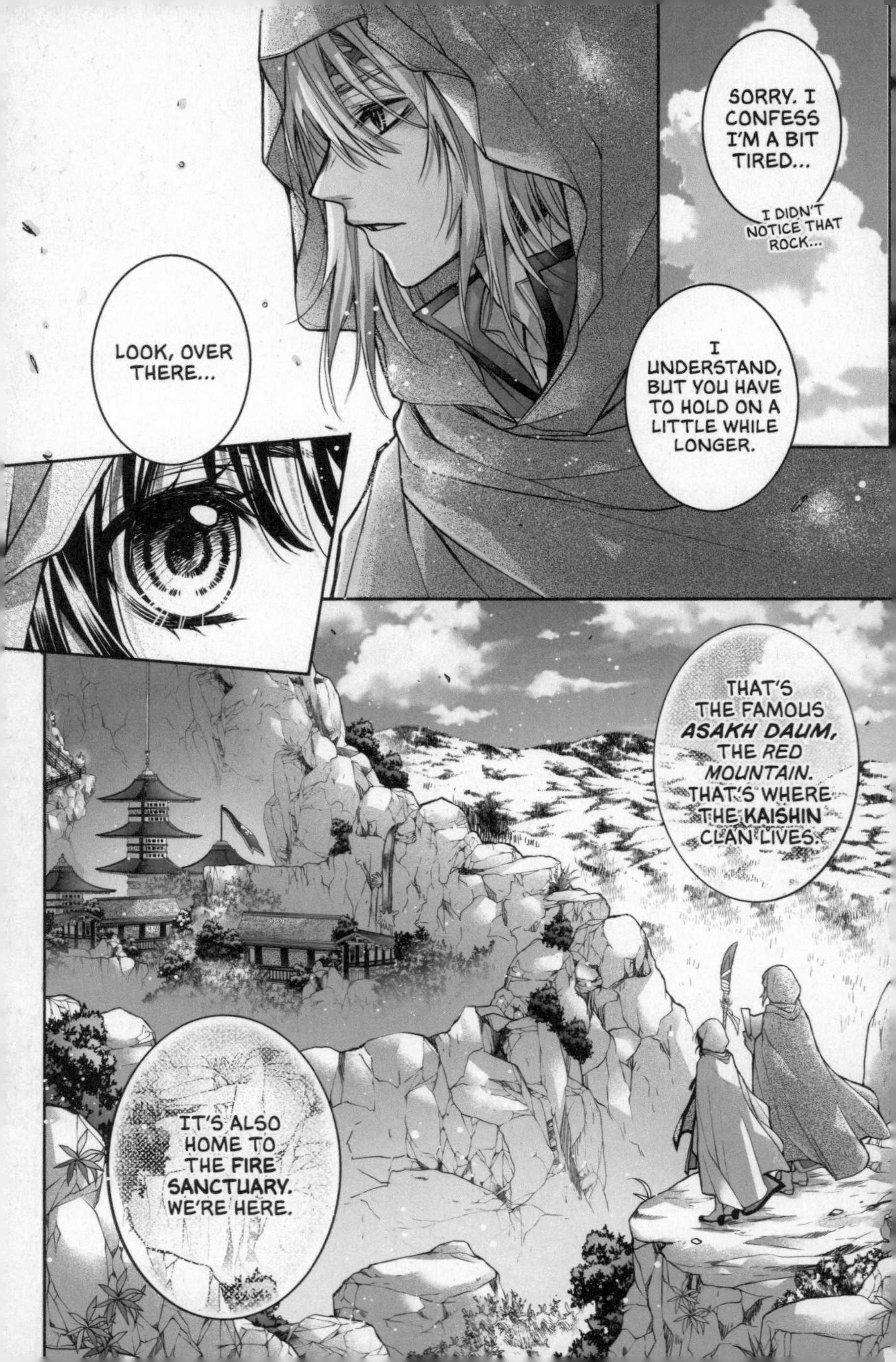
SORRY. I CONFESS I'M A BIT TIRED...
I DIDN'T NOTICE THAT ROCK...
I UNDERSTAND, BUT YOU HAVE TO HOLD ON A LITTLE WHILE LONGER.
LOOK, OVER THERE...
THAT'S THE FAMOUS *ASAKH DAUM*, THE *RED MOUNTAIN*. THAT'S WHERE THE KAISHIN CLAN LIVES.
IT'S ALSO HOME TO THE FIRE SANCTUARY. WE'RE HERE.

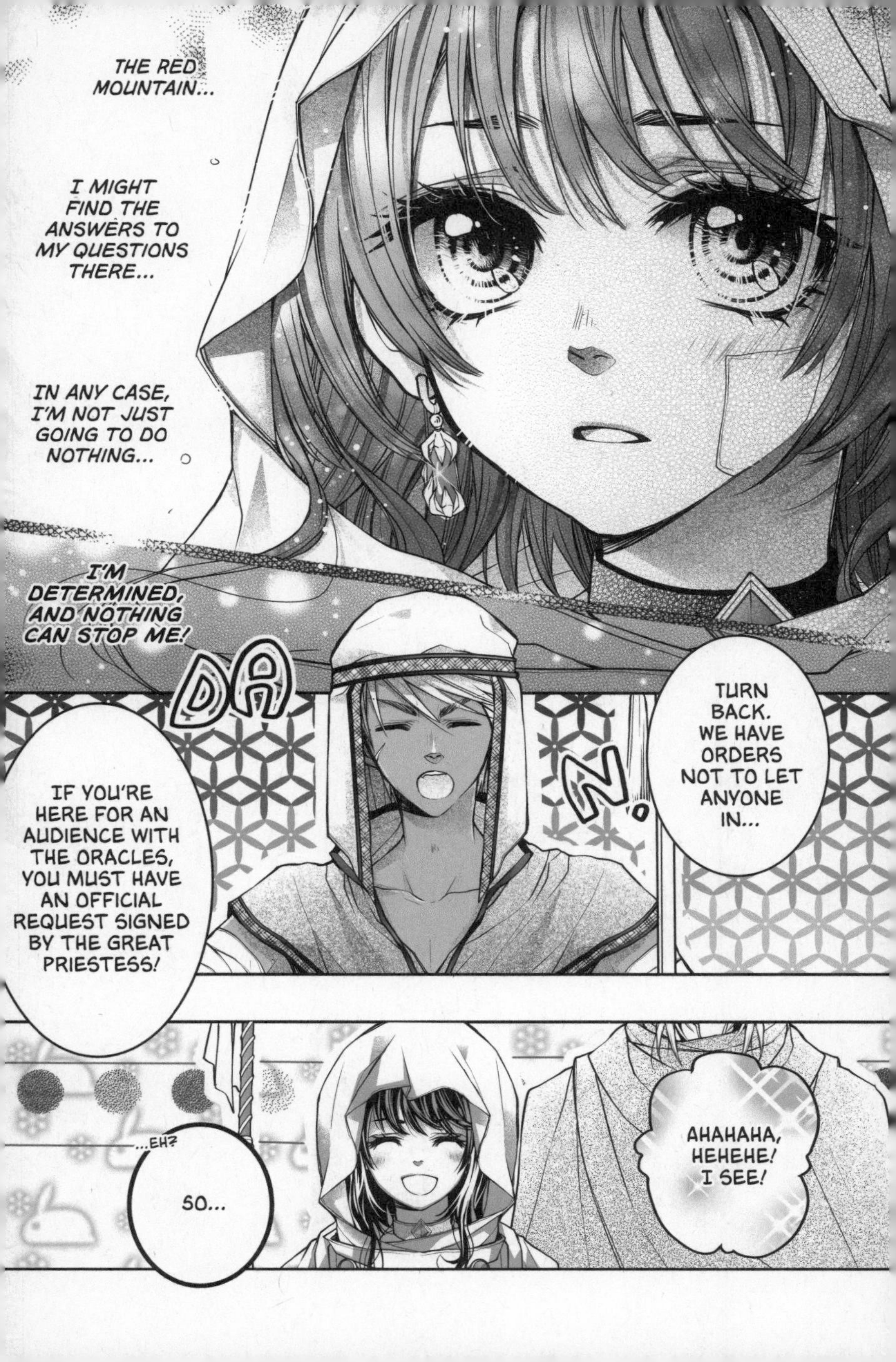
THE RED MOUNTAIN...
I MIGHT FIND THE ANSWERS TO MY QUESTIONS THERE...
IN ANY CASE, I'M NOT JUST GOING TO DO NOTHING...
I'M DETERMINED, AND NOTHING CAN STOP ME!
DA
N!
TURN BACK. WE HAVE ORDERS NOT TO LET ANYONE IN...
IF YOU'RE HERE FOR AN AUDIENCE WITH THE ORACLES, YOU MUST HAVE AN OFFICIAL REQUEST SIGNED BY THE GREAT PRIESTESS!
AHAHAHA, HEHEHE! I SEE!
...EH?
SO...

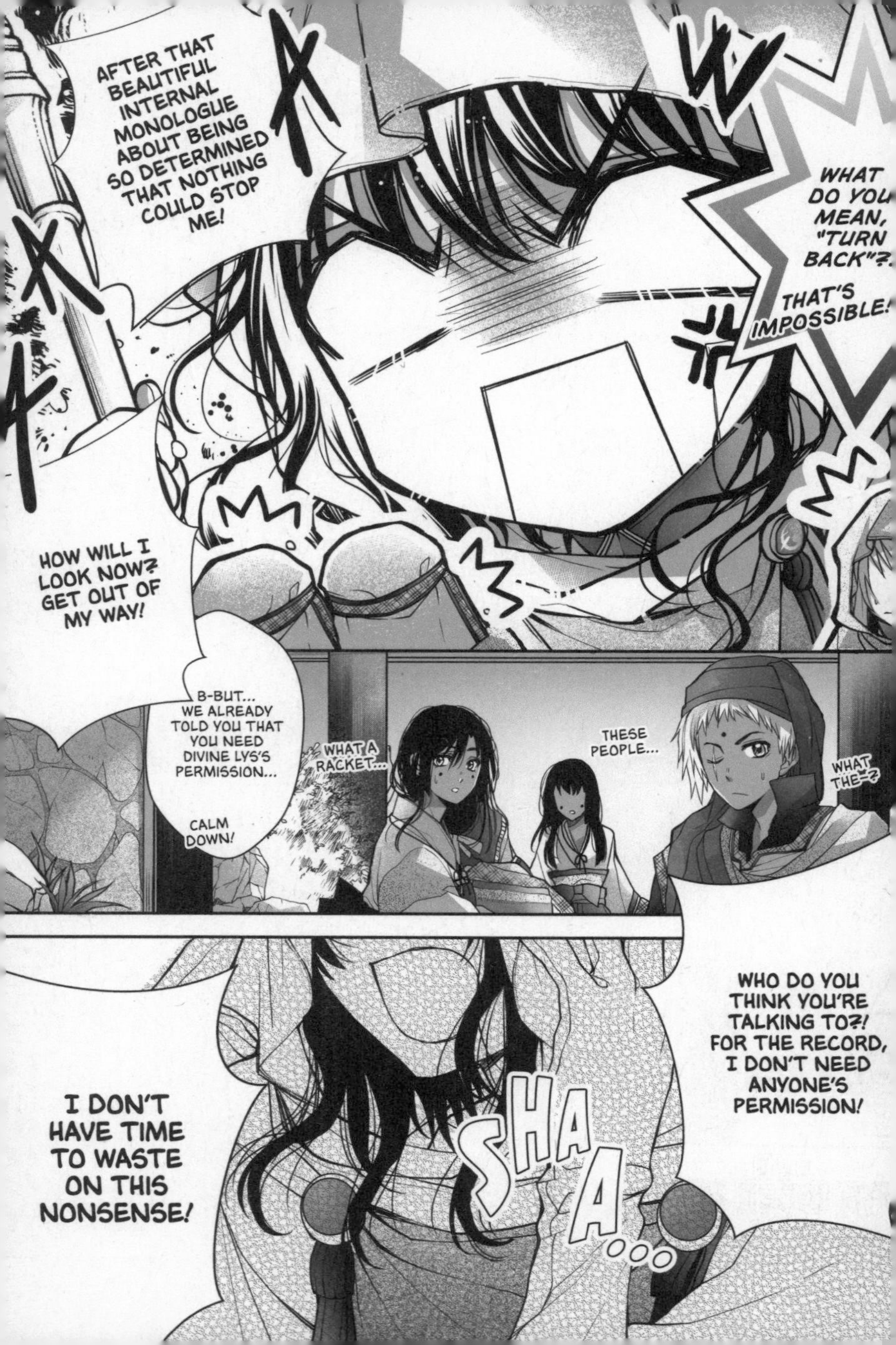
WHAT DO YOU MEAN, "TURN BACK"?! THAT'S IMPOSSIBLE!
AFTER THAT BEAUTIFUL INTERNAL MONOLOGUE ABOUT BEING SO DETERMINED THAT NOTHING COULD STOP ME!
HOW WILL I LOOK NOW?! GET OUT OF MY WAY!
WHAT THE-?!
THESE PEOPLE...
WHAT A RACKET...
B-BUT... WE ALREADY TOLD YOU THAT YOU NEED DIVINE LYS'S PERMISSION...
CALM DOWN!
WHO DO YOU THINK YOU'RE TALKING TO?! FOR THE RECORD, I DON'T NEED ANYONE'S PERMISSION!
SHAA...
I DON'T HAVE TIME TO WASTE ON THIS NONSENSE!

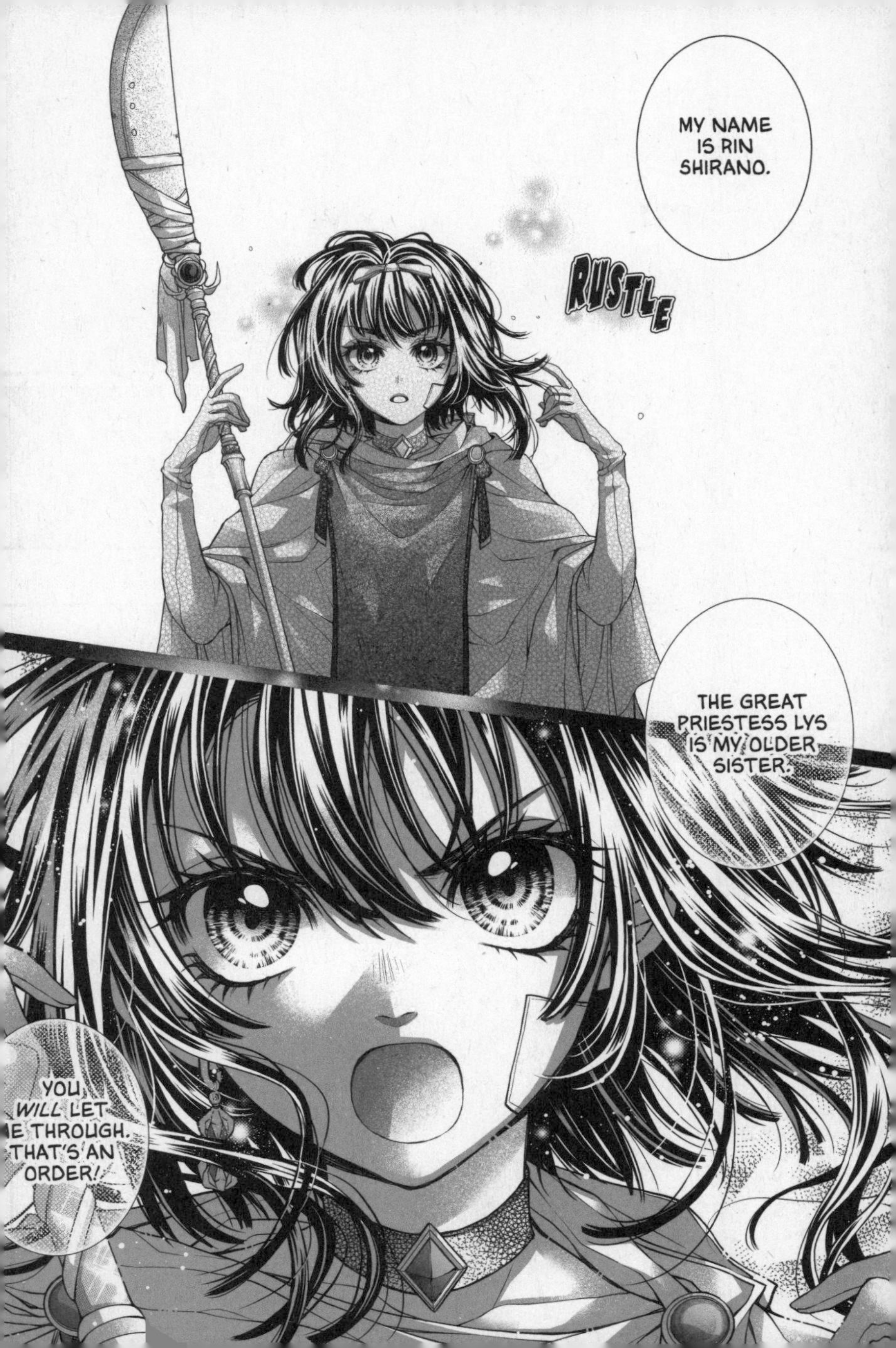
MY NAME IS RIN SHIRANO.
RUSTLE
THE GREAT PRIESTESS LYS IS MY OLDER SISTER.
YOU, WILL LET E THROUGH. THAT'S AN ORDER!

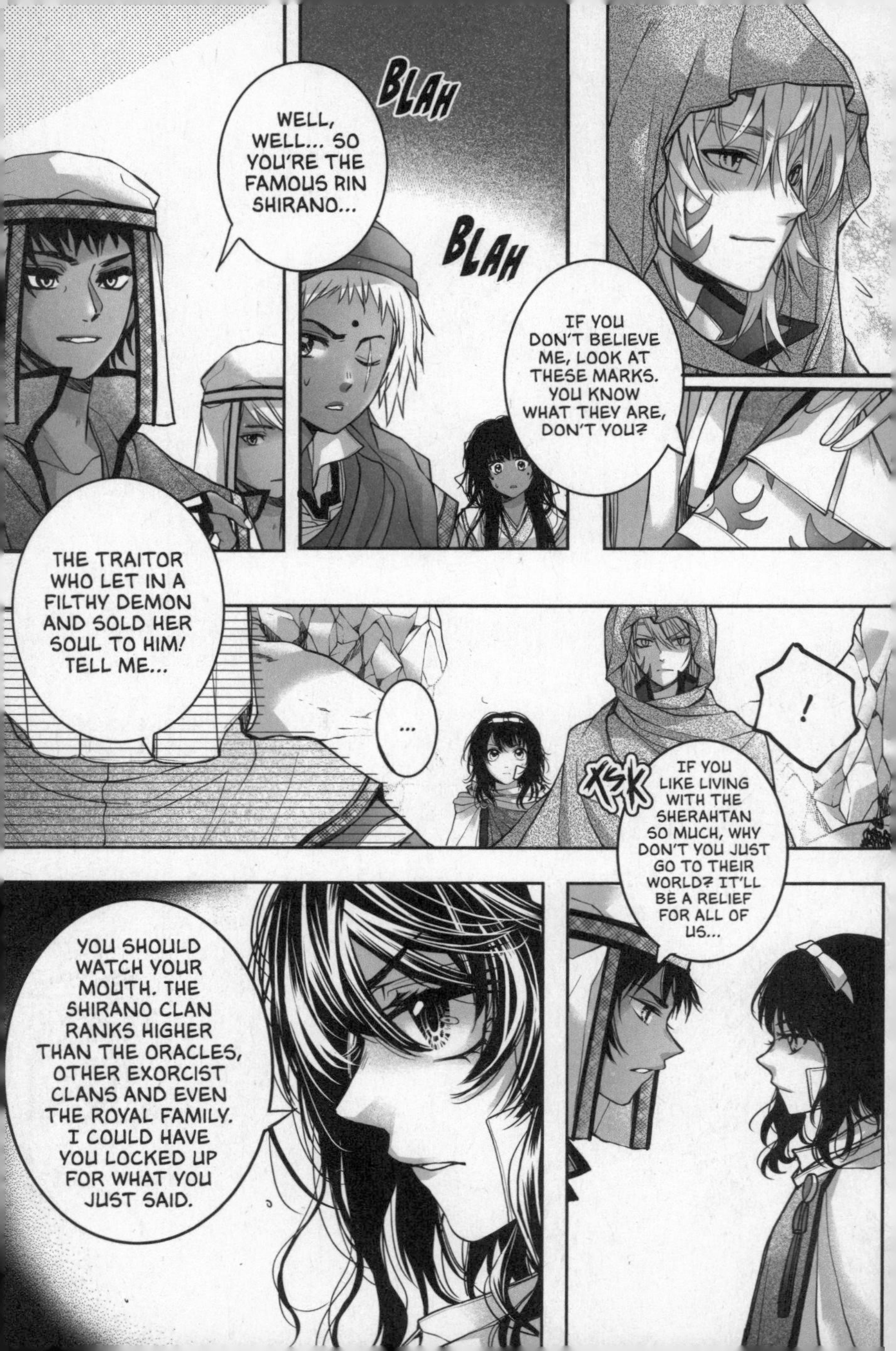

IF YOU DON'T BELIEVE ME, LOOK AT THESE MARKS. YOU KNOW WHAT THEY ARE, DON'T YOU?
BLAH
BLAH
WELL, WELL... SO YOU'RE THE FAMOUS RIN SHIRANO...
THE TRAITOR WHO LET IN A FILTHY DEMON AND SOLD HER SOUL TO HIM! TELL ME...
!
TSK
IF YOU LIKE LIVING WITH THE SHERAHTAN SO MUCH, WHY DON'T YOU JUST GO TO THEIR WORLD? IT'LL BE A RELIEF FOR ALL OF US...
...
YOU SHOULD WATCH YOUR MOUTH. THE SHIRANO CLAN RANKS HIGHER THAN THE ORACLES, OTHER EXORCIST CLANS AND EVEN THE ROYAL FAMILY. I COULD HAVE YOU LOCKED UP FOR WHAT YOU JUST SAID.

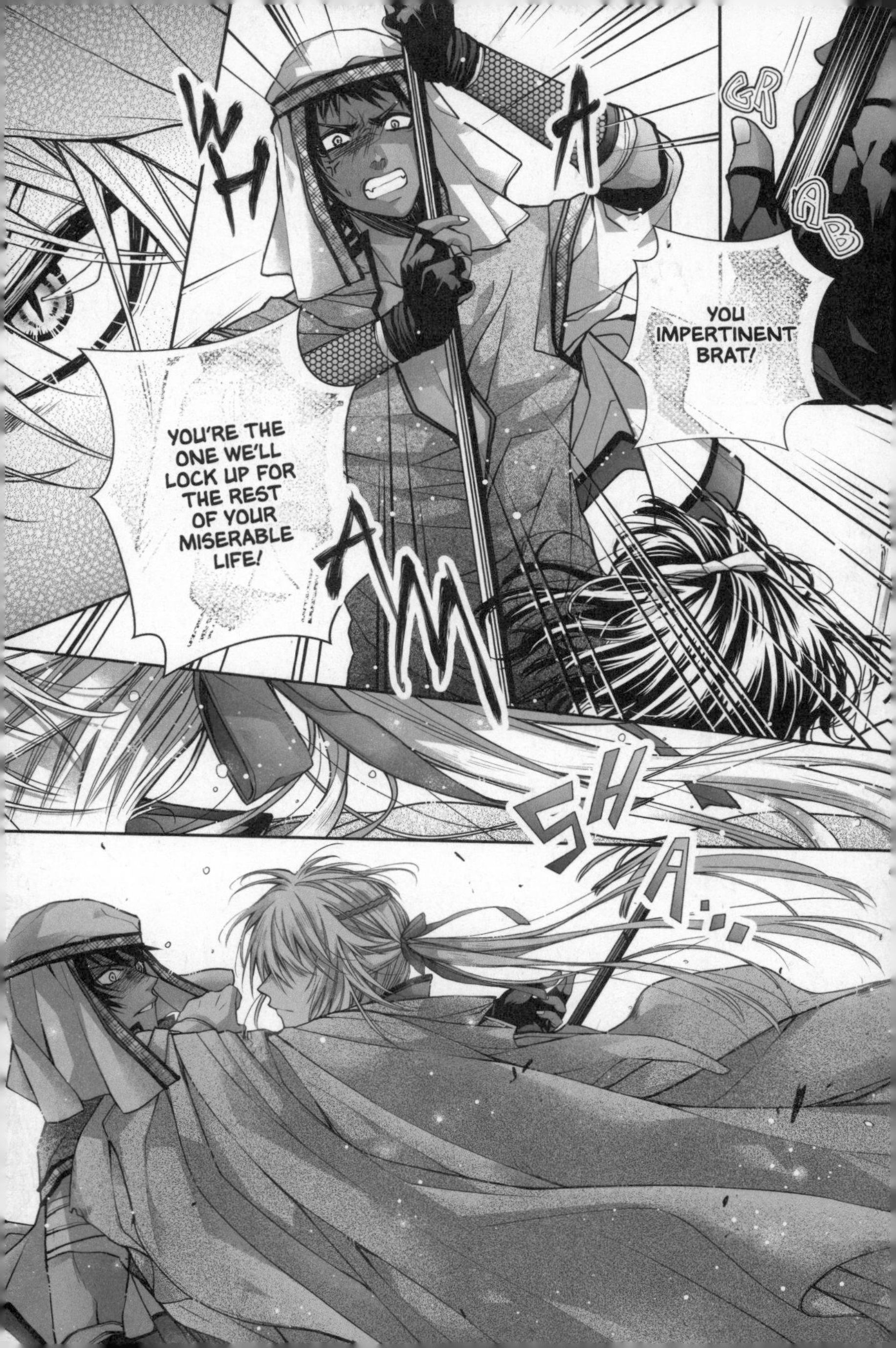
GRAB
YOU IMPERTINENT BRAT!
WHAAM
YOU'RE THE ONE WE'LL LOCK UP FOR THE REST OF YOUR MISERABLE LIFE!
SHA...

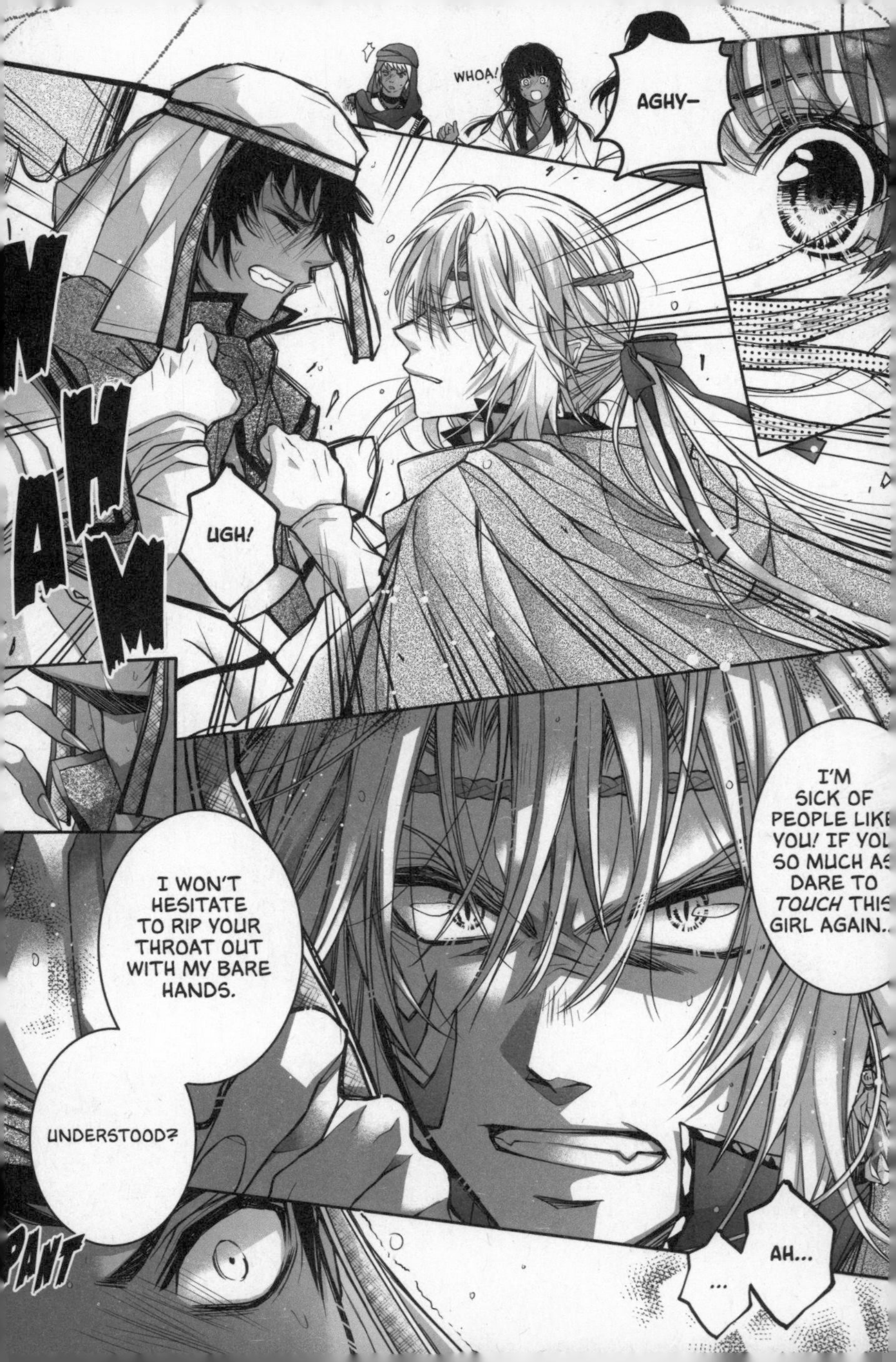
AGHY–
WHOA!
UGH!
I'M SICK OF PEOPLE LIKE YOU! IF YOU SO MUCH AS DARE TO *TOUCH* THIS GIRL AGAIN...
I WON'T HESITATE TO RIP YOUR THROAT OUT WITH MY BARE HANDS.
UNDERSTOOD?
AH...
...
PANT

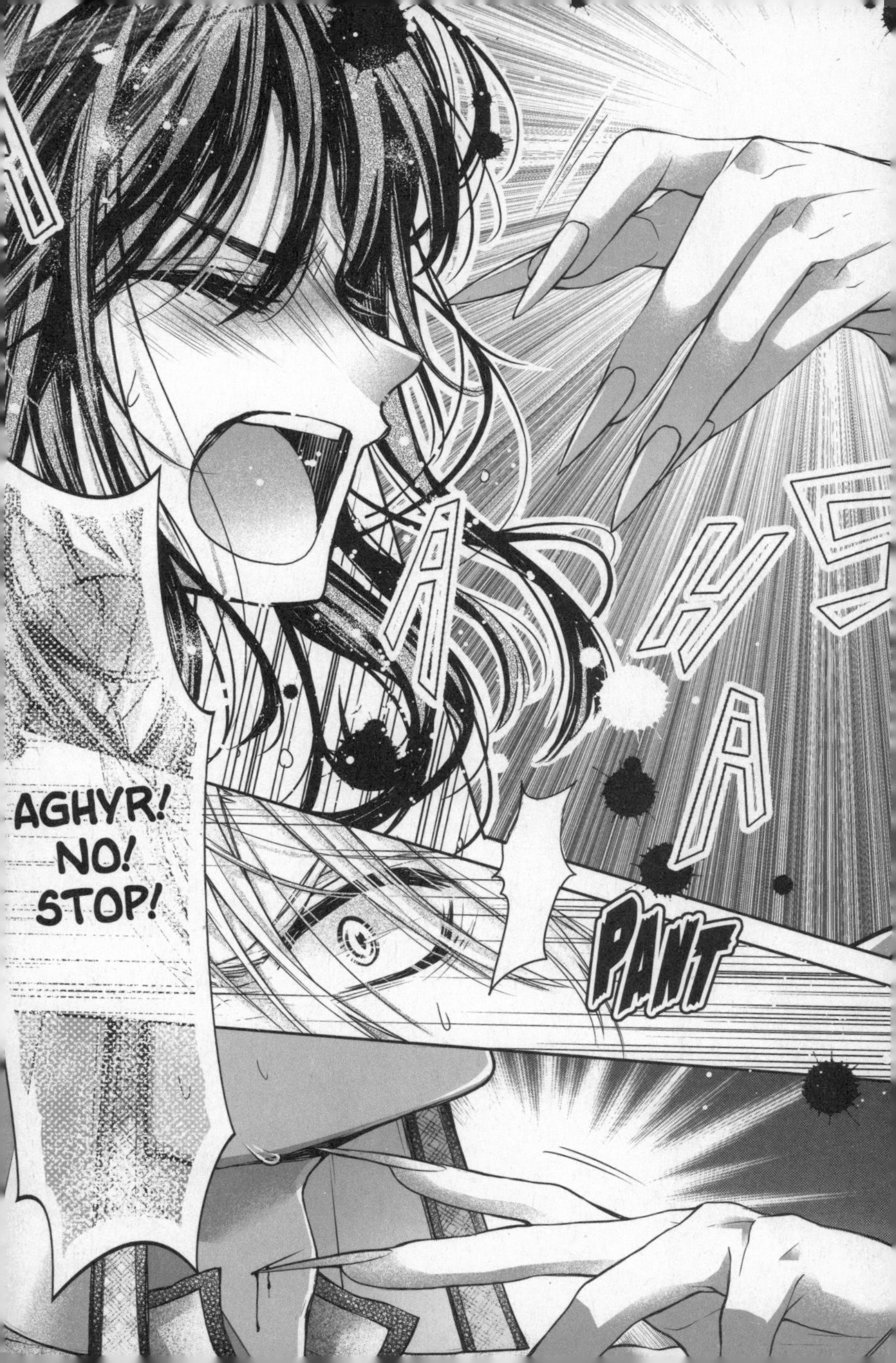
AGHYR! NO! STOP!
PANT

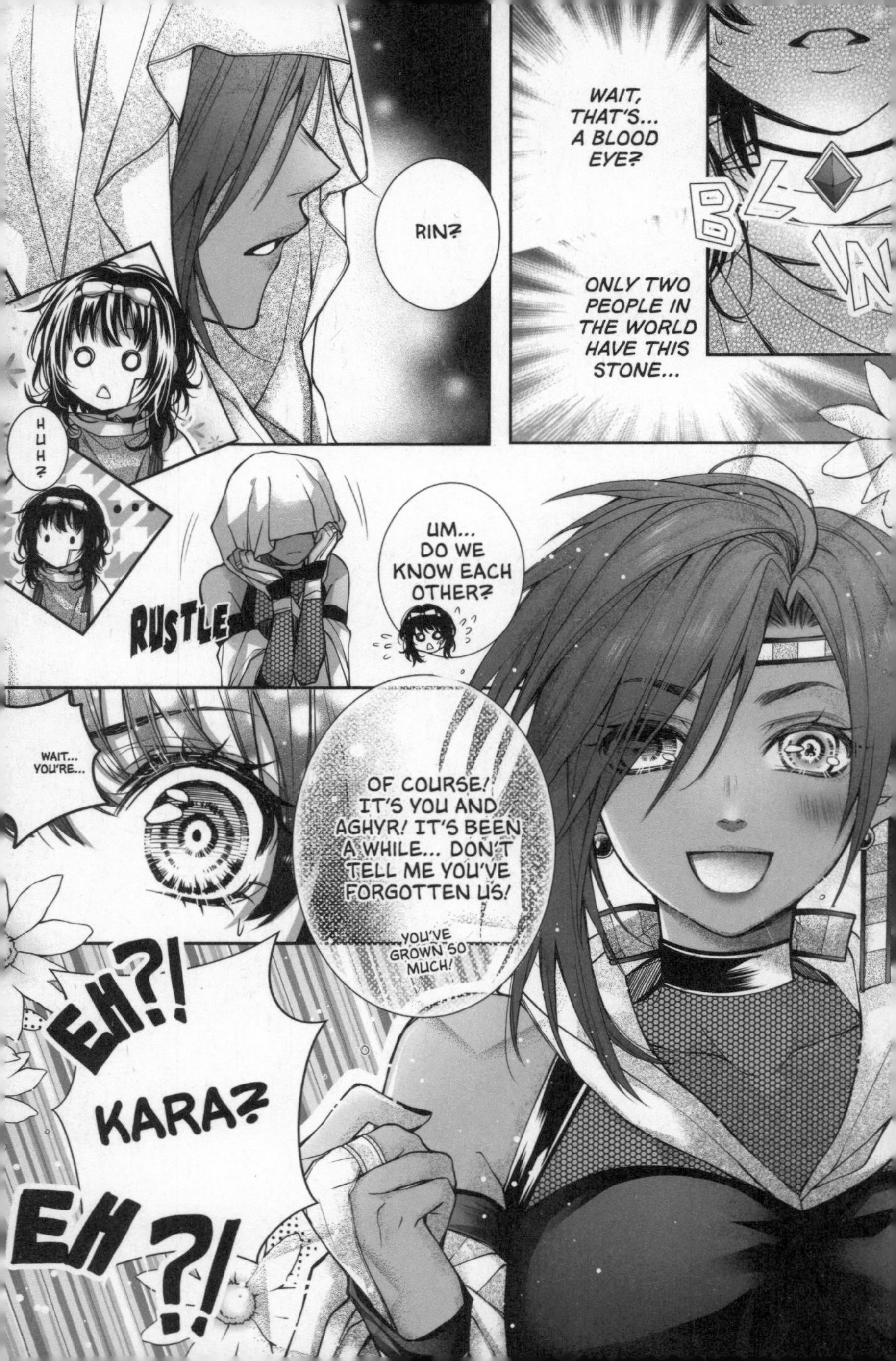
WAIT, THAT'S... A BLOOD EYE?
BLIN
ONLY TWO PEOPLE IN THE WORLD HAVE THIS STONE...
RIN?
HUH?
UM... DO WE KNOW EACH OTHER?
RUSTLE
...
OF COURSE! IT'S YOU AND AGHYR! IT'S BEEN A WHILE... DON'T TELL ME YOU'VE FORGOTTEN US!
YOU'VE GROWN SO MUCH!
WAIT... YOU'RE...
EH?!
KARA?
EH?!

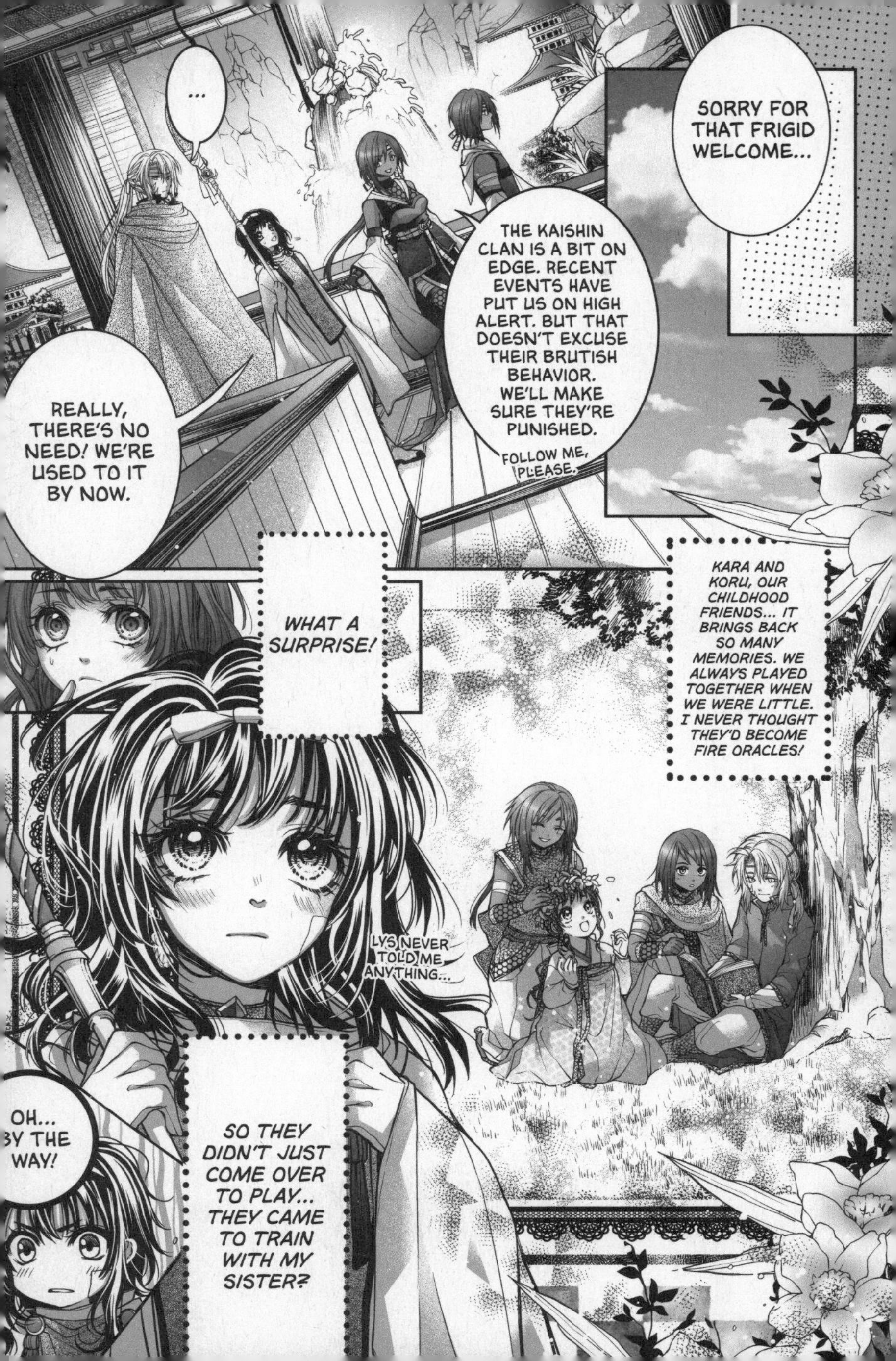
SORRY FOR THAT FRIGID WELCOME...
THE KAISHIN CLAN IS A BIT ON EDGE. RECENT EVENTS HAVE PUT US ON HIGH ALERT. BUT THAT DOESN'T EXCUSE THEIR BRUTISH BEHAVIOR. WE'LL MAKE SURE THEY'RE PUNISHED.
FOLLOW ME, PLEASE.
...
REALLY, THERE'S NO NEED! WE'RE USED TO IT BY NOW.
KARA AND KORU, OUR CHILDHOOD FRIENDS... IT BRINGS BACK SO MANY MEMORIES. WE ALWAYS PLAYED TOGETHER WHEN WE WERE LITTLE. I NEVER THOUGHT THEY'D BECOME FIRE ORACLES!
WHAT A SURPRISE!
LYS NEVER TOLD ME ANYTHING...
SO THEY DIDN'T JUST COME OVER TO PLAY... THEY CAME TO TRAIN WITH MY SISTER?
OH... BY THE WAY!

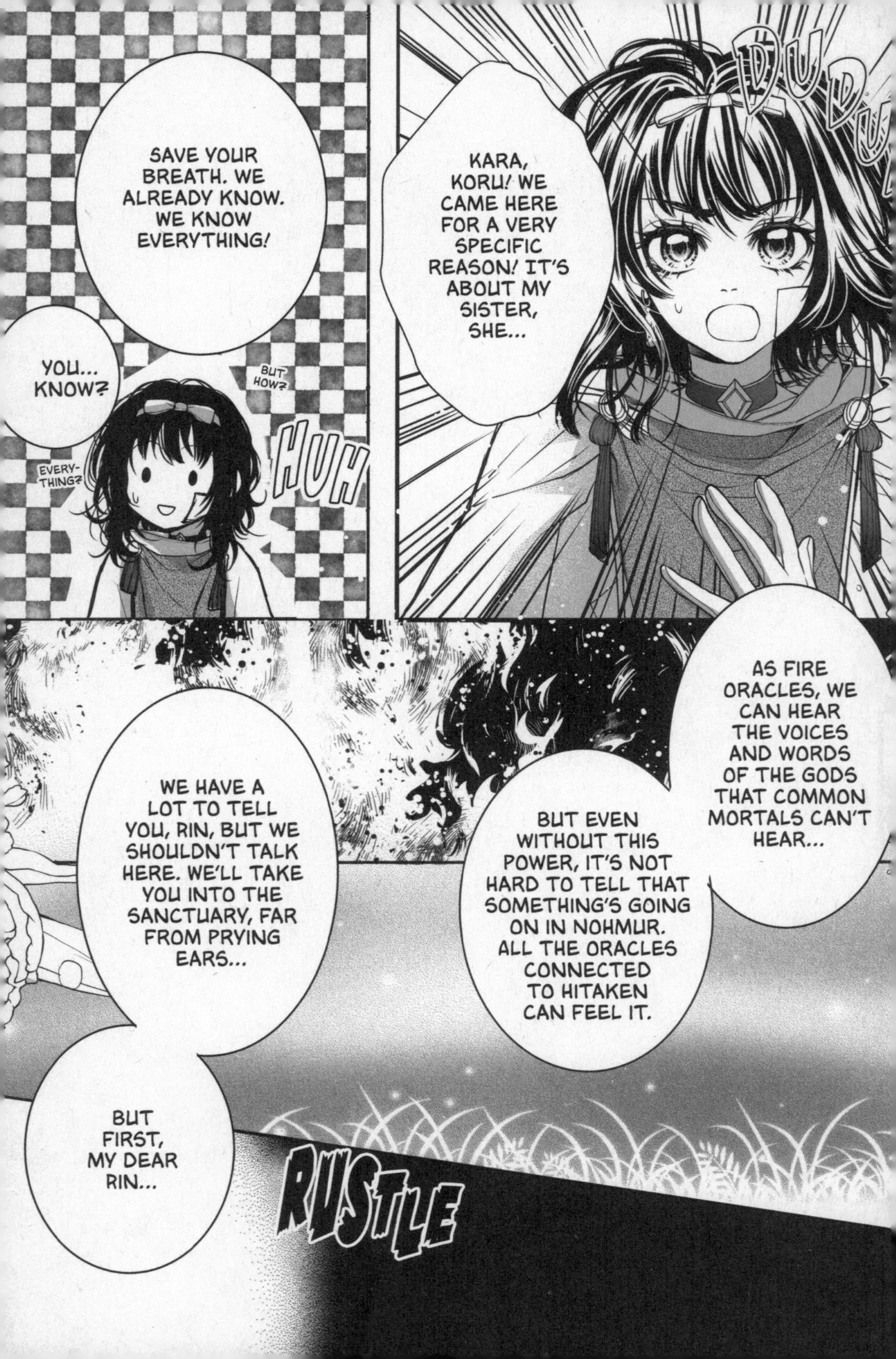
DUDU
KARA, KORU! WE CAME HERE FOR A VERY SPECIFIC REASON! IT'S ABOUT MY SISTER, SHE...
SAVE YOUR BREATH. WE ALREADY KNOW. WE KNOW EVERYTHING!
BUT HOW?
HUH
YOU... KNOW?
EVERY-THING?
AS FIRE ORACLES, WE CAN HEAR THE VOICES AND WORDS OF THE GODS THAT COMMON MORTALS CAN'T HEAR...
BUT EVEN WITHOUT THIS POWER, IT'S NOT HARD TO TELL THAT SOMETHING'S GOING ON IN NOHMUR. ALL THE ORACLES CONNECTED TO HITAKEN CAN FEEL IT.
WE HAVE A LOT TO TELL YOU, RIN, BUT WE SHOULDN'T TALK HERE. WE'LL TAKE YOU INTO THE SANCTUARY, FAR FROM PRYING EARS...
BUT FIRST, MY DEAR RIN...
RUSTLE

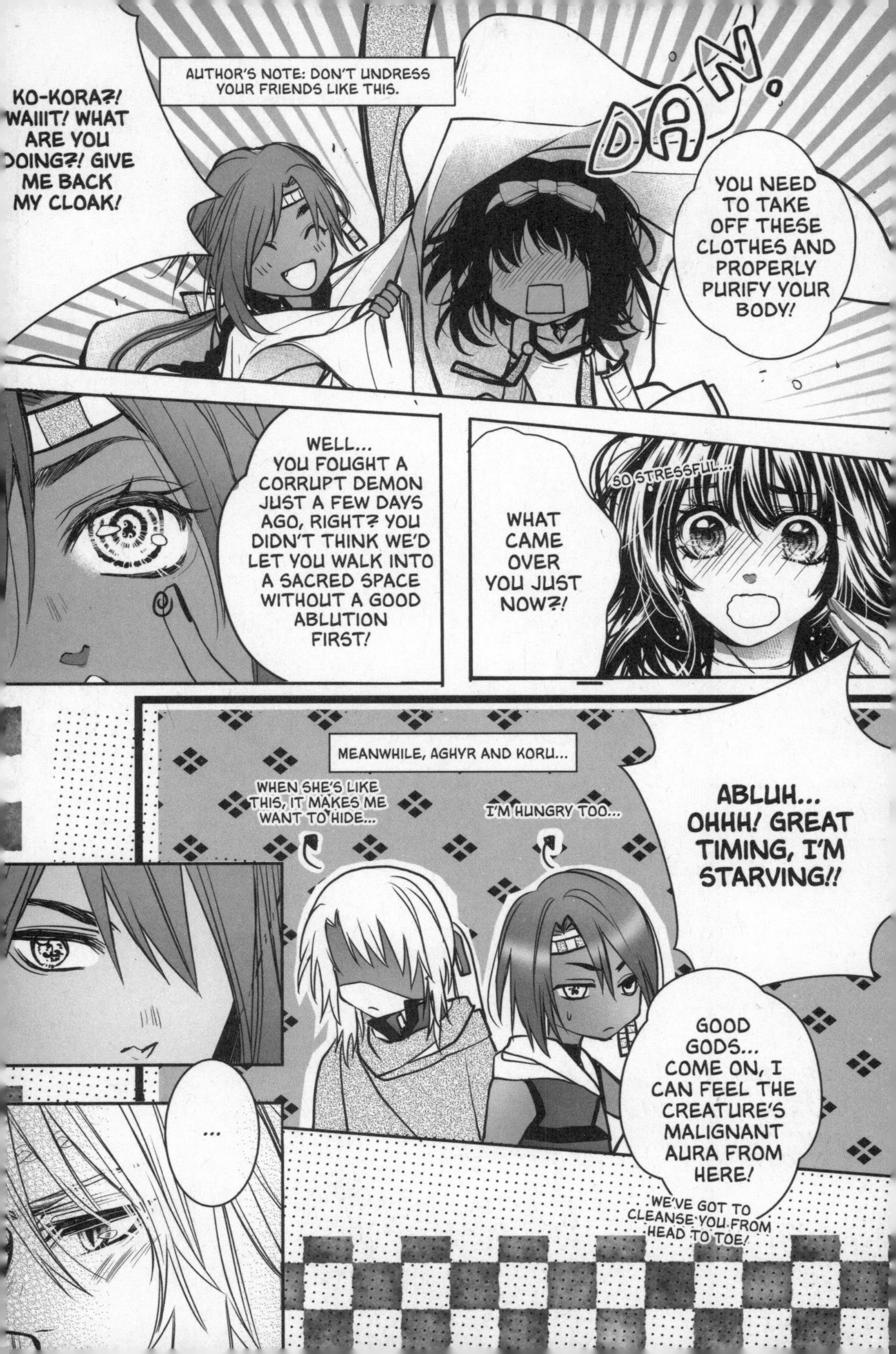

AUTHOR'S NOTE: DON'T UNDRESS YOUR FRIENDS LIKE THIS.
DAN.
YOU NEED TO TAKE OFF THESE CLOTHES AND PROPERLY PURIFY YOUR BODY!
KO-KORA?! WAIIIT! WHAT ARE YOU DOING?! GIVE ME BACK MY CLOAK!
SO STRESSFUL...
WHAT CAME OVER YOU JUST NOW?!
WELL... YOU FOUGHT A CORRUPT DEMON JUST A FEW DAYS AGO, RIGHT? YOU DIDN'T THINK WE'D LET YOU WALK INTO A SACRED SPACE WITHOUT A GOOD ABLUTION FIRST!
ABLUH... OHHH! GREAT TIMING, I'M STARVING!!
GOOD GODS... COME ON, I CAN FEEL THE CREATURE'S MALIGNANT AURA FROM HERE!
WE'VE GOT TO CLEANSE YOU FROM HEAD TO TOE!
MEANWHILE, AGHYR AND KORU...
I'M HUNGRY TOO...
WHEN SHE'S LIKE THIS, IT MAKES ME WANT TO HIDE...
...

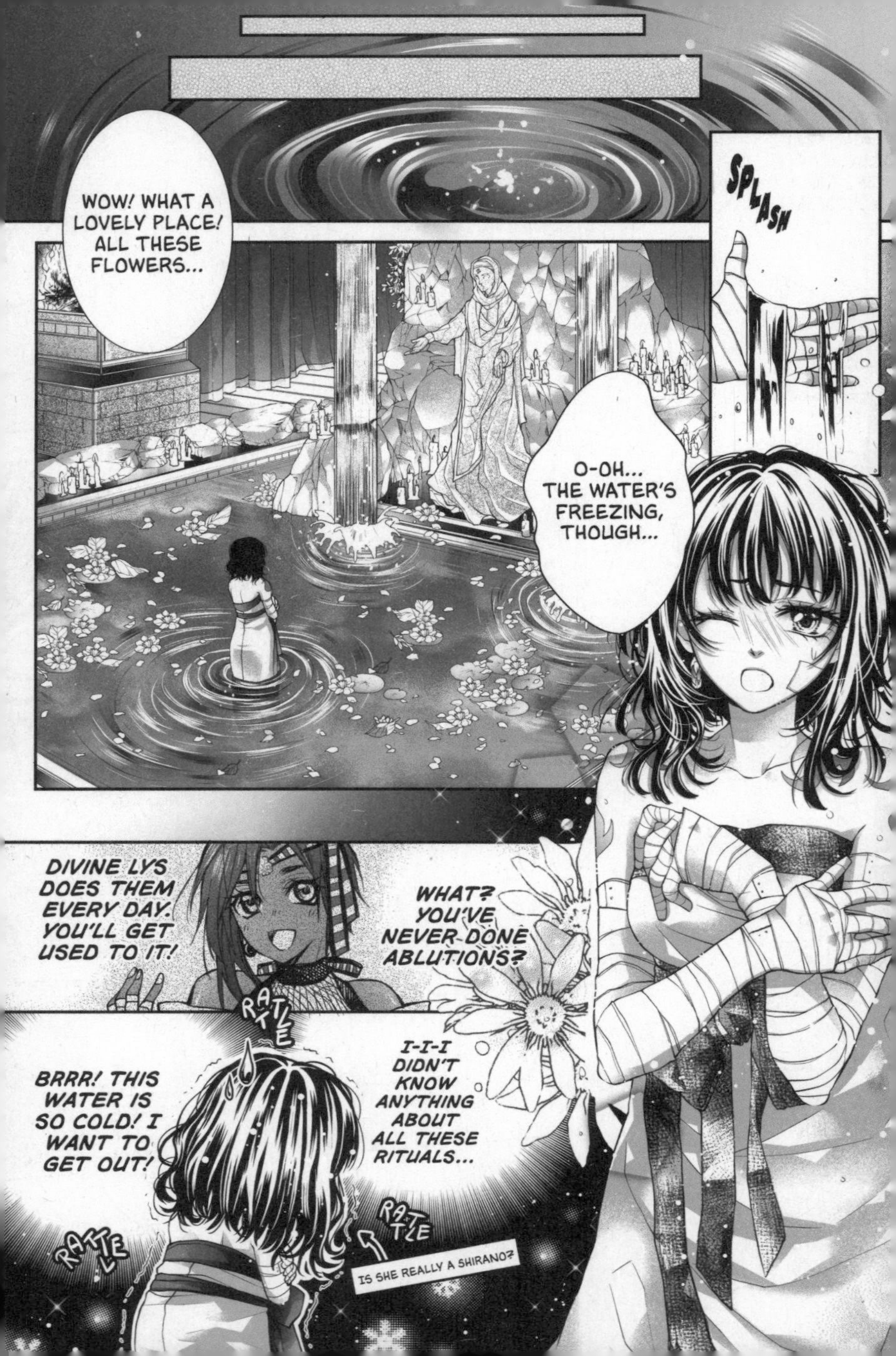
WOW! WHAT A LOVELY PLACE! ALL THESE FLOWERS...
SPLASH
O-OH... THE WATER'S FREEZING, THOUGH...
WHAT? YOU'VE NEVER DONE ABLUTIONS?
DIVINE LYS DOES THEM EVERY DAY. YOU'LL GET USED TO IT!
RATTLE
I-I-I DIDN'T KNOW ANYTHING ABOUT ALL THESE RITUALS...
BRRR! THIS WATER IS SO COLD! I WANT TO GET OUT!
RATTLE
RATTLE
IS SHE REALLY A SHIRANO?

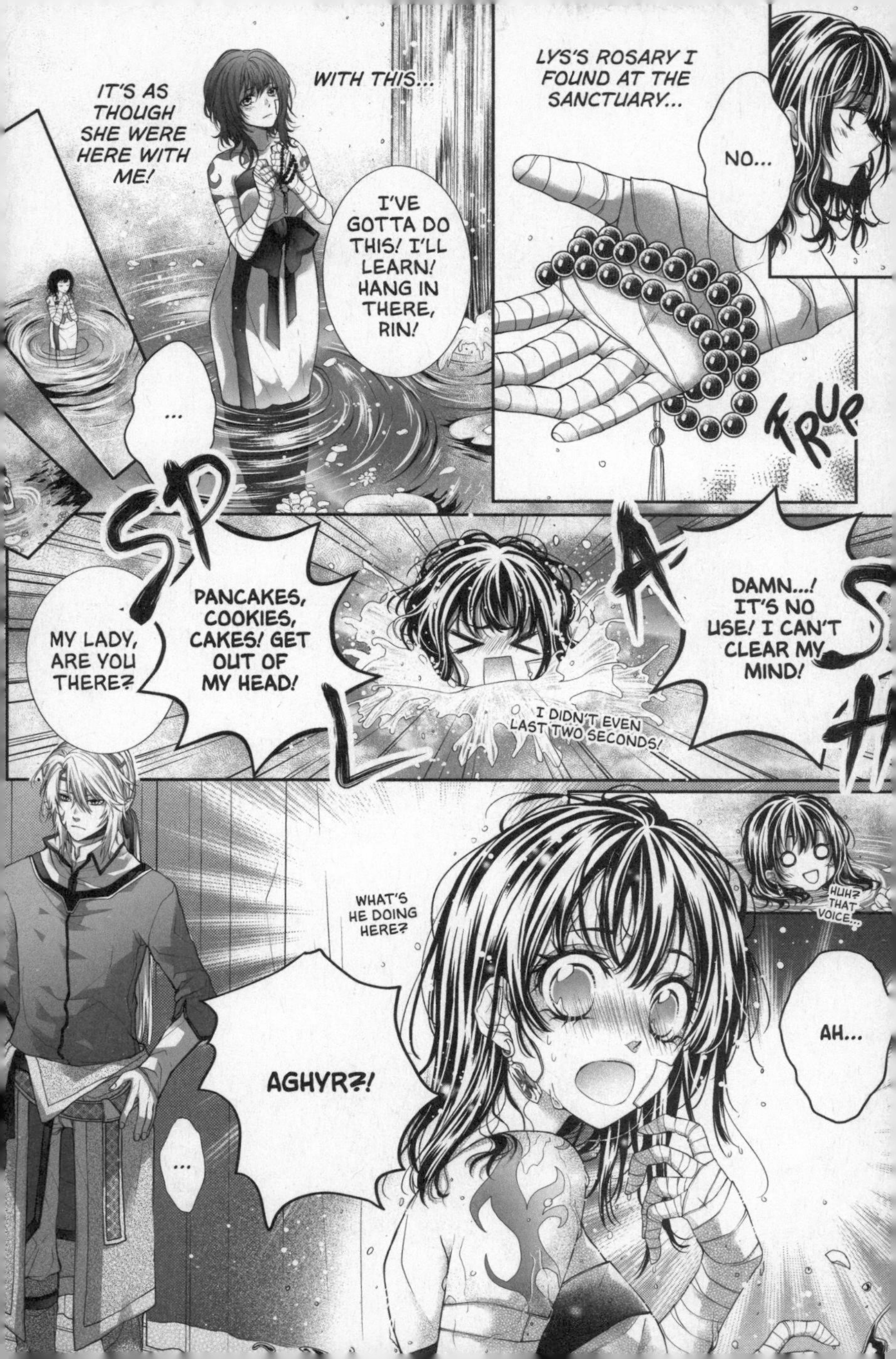
LYS'S ROSARY I FOUND AT THE SANCTUARY...
NO...
FRUP
WITH THIS...
IT'S AS THOUGH SHE WERE HERE WITH ME!
I'VE GOTTA DO THIS! I'LL LEARN! HANG IN THERE, RIN!
...
SPLASH
DAMN...! IT'S NO USE! I CAN'T CLEAR MY MIND!
I DIDN'T EVEN LAST TWO SECONDS!
PANCAKES, COOKIES, CAKES! GET OUT OF MY HEAD!
MY LADY, ARE YOU THERE?
HUH? THAT VOICE...
AH...
WHAT'S HE DOING HERE?
AGHYR?!
...

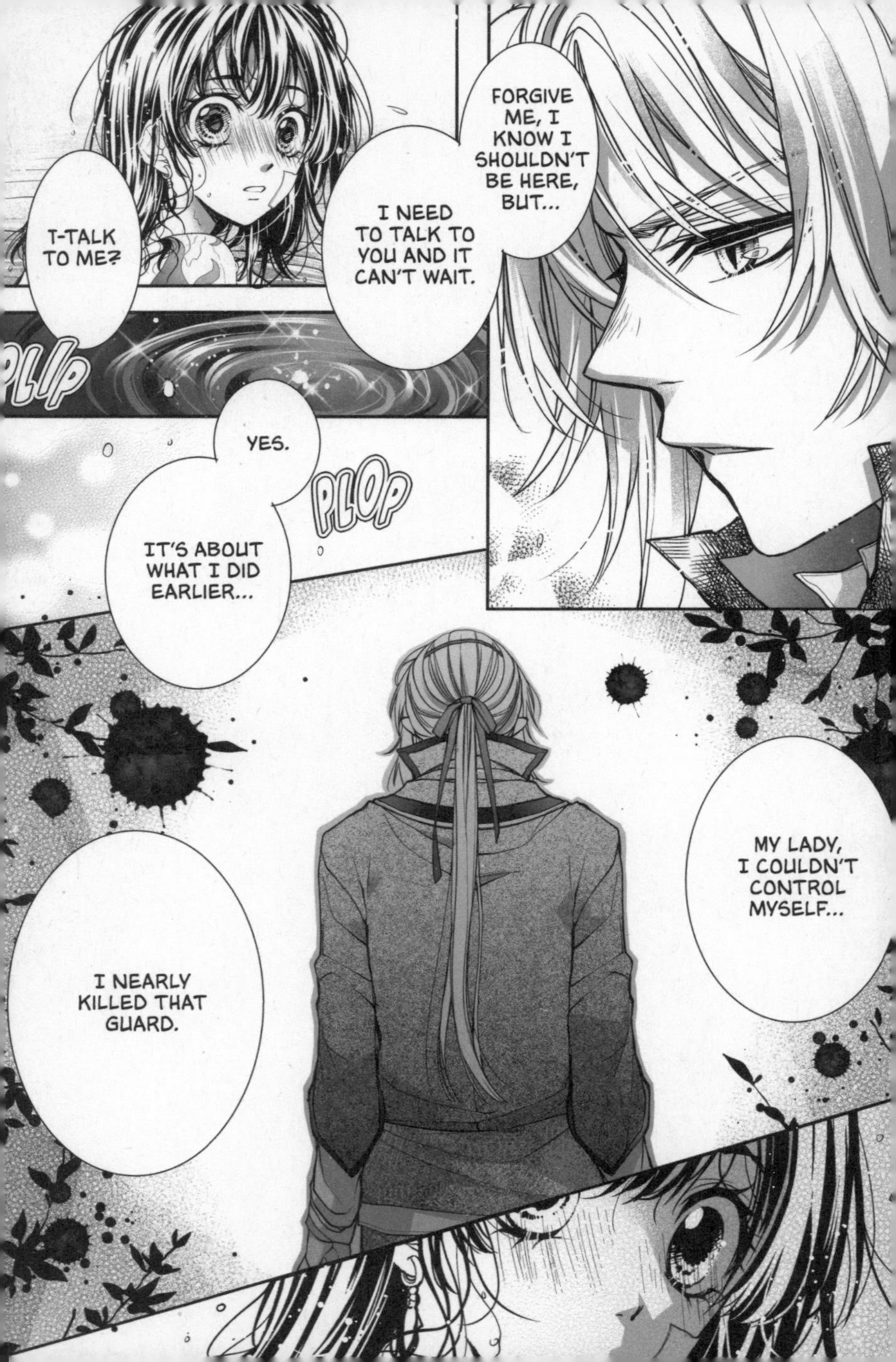
FORGIVE ME, I KNOW I SHOULDN'T BE HERE, BUT...
I NEED TO TALK TO YOU AND IT CAN'T WAIT.
T-TALK TO ME?
PLIP
YES.
PLOP
IT'S ABOUT WHAT I DID EARLIER...
MY LADY, I COULDN'T CONTROL MYSELF...
I NEARLY KILLED THAT GUARD.

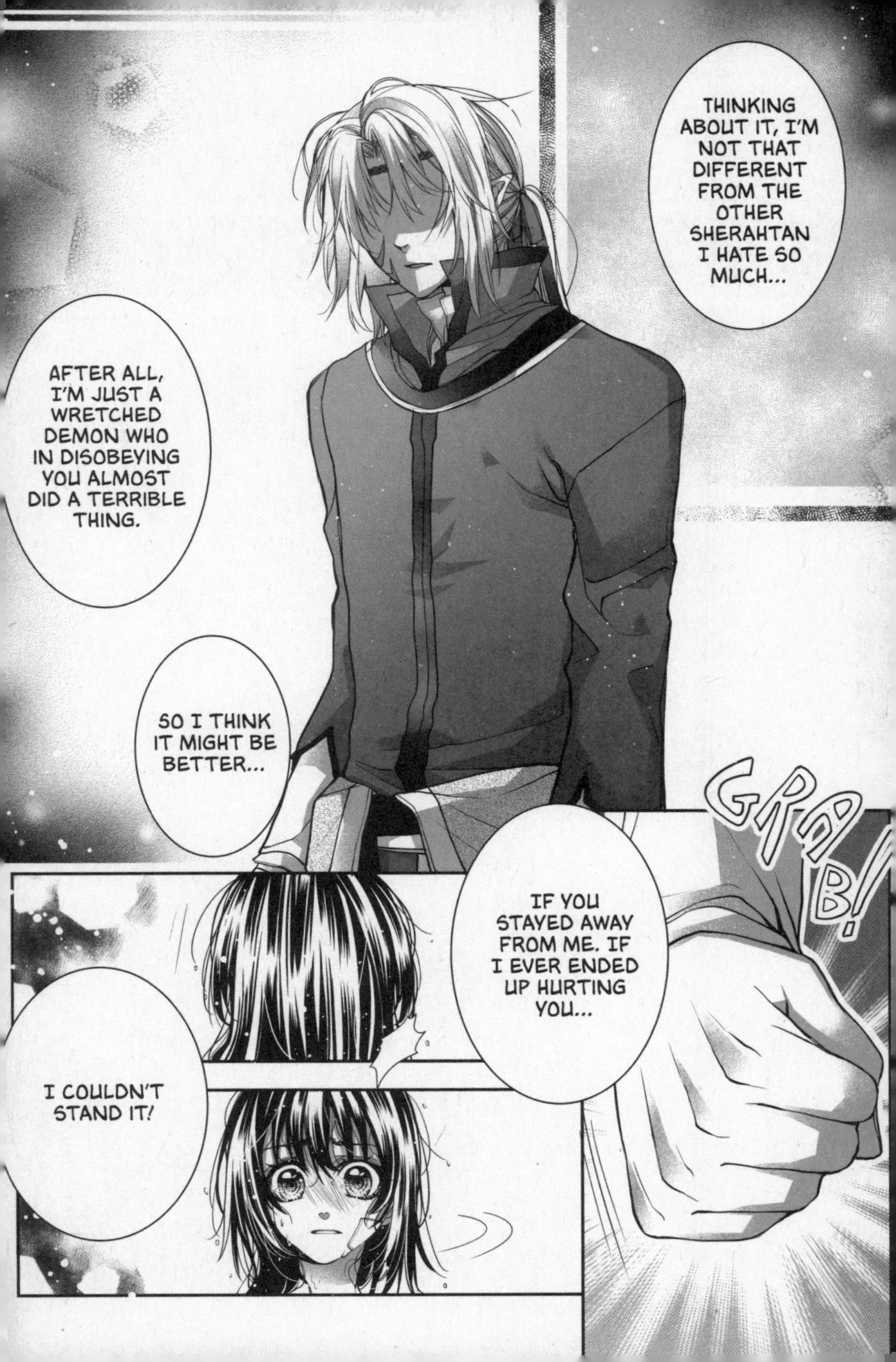
THINKING ABOUT IT, I'M NOT THAT DIFFERENT FROM THE OTHER SHERAHTAN I HATE SO MUCH...
AFTER ALL, I'M JUST A WRETCHED DEMON WHO IN DISOBEYING YOU ALMOST DID A TERRIBLE THING.
SO I THINK IT MIGHT BE BETTER...
IF YOU STAYED AWAY FROM ME. IF I EVER ENDED UP HURTING YOU...
GRAB!
I COULDN'T STAND IT!

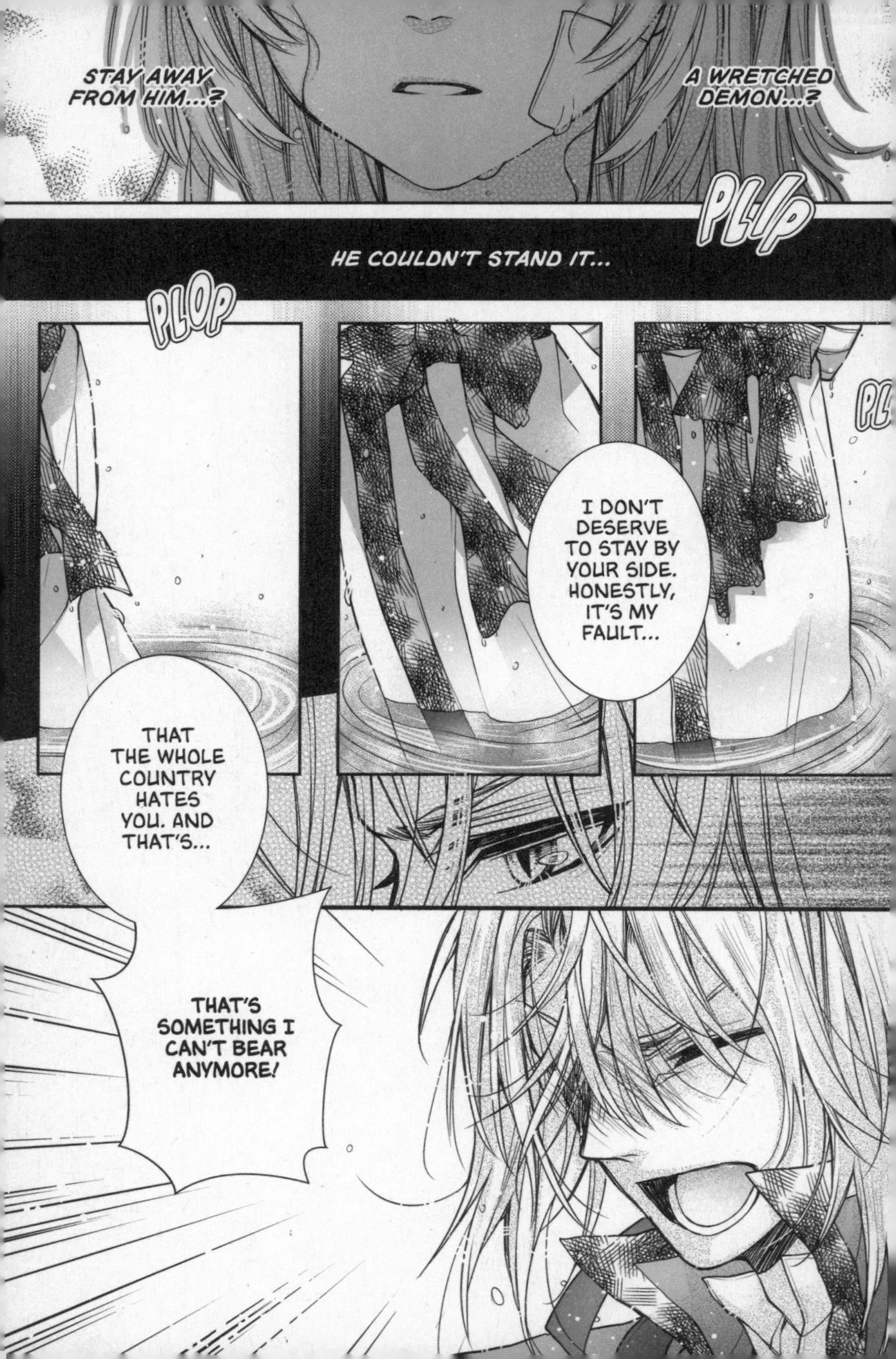
A WRETCHED DEMON...?
STAY AWAY FROM HIM...?
PLIP
HE COULDN'T STAND IT...
PLOP
I DON'T DESERVE TO STAY BY YOUR SIDE. HONESTLY, IT'S MY FAULT...
THAT THE WHOLE COUNTRY HATES YOU. AND THAT'S...
THAT'S SOMETHING I CAN'T BEAR ANYMORE!

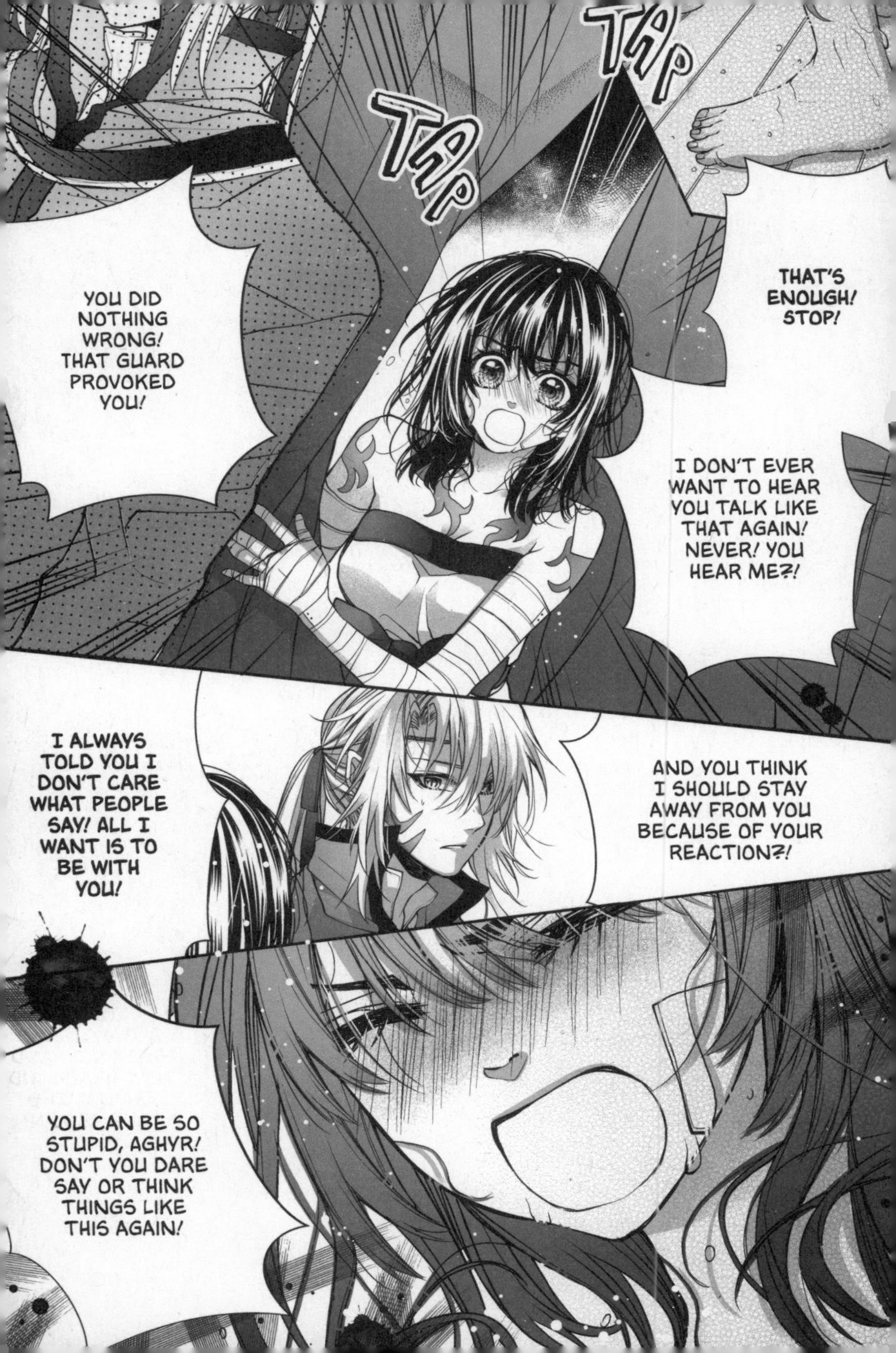
TAP
TAP
THAT'S ENOUGH! STOP!
YOU DID NOTHING WRONG! THAT GUARD PROVOKED YOU!
I DON'T EVER WANT TO HEAR YOU TALK LIKE THAT AGAIN! NEVER! YOU HEAR ME?!
AND YOU THINK I SHOULD STAY AWAY FROM YOU BECAUSE OF YOUR REACTION?!
I ALWAYS TOLD YOU I DON'T CARE WHAT PEOPLE SAY! ALL I WANT IS TO BE WITH YOU!
YOU CAN BE SO STUPID, AGHYR! DON'T YOU DARE SAY OR THINK THINGS LIKE THIS AGAIN!

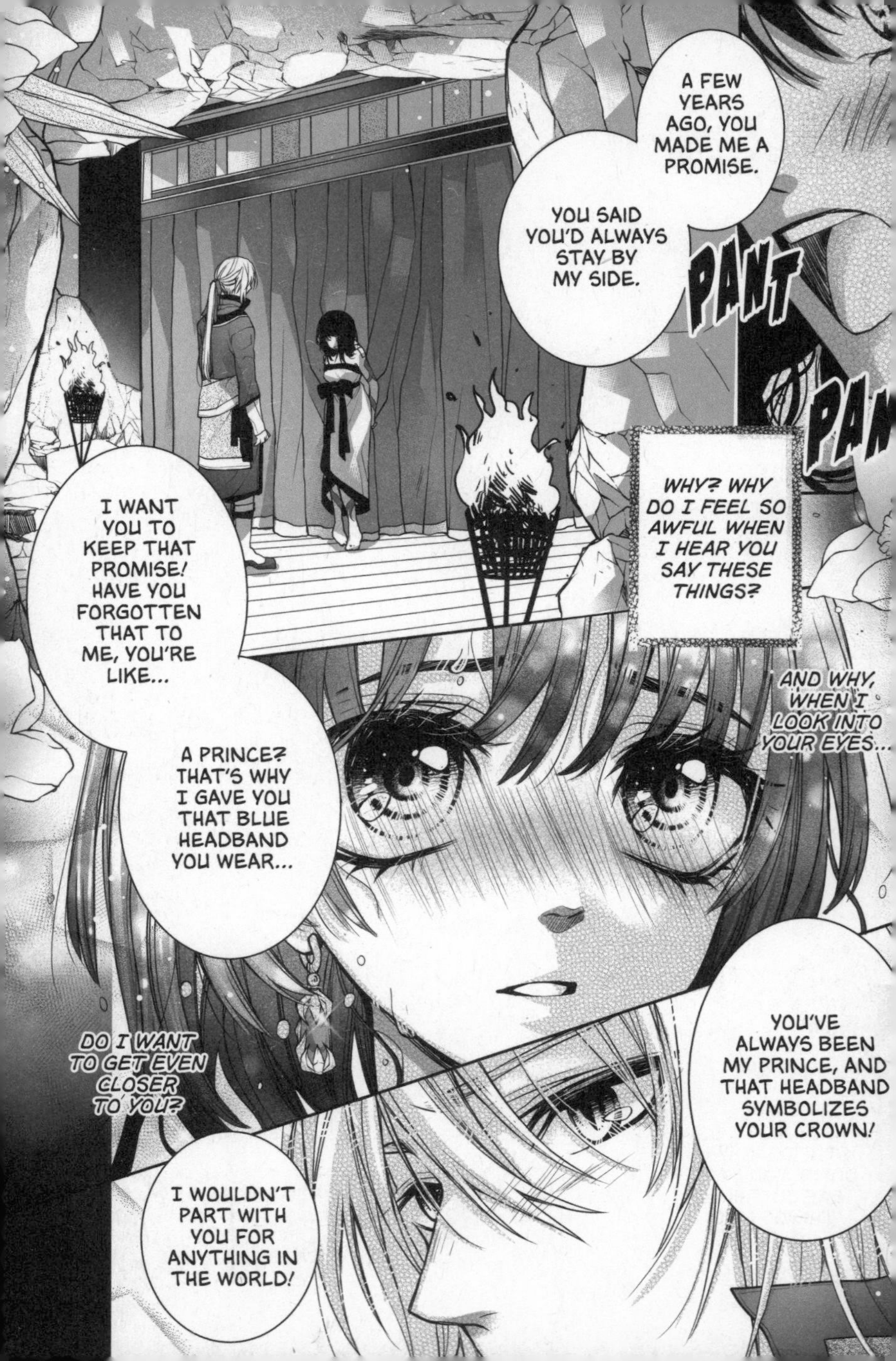

A FEW YEARS AGO, YOU MADE ME A PROMISE.
YOU SAID YOU'D ALWAYS STAY BY MY SIDE.
PANT
PAN
WHY? WHY DO I FEEL SO AWFUL WHEN I HEAR YOU SAY THESE THINGS?
I WANT YOU TO KEEP THAT PROMISE! HAVE YOU FORGOTTEN THAT TO ME, YOU'RE LIKE...
AND WHY, WHEN I LOOK INTO YOUR EYES...
A PRINCE? THAT'S WHY I GAVE YOU THAT BLUE HEADBAND YOU WEAR...
DO I WANT TO GET EVEN CLOSER TO YOU?
YOU'VE ALWAYS BEEN MY PRINCE, AND THAT HEADBAND SYMBOLIZES YOUR CROWN!
I WOULDN'T PART WITH YOU FOR ANYTHING IN THE WORLD!

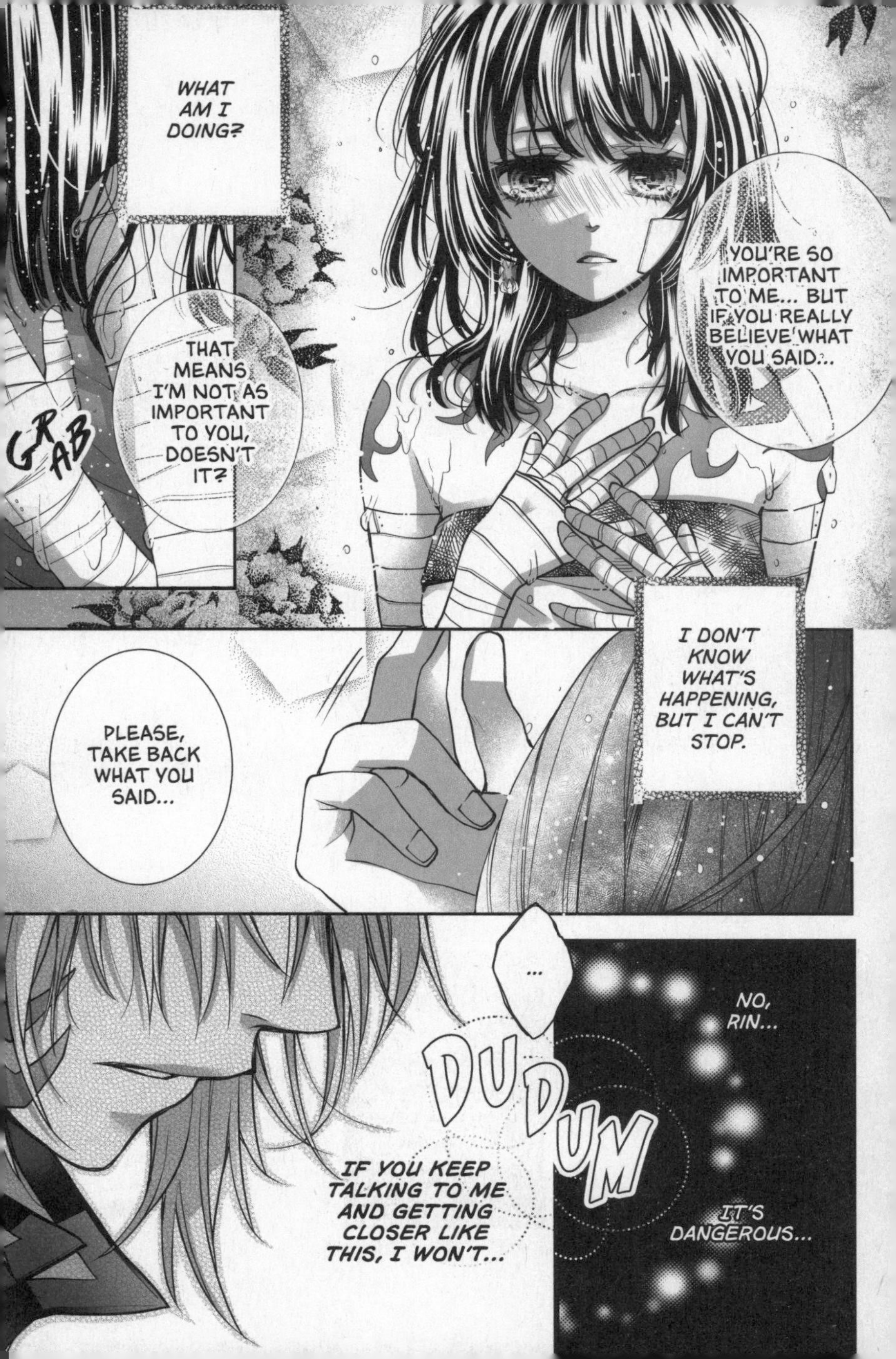
YOU'RE SO IMPORTANT TO ME... BUT IF YOU REALLY BELIEVE WHAT YOU SAID...
THAT MEANS I'M NOT AS IMPORTANT TO YOU, DOESN'T IT?
GRAB
WHAT AM I DOING?
I DON'T KNOW WHAT'S HAPPENING, BUT I CAN'T STOP.
PLEASE, TAKE BACK WHAT YOU SAID...
NO, RIN...
IT'S DANGEROUS...
...
DUDUM
IF YOU KEEP TALKING TO ME AND GETTING CLOSER LIKE THIS, I WON'T...

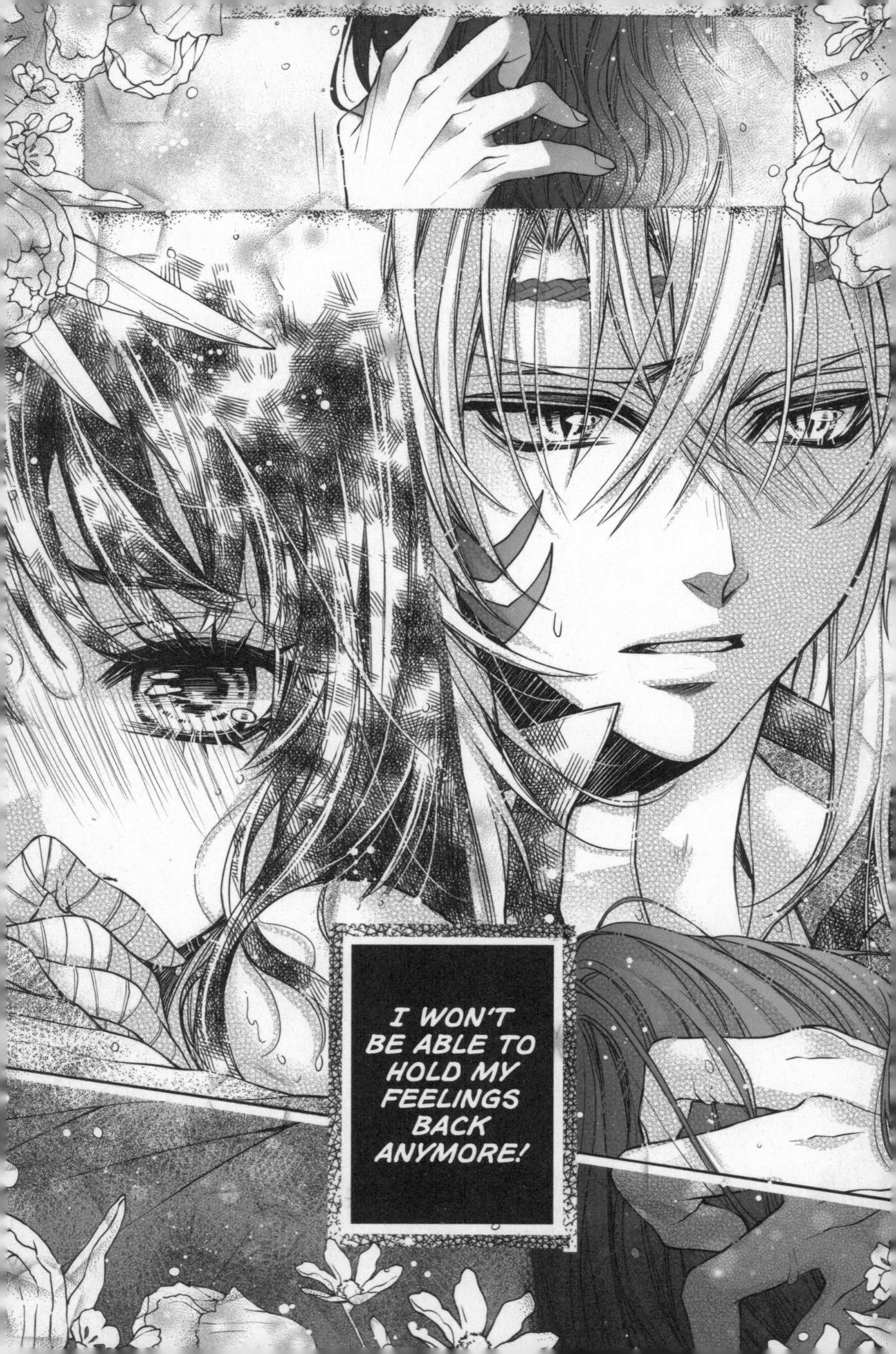
I WON'T BE ABLE TO HOLD MY FEELINGS BACK ANYMORE!

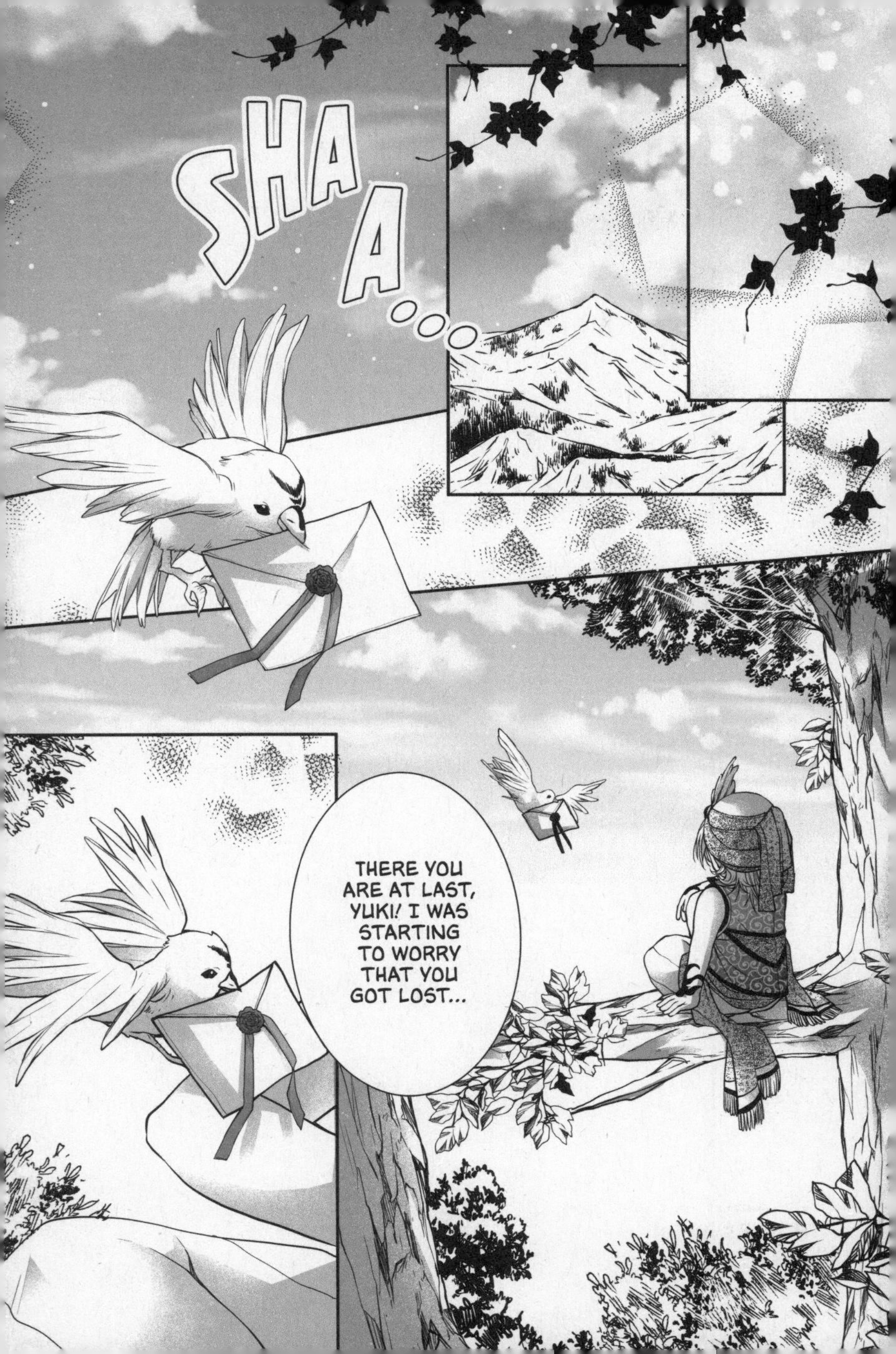
SHA A...
THERE YOU ARE AT LAST, YUKI! I WAS STARTING TO WORRY THAT YOU GOT LOST...

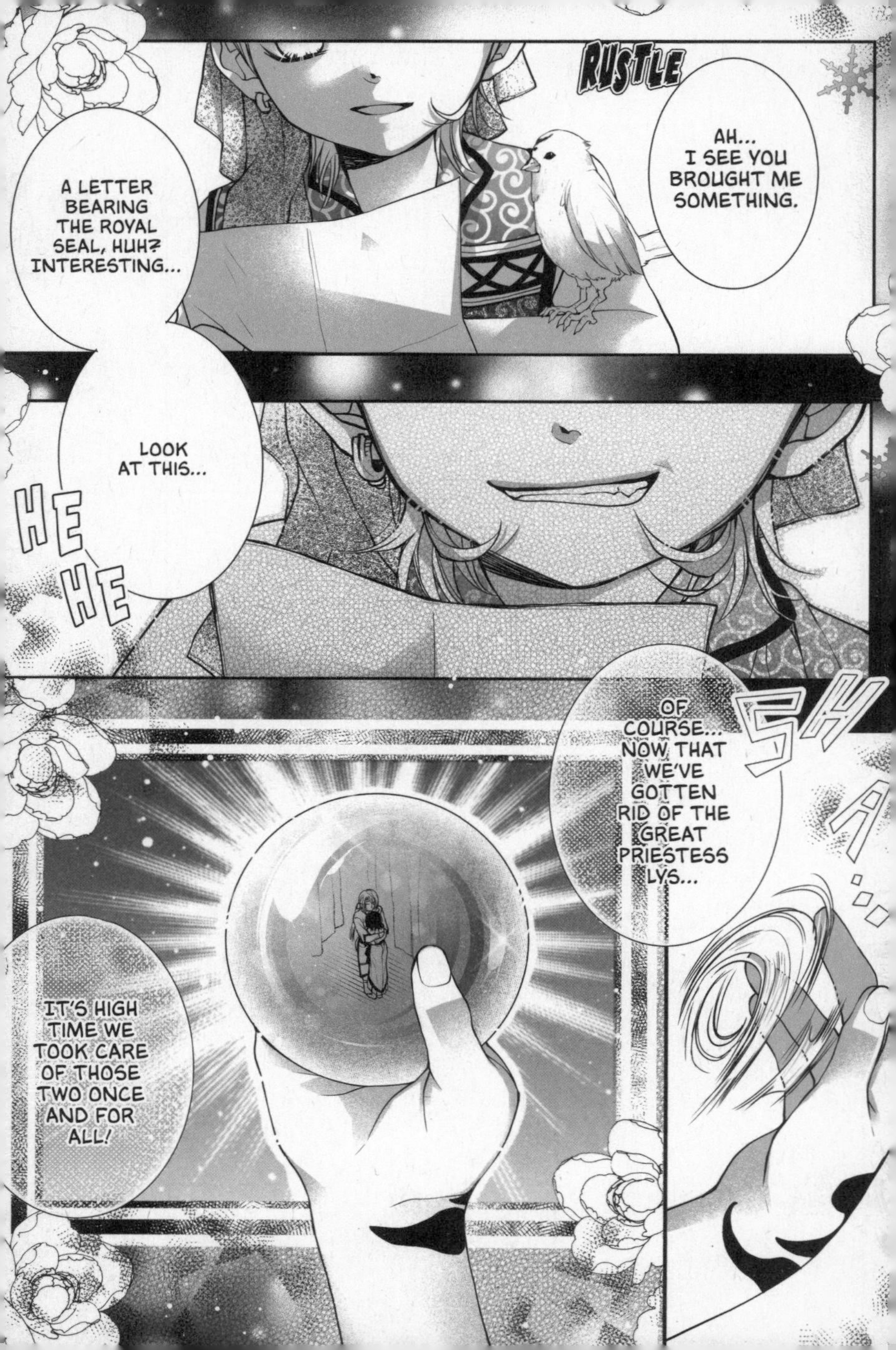
RUSTLE
AH... I SEE YOU BROUGHT ME SOMETHING.
A LETTER BEARING THE ROYAL SEAL, HUH? INTERESTING...
LOOK AT THIS...
HEHE HEHE
OF COURSE... NOW THAT WE'VE GOTTEN RID OF THE GREAT PRIESTESS LYS...
SHA...
IT'S HIGH TIME WE TOOK CARE OF THOSE TWO ONCE AND FOR ALL!

SCARLET SOUL

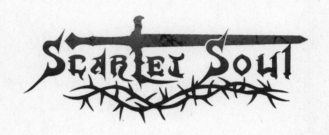

VOLUME 1 - END

BONUS

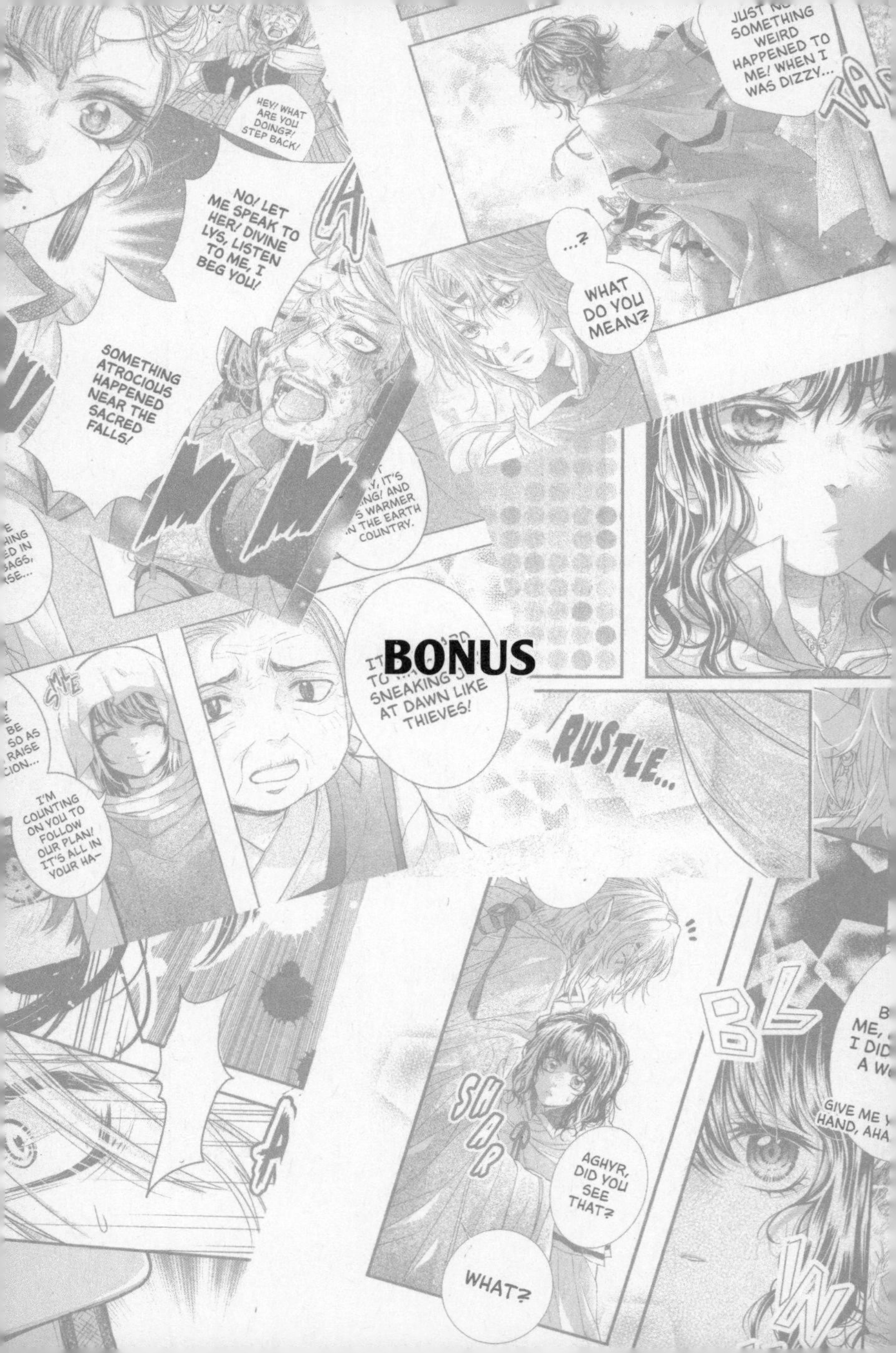

SOMETHING WEIRD HAPPENED TO ME! WHEN I WAS DIZZY...
...?
WHAT DO YOU MEAN?
HEY! WHAT ARE YOU DOING?! STEP BACK!
NO! LET ME SPEAK TO HER! DIVINE LYS, LISTEN TO ME, I BEG YOU!
SOMETHING ATROCIOUS HAPPENED NEAR THE SACRED FALLS!
SNEAKING AT DAWN LIKE THIEVES!
RUSTLE...
I'M COUNTING ON YOU TO FOLLOW OUR PLAN! IT'S ALL IN YOUR HA-
AGHYR, DID YOU SEE THAT?
WHAT?

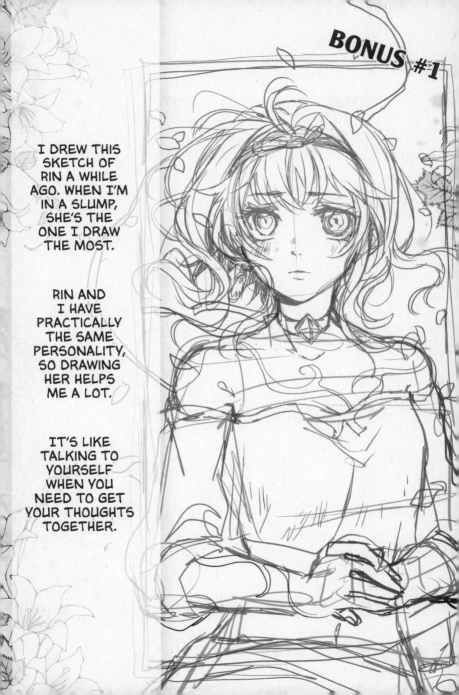

BONUS #1

I DREW THIS SKETCH OF RIN A WHILE AGO. WHEN I'M IN A SLUMP, SHE'S THE ONE I DRAW THE MOST.

RIN AND I HAVE PRACTICALLY THE SAME PERSONALITY, SO DRAWING HER HELPS ME A LOT.

IT'S LIKE TALKING TO YOURSELF WHEN YOU NEED TO GET YOUR THOUGHTS TOGETHER.

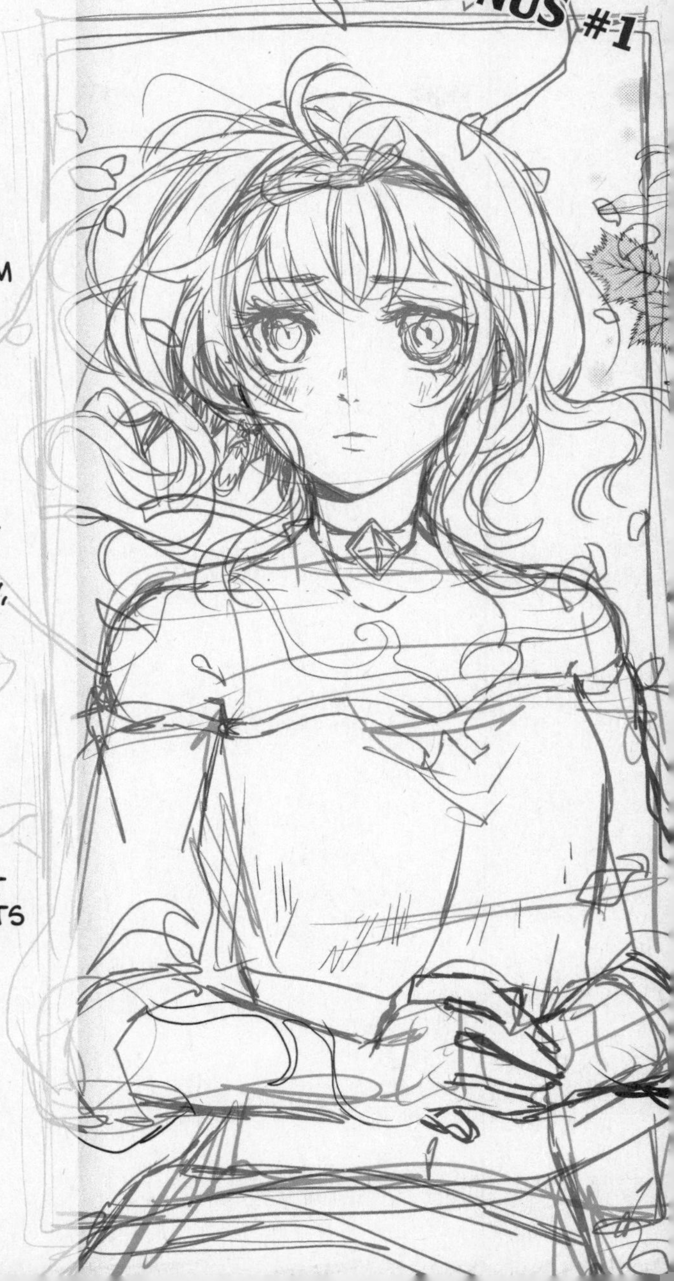

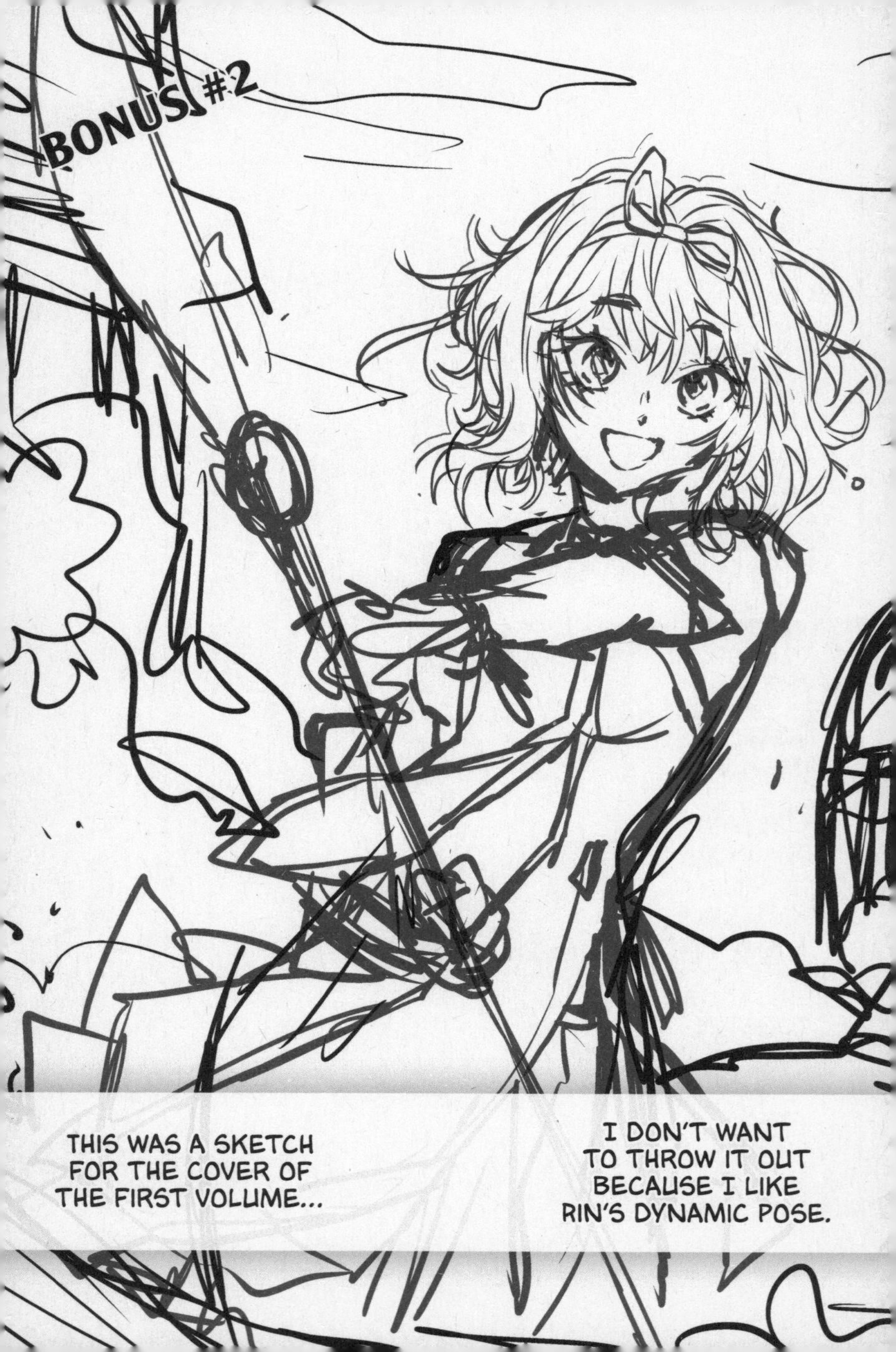
BONUS #2
THIS WAS A SKETCH FOR THE COVER OF THE FIRST VOLUME...
I DON'T WANT TO THROW IT OUT BECAUSE I LIKE RIN'S DYNAMIC POSE.

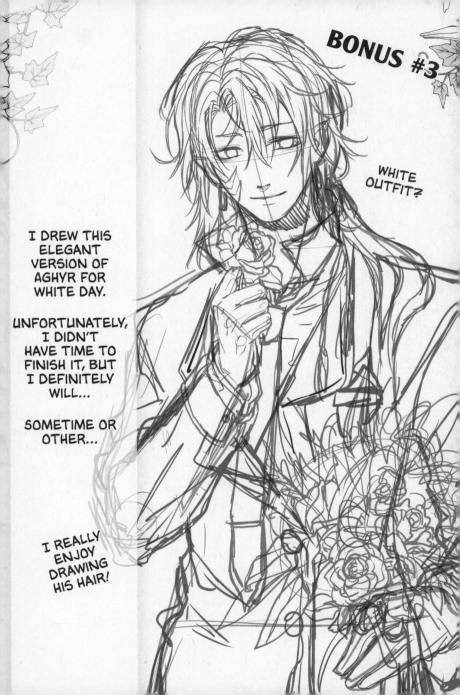

BONUS #3

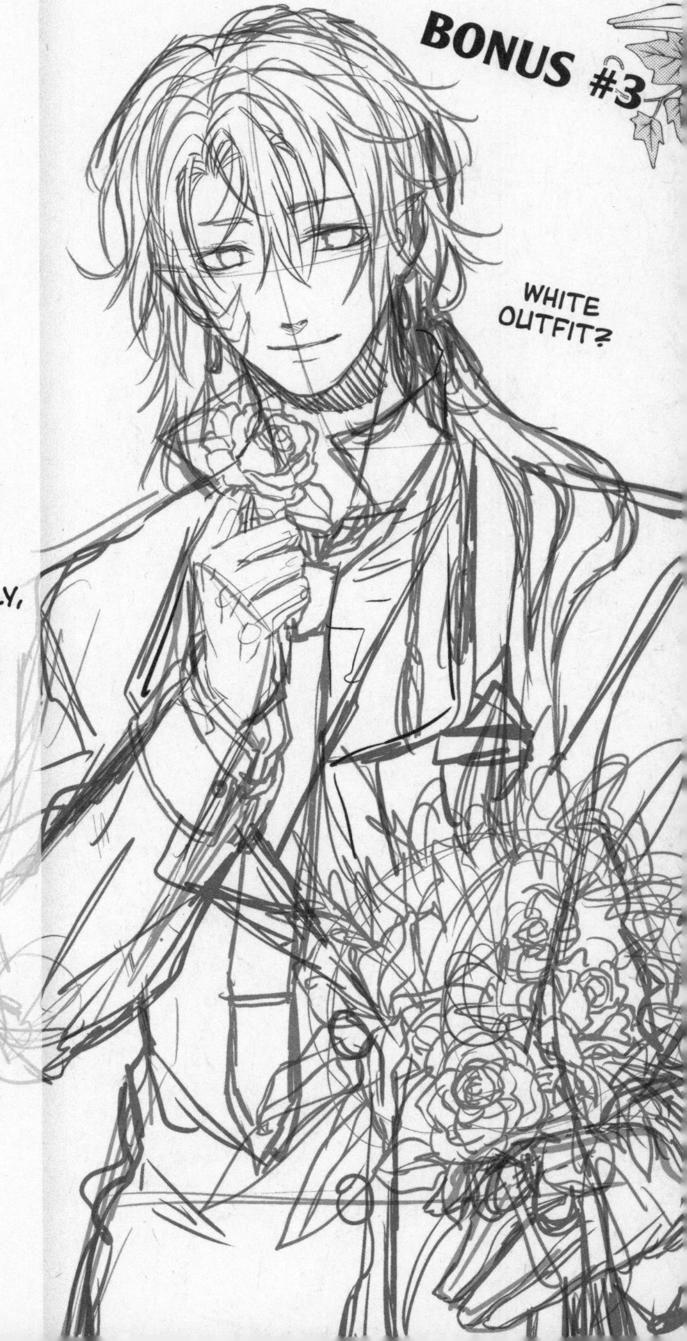
WHITE OUTFIT?

I DREW THIS ELEGANT VERSION OF AGHYR FOR WHITE DAY.

UNFORTUNATELY, I DIDN'T HAVE TIME TO FINISH IT, BUT I DEFINITELY WILL...

SOMETIME OR OTHER...

I REALLY ENJOY DRAWING HIS HAIR!

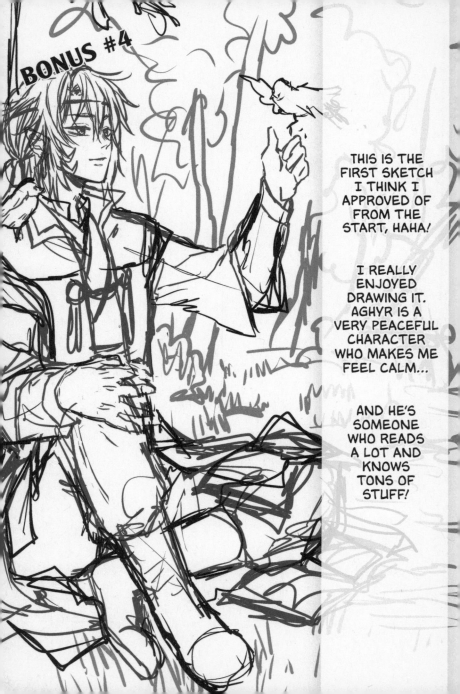

BONUS #4

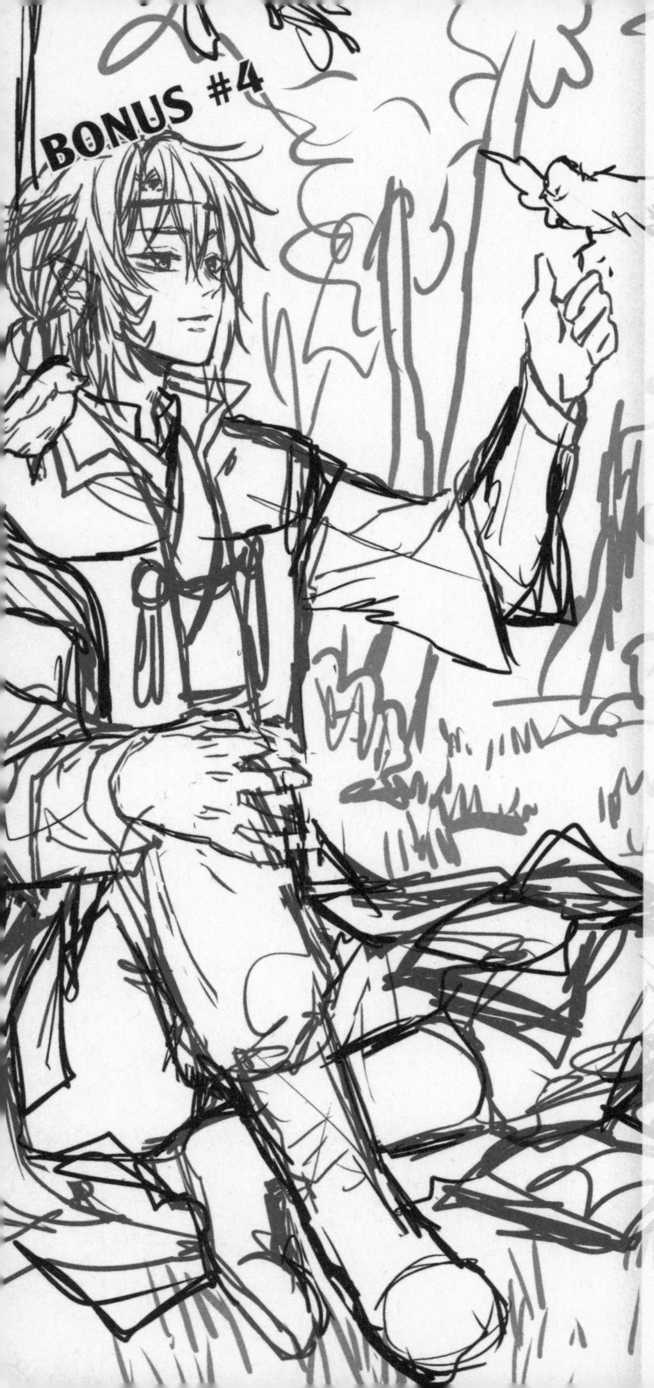

THIS IS THE FIRST SKETCH I THINK I APPROVED OF FROM THE START, HAHA!

I REALLY ENJOYED DRAWING IT. AGHYR IS A VERY PEACEFUL CHARACTER WHO MAKES ME FEEL CALM...

AND HE'S SOMEONE WHO READS A LOT AND KNOWS TONS OF STUFF!

Scarlet Soul

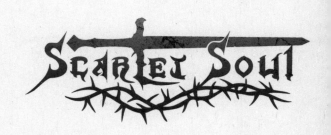

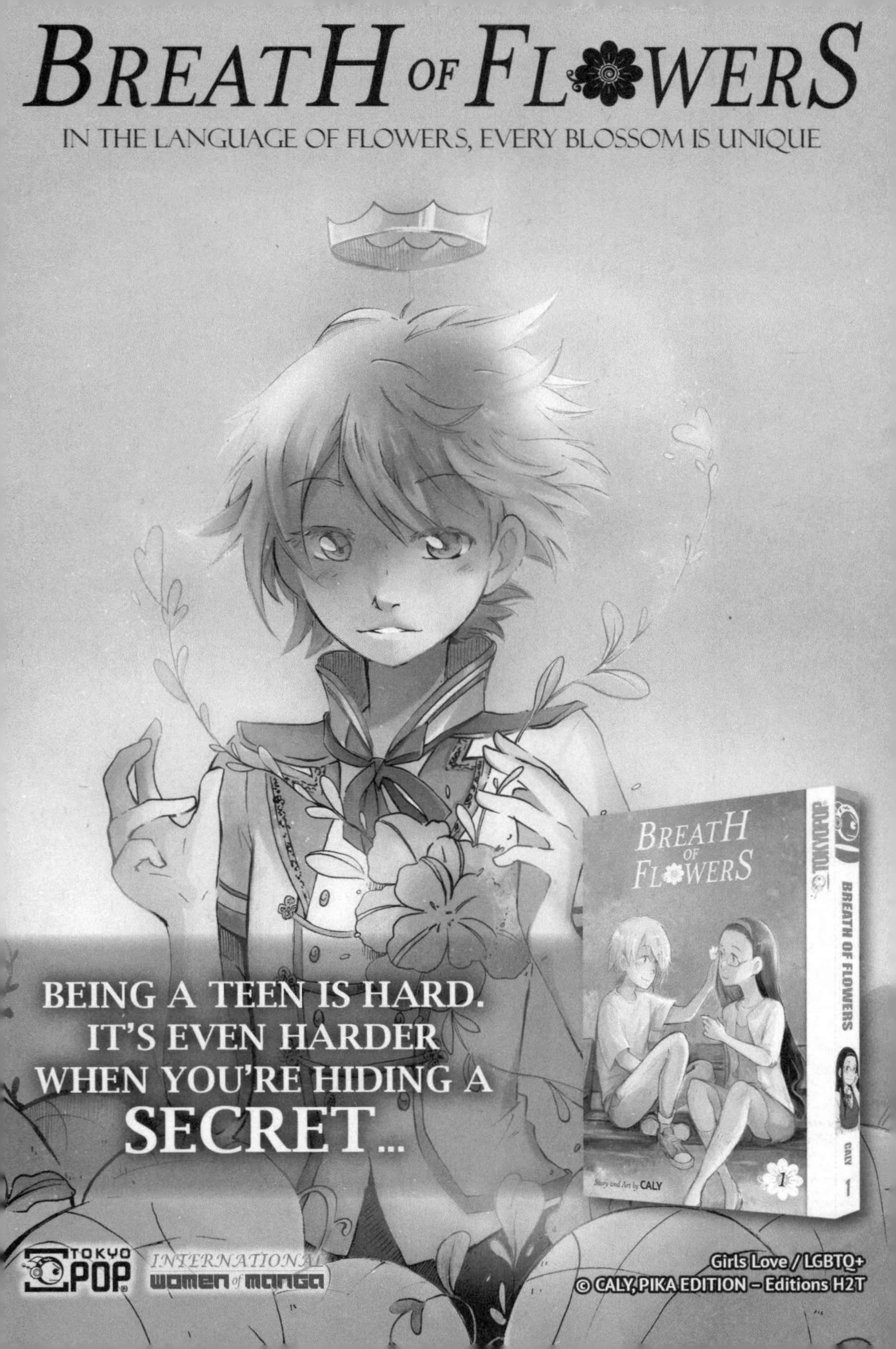
BREATH OF FLOWERS
IN THE LANGUAGE OF FLOWERS, EVERY BLOSSOM IS UNIQUE
BEING A TEEN IS HARD.
IT'S EVEN HARDER
WHEN YOU'RE HIDING A
SECRET...
BREATH OF FLOWERS
Story and Art by CALY
1
TOKYOPOP
BREATH OF FLOWERS
CALY
1
TOKYO POP
INTERNATIONAL
Women of Manga
Girls Love / LGBTQ+
© CALY, PIKA EDITION – Editions H2T

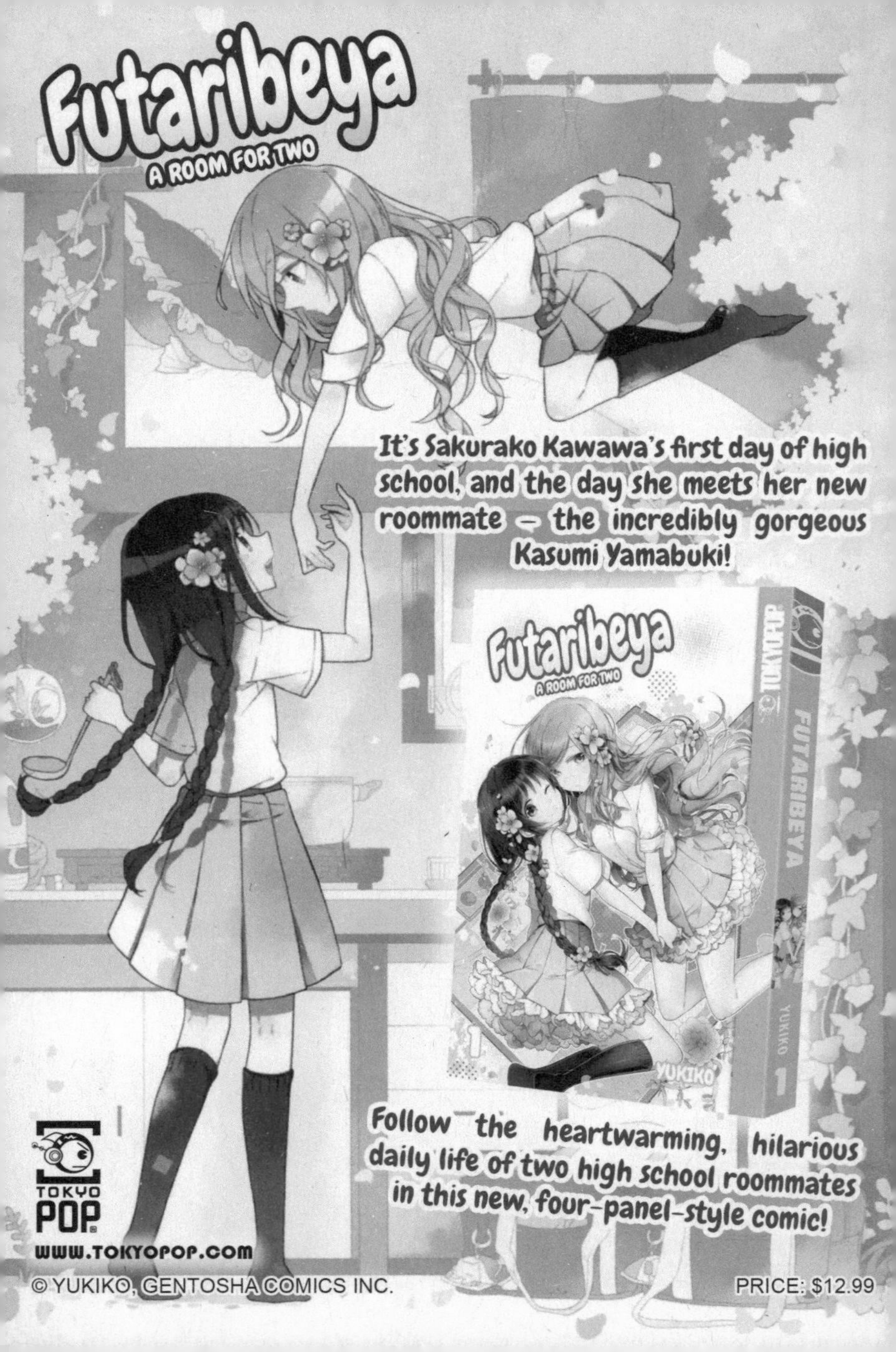
Futaribeya
A ROOM FOR TWO
It's Sakurako Kawawa's first day of high school, and the day she meets her new roommate – the incredibly gorgeous Kasumi Yamabuki!
Futaribeya
A ROOM FOR TWO
TOKYOPOP
FUTARIBEYA
YUKIKO
1
Follow the heartwarming, hilarious daily life of two high school roommates in this new, four-panel-style comic!
TOKYO POP
www.TOKYOPOP.com
© YUKIKO, GENTOSHA COMICS INC.
PRICE: $12.99

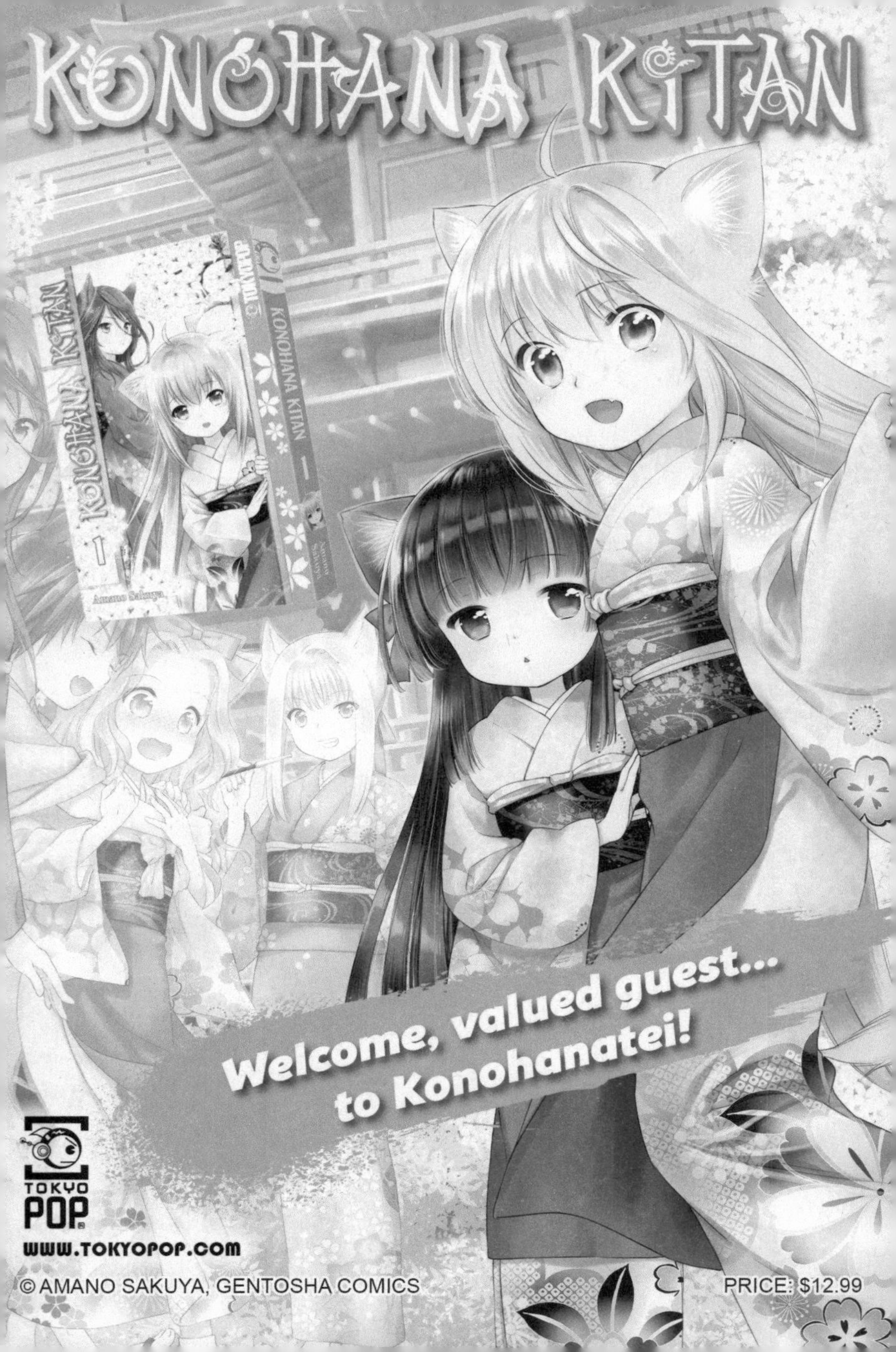
KONOHANA KITAN
KONOHANA KITAN
1
Amano Sakuya
TOKYOPOP
KONOHANA KITAN
Welcome, valued guest...
to Konohanatei!
TOKYO POP
WWW.TOKYOPOP.COM
© AMANO SAKUYA, GENTOSHA COMICS
PRICE: $12.99

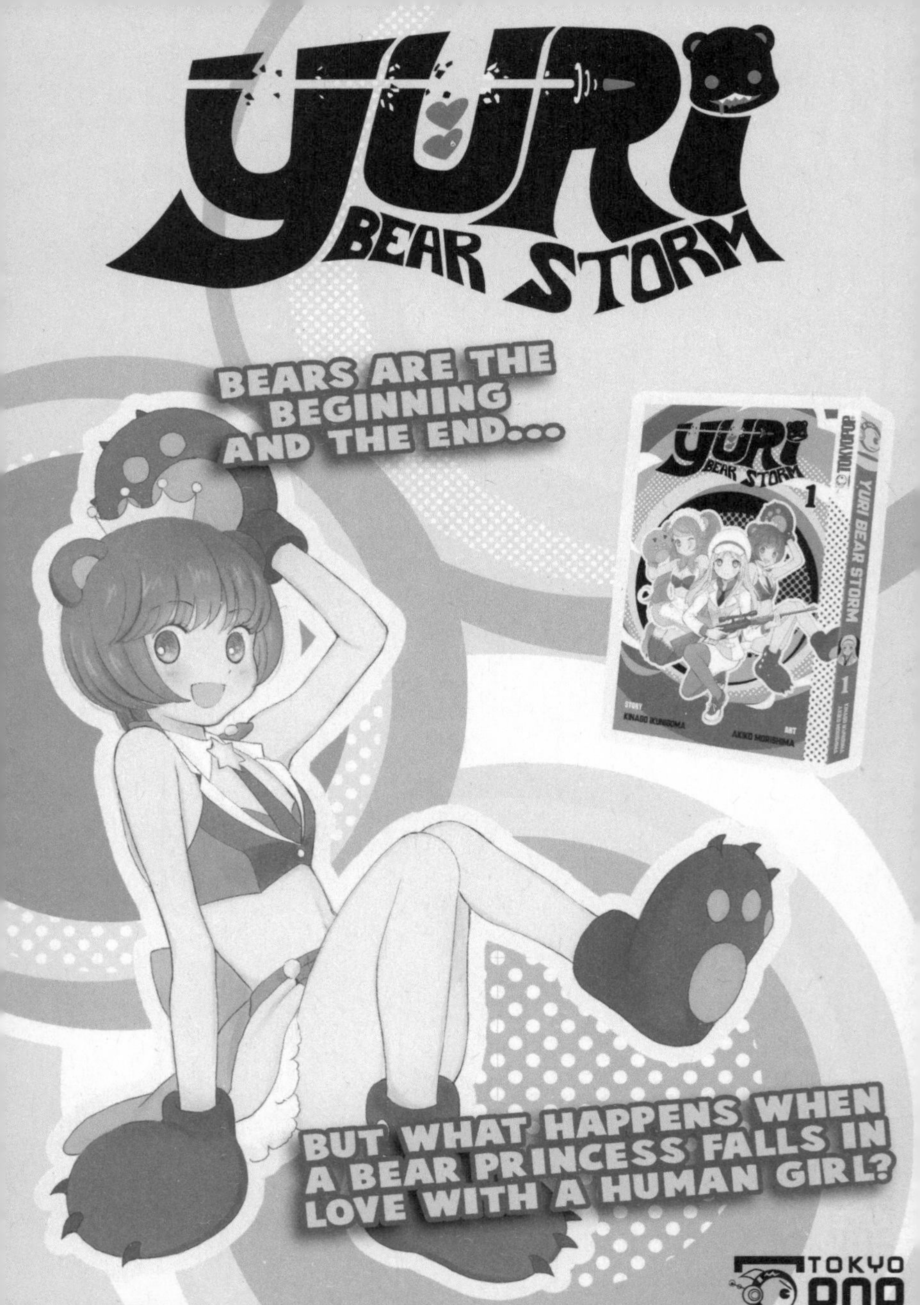
YURI BEAR STORM
BEARS ARE THE BEGINNING AND THE END...
YURI BEAR STORM 1
BUT WHAT HAPPENS WHEN A BEAR PRINCESS FALLS IN LOVE WITH A HUMAN GIRL?
TOKYO POP

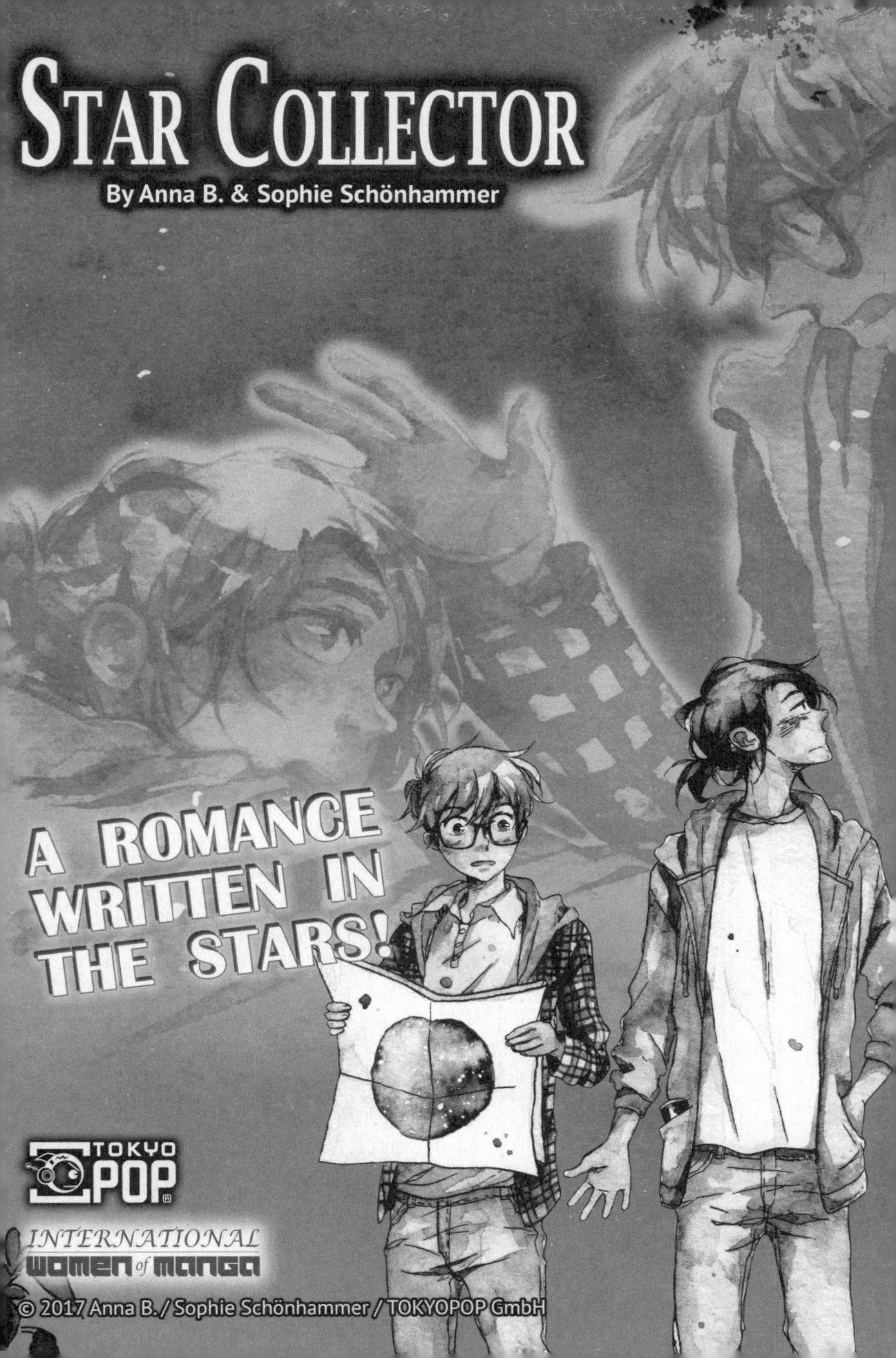
STAR COLLECTOR
By Anna B. & Sophie Schönhammer
A ROMANCE WRITTEN IN THE STARS!
TOKYO POP
INTERNATIONAL WOMEN of MANGA
© 2017 Anna B. / Sophie Schönhammer / TOKYOPOP GmbH

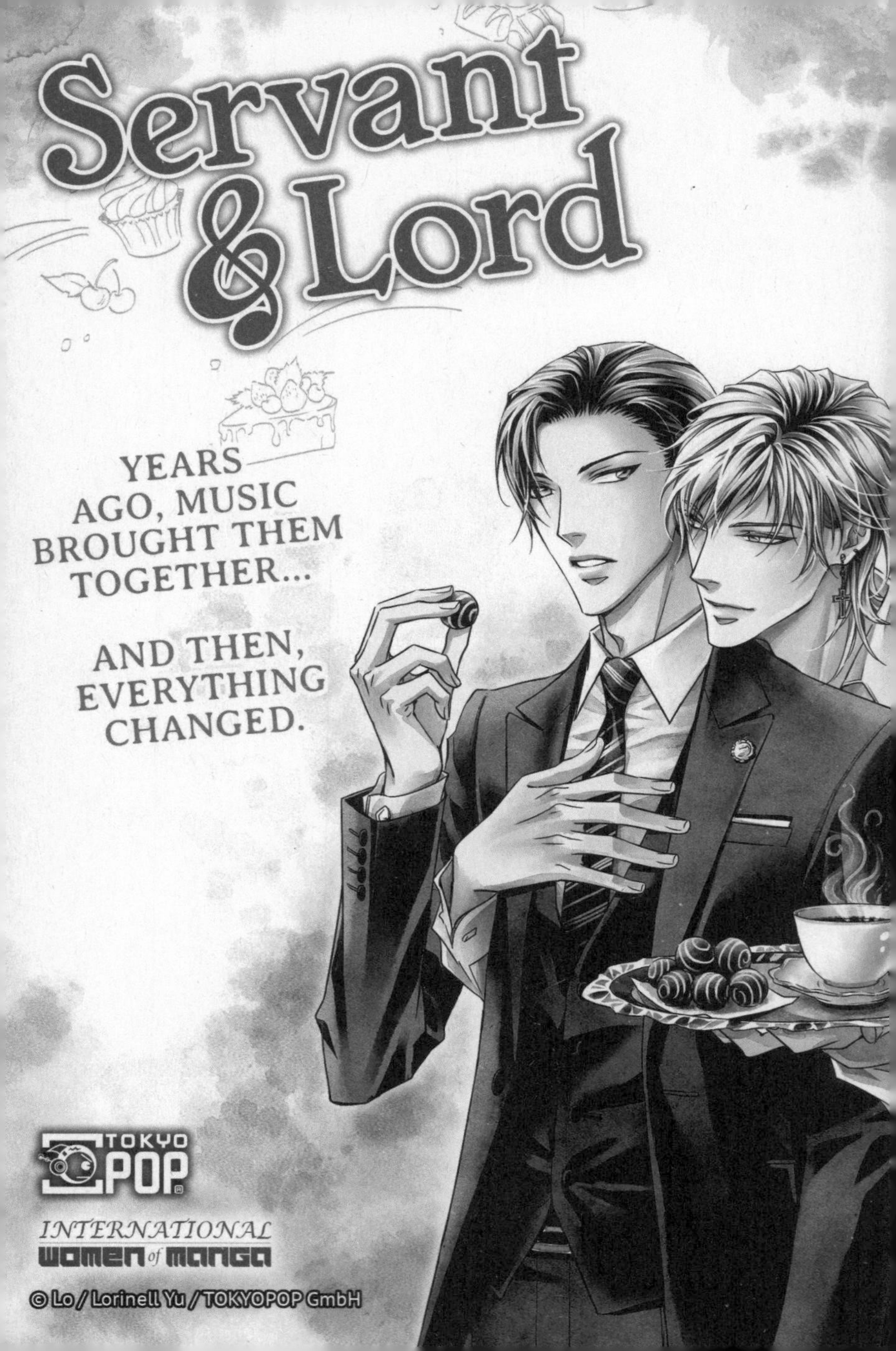
Servant & Lord
YEARS AGO, MUSIC BROUGHT THEM TOGETHER...
AND THEN, EVERYTHING CHANGED.
TOKYO POP
INTERNATIONAL WOMEN of MANGA
© Lo / Lorinell Yu / TOKYOPOP GmbH

A R I A The MASTERPIECE

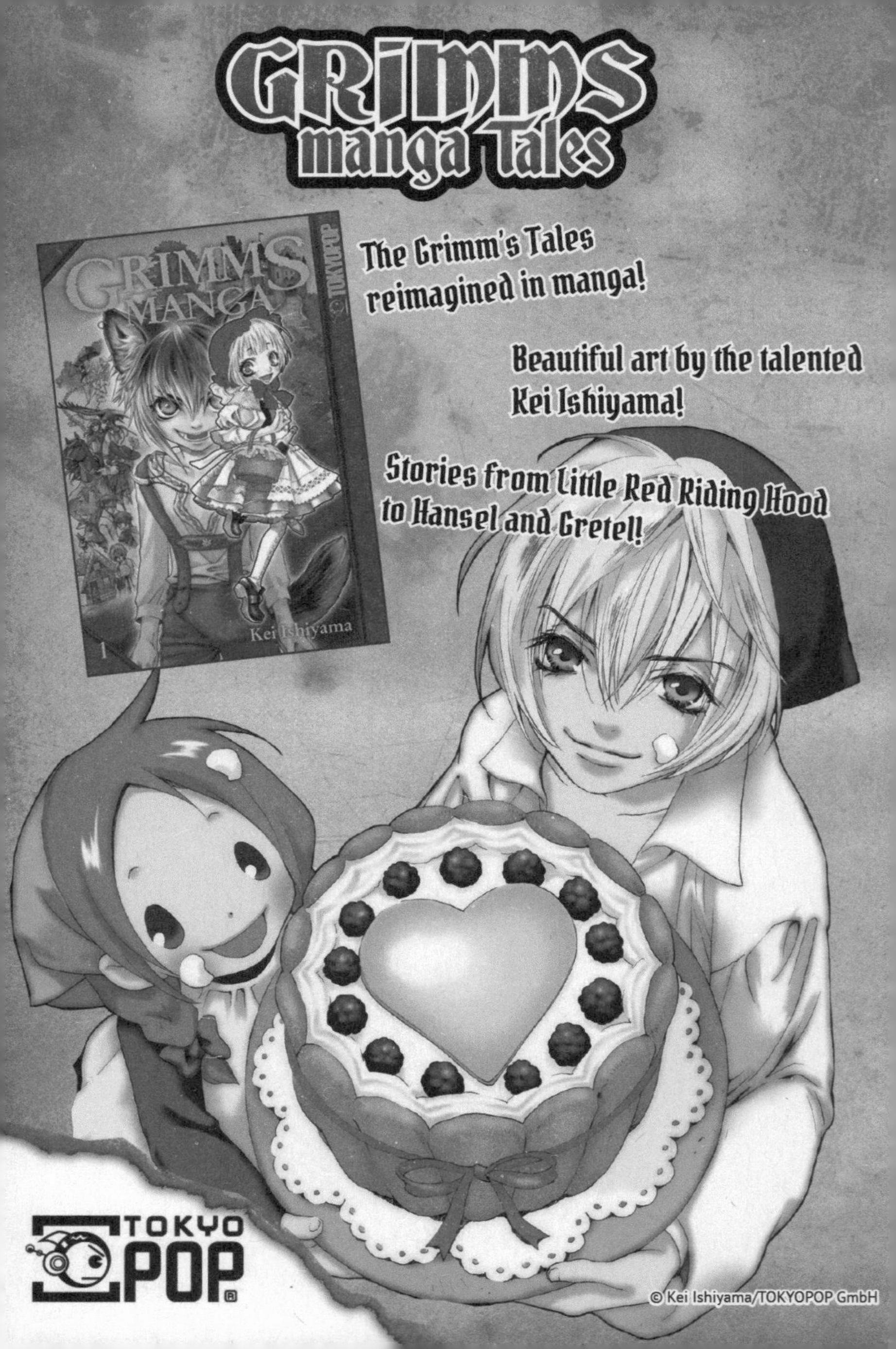

GRIMMS manga Tales
GRIMM'S MANGA
TOKYOPOP
Kei Ishiyama
1
The Grimm's Tales reimagined in manga!
Beautiful art by the talented Kei Ishiyama!
Stories from Little Red Riding Hood to Hansel and Gretel!
TOKYO POP
© Kei Ishiyama/TOKYOPOP GmbH

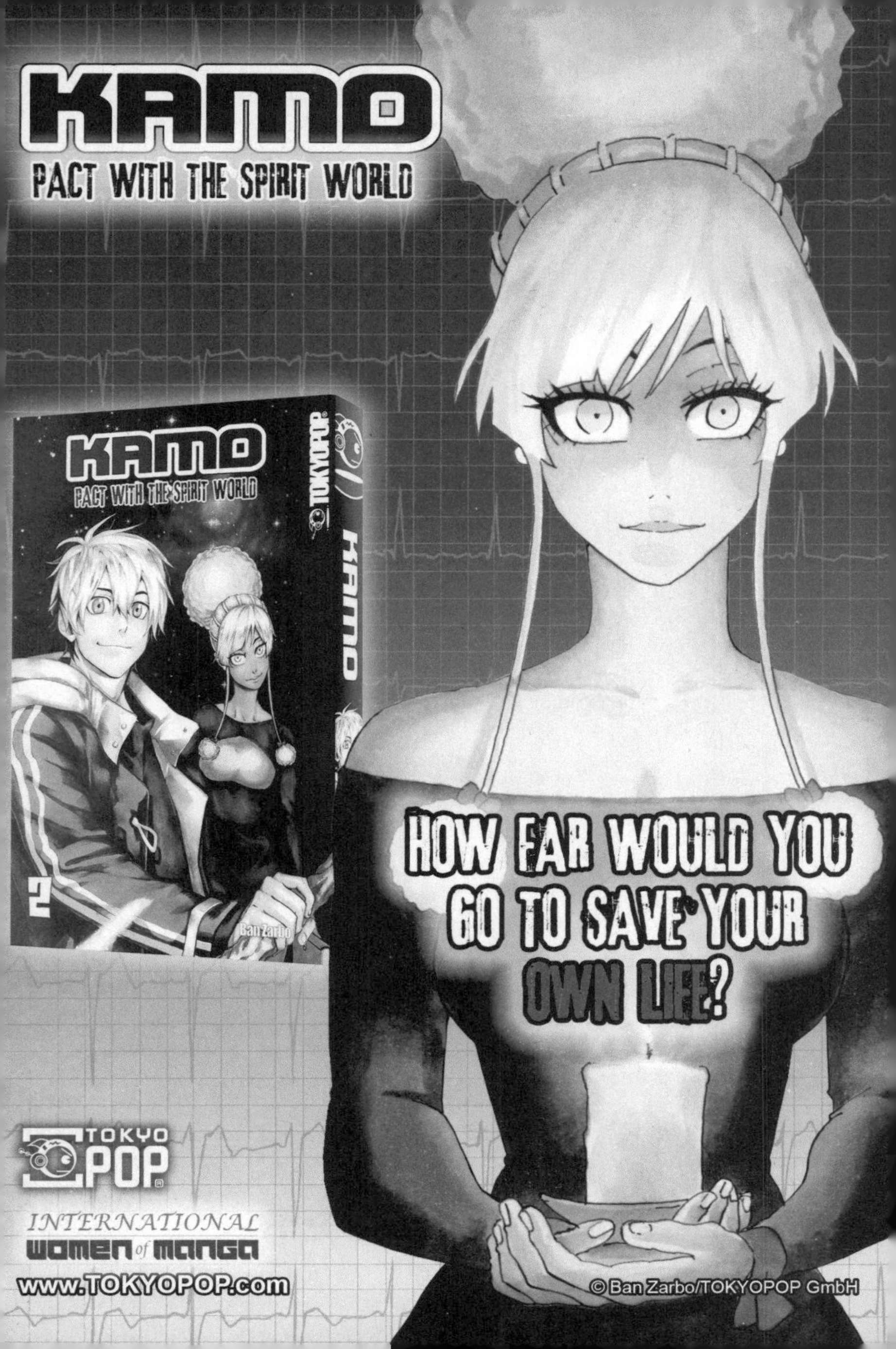
KAMO
PACT WITH THE SPIRIT WORLD
KAMO
PACT WITH THE SPIRIT WORLD
TOKYOPOP
KAMO
2
Ban Zarbo
HOW FAR WOULD YOU GO TO SAVE YOUR OWN LIFE?
TOKYO POP
INTERNATIONAL
WOMEN of MANGA
www.TOKYOPOP.com
© Ban Zarbo/TOKYOPOP GmbH

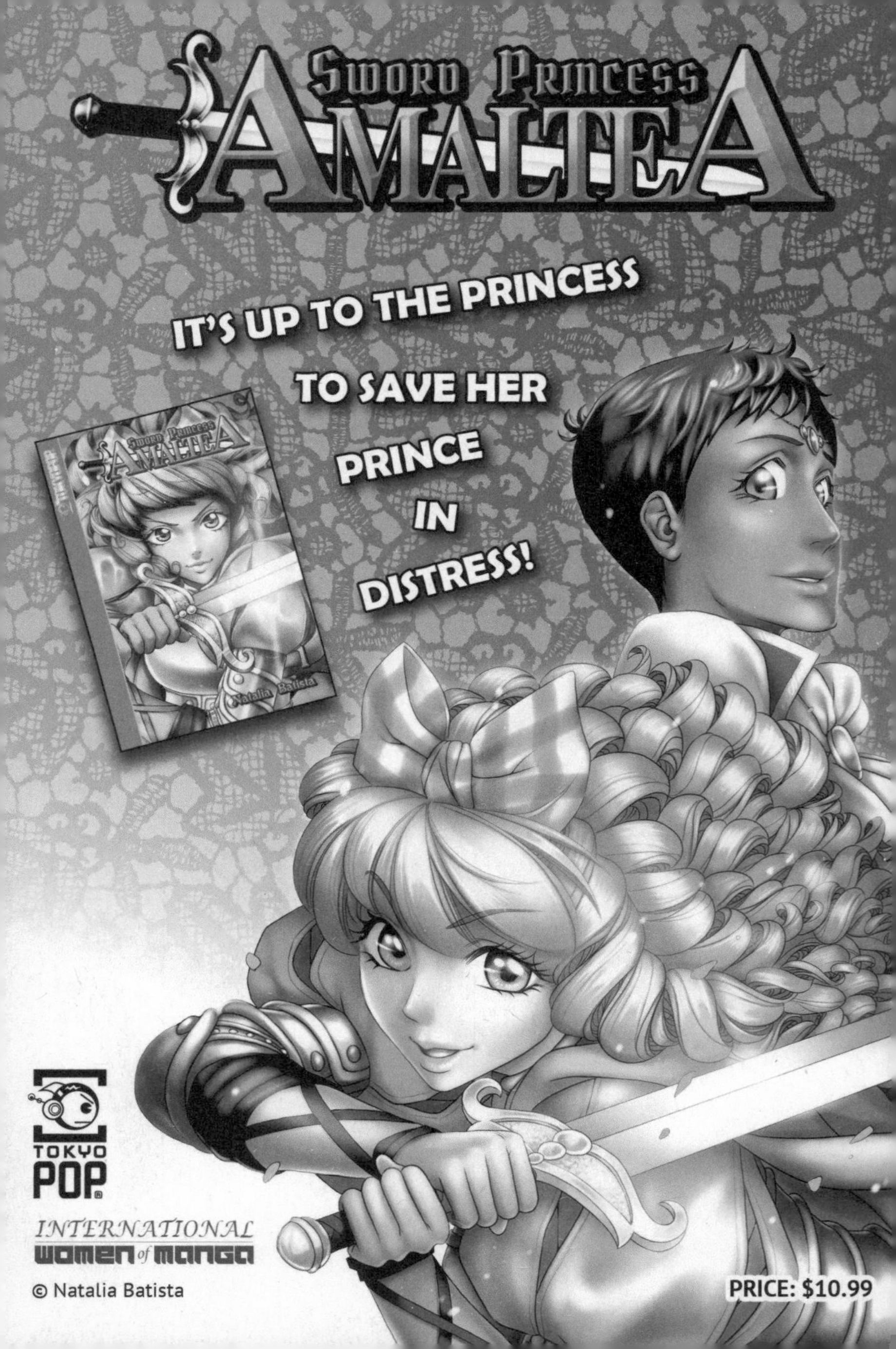

Sword Princess
AMALTEA
IT'S UP TO THE PRINCESS
TO SAVE HER
PRINCE
IN
DISTRESS!
Sword Princess AMALTEA
Natalia Batista
TOKYO POP
INTERNATIONAL
women of manga
© Natalia Batista
PRICE: $10.99

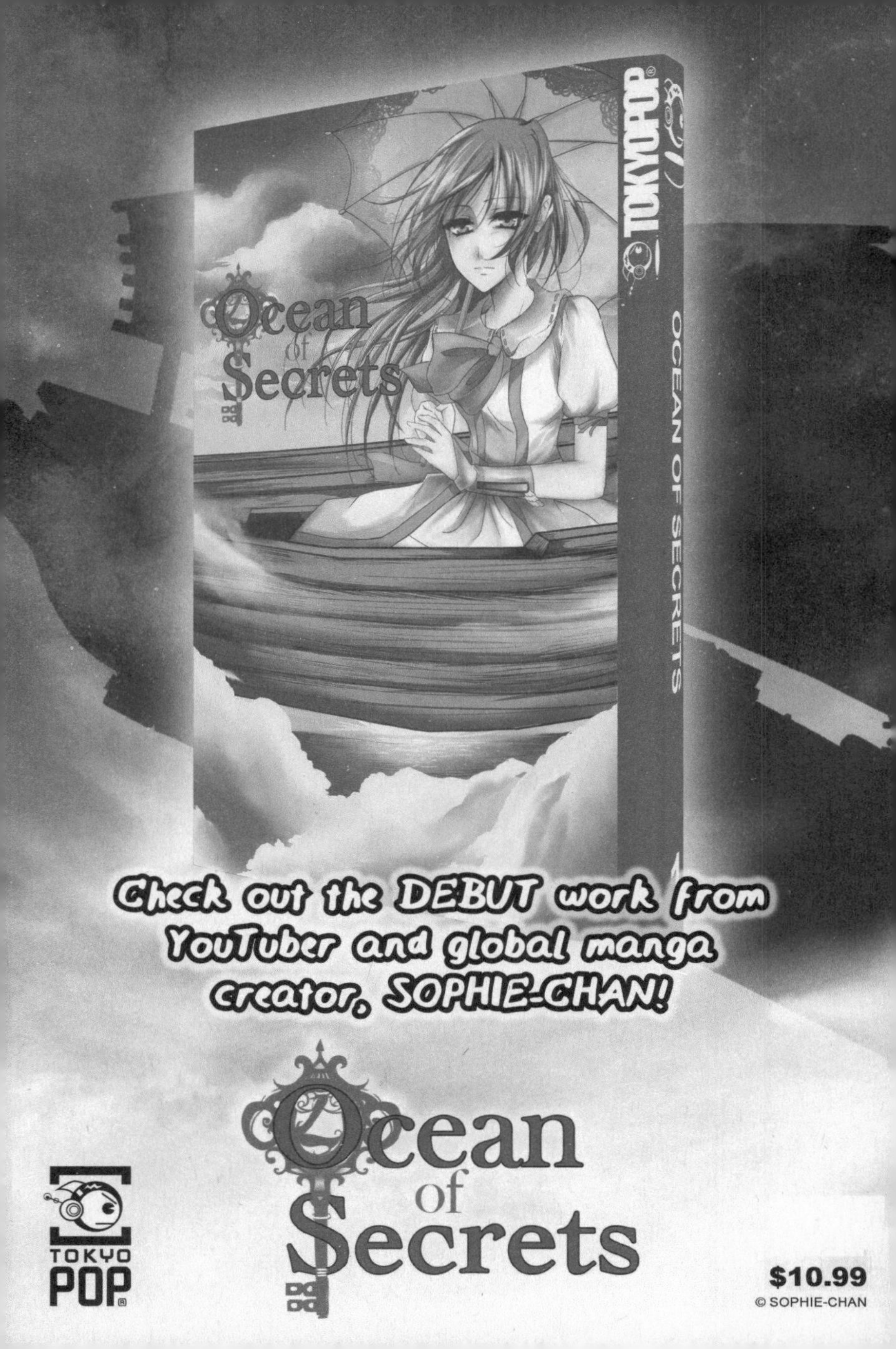
Ocean of Secrets
TOKYOPOP
OCEAN OF SECRETS
Check out the DEBUT work from YouTuber and global manga creator, SOPHIE-CHAN!
Ocean of Secrets
TOKYO POP
$10.99
© SOPHIE-CHAN

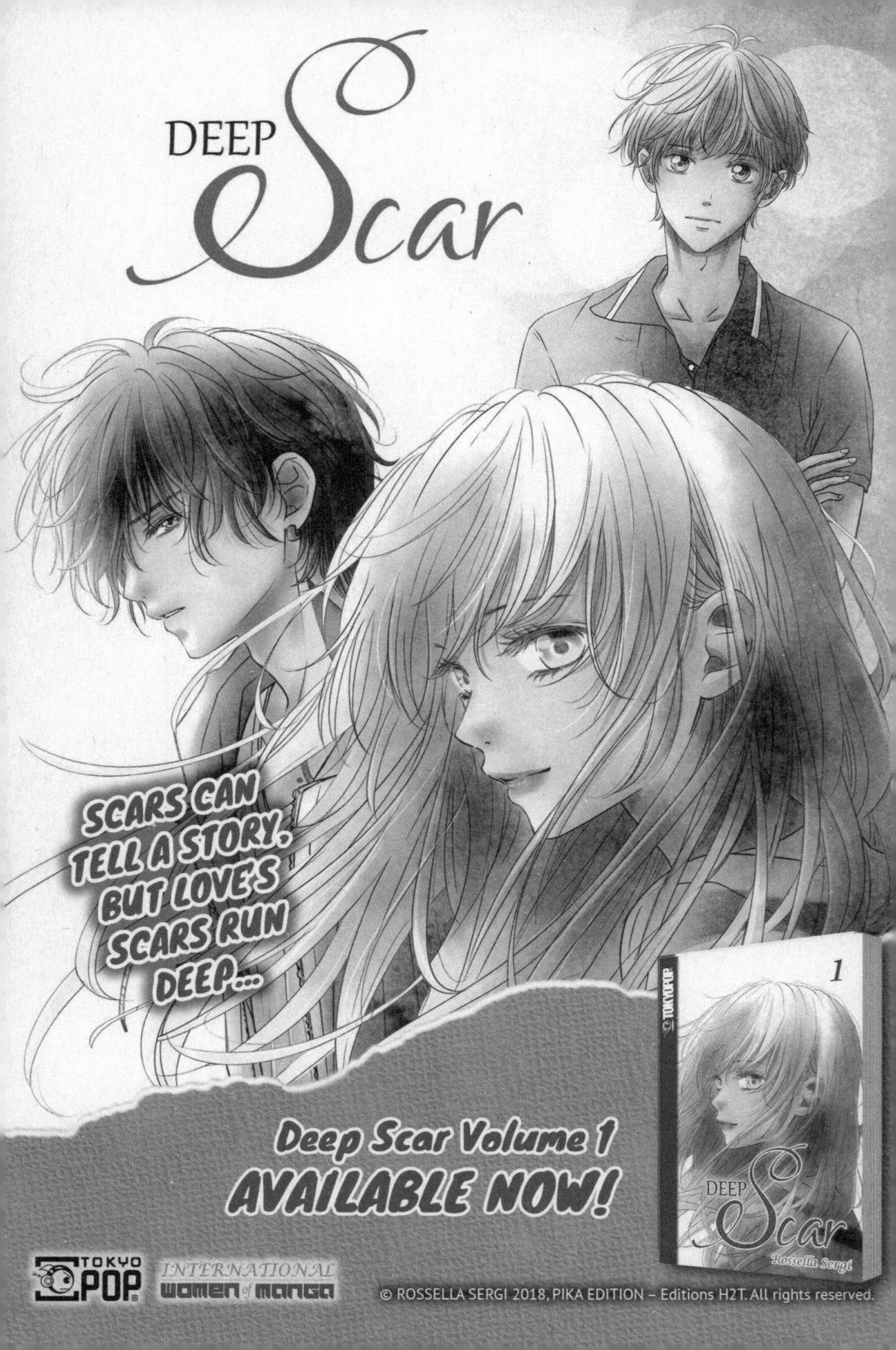
DEEP Scar
SCARS CAN TELL A STORY, BUT LOVE'S SCARS RUN DEEP...
Deep Scar Volume 1
AVAILABLE NOW!
1
TOKYOPOP
DEEP Scar
Rossella Sergi
TOKYO POP
INTERNATIONAL
Women of Manga
© ROSSELLA SERGI 2018, PIKA EDITION – Editions H2T. All rights reserved.

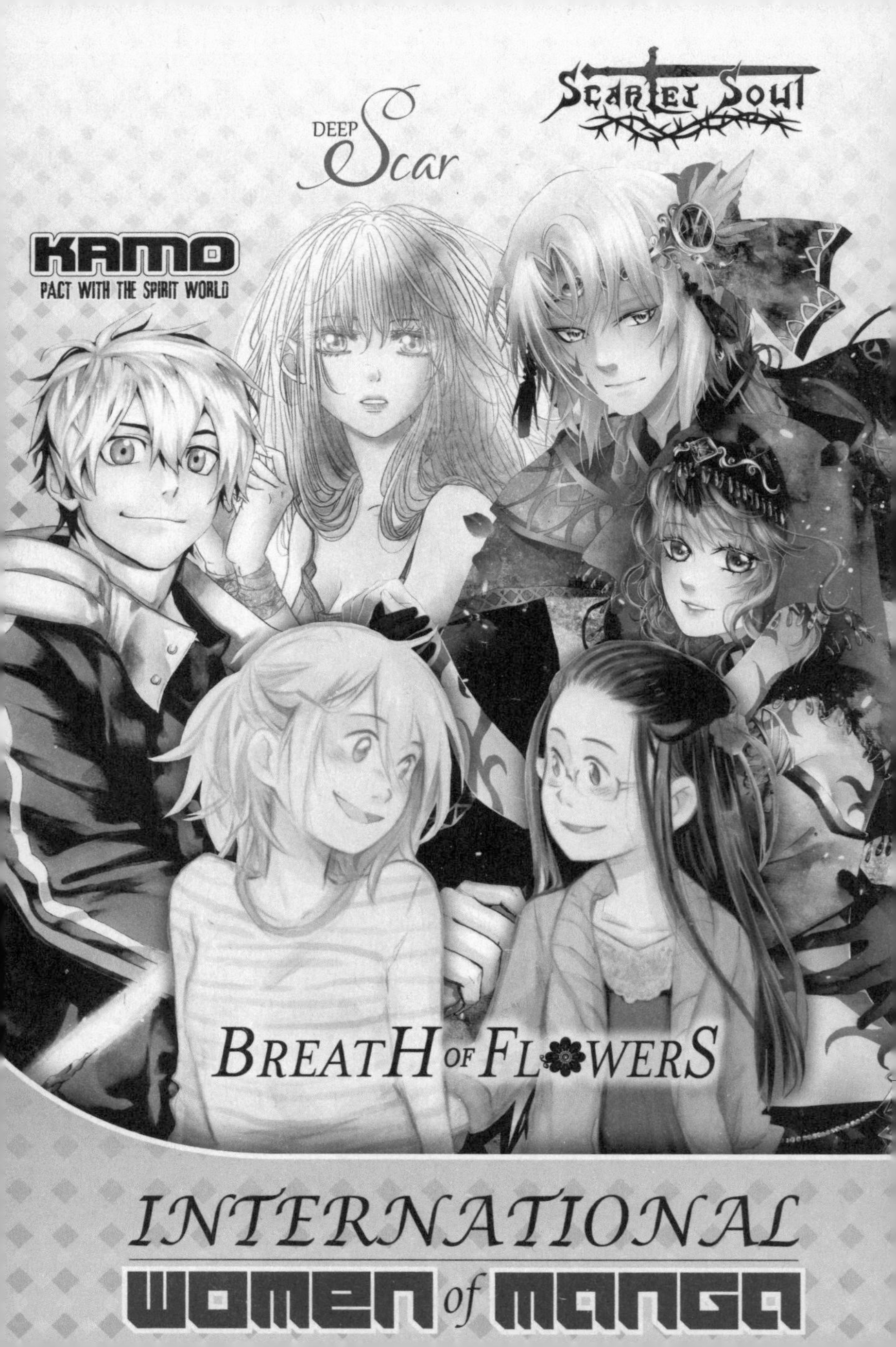
Scarlet Soul
Deep Scar
KAMO
PACT WITH THE SPIRIT WORLD
BREATH OF FLOWERS
INTERNATIONAL
WOMEN of MANGA

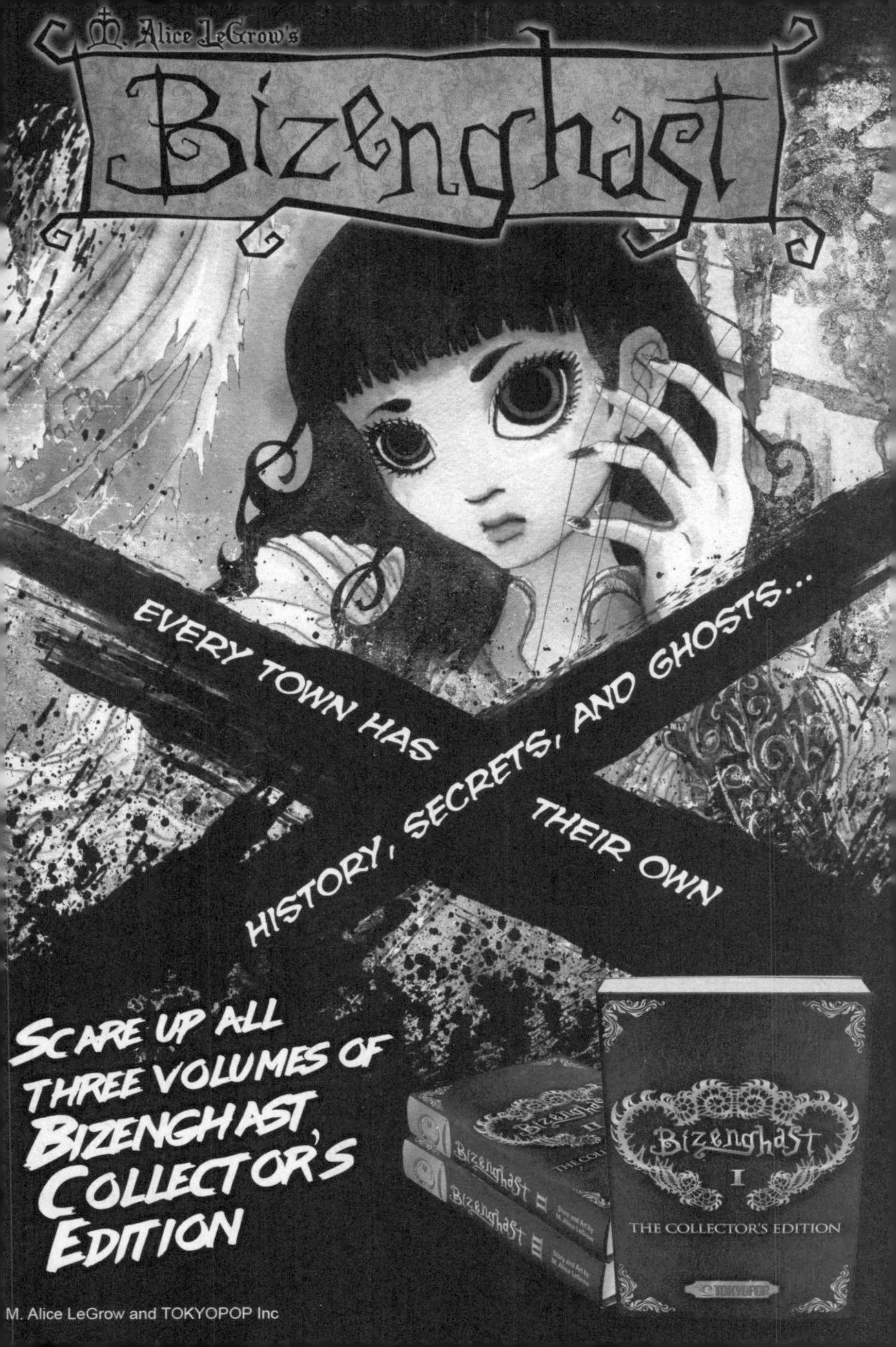
M. Alice LeGrow's
Bizenghast
EVERY TOWN HAS
HISTORY, SECRETS, AND GHOSTS...
THEIR OWN
SCARE UP ALL THREE VOLUMES OF BIZENGHAST, COLLECTOR'S EDITION
Bizenghast
I
THE COLLECTOR'S EDITION
TOKYOPOP
Bizenghast II
Bizenghast III

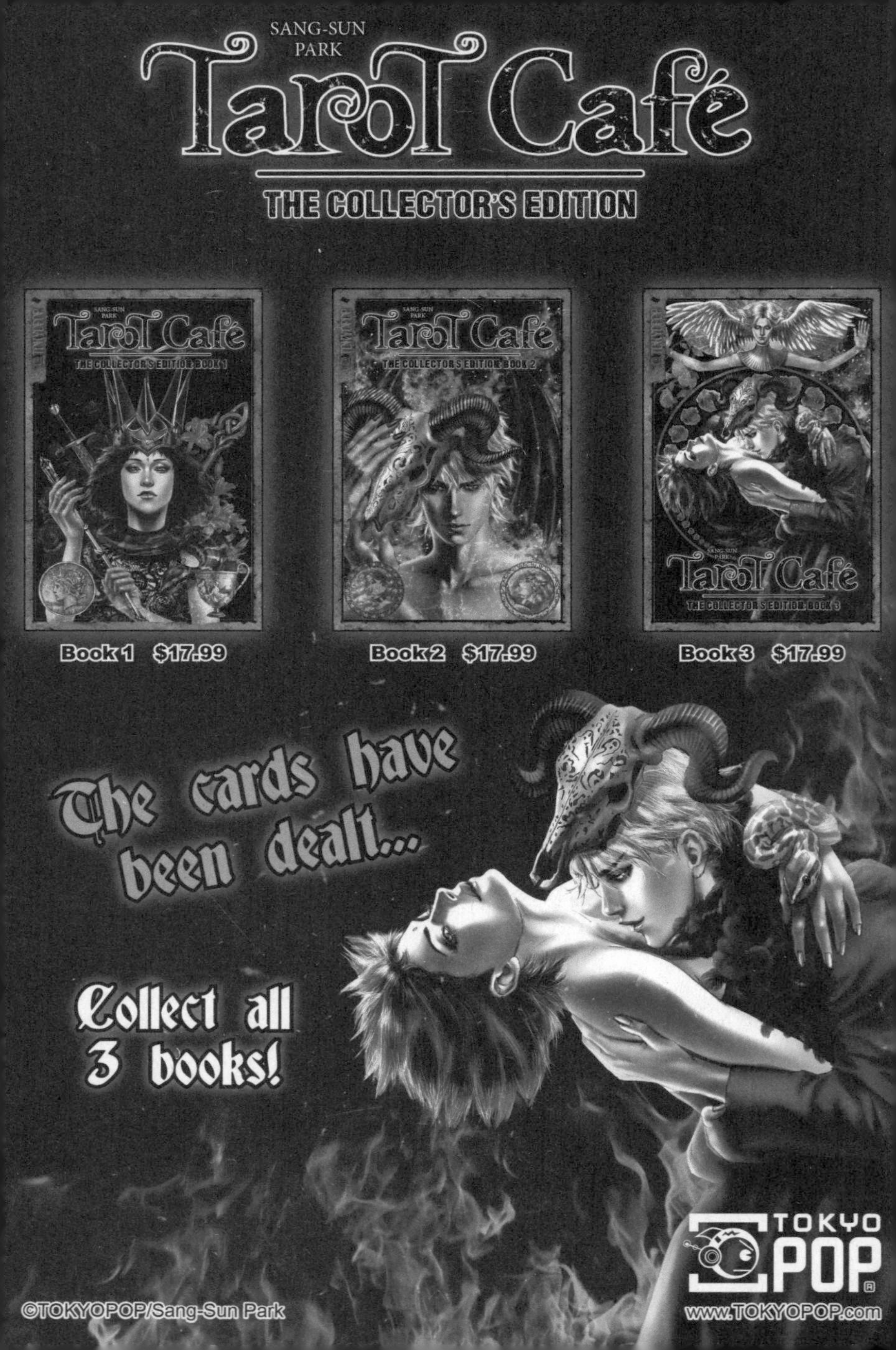
SANG-SUN PARK
Tarot Café
THE COLLECTOR'S EDITION
Book 1 $17.99
Book 2 $17.99
Book 3 $17.99
The cards have been dealt...
Collect all 3 books!
TOKYO POP
©TOKYOPOP/Sang-Sun Park
www.TOKYOPOP.com

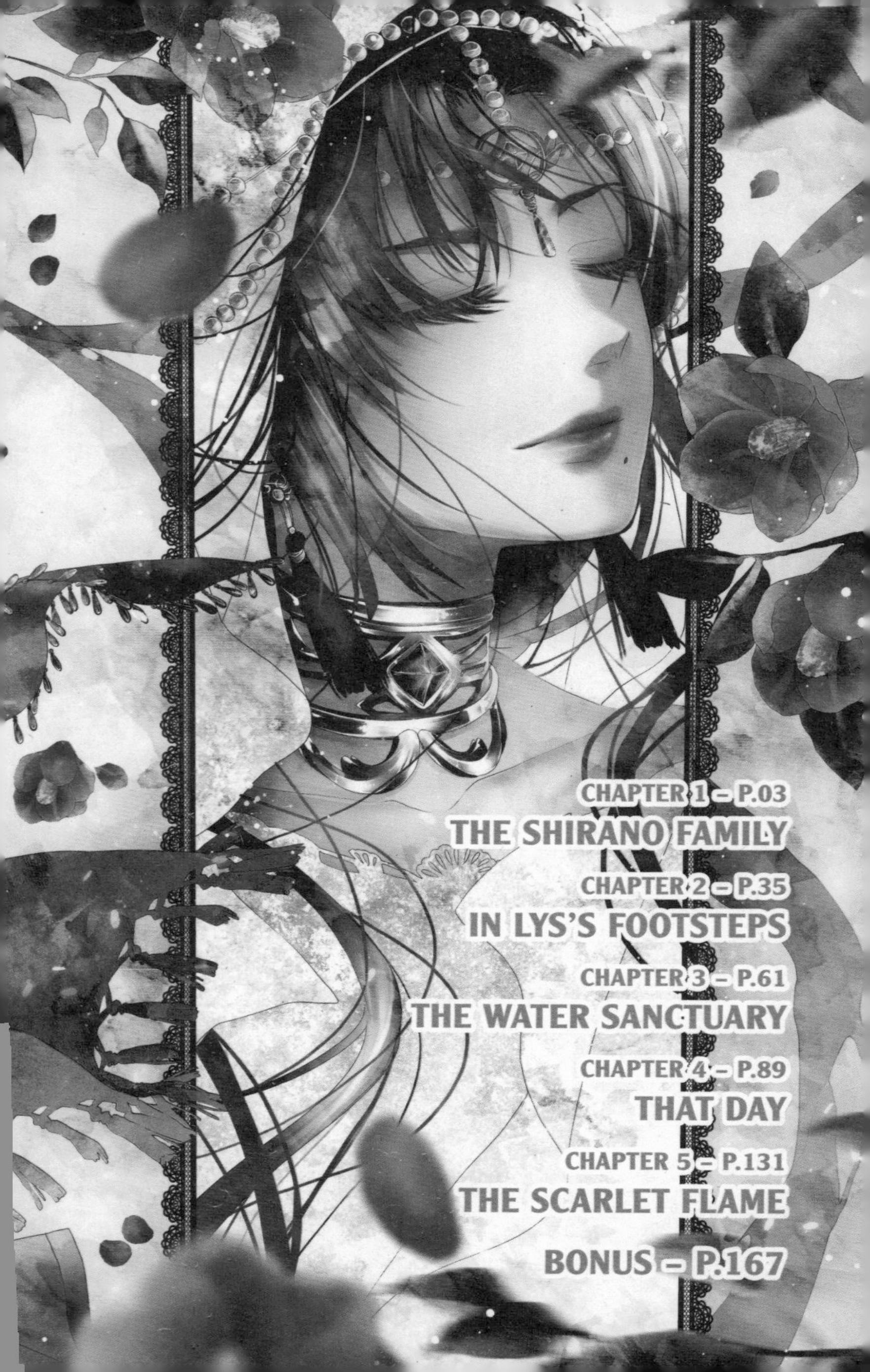

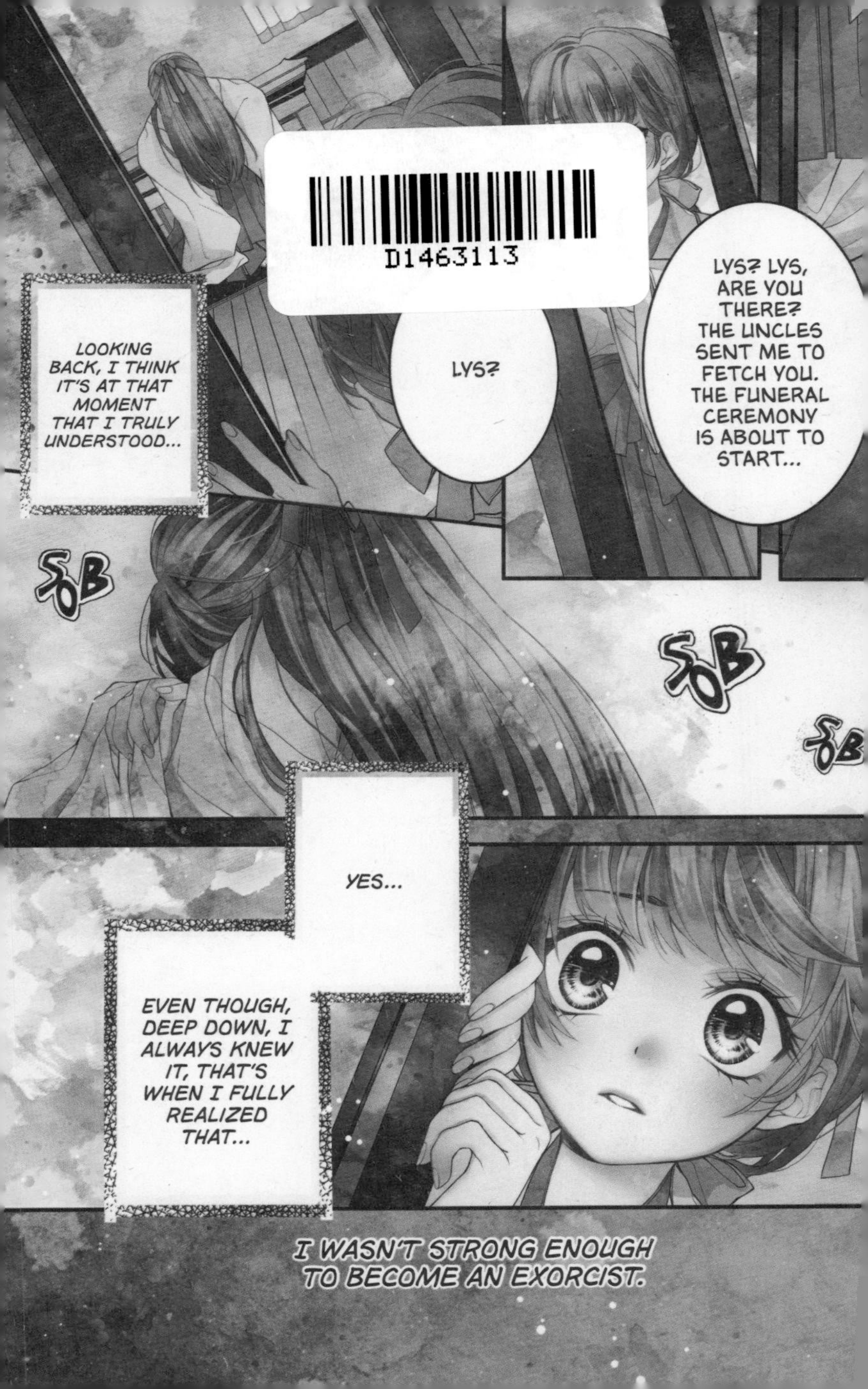
LYS? LYS, ARE YOU THERE? THE UNCLES SENT ME TO FETCH YOU. THE FUNERAL CEREMONY IS ABOUT TO START...
LYS?
LOOKING BACK, I THINK IT'S AT THAT MOMENT THAT I TRULY UNDERSTOOD...
SOB
SOB
SOB
YES...
EVEN THOUGH, DEEP DOWN, I ALWAYS KNEW IT, THAT'S WHEN I FULLY REALIZED THAT...
I WASN'T STRONG ENOUGH TO BECOME AN EXORCIST.